Retreat from the Finland Station

Retreat from the Finland Station

➤➤➤ ⬅⬅⬅

Moral Odysseys in the Breakdown of Communism

Kenneth Murphy

THE FREE PRESS
A Division of Macmillan, Inc.
NEW YORK
Maxwell Macmillan Canada
TORONTO
Maxwell Macmillan International
NEW YORK—OXFORD—SINGAPORE—SYDNEY

The Free Press
A Division of Macmillan, Inc.
866 Third Avenue, New York, N.Y. 10022

Maxwell Macmillan Canada, Inc.
1200 Eglinton Avenue East
Suite 200
Don Mills, Ontario M3C 3N1

Macmillan, Inc. is part of the Maxwell Communication Group of Companies.

Printed in the United States of America

printing number
1   2   3   4   5   6   7   8   9   10

Sincere appreciation is extended to the individuals and companies concerned for permission to reproduce the following material.

Chapters 2, 3, 7, and 8: Quotations from *Bukharin and the Bolshevik Revolution* by Stephen F. Cohen. Copyright © 1971, 1973 by Stephen F. Cohen. Reprinted by permission of Alfred A. Knopf, Inc.

Chapters 9, 10, and 11: Quotations from *The God That Failed* by Richard Crossman. Reprinted by permission of Anne Crossman for the Estate of Richard Crossman.

Chapter 13: Excerpts from *The New Class* by Milovan Djilas, copyright © 1957 by Harcourt Brace Jovanovich, Inc. and renewed 1985 by Milovan Djilas and Harcourt Brace Jovanovich, Inc., reprinted by permission of the publisher.

Library of Congress Cataloging-in-Publication Data

Murphy, Kenneth.
    Retreat from the Finland station: moral odysseys in the breakdown of Communism / Kenneth Murphy.
        p.   cm.
    Includes bibliographical references and index.
    ISBN 0–02–922315–6
    1. Communism—History—20th century. 2. Soviet Union—Politics and government—1917–   3. Europe, Eastern—Politics and government—1945–1989.   I. Title.
HX40.M848   1992
335.43′09′04—dc20   92–4707
                                                            CIP

For my parents

Contents

Part Four

Preface

Terror once had a precise home address. It could be found at 2 Malaya Lubyanka Street, a gloomy path behind Moscow's Dzerzhinsky Square, as if the Lubyanka Prison were merely some sort of boardinghouse or single-room occupancy hotel, full of "guests" occupying rooms according to the degree of interest aroused in the building's landlord, the KGB. The once elegant square was open to the public, but Muscovites habitually went out of their way to shun it; those waiting for word of the building's prisoners shuffled in silence, "lips blue from the cold,"[1] beneath a huge black statue of Feliks Dzerzhinsky, patron saint of secret policemen.

The Lubyanka was both a prison and a laboratory, a charnel house of the mind in which the technical genius of the modern age was applied to the science of confinement and pain. For seven decades in the Soviet Union the very mention of its name suggested an immense Gothic mausoleum of darkness and secrecy, a place into which men and women would disappear without warning and never again see the light of day. By the summer of 1991, as the reality of the Lubyanka became something of an anachronism under the reformist rule of Mikhail Gorbachev, its demonology became ever more important in defining opposition to Communist power. If communism came more and more to be depicted (with full justice) as arbitrary, obsessed with secrecy and vested with capricious powers of life and death, the Lubyanka was the perfect symbol of those deadly traits. If it had not existed at the time of the failed coup against Gorbachev of August 19–22, 1991, it would have had to be invented.

But exist it did, and on the night of August 23, the funeral rites for communism in Europe were marked at Dzerzhinsky Square with a bizarre literalness. Such was the symbolic power of the Lubyanka to gather to itself all the miseries for which communism was, with the coup's demise, at last to be held accountable, that all of the hatred which to a large degree had been spared Moscow during the bungled rising became concentrated on the statue of Dzerzhinsky. The old Chekist gave a shape and an image to all the terrors by which the revolution against communism defined itself. As witnesses and celebrants, a mob gathered at the foot of the statue soon after the coup collapsed. Light would disintegrate this citadel of darkness. A crane was brought in. Like a huge noose, an iron chain was lowered. The colossus of Dzerzhinsky was lynched.

What died with the demolition of Dzerzhinsky's monument, what died with Nicolae Ceauşescu before an impromptu firing squad in December 1989, what died in the peaceful revolutions of Berlin, Prague, Budapest, and Sofia of that year, was the totalitarian pretense, the claims of Marx and Lenin and their myriad of followers in this century, to have broken all of history to the saddle of the Communist party's unremitting political will.

In 1940, when Marxism-Leninism still enjoyed prestige as a moral and intellectual force, Edmund Wilson published what was, perhaps, his most famous and influential work—*To the Finland Station*. From a set of ideas conceived in the eighteenth-century mind of Giovanni Vico, through their development in Michelet, Saint-Simon, and Marx, Wilson traced the growth of the idea of socialism, the sweeping prophecy of the inevitability of socialism as history's endpoint, up to the moment when that theoretical triumph appeared to become a reality with Lenin's arrival in a sealed train at Saint Petersburg's Finland Station. Having devised strategies for organizing cadres and parties, Lenin was portrayed as the physical completion of the socialist idea. The originality of Wilson's study, however, lay not in its narrative—for Wilson says almost nothing about the Bolshevik coup itself—but in its concern with history as a human phenomenon. The task which Wilson set himself was to follow, by examining the lives of its instigators and architects, that century of conspiracy which ended with the tiny Bolshevik party's lunge for power in October, 1917: yielding what Wilson, with more than a little sorrow, called in 1971 "one of the most hideous tyrannies that the world has ever known."[2] Where Wilson's purpose was to trace the birth and maturation of the idea of socialism, my purpose is to biopsy that idea in its decline and fall in Europe. To be sure, Marx continues to be worshipped—in China and Cuba and other outposts of the impoverished, because his ideas (as distilled by Lenin) offered a perfect means to centralize all political and economic power; and on some university campuses the socialist idea retains a curious, mystical hold—but among those people who have lived longest with the real-life consequences of Marx's vision, his system is as dead as that of the divine right of kings.

Retreat from the Finland Station, too, explores the power of ideas: their power to attract and enslave. Three arguments will be developed in the course of this exploration. The first concerns the troubling relations between abstract ideas and their practical consequences, which, in the course of the Communist experiment, turned into a brutal competition between an all-powerful state and the effervescence of politics. The second takes to task the socialist notion of the perfectibility of human society. Marx tells us that once the class war is over and true history allowed to begin, all problems will generate their own solutions, which will be realized through the harmonious workings of a classless and propertyless society. We will see, however, that this theory yields a world in which man's inner life, all that is moral and spiritual and imaginative, must be made mute. "I know what you need," the true socialist says, "I know what all men need. If you resist, then you must be broken. And if necessary hundreds of thousands may have to perish so that men can be made happy for all time." Finally, this book attempts to confront directly the painful problem of self-deception among those who adopted communism, that "idea with an army at its back,"[3] to borrow Sir Isaiah Berlin's bitter phrase. For the men we are to examine turned away in horror when at last they came to realize that there was no limit to the blood that would be shed to build the socialist future. Anxious lest they be lumped together with anti-Communist witch-hunters, most historians have erred on the side of squeamishness in dealing with this issue. Here it becomes a central focus of the story because such self-inflicted fantasies were not merely an unfortunate waste product of faith in socialism, or the all-too-easy device by which guilty men soothe their consciences: in a depressingly fundamental sense, self-deception was an inherent part of the socialist idea itself.

Political intoxication, a madness of words, is the source of the self-deception that plays so remarkably large a role in the history of socialism. It consists in assessing a situation in terms of fixed notions while ignoring or rejecting any and all contrary signs. Such romantic and ideological hysteria denies the power of argument. For a true believer, man's destiny is known; it cannot be challenged. Frothing ideology, in the face of contravening facts, Marxist mystics endlessly repeat the same thing. They act according to wish and prophecy, and will not allow themselves to be deflected by facts, no matter how stunning or harsh. This is the central attribute of that "Captive Mind" described some forty years ago in a book of that title by the Polish poet, diplomat, and lapsed Communist, Czezlaw Milosz: every man his own thought police.

Self-delusion also encompasses refusal to benefit from experience, a special strain of religious mania. Beliefs become delusions when they are maintained by sacrificing one's sense of reality. Marxists use or discard reality as they please. The wish to return to the shelter of absolute certainty and to make of its limits the limits of the world, stands behind the mystical attitude of Marx's adherents. Self-delusion becomes a dangerous disease because it fosters habits of mind that divides men into friends and foes, into masters and slaves.

A principle that will emerge is that the socialist delusion is a child of hope—hope for the future, hope for future power. From unending repetition of Lord Acton's dictum we all know that power corrupts. We are less aware that the yearning for it breeds delusion; that the absolute power to forge society anew inevitably causes failure to reason. A duty of any political leader is to stay well-informed, to heed information, to discover and submit to facts, to keep mind and judgment open and to resist the insidious spell of ideological blindness. In order to illustrate the danger of such intoxication, I have chosen to follow the disintegration of the socialist idea in the form of linked, brief biographies. For if, in fact, the death of socialism as a viable idea for government was a tremendously chaotic event and much more the product of human energy than of any sort of structural conditioning, as Marx would argue, the human focus seems indispensable in making the twists and turns intelligible. *Retreat from the Finland Station* returns, then, to Wilson's method of exploring an idea by tracing its growth and effect upon men, who allow different interests and issues to shape the story as they arise, year after year, month after month.

Wilson's subjects are born when their yearning minds make their act of discovery. So Vico, the modest Italian scholar who finds his academic career blocked because of his humble origins and because he is thought to be a crank, discovers the subversive idea that society is organic: "I speak of this incontestable truth: the social world is certainly the work of men."[4] This is in 1725. Then Wilson leaps to 1824, when Michelet, the son of a poor printer persecuted by Napoleon, finds Vico's name in a translator's note and—in brisk Wilsonian phrase—"immediately set out to learn Italian."[5] History is born, and here, with Michelet as master, Wilson acquired his method and struck his subject. As it is the method I intend to follow, I should like to take this opportunity to explain it.

Michelet claimed that he dashed off his *Introduction to Universal History* when he was fresh from "the burning pavements"[6] of Paris and the workers' riots before Charles X abdicated, in 1830, and in the fervent chapters on Michelet's life and work we can see how much of Wilson's method was extracted and adapted from the French historian. The main difference between Michelet's method and that of the ordinary historian, Wilson says, is this:

> The ordinary historian knows what is going to happen in the course of his historical narrative because he knows what has really happened, but Michelet is able to put us back at upper stages of the stream of time, so that we grope with the people of the past themselves, share their heroic faiths, are dismayed by the unexpected catastrophes, feel, for all our knowledge of after-the-event, that we do *not* know precisely what is coming. Michelet responds with the sensitivity of a poet to every change of tempo, movement or scope and he develops an infinitely varied technique to register different phases. . . . To give us a final symbol for the monarchy, Michelet has only to describe without comment the expense and the clumsy complication of the great waterworks at Marly which make the Versailles fountains agonised creakings and groanings.[7]

So, in Wilson's book, Michelet the historian is seen as a character playing a creative part in history. He is a human continuation of it. Very early on in the book, we see him as both man and symbol. There he stands for us—the laborious and fervid son of a printer worshipping his father's printing press itself. The press represents enlightenment and liberty. It might be some allegorical object out of Balzac. When Napoleon's police took the whole family off to jail and put seals on the machine, "the incident caused Jules such anguish that he afterwards made a stipulation in his will that his wife should not be obliged to seal his coffin."[8] When Wilson moves on to Renan, Taine, Anatole France and, briefly, to the Symbolists in order to show the ossification of the once Romantic impulse, the biographical detail links their thinking to their lives. The idea of socialism grows with each subject, like a family inheritance nurtured and expanded over the generations.

This is a method even more appropriate for coming to an understanding of the decline and death of the idea of socialism. In 1917 and for decades after, the idea of the socialist utopia was addictive for many intellectuals. As communism's aim was the abolition of private property and the redistribution of the world's goods to provide everybody with enough, it was a natural home for the liberal-minded. The Marxist doctrines of *Verelendung* (pauperization, or increasing misery) and *Zusammenbruch* (collapse) was the religious formula of communism, equivalent to the "God is One" of another religion. Property had lasted too long, filling the world with wickedness, turning men against each other. The time for overturning had come. The social evils produced by capitalism would be wiped out and replaced by social harmony. Freed from false patriotism, workingmen linked by their underlying brotherhood would no longer fight each other. Freed from the greeds and frustrations imposed by capitalism, under socialism every individual was guaranteed sufficient means to fulfill himself. This goal gave an excitement, a meaning, a glow to Communist lives. Communism was a cause, not a career.

Retreat from the Finland Station will begin with the Russian Revolution and the sense of euphoria it created among many intellectuals. It will do so by concentrating on the figure of Nicolai Bukharin, a leading Bolshevik, who joined the Party because of its promise that men had it in their power to make the world anew. But Bukharin began to doubt, and his doubts—like spoors scattered in the wind—began to spread, to grow, until now, seventy-odd years after the Russian Revolution, the idea of socialism has been choked off, and the communist party abolished throughout all the former territories of the U.S.S.R.

Ruins of the socialist dream, indeed, litter the twentieth-century's landscape. That all socialist experiments failed (some, like China, Vietnam, Cuba, and North Korea, continuing in a strange half-life of rote revolutionary fervor and reflex thuggery) we now take for granted; in fact, we have become so accustomed to anticipating and accepting the disintegration of utopian schemes that we find it hard to understand our parents and our grandparents, many of whom believed, with the utmost devotion, that socialism's historical destiny was to conquer the world. If we are to understand and resist the utopian impulse when it returns—as it surely will, in one guise or another—it is necessary to understand the seductive power of the socialist vision. The great delusion was the notion that men can create workable utopias. Men, however, are too complex to have all the future planned for them; their needs are not readily quantifiable. What seems obvious now was rank heresy to the socialist true believers we are to examine: the fact that men and society cannot be "purified" without countless grating invasions of liberty; that the political visionary's moral charter must include the duty to work with the real world and its inherited content. Memory is reality. It is better to recycle what exists, to avoid mortgaging a workable past to a non-existent future, and to think small. In the life of society, only gradual reform is sanity. It has taken a century of hideous crimes to arrive at such a point. The socialist experiment, one may hope, will not be repeated; the Utopian buck stops here. But I suspect we may not be so lucky.

In tracing the decline and death of the socialist idea my approach has been, I admit, highly selective. I am conscious on finishing this book that it could have been written all over again under the same title with entirely other subject matter; and perhaps a third time, still without repeating. There could be chapters on Trotsky, on Bertrand Russell's or Rosa Luxemburg's early critiques of bolshevism, on George Orwell, André Malraux, James T. Farrell, Richard Wright, or Edmund Wilson himself. There could have been chapters on the Sartre-Camus feud, on the opponents of totalitarianism, Whittaker Chambers, Hannah Arendt, Raymond Aron, and Sir Karl Popper, or the tardy *mea culpas* of Susan Sontag, Jorgé Semprun, and Boris Yeltsin. Too, there could have been a slightly digressive look at some ordinary communist cadre, so that the breakdown of socialist loyalty among the anonymous ranks of the Communist party could have been exhibited. Alas, I never found him.

Thus I think I owe the reader a word about my process of selection. In the first place, I tried to confine myself to that same European world that Edmund Wilson studied, leaving aside the gestation of socialism in America and in the Third World which, however important, are separate traditions. In choosing subjects the criterion I used was that each must be truly both representative of and engaged in the disillusion that brought about, step by step, socialism's downfall as an idea. I know that what follows is far from the whole story. It is not false modesty which prompts me to say so, but simply an acute awareness of what I have not included. The faces and voices of all those that I have left out crowd around me as I reach the end.

Marnac por St. Cyprien/Lake Mohawk
1992

*Part
One*

1

❧❧❧ ❦❦❦

Lenin Decrees
the Socialist Order

In 1917 the great Marxist prophecy, Revolution, suddenly became
flesh—in the wrong way, and in the wrong country. Russia had not
reached the highly industrialized stage which Marx postulated as necessary for capitalist collapse. The rising, moreover, was not the work of
some self-conscious and disciplined proletariat but simply of men and
women at their breaking point. Everyone—including Lenin—was
shocked that the Bolsheviks succeeded in hijacking the revolution
against Tsar Nicholas II, but the most extraordinary aspect was that,
with victory, the meaning of socialism changed forever.[1]

In the nature of things, the start of the Bolshevik *coup d'état* on
November 7, 1917, should have been a day of terrible and serious
drama, and so it was in many ways; and yet there was also a high,
strained note of absurdity, cowardice, and luck in much that happened,
almost an element of farce. The infiltrating process, that stealthy almost
accidental manner in which the Bolsheviks, under the direction of
Vladimir Lenin and Leon Trotsky, pounced on one military and political
stronghold after another, until like a house that has been eaten out by
white ants the whole edifice of the Provisional Government, then under
the leadership of the autocratic and slightly hysterical Alexander Kerensky, collapsed, was a thing of improvisation, with the Bolsheviks only
slightly less incompetent than their hated rivals.

A good deal of the white-anting had been done during the night. By
daybreak on November 7, the Bolsheviks had seized Petrograd's train
stations, the state bank, the power stations, the bridges across the
Neva, and finally the telephone exchange. The cruiser *Aurora* was in
the river; with two torpedo boats she had come up to the Nicholas
Bridge and had put ashore a party of sailors. There had been no resistance anywhere except for a few shots along the river, and the Cossack
patrols were behaving with that air of appearing to notice nothing which

3

usually overtakes policemen and soldiers who, in a crisis, are without leadership or definite orders.

At 10 A.M. on November 7 a proclamation was issued by Trotsky's Military Revolutionary Council stating that Kerensky's Provisional Government had fallen, and that power had passed to itself. This was nothing more than political bluff, but it was rapidly becoming true, at any rate as far as Petrograd was concerned. The government ministers Kerensky left in the Winter Palace as he went out to rally troops were quite powerless. While they sat and debated, one district after another went over to the Bolsheviks, and still the government's loyal Cossack troops did nothing. By midday it was apparent that there was nothing much they could do: almost all of the rest of the city garrison was either neutral or actively supporting the rising, some twenty thousand Red Guards were in the streets, and a squadron of seven rebel warships was on the way from Kronstdadt naval base. In addition, several trainloads of armed sailors came in from Helsingfors in what was then Russian Finland, where the Bolshevik party was very strong.

The embryo parliament (composed of the various parties that organized the Tsar's fall) might have made a center of resistance, but it was overcome by violence; a gang of armed soldiers and sailors walked into its assembly room in the Mariinsky Palace and ordered the delegates to disperse. The delegates had to obey. After this collapse became general, and by seven o'clock that evening only the Winter Palace was holding out. Its position was precarious. Throughout the day there had been a steady stream of desertions from the palace garrison, and those that remained numbered barely a thousand, of whom 130 were women and the rest mainly officer cadets. After Kerensky's departure the thirteen remaining ministers continued in session in one of the rooms on the river side of the palace. They placed their faith in the expected arrival of loyal troops. But through the windows of their room they could see the *Aurora* in the river, with the guns of the St. Peter and St. Paul fortress just beyond. By 6 P.M. the palace itself was surrounded by Bolshevik troops. Artillery could be seen taking up positions in the main courtyard.

Two blank shots fired at 9 P.M., one from the *Aurora,* the other from the fortress of St. Peter and St. Paul, were the signal for action, and a desultory shelling of the palace began. It was not very effective—a few windows were smashed, a few stones were knocked down—but it was too much for a battalion of women militia. They came out to surrender and were soon followed by other deserters. Small parties of Red Guards began to break into the outer rooms of the huge building, and those who did not become lost in the ornate corridors that stretched away like streets into the distance engaged in a series of hand-to-hand skirmishes with the officer cadets. Neither side seems to have been very certain of itself: at one stage a Red Guard is said to have suddenly found himself confronted with the reflection in a huge mirror of a painting of a horseman and with a horrified cry of "the cavalry" he turned and bolted with his men. Huge crowds had gathered near the palace, and all who could surged forward. Armored cars with the word "Bolshevik" daubed on their sides cruised about before the main entrance. The American communist John Reed and some friends, with the aid of their passports however, had no difficulty in getting into the building. Porters on duty at the door, wearing brass-buttoned uniforms with red and gold collars, politely took their coats as they entered to witness the chaos within.

After an hour's pause, shelling resumed at 11 P.M. No one was hurt, but the psychological effects were profound. The slow solemn booming of the cannon became intolerable, and toward midnight the members of the Petrograd city Duma could stand it no longer. They chose to march on the palace and die with the provisional Government. Indeed, it is said that the mayor, armed with an umbrella and a lantern, did set out with a few followers. At the palace gates, Red sailors brusquely told them that they could not pass and eventually they returned to their homes.

At 1 A.M. on November 8 the last phase of the siege began. Red Guards infiltrated the corridors of the palace, and soon after 2 A.M. they rushed the inner room where the civilian ministers of the cabinet—the military members had already surrendered—were meeting. These men, who behaved with some courage and dignity throughout, were arrested and taken off to the dungeons of St. Peter and St. Paul. No one resisted; "The Red Guards raped half of the female unit guarding the palace and looted its chambers. Only two soldiers were shot, and one drowned in the wine cellar."[2]

During these events the conspirators at Bolshevik headquarters at the Smolny Institute had had a momentous day. Lenin appeared at a meeting of the Petrograd Soviet that afternoon—a rapturous moment for his followers—and the frantic Trotsky had announced triumphantly that the revolution was proving bloodless. Telegrams had been sent off to the army facing the Germans on the Eastern front, announcing the fall of the Provisional government. Late in the evening the Second All-Russian Congress (the legislature that gave popular legitimacy to Kerensky's cabinet) opened, and it was hardly possible for the delegates to breathe as they stood in one congested mass, a dense cloud of tobacco smoke floating over their heads. But they were living on excitement now. The

result of the election of the new presidium was no surprise to anybody—
the Bolsheviks scored an overwhelming majority. The old presidium
stepped down and the new one moved onto the platform. It consisted of
fourteen Bolsheviks, seven Left Revolutionaries, and one representative
from the Ukraine. Three Mensheviks and one Menshevik Internationalist who had also been elected refused to serve. The old rebel Lev
Kamenev took the chair. For the first time in its existence the word
"Bolshevik" ceased to be a lie: at this meeting at least the party had a
genuine majority at last.

An uneasy stillness settled on Petrograd during the remaining hours
of darkness. On this of all nights no holdups or robberies occurred.
Except for the continuous commotion at Smolny no move of any consequence was made by either side. Searchlights played on the walls of
the Winter Palace, and soldiers tramped through the halls and corridors
within, but there was no further disturbance. At the front the next day
Kerensky met with treachery. No troops rallied to him. Bolshevik agents
had infiltrated the army. As he travelled from base to base, the vital
hours slipped away. The cause of democracy was lost.

At Smolny the Bolsheviks were rushing ahead before their opponents
could guess what was happening. At 8:40 on the evening of November
8 the Congress assembled, and this time Lenin himself went onto the
platform with the presidium. There was the usual commotion. At last
Lenin got up to speak. He stood there, says Reed, "gripping the edge of
the reading stand, letting his little winking eyes travel over the crowd
. . . apparently oblivious to the longrolling ovation, which lasted several
minutes. When it finished he said simply, 'We shall now proceed to
construct the Socialist order.' Again that overwhelming human roar."[3]

2

⇢⇢⇒ ⇐⇐⇐

Bukharin Sees Leviathan

Nicholai Bukharin was one of many who believed Lenin never uttered that lapidary phrase about the Socialist order. As leader of the Moscow Bolsheviks, he presided over the uprising in that city, a far bloodier affair than the coup in Petrograd. Afterwards, he wired Smolny for instructions on how to establish socialism in Moscow. No reply. Revolutionary improvisation was the order of the day.

Although Reed did falsify Lenin's words, he indicated precisely what Lenin sought to do, except that it was Lenin and not the All-Russian Congress who did the constructing. On the Eastern front there was to be peace, immediate peace, peace without annexations or indemnities. The secret treaties the Tsar had struck with the Allies were repudiated and the self-determination of the empire's constituent peoples guaranteed—on paper, that is. As to the "Socialist order," only one decree went out. Private ownership of land was abolished. No compensation was to be paid. The Constituent Assembly was called to Petrograd. It convened on January 18, 1918, in the Tauride Palace, supposedly to write a republican constitution. It says something for the courage of the non-Bolsheviks that they attended at all. Once inside they quite expected to be besieged. So they brought food with them and candles in case of a power failure. "Thus," says Trotsky, "democracy entered upon the struggle with dictatorship heavily armed with sandwiches and candles."[1]

Lenin's dictatorship had come to the meeting much better prepared. It packed the corridors and galleries of the main hall with Latvian guards and sailors from the *Aurora*. All carried loaded rifles. Hand grenades and cartridge belts were stacked in the anterooms.

When the vote was taken to elect the chairman, the Bolsheviks found themselves in the minority once more. The leader of the Right Social Revolutionaries, Viktor Chernov, was elected by a vote of 244 to 151. The debate that followed bordered on lunacy. Every speech was interrupted by Bolshevik howls, catcalls, and jeers. During most of the speeches Lenin lolled about on the steps leading to the platform and at one point curled up on a bench and pretended to go to sleep. After many hours of this the guards and sailors lost control. Some dropped into the body of the hall and tried to break up the meeting. Others amused themselves by aiming their rifles directly at the deputies. It was while Chernov was reading out the land decree that a sailor came up and, putting a hand on his arm, told him that the meeting must disperse as the guard was tired. Chernov was trying to reply when the lights were turned out. A massacre might have ensued, but the Bolsheviks—acting on orders from Lenin—saved the situation. Bolsheviks who remained in the corridors managed to hold back the sailors and soldiers loyal to them, while small groups of Social Revolutionaries were escorted from the building. They scattered into the freezing night, some of them to go immediately into hiding, others to leave Russia for good. The Assembly never met again. "The simple, open, brutal breaking-up of the Constituent Assembly," Trotsky later wrote, "dealt formal democracy a finishing stroke from which it . . . never recovered."[2]

Nicolai Bukharin did not witness the events in Petrograd but he would not have been surprised. Bukharin believed in class war to the end. He equated Social Revolutionaries and Mensheviks with aristocrats, as just another face of the employing class. At the outset of the revolution, Bukharin imagined a revolutionary state responsible for little more than keeping "the overthrown classes in leash."[3] Bukharin believed that with property, the monarch of all evil, eliminated, no man could again live off the labor of another and mankind would be released to seek its natural level of justice. To this end, any reform of existing social evils through votes of persuasion was futile, for the ruling class would never give up its property or the powers and laws which protected ownership of property. Therefore, the violence and contempt of the Bolshevik coup was necessary. Only revolutionary overthrow of the entire malignant existing system would accomplish the desired result. Once the old structure was in rubble, Bukharin believed, a new social order of utter equality and no authority, with enough of everything for everybody, would one day settle smilingly upon the earth.

How to reach that point was the problem Bukharin identified from the start of the revolution. One of the myths of the Bolshevik coup was the notion that the Party came to power with a set program to remake Russian society. Savage disputes within the Party over the next twelve years resulted, in part, because the very opposite was true. The Bolsheviks seized power without a coherent plan to bring about industrial socialism in a largely backward land.

Although every revolution is fought in the name of social justice, there is a tendency among Marxist revolutionaries to define justice as the absence of social opposition to the cause and to confuse such an absence with military victory. To discuss the post-revolutionary world during the revolution seems indecent, as if admission that the revolution will one day end could cause a slackening of effort. This is no accident. The logic of revolution is power, and power has no inherent limit.

A just social order, however, demands proportion, and proportion implies limitation. Total victory is the measure of a revolution's success; a just social order requires consensus and stability. The conditions for total victory are absolute commitment and submission, the condition for a just social order is self-restraint. The motivation of revolution is extrinsic: hate and fear of class enemies. The motivation of a stable social order is intrinsic: a balance of social forces and the acceptance of the legitimacy of all social groups and classes. Without enemies, socialist revolution is inconceivable; a social order built on the myth of enemies within is merely an armed truce. The first temptation of socialist revolution is to punish; it is the task of governance to construct. Power demands to sit in judgment, but governments must look to the future.

Such contradictions are the inevitable problems faced by successful revolutionaries of the Communist sort. Barbarity and suffering lead to a conception of the revolution in personal terms, of the enemy as the *cause* of all misfortune, of the defeat of class rivals as the moment for retribution. The greater the suffering, the more the revolution will be conceived as an end in itself and the bitter rules of insurrection applied to the task of social construction. The more total the revolutionaries' commitment, the more natural unlimited claims appear to be. Suffering leads to self-righteousness more often than to humility, as if it were a badge of courage and commitment, as if only the innocent can suffer. Revolutionaries live only for violence, the idea of the enemy and the traitor, grudge and complaint, like a complete expression of their faith. Every revolutionary government is thus confronted with determining the fate of its enemies and with the more fundamental problem of whether the experience of revolution has made it impossible to conceive of a world without enemies.

The absence of any pre-revolutionary notions of what the post-revolutionary world would look like made it impossible for the Bolsheviks to resist the temptation for punitive governance. History, as dictated by Marx, had granted them all the legitimacy they needed. Their coming to power was supposedly pre-ordained. There was no need to seek justice. So passionate had been the conduct of their revolution, so improvisational its success that, although the revolution was an accidental victory, it did not seem so. A dream once achieved loses its terrors and succumbs to its temptations. For Marxist revolution has its own legitimacy: total victory, not social peace. Compromise becomes acquainted with blasphemy and petty calculation, and is perceived as a threat to the exhilaration that brought about success. A successful socialist must identify the post-revolutionary order with his will; he must create a social order safeguarded solely by the purity of his doctrines. Moderation in an hour of triumph is appreciated only by posterity, rarely by revolutionary comrades who despise it as supine surrender.

Among the Bolshevik leadership, discussion of the future had almost always been political. Lenin talked of war. His writings were primers on how to destroy, not build. His remarks on economic policy throughout the long years of exile were, in contrast, sketchy, infrequent, and incidental, amounting to little more than plans to nationalize banks and land, and to give the working class control over industry. The reason for this gap is that all his actions were completely subservient to Marx's historical prophecy, and as Lenin admitted, "there is hardly a word on the economics of socialism to be found in Marx's work"[4]—apart from such useless slogans as "from each according to his ability, to each according to his needs."

Lenin was blind to industrial growth in Russia before the Great War. All his plans involved control and regulation, not transformation. Before 1917, the Party's leaders concentrated on the political struggle, not the remote fancy of building the socialist order. The February, 1917, overthrow of the Tsar caught Lenin napping, for in its aftermath he spent months debating among his circle the prospect of coming to power, not what to do with it. Again, this mimicked Marx, who viewed economic modernization as the historical function of capitalism, and thus did not see any role for socialists in that struggle. All Marx's writings described the capitalist economy; what the socialist economy would look like he never ventured to say. It would, Marx remarked vaguely, be organized by society. All that he was certain about was that once "all elements of production" were "in the hands of the state, i.e. of the proletariat organized as the ruling class," then "productive forces would reach their peak and the sources of wealth flow in full abundance."[5] Here is the irrational element of socialism, the source of its inspiration and its ultimate failure. Socialists need not concern themselves with the humdrum details of real work or argument; their duty was to annunciate a prophecy and act upon it. History was on their side. Everything would fall into place.

For socialists, collective ownership (meaning state ownership) was the answer to the terrible paradox posed by the nineteenth century: that the greater the material progress, the wider and deeper the resulting poverty. Marx drew from this conundrum the central principle of his system: that this inherent contradiction within capitalism would bring about its ultimate breakdown. The capitalist's accumulation of profits derived from the surplus value of the worker's product. Exploiters were becoming richer and the exploited poorer. The process could only end in the violent collapse of the existing order. Trained and prepared for this event, at the moment of ripeness the Bolsheviks had no scheme to usher in Lenin's putative new order.

None of these notions fully explain why the Bolshevik leaders failed to think seriously about an economic program. But the events at hand revealed the major dilemma that quickly confronted the Bolsheviks. Despite his persistent advocacy of socialist revolution, Bukharin understood that Russia was a profoundly backward society. How could it play host to a revolution designed to overthrow an advanced industrial order? For him the initial answer presumed an organic relationship between revolution in Russia and revolution in the advanced countries like Germany, England, and France. Instead of confronting the bitter implica tions of socialism in Russia alone, Bolsheviks fell back on the Marxist dogma that, like its capitalist precursor, proletarian revolution would be an international event. Russia's social and economic immaturity— Bukharin and other Bolsheviks reasoned, would be cured by comradely aid and copycat uprisings that never seemed to come. "There is no doubt whatsoever," Bukharin declared, "that the Russian revolution will spread to the old capitalist countries and that sooner or later it will lead to the triumph of the European proletariat."[6] International revolution would result in a single "fraternal economy."[7] But the notion of international revolution was an hallucination. While the Bolsheviks kept on talking about it and believing in it, they were dealing more in a wish than in a reality.

Bukharin, more than any of the other Communist leaders, should have understood such thinking as fantasy. For of the two classes of Bolshevik revolutionary, the bullnecked and the consumptive, Bukharin belonged to the second. A small-boned, goateed little man, laconic and expressionless except for alert dark eyes, merry behind his aviator's glasses, effete in appearance, correct and yet garrulous in manner, he is remembered as having concentrated with such single-mindedness on his revolutionary goals that when an aide, at the end of an all-night working session, pointed out to him the beautiful leather binding of one of the books in his study, Bukharin gave a brief, dismissive look in reply. Equally trivial, he would soon decide, was any notion of placing limits upon the revolutionary will.

Bukharin had devoted all his adult life to understanding the capitalist world he sought to overthrow. The niceties of governance were second-ary. To speed the socialist plough was essential. Time counted above all else. Anything that obstructed that goal he condemned. For Bukharin arose from the same embittered, mandarin class that had nurtured Lenin in hatred and haste. The habit of struggle against the odds was bred into Bukharin's blood.

Born in 1888, Nicolai was the second of three sons born to Ivan Gavrilovich and Liubov Ivanovna Bukharin, and he had a conventional Moscow boyhood. His father rose steadily in his career as a teacher and tax inspector until losing his position in 1897. The old man, who was ambitious and truculent, then moved successively to ever more demean-ing posts, embittering his son and marking him for life. Still, the Bukharin children did well at school, Nicolai winning a gold medal. They were religious, hard-working, and none of the children received any revolutionary notions from their serious-minded parents. Bukharin's elder brother Vladimir, we are told, had a liking for Dostoevsky and Nicolai for Turgenev. There is no mention in the family history of Marx.

Bukharin's career as a revolutionary sprang from the failed uprising of 1905, which took place during Nicolai's first year as a law student at Moscow University. With the Tsar's betrayal of the reforms he reluc-tantly began in the face of the rising—including the establishment of the Duma, Russia's first elected assembly—the results were cabinets of all colors going up and down, money going only down, food scarce, national faith scarcer, and the emergence all over the land of little groups of men, each fired with a new brand of patriotism which, if they could only build it to power, was to be the country's single salvation. It was thus, in 1906, that Bukharin found his way into the socialist student under-ground, attracted by the belief that the revolution was not yet over but would rise again. From this moment on he did not look back. Abandon-ing his former student liberalism, he emerged a ferocious critic of every form of monarchy, constitutional or not, and of capitalism, which he now equated with arbitrary power. He gravitated toward the Bolshevik faction. Hopes for a gradual transition to a democratic society had been shattered by the satanic forces of Siberian exile and Cossack blades: the world could be rebuilt, Bukharin learned in his fevered underground meetings, only by cutting off all the heads of the tyrannical capitalist hydra in their many disguises. Two worlds were meeting in mortal combat. He chose his side and meant to give no quarter. Without this battleship of an ego, Bukharin could not long have survived in the revolutionary underground, or in his protracted struggle with Stalin that would begin in the 1920s and end with his execution in 1938.

Bukharin embraced the subterranean revolutionary Left, and never relaxed until his judicial murder three decades later. He plunged into conspiratorial activities, arranging demonstrations and staging guerrilla raids into university lecture halls to preach the gospel of socialism as interpreted by Lenin. His early underground years were one long flight from authority, on the run, working under pressure. Mythmaking about this period contributed mightily to Bukharin's standing in the party at the time of the revolution. He was an intellectual among the common conspirators with their dirty feet and ragged sleeves. The movement, with its craving for leaders with a curse on them, devoured Bukharin's deliberately cultivated image—saturnine, overpeppered with ideas, and on the lam from the Okhrana, the Tsar's political police.

On a charge of incitement to treason he was arrested in 1909. He was betrayed by a friend who was also an informer, but one suspects that he could not have escaped the police much longer anyway. A strong tendency to recklessness—almost a desire to be persecuted and perhaps martyred—stamps all the early Bolshevik revolutionaries. There must also have been a certain pleasure in the game of out-witting the police, in all the exciting business of false-bottom suitcases, elaborate codes, messages hidden in the spines of books, certain significant letters in the books marked with dots, conspiratorial names, and disappearing inks like milk which, when dipped into tea and heated, reappeared in a brownish color.

Confined in Moscow's Butyrka and Sushchevka prison for over six months, he was exiled to Onega in the remote province of Arkhangelsk, a punishment often effective in producing committed communists. Under the Tsars, internal exile was not nearly such a tragedy as it later became. If a prisoner had permission and the means to pay for his own passage, he proceeded like a normal traveller to his destination. There were no guards; he simply reported to the authorities en route and at the journey's end he set up his own household in the village to which he was assigned. He could not move about without permission, but within his own province he was more or less a free man. He could take jobs, get married, visit his friends, and the only real prison walls were the vast distances which isolated him from the outer world. By the time Bukharin arrived, Arkhangelsk had become a training ground for revolutionary intellectuals. Almost all the leading Bolsheviks spent several years in similar conditions, and as a rule they profited greatly from it. They had time to think and write and scheme. Up from the underground their health usually improved: and although they may not have welcomed the experience, it provided them with a certain toughness for the struggles ahead. It was only when the prospect of transfer to a penal colony deep in outermost Siberia greeted Bukharin that he made his escape, in 1911.

There now began for Bukharin a roaming, rootless life which was to continue until the November 1917 uprising. Imagine how he moves from Germany to Austria to England and the United States; and nearly always it is the same thing, the same dark room in some decrepit lodging-house, the same revolving haze of intellectual argument. One has a queer picture of the Bolshevik exiles in these years awaiting revolution. They hunt in packs. They coalesce only to split up again and form new patterns in another way. The best of friends turn into the worst of enemies. They drift throughout Europe, and when they are not together they wrangle at a distance in their newspapers. And all of them from time to time suffer the chronic melancholy of the exile: the ennui and frustration of never being on their native soil, of watching the years go by with nothing accomplished. The need for money presses on them continually, and every city where they pause briefly on their wanderings is like any other: the same back room in the same doss-house in the same back street. They live life at second hand, constantly talking about the Russia they cannot see and the revolution that has not happened, endlessly reading newspapers and awaiting news from home. But Russia keeps receding.

Bukharin suffered from this demoralization as much as anyone else, since his was a mind trained on a single objective, from which he could not be easily distracted. This narrowness of vision precluded Bukharin from developing some of the skills of his later rivals and colleagues within the Bolshevik leadership. He had none of the fire of the great agitators like Trotsky; he was not a ruthless judge and connoisseur of human weakness like Stalin, nor did he possess Lenin's tub-thumping oratory; the greater part of Bukharin's revolutionary career was spent in comparative obscurity at a writing table. Although he contributed to the socialist mythmaking, his life failed to stir the imagination or evoke the boundless devotion, the intense, almost religious worship, with which Lenin and Trotsky were regarded by their followers. On the few occasions on which he addressed meetings of the faithful, his speeches were overloaded with facts, and delivered with a combination of monotony and timidity, which diminished the respect of his audience. Bukharin was by temperament a theorist and an intellectual, and instinctively avoided contact with the masses and the Party rank and file, although his entire life was supposedly devoted to studying and supporting their interests. Within the Party he appeared as a dogmatic if kindly schoolmaster, prepared to repeat his thesis indefinitely, with great patience, until its essence became embedded in his followers' minds. He wrote slowly and painfully, as sometimes happens with rapid and fertile thinkers, scarcely able to cope with the speed of their ideas, impatient at once to communicate a new doctrine, and to anticipate all objections; the published versions of his books are generally turgid, clumsy, and obscure in their details, although the central idea is never in serious doubt. By nature, Bukharin was not introspective, and took little interest in people or states of mind or soul; a failure quite consistent with many of his contemporaries, who could assess all the sins of the world, but never spot the mote in Stalin's eye when there was still time to do something to avert the danger.

Nevertheless, he was endowed with a powerful, active, and usually unsentimental mind, an acute sense of injustice, and was repelled as much by the aimless chatter of mob leaders as by the stupid herd instinct of the mob which he viewed as proof that the masses could never be trusted to make the revolution on their own.

If his attitudes in public were seemingly austere and cold, in the intimate circle composed of family and longtime friends, in which he felt completely secure, he was considerate and gentle; his married life was not unhappy, for his widow would remain ever faithful to him after his execution, almost two decades of which she would spend in the gulag. He treated lifelong friends with loyalty and devotion. All his life Bukharin remained an oddly isolated figure within the party. He differed from his comrades and rivals by making his political appeals, at least in his own view, solely on the basis of argument, denouncing only intellectual vice or blindness, and insisting that all anyone needed, in order to know how to save the revolution from chaos, was to seek to understand the underlying conditions; he believed that a correct estimate of the balance of forces in play would itself indicate the immediate policy that should be pursued. Yet, designed though his writings were to appeal to the intellect, his language was often that of the herald or prophet, speaking in the name not of men but of universal laws of history, seeking not to rescue, nor to improve, but to warn and to condemn, to reveal what he *knew* in his mind if not in his heart to be the truth, and above all to refute falsehood. *Destruam et aedificabo* (I shall destroy and I shall build), which Pierre Proudhon had placed at the head of one of his books, far more aptly describes Bukharin's conception of his own annointed task.

In his various places of exile, Bukharin remained almost totally unaffected by his surroundings, living encased in his own, largely Russian, world, formed by a small group of intimate friends and political cronies. He met few Germans during his time in Hanover, few Viennese when in Austria, few Americans when in New York. Bukharin was a man unusually impervious to the influence of his surroundings: he saw little that was not printed in newspapers or books, and remained until the time when his execution was fast approaching relatively immune to the quality of life around him. As far as his intellectual development was concerned, he might just as well have spent his exile in Timbuktu, provided that a regular supply of books, journals, and government reports could have been secured. His journalism and pamphlets written in exile are, at times, sharp, lucid, and mordant. And his fixation on the power of argument left him remarkably unconcerned with developing the conspiratorial skills that so many of his rivals were acquiring in the years before the revolution. This failing would have fatal consequences in the long struggle with Stalin that was to come.

After his flight from Russia in 1911, Bukharin postponed the customary pilgrimage to Lenin, then living in Cracow, and went to Hanover, in Germany. Over the next six years his stream of convincing and passionate polemics, his active work with the Bolshevik underground all over Europe and in New York too, all topped by his theoretical works, made him one of Lenin's recognized apostles. Nevertheless, their relations were almost always strained, due partly to Lenin's instransigence and suspicion of ideological innovation, and partly to Bukharin's independence.

The truth is, Bukharin was too impatient to be an orthodox anything. He "appreciated" non-Marxist theories and tried to incorporate them into his thought. He was groping for an understanding of capitalism's continued vigor. His journeys on the Continent revealed facts contrary to Marx: the middle class was not disappearing; the number of propertied persons was increasing, not decreasing. In Germany the working class was not sinking in progressive impoverishment but slowly making gains. Capital was not accumulating among a diminishing number of capitalists but was rather being diffused over a wider ownership through the medium of stocks and shares. Increased production was not all being consumed by capitalists but was spreading into increased consumption by the middle class and even, as they earned more, by the proletariat. The wider the dispersal of capital, the less chance of any single economic crisis bringing about a final crash. If socialists waited for that, Bukharin suspected, they might wait forever.

In place of inevitable collapse, Bukharin foresaw a fearsome prospect: a capitalist economy capable of expansion and adjustment so as to rule out the pre-ordained Marxist breakdown. He drew his inspiration for this not from Lenin but from Rudolph Hilferding's *Finance Capital: The Newest Phase in the Development of Capitalism*. Hilferding's achievement was to relate the rise of imperialism to the far-reaching structural changes within capitalist systems that had taken place since Marx's death. Laissez-faire capitalism had mutated into monopoly capitalism. Here was a world of trusts and cartels, outwardly inspiring a new prosperity in Europe, but secretly devouring and supplanting smaller capitalist units.

Even today, we can feel something of Bukharin's fascinated terror. Hilferding's text is filled with horrifying and haunting images: capitalist cartels, like writhing serpents, 'strangle the globe; a *danse macabre* performed by blindfolded workers teased by the capering skeleton of capital. A powerful sense of approaching apocalypse is portrayed.

Hilferding paid special attention to the new role of banks in the remorseless spread of monopolies. Capital's concentration had followed the concentration and centralization of the banking system. Banks emerged as the dominant owners of industry's capital. Here Hilferding introduced a new concept—finance capital: "bank capital—that is, capital in monetary form—which has in its way been transformed into industrial capital."[8] Mature capitalism was for him finance capitalism, a system distinguished by its organizing tendencies. As finance capital permeated an entire economy and large trusts became dominant, regulation would eliminate the unfettered competition of smaller units. And once home markets were monopolized and in chains, finance capital would move abroad in search of other game.

Bukharin usurped this principle and projected its actions into the future. Elimination of weak competitors, coupled with the relentless organizing energies of finance capital, transforms "the entire national economy into a combined enterprise with an organisational connection between all branches of production."[9] Because the making of trusts involves the fusion of industrial and banking interests with the power of the state itself, Bukharin called this new Leviathan "state capitalism."[10] The state ceases to be a capitalist tool. It becomes a living tyrant, a direct owner and organizer of the economy, with a "colossal, almost monstrous power."[11] Laissez-faire capitalism gives way to a form of "collective capitalism," whose predatory "finance capitalist oligarchy" conducts its raids directly through the state, "which more and more becomes a direct exploiter, organising and directing production as a collective capitalist."[12] As state control rampages, "the process of organisation continually eliminates the anarchy of the separate parts of the 'national economic' mechanism, placing all of economic life under the iron heel of the militaristic state."[13]

Driven by insatiable lust, the state penetrates all areas of social life. Separation of state and society is systematically abridged: "It can even be said with some truth that there is not a single nook of social life that the bourgeoisie can leave unorganised."[14] All groups and organizations become mere "divisions of a gigantic state mechanism,"[15] until the state stands alone, omnivorous and omnipotent. Bukharin's vision is nightmarish:

> Thus arises the final type of the contemporary imperialist robber state, an iron organisation which envelops the living body of society in its tenacious, grasping paws. It is a new Leviathan, before which the fantasy of Thomas Hobbes seems child's play. And even more *"non est potestas super terram quae comparetur ei"* (there is no power on earth that can compare with it).[16]

In his description of an all-powerful state, Bukharin foresaw the structure of what Hannah Arendt later called the "totalitarian state." He also anticipated the agonizing question this development was to pose for Marxists. Was it possible that "statization" could become so pervasive that the prospect of revolution would be diminished? Was a third way, neither capitalist nor socialist, imaginable for man's future? Yes, was his answer. "Such an economic structure would," he mused, "resemble a slave-owning economy where the slave market is absent."[17]

If this was possible, post-capitalist society would only usher in an even crueler system of exploitation, not the promised land of pure communism. This was a stake plunged deep into the heart of socialist theory. But Bukharin did not shrink from it. Like a Baptist beginning to doubt the biblical story of creation, Bukharin was assailed by the agonies of dialectical doubt. Imagine how for the first time, if imprecisely,

Bukharin senses the violence and fanaticism which are to be unleashed upon the world when the state absorbs all the levers of economic power. Coercive power is the terrible and eternal law of economic and political monopoly. What this hideous new state will demand is not conditional loyalty and subservience, it is a dissolution of the individual within the state. All individual efforts in the name of imaginary rights threaten the very survival of the new Leviathan, which alone must have the power of life.

Six decades of socialist thinking went into the making of Bukharin's vision in which the seed of dictatorship (and personal self-destruction) lay embedded, waiting for its hour. The voice was Bukharin's, but the thoughts were those of Karl Marx who saw the working class chosen by History to occupy the supreme place in human development, of Plekhanov who saw them leading the world to a glorious destiny of compulsory equality, of Lenin who told them that their vanguard—the Communist party that he led—was above ordinary controls, of Trotsky who decreed the increase of power as the highest moral duty of the revolutionary state. What constituted Bukharin's vision of Leviathan was the body of accumulated egoism which drove Party members and energized the movement.

Thus Bukharin's mind, like a heart, contained two valves: one pumped spirit into theory; the other circulated insight and foreboding. As Bukharin peered into the future his mood grew black with inchoate doubts. The great application of his theories was about to be exacted upon mankind.

3

֎ ֍

Bukharin
Embraces Leviathan

Frustrated, frightened by the chaos unleashed through revolution, Bukharin's vision soon exerted a strong pull upon the Bolshevik leadership.

For the early months of 1918 brought a steady drumbeat of calamity. Within weeks of each other, the Bolshevik leaders heard of the eastward advance of the German army, the formation of the rebel White army, composed mainly of Cossacks still loyal to the Tsar, and national uprisings in Georgia and the Ukraine. Report after report described Red army units dissolving on contact with the enemy; volunteers demoralized and disorderly, deserting or taking to their heels; the red flag trampled in the mud. When Bukharin returned from the front, he brought with him a gloom as dark as the days before the November rising. If the armies continued to disintegrate, he warned, there was nothing between the Germans and the capital. To many Bolsheviks there could be only one explanation for this sorry trail of disasters: conspiracy among socialism's enemies.

Faced with this military landslide, the Communist Party Central Committee, with very few exceptions, acknowledged that the powers of the state had to be strengthened. Without an effective executive and a coherent chain of command, centrifugal forces would pull Russia apart. Lenin set about creating strong organs of central authority authorized to do the revolution's bidding without endless reference to the soviets. The Central Committee was transformed into a Bolshevik Committee of Public Safety and, like its French revolutionary ancestor, it was to be the key organ of the terror. The Bolsheviks were seeking to achieve something that had eluded every government since the Tsar's fall: recapture the state's monopoly of authorized violence. To accomplish this it was necessary to do a number of things. First, as Lenin recognized, it was essential that the Bolshevik state take into its hands the kind of punitive powers needed to assuage the general urban thirst for symbols of conspiracy. It had to be prepared to use those powers, publicly and demonstratively, if lynch mobs and improvised murder gangs were to be denied their prey. Second, the endless factionalism, which made it repeatedly possible for the Central Committee to be outflanked by a disaffected group appealing to the streets or mutinous soldiers, had to be ended.

Redirection of revolutionary energies was all the more urgent because, in addition to military reverses, the revolution faced in the late winter and early spring of 1918 another disruptive threat in the shape of acute economic crisis. Disorder was spreading in the countryside among disaffected peasants who had not benefitted from the nationalization of land. Grain barges and wagons were being stopped everywhere. Consumers in the cities were seeing dramatic price rises for basic foodstuffs. Bread riots were roundly denounced by all factions in the Central Committee. Trotsky thought the public's concentration on coffee or sugar evidence of an aristocratic plot. Stalin berated rioters for debasing the sacred value of insurrection. But even though some Bolsheviks, like Bukharin, understood the inflationary causes of the disorders, the Central Committee seemed impotent to correct them.

The stages by which Lenin created a Leviathan state along the lines envisioned by Bukharin are worth describing, for they became the grim definition of every socialist system ever established. In 1902, garbed in mildly reformist tones, Lenin's *What Is to Be Done?* set out to create the image of the socialist revolution that did not yet exist. Its architecture would not resemble the muddled scrum of any democratic party then in existence in Europe but the rigid environment conjured up by the great army of Wilhelmine Germany: all hierarchy and professional foot soldiers, with their solitary purpose the overthrow of the Tsarist order. To fix this goal ineradicably, dissent within the socialist movement had to be eliminated. As Richard Pipes has said, *"What is to be Done?* overturned, in the name of orthodox Marxism, the basic tenets of Marxist doctrine and rejected the democratic elements" of Western social democratic groups. "In plain language," Pipes continued, Lenin "translated into programs of action the ideas which his socialist rivals, lacking the courage of their convictions, hedged with countless qualifications."[1]

For the central question that concerned Lenin was this: was the revolution to organize itself as a democracy or a dictatorship? Was every Party member to share power or was control to be given to one central committee? From the start, Lenin was in no doubt as to his answer. His tactics in building up his own faction before the revolution had a certain ruthless clarity about them that prefigured his deeds after October 1917. Everything was to be subordinate to the party—meaning Lenin's—will.

Nicolai Bukharin accepted the martial strain of Lenin's thinking with an almost complacent blindness. Because he worshipped Lenin as both a man and a thinker, he accepted his leader's militarization of party thinking and behavior. Lenin's will was his mental barbed-wire fence. For Bukharin perceived that dictatorial discipline within the revolution was necessary as a bulwark against diffusion of the Party's energy. To be sure, Bukharin was a personality and a thinker of a different cast from Lenin. His light was no less focused, his intellectual core equally hard and icy, but his vision of the socialist future was less violent, indeed less sinister, than any within Lenin's narrow, driven horizon. Bukharin did not understand, as Lenin gave every sign of doing, the terrifying contours of the new world which the revolution brought into being. Everything evil in the revolutionary cause was merely a temporary aberration in Bukharin's eyes. But in Lenin's vision of the socialist order—framed in the language of prophecy—there was at its core a blood-freezing concept of the future. Only when it was too late would Bukharin vaguely suspect that terror lay at the heart of Lenin's gospel, as well as Stalin's.

But in the early days of revolutionary power Bukharin believed fervently in the notion that everyone had to submit to the Party's authority. People were too corrupt, too enfeebled, to create the communist utopia on their own; without absolute guidance the revolution would collapse into anarchy and the cause of communism would be lost. No revolution can govern itself; such a notion is sheer idiocy: the revolution can only be assured through some unquestioned coercive authority. Disintegration of revolutionary purpose can only be stopped by something from which there is no appeal. It may be party custom or conscience, dictate or a dagger, but it must be something absolute. Capitalism has so confused the minds of men, Bukharin believed, that they cannot be freed of their chains immediately: crippled by years of oppression, they can be remade only by the revolutionary state, which suppresses and surgically removes the aberrations of history—an intellectual lobotomy. And such a state cannot be created by, or on the basis of, a written constitution guaranteeing individual liberties: a constitution may be obeyed, but it will not be worshipped. Without worship, the revolution will not stand. What Bukharin learned from his love of Lenin was not conditional obedience, but the submission of the individual to the cause. Time and again, when Lenin dismissed his ideas, Bukharin might argue his cause for a while, but he was destined to surrender. Infected as Russian society was by all sorts of spineless, corrupt, and compromised creatures from the old regime, only implacable authority could prevent the rebirth of backsliders and hypocrites. A new Sparta was needed. The revolution, Bukharin believed, must be ever vigilant. The Bolsheviks had to be terrible if they were to prevail, and those who led the revolution must never, ever relax their guard. In the Bukharin of the underground years and of 1917 we hear echoes of Saint Just: "Those who would make revolutions in the world, those who want to do good in this world must sleep only in the tomb."[2]

Lenin's aims in centralizing all state authority were fourfold. First, to destroy all opposition outside the party; second, to place all power, including government, in party hands; third, to destroy all opposition within the party; fourth, to concentrate all power in the party in himself and those he chose to associate with him. All four objectives were pursued simultaneously, though some were attained more quickly than others.

Elimination of non-party opposition posed few problems once Lenin had established his own secret police, the Cheka. The 1918 constitution, drafted by Stalin on Lenin's instructions, embodied the "dictatorship of the proletariat," which Lenin once brutally described as a "special kind of cudgel, nothing else."[3] It contained no constitutional safeguards and gave no one any rights against the state. The power of the state was unbounded, indivisible—no separation of legislative and executive function, no independent judiciary—and absolute. Lenin scorned the antithesis between the individual and the state as the heresy of the class society. In a classless society, the individual *was* the state, so how could they be in conflict, unless of course the individual were an enemy of the state? The constitution listed among its "general principles" the laconic observation that:

> In the general interest of the working class, [the state] deprives individuals of separate groups of any privileges which may be used by them to the detriment of the socialist revolution.[4]

Party membership became essential to holding any important position in the state and its endlessly replicating organs. "As the governing party," Lenin wrote, "we could not help fusing the Soviet 'authorities' with the party 'authorities'—with us they are fused, and they will be."[5] Communists were instructed to take over the "network of the state administration (railways, food supplies, control, army, law-courts, etc.), trade unions, and all factories and workshops, even public baths and dining rooms and other welfare organs, schools and housing committees."[6] Leviathan's tentacles reached everywhere.

Thus there came into being what became the determining characteristic of socialism in practice: the hierarchy of Party organs in town, district, region, and republic, placed at each level in authority over the corresponding organs of the state. The vanguard of the revolution now transformed itself into a vanguard of eternal rule, the Party becoming and remaining what Lenin called the "leading and directing" force in Soviet society.

One ruling class had been displaced by another. This meant, however, crushing all opposition within that class, the third stage in the building of Lenin's Leviathan. To do Lenin justice, he always made it clear that he believed in a small, centralized party, real decisions in the hands of a few. He had set this all down in a letter to party workers in 1902. His notions of democratic centralism were clear and well known. He gave the Central Committee "full powers . . . to apply all measures of party sanctions, including expulsion from the party," when any "breach of discipline or revival or toleration of fractionalism"[7] took place. Such expulsion could even apply to members of the Committee. Moreover, factionalism was made an offense comparable to counterrevolution, so that all the new forces of repression, hitherto reserved for enemies of the Party, could now be used against Party members, who would be tried and condemned in secret. Some of the Bolshevik leaders were fretful. "In voting for this," said Karl Radek, "I feel that it can well be turned against us. . . . Nevertheless I support it. . . . Let the Central Committee in a moment of danger take the severest measures against the best party comrades if it find this necessary. . . . Let the Central Committee even be mistaken! That is less dangerous than wavering."[8] Unwittingly, party democracy was signing its death warrant. What Bukharin and those who voted for the measure failed to realize was that they were signing their own future death warrants, too.

Doubtless this was because the extent to which the Central Committee itself had forfeited power to groups within it, including its own bureaucracy, was not yet realized, even in the highest reaches of the Party. The party bureaucracy was a deliberate creation of Lenin's. Not only did he distrust the old imperial bureaucracy, he loathed it, not least because the party's lack of trained administrators forced him to use it. He wanted his own minions, rather as the Tsar used a "personal chancery" to get around the old system of cabinets and responsible government. On April 9, 1919, in order to counter the evils of the old bureaucracy, Lenin issued a decree setting up a People's Commissariat of State Control, to keep a watchful eye over state officials, and replace them when necessary with reliable people. As commissar of this bureau he appointed a sullen and obscure young man who had taken for himself the name of Stalin.

What Lenin liked about Stalin was his capacity for endless drudgery behind a desk. Men like Bukharin and Trotsky were happy enough in violent action, or in violent polemics in speech and print. But they lacked a willingness to engage, day after day and month after month, in the hard slog of running the Party or state machinery. Stalin had a ravenous appetite for this, and since he appeared to possess no ideas of his own, or adopted Lenin's the moment they were explained to him, Lenin strapped more and more offices and detailed bureaucratic work upon this eager beast of burden. At the Eighth Party Congress in the spring of 1919, three new bodies of importance emerged. These were a six-member Secretariat of the Central Committee, an Organization Bureau (Orgburo) to run the Party on a day-to-day basis, and a Political Bureau or Politburo of five, to take decisions on questions not permitting delay. To avoid fights between these three bodies, interlocking membership was arranged. Stalin's name appeared on the Politburo and the Orgburo lists.

Holding a myriad of posts, exercising to the full his capacity for work, Stalin began to move men around and within the labyrinthine hierarchies of Party and government, with a view to securing a disciplined and docile machine responsive to Lenin's will. He was Lenin's perfect instrument—the born bureaucrat, and he had found his perfect master, with a huge will and an absolutely clear sense of direction.

Just as the "vanguard elite" had to take the place of the proletariat in forcing the revolution, so too it would have to represent it in running the economy.[9] And since Lenin believed in ultracentralism in political matters, and had created a machine with precisely this in view, there had to be central control in industry, with the Party exercising it.

Bukharin's idea of a Leviathan, which created a society of marionettes, was thus expropriated by Lenin. Russia acquired a centralized "planned" economy which became a byword for socialism. As usual, Lenin thought entirely in terms of central economic control; not of production. Provided he got the system of control right, with the Politburo taking all key decisions, the desired results would flow inevitably. Lenin was wholly ignorant of the process whereby wealth was created, and no one in his circle was able to enlighten him. What he liked were figures: all his life he hungered for bluebooks. One suspects that inside

Lenin there was a bookkeeper of no mean genius struggling to emerge and bombard the world with ledgers. In all his remarks on economics once he achieved power, the phrase which occurs most frequently is "strict accounting and control." Statistics were evidence of success. So the new ministries, and the new state-owned factories, produced statistics in enormous quantities. Columns and columns of statistics became the most gaudy characteristic of socialist industry. The manufacture of goods was another matter.

Leviathan's shape was also determined by an external vision. This was the German war-producing machine. During the embryonic phase of the Bolshevik regime, Russia was first the negotiating partner, then the economic puppet, of Germany. By 1917, the Germans, under General Erich von Ludendorff's growing influence, had seized upon the model of state capitalism envisioned by Bukharin and fused it with their own state, now run by the military. They called it "war socialism." Lenin's first industrial tsar, a former Menshevik named Larin, became an enthusiastic exponent of German methods, as they fitted neatly with Lenin's notions of central control. Larin began to hire German experts. When other Bolsheviks objected, Lenin replied with his pamphlet *On Left Infantilism and the Petty Bourgeois Spirit*:

> Yes: learn from the Germans! History proceeds by zigzags and crooked paths. It happens that it is the Germans who now, side by side with bestial imperialism, embody the principle of discipline, organisation, of working together, on the basis of the most modern machinery, of strict accounting and control. And this is precisely what we lack.[10]

German state capitalism was a step forward on the path to socialism, he said. History had played a "strange trick." It had given birth to "two separate halves of socialism, side by side, like two chickens in one shell": political revolution in Russia, economic organization in Germany. Both were key to the socialist future. Fusion was necessary. Thus the new Russia must study the "state capitalism of the Germans" and "adopt it with all possible strength, not to spare dictatorial methods in order to hasten its adoption even more than Peter [the Great] hastened the adoption of westernism by barbarous Russia, not shrinking from barbaric weapons to fight barbarism."[11]

Meanwhile Bukharin, that inveterate interpreter of the wills of Marx and Lenin, and Pharisee for the faithful, now expressed all the confusions of the revolution's lust for power and made them appear a permanent article of the faith. Capitalism could not be mastered. It was to be rejected; at the same time its most pernicious aspects were to be incorporated. At the heart of Bukharin's vision of the economy is a doctrine of violence, a belief that economic progress must pass through a phase (of undetermined length) when the chains of concentrated power curb man's self-destructive instincts.

Bukharin's willingness to establish an all-powerful state arose, in large measure, from his understanding of the failure of the French Revolution. The French regicides had had liberty, equality, and justice within their sight, but their own failure to understand the true nature of property permitted resistance to the revolution to begin and to mushroom. Rule by the mob, the fanaticism of the Committee of Public Safety, the overthrow of moderation and reason, the Terror—none of these things had contributed to the revolution's collapse. Or so Bukharin believed. The failure came from the revolutionaries' inability to manipulate the economy, which proved suicidal. A revolution founded on an impotent state would inevitably fail in its purpose. Usurpation of all power by the socialist state in the name of the people was but the just reverse of the original wicked usurpation by kings and capitalists. Armies obey orders and go to their death; and as discipline is to armies, so it must be to a revolutionary society. The Kaiser's generals were certainly criminals, Bukharin believed, but they knew how to maximize power and make the economy under them hum. Such disciplined force commanded his respect. For he despised all signs of weakness among the Bolsheviks. The Jacobins were budding failures, but with the Terror they succeeded, at least for a time, in re-establishing the revolution's authority. And the German general staff had restored the will to fight by centralizing power. Each therefore stood higher in Bukharin's estimation than liberals and idealists who let power slip from their grasp. Thus Ludendorff provided the new model he adopted as the Bolsheviks confronted a revolutionary chaos far more endemic than that confronted by Robespierre.

And German "war socialism" did not shrink from barbarity. In January 1918, Ludendorff crushed a Berlin factory strike by drafting tens of thousands of workers and sending them to the Western front. This ruthlessness caught Lenin's and Bukharin's fancy. Like Ludendorff, they wanted a docile labor force, and set about getting it. The workers' soviets, which had taken over the factories during the revolution, were stripped of all authority. Lenin's trade union spokesman, Lozovsky, warned: "The workers in each enterprise should not get the impression that the enterprise belongs to them."[12] No fear of that with Lenin in control! "Disturbers of discipline," he said, "should be shot."[13] Here was a sentiment worthy of the most blood-thirsty Tsar. By January 1918, the Bolsheviks had taken over the unions and brought them into the government as another organ "of social power." Worker participation in such unions was part of their "duty to the state."[14] In short, they became company unions of the most debased kind, the company being the state. In this corporatist system their main task became "labour discipline," and shop stewards found themselves acting as industrial cops.

Such policing was necessary as Lenin applied his notion of "universal labour service"[15] along lines similar to a military draft. Unions set to work issuing regulations to "fix the norm of productivity." Rebellious workers were expelled from the union, with a corresponding loss of ration cards. "He who does not work," Lenin said, "neither shall he eat."[16] Strikes were outlawed; strike funds confiscated. The first: labor camps emerged. Undisciplined workers, hooligans, social parasites, the disaffected and the idle could be sent off on the simple say-so of the Cheka, revolutionary tribunals, or the Narkomtrud, the body responsible for mobilizing labor. Anyone could be called up for compulsory labor. As a Narkomtrud spokesman put it: "We supplied labour according to plan, and consequently without taking account of individual peculiarities or qualifications or the wish of the worker to engage in this or that kind of work."[17] The wheel had turned almost full cycle from Nicholas II to Lenin, from autocracy back to autocracy again. The Bolsheviks had betrayed or were soon to betray nearly every political slogan that had brought them to power. They had promised the freedom of the individual worker and instead locked him within the factory gate, forbade strikes, and set up a secret police.

The whole performance was a triumph of calculated purpose. In the fire of civil war, the dream of the state withering away expired. It was left to Bukharin to call this new dictatorship socialism. Here Saint Just's justification of the Terror applies: "One must rule with iron when one cannot rule with law."[18]

No one grasped the theoretical opportunities offered by the growth of the Bolshevik state, the appearance of Lenin's "war communism," better than Bukharin. He became, simultaneously, both inventor and impresario of the new soviet-style socialism, which Stalin would perfect in the next decade. It was Bukharin's concept of the socialist version of Thomas Hobbes' Leviathan that was used time and again to justify the ever-widening scope of socialist state control. Deconstructing the edifice of Marxian economics, with its essential claim that the state would atrophy and die, he reconstructed a myth of the Leviathan state which, packaged, propagandized, and distributed around the globe, became the socialist idea itself.

Bukharin understood, and here he was not alone, that the revolution demanded a new kind of state. But this craving had to be related to existing doctrine. Bukharin was aware that he was, as Stephen Cohen has said, "responsibile for the theoretical integrity of Bolshevism."[19] In the mushrooming growth of state power, in the withering of intermediary institutions between state and society, he discerned the road on which Russia was hurrying from capitalism to socialism. Where Marxism was merely a theory that explained and unified everything, Bukharin offered the socialist state as not only the agent of that theory, but as its very embodiment.

Bukharin was not blind to the implications of abandoning the theory of the state withering away. But power was in the air and he felt its intoxicating force. The facts of political life made a necessity of revising party doctrine, whether Marxists liked it or not. The state's "fundamental meaning," he now claimed, was "precisely that it is the lever of economic revolution."[20] In the past the Bolsheviks had insisted that revolution and dictatorship of the proletariat would usher in immediately the communist utopia. This had been the source of their schism with the Mensheviks, who believed utopia could not be achieved until Russia passed first through a bourgeois stage of parliamentary government, during which socialists would have to collaborate with liberal parties. By means of a super-state, Bukharin now argued, Russia would leap in a single bound into socialism.

While acceptance of the state as an agent of modernism was essential to an understanding of Marx's writings on capitalism, to say that it was the midwife of socialism called into question the dogmatic Marxist assertion that the state was subordinate to the economic base of society. Here was the terrible horizon of state-sponsored socialism. "If the proletariat's state power is the lever of economic revolution," Bukharin argued,

> then it is clear that "economics" and politics must merge here into a single whole. Such a merging exists under the dictatorship of finance capital . . . in the form of state capitalism. But the dictatorship of the proletariat reverses all the relations of the old world—in other words, the political dictatorship of the working class must inevitably be its economic dictatorship.[21]

This was a classic statement of totalitarianism before Hannah Arendt tagged it with a name.

Where was the voice of the worker, the man directly concerned, in all this talk of state socialism? It was not heard, and Bukharin was unmoved. War communism's very success in extending state control of industrial production and the distribution of goods turned his sight away from the utopian program, toward the minimum and the possible. Communism's red dawn receded. Old Marxist slogans were repeated with untamed ardor, but conviction had passed to faith in the state as an organized socialist economy. That this was a biased glance at a predominantly farm economy was evident from Bukharin's own less fanciful observations about peasant agriculture. Small peasants, he emphasized, were not to be expropriated or forcibly collectivized; "many intermediate forms of agricultural production" were still necessary. And he warned the party not to "spit on the muzhik,"[22] although spitting on the peasants (forcible requisitioning) was in fact a lynchpin of war communism. The impulse came from the compelling lure of an almighty state. Having seized office with no preconceived economic program, Bukharin and the Bolsheviks embraced the first one that appeared to arise out of and correspond to actual events. An internal logic—what Marxists call "regularity"—seemed discernible in the kaleidoscope of revolution and civil war. Class war, civil war, foreign intervention, the economic and political "dictatorship of the proletariat"—in order to demonstrate that the revolution conformed to Marx's prophecy, each had to be reconciled with the party's pre-revolutionary doctrines. War communism had to be shown as validating old theory. What set Bukharin apart from his comrades, what made him seem an archangel of the state, was his literary monument to collectivist folly, *The Economics of the Transition Period,* a tract grounded in the blindness of the period, the belief that "civil war lays bare the true physiognomy of society."[23]

Locking himself in his study, Bukharin worked relentlessly for six months, mastering the intricacies and mysteries of government statistics and publishing his document in May 1920. He intended the book to be a study of "the process of the transformation of capitalist society into communist society."[24] Instead it became the classic apology for totalitarianism.

For Bukharin's theoretical model of socialism defined a new allegiance. He spawned, in fact, a dogma for worship of the state. His faith lay in the collective moral purity and vision of the revolution being preserved into the future by a state in which virtue and freedom would be mutually sustained.

Just how this was to be accomplished remained, in all Bukharin's writings, notoriously obscure. In his lifetime he had shown himself circumspect about, if not downright hostile to, overt suggestions of bloody permanent dictatorship. What he invented was not a blueprint for totalitarianism, but the idiom in which its lusts could be voiced and its goals articulated. Most of all he provided a way for limitations on state power to be stripped away, and the deed justified. In place of an irreconcilable opposition between the individual, with his freedom intact, and a government eager to curtail it, Bukharin substituted a state in which liberty was not alienated but, as it were, placed in trust. The surrender of individual rights to the collective state was supposedly conditional on that entity preserving them. But the impossibility of that bargain was soon revealed to all.

In abstract language—"almost in algebraic formulas"[25]—Bukharin nailed his thesis to the Kremlin's door. Key ideas and concepts were frequently muddled and occasionally inconsistent, but as a first audacious attempt to go beyond the existing body of Marxist thought *The Economics* was an immediate success. It put to rest the old assumption that the transition to socialism would be relatively painless. He dismissed the nagging question of Russian backwardness, and emphasized the "human apparatus" as the essential element to building communism, the decisive factor being a revolutionary class willing to carry out "social and organisational tasks."[26]

This line plunged Bukharin to the heart of the Bolsheviks' dilemma. Spurned was the traditional Marxist assumption that socialism grows in the womb of the old order. He contrasted the growth of socialism to the growth of capitalism:

> They [the bourgeoisie] did not build capitalism, it built itself. The proletariat will build socialism as an organised system, as an organised collective subject. While the process of the creation of capitalism was spontaneous, the process of building communism is to a significant degree a conscious, i.e., organised process. . . . The epoch of Communist construction will therefore be an epoch of planned and organised work; the proletariat will solve its task as a social-economic task of building a new society.[27]

Because the socialist state considers existing classes and structures oppressive, relations between it and other forces in society must be revolutionary. It is not adjustment of differences within the existing system that is at issue, but the very system itself. Adjustments may be possible, Bukharin conceded, but they are mere tactical maneuvers intended to consolidate socialism's power, or tools designed to undermine the morale of the state's antagonists. Self-defense may at times truly be the motivation of the revolutionary state; for Bukharin was sincere in his protestations of feeling threatened by remnants of the past. After all, Tsarist officers were preparing their counterstrike that would lead to civil war. But the distinguishing feature of a revolutionary state which Bukharin reveals (quite unintentionally) is not that it feels threatened, but that *nothing* can appease it. Only absolute security—the neutralization of all opponents—can be a sufficient guarantee of survival, and thus the state's desire for absolute security to build socialism meant absolute insecurity for all other sectors of society.

In such an environment, power cannot be restrained. Opponents of the state can meet with it, but they cannot persuade it to limit its power, for they do not speak the same language. For Bukharin, it is the essence of revolutionary socialist governance that it possesses the courage of its convictions. It is willing, indeed eager, to push its convictions to their ultimate conclusion. Whatever else revolutionary government achieves, it must erode the legitimacy of all social structures inherited from the previous order, and put an end to the restraint with which that order operated. All political and economic contests become doctrinal. Sole responsibility for translating the moral claims of the revolution into reality resides with the socialist state. To succeed, it must disintegrate not only the system of legitimacy derived from the Tsar, but with that all the intermediate social structures and safeguards which, to Bukharin's contemporaries at least, seemed the prerequisite of social stability. Coercion and force replace social obligation. For both the revolution and the construction of socialism depend on revealed truth and a special reading of history; both require absolute faith. And both are fed by the same passions: justice, communion, vengeance.

Dictatorship was the only possible response to the problem of management in the post-revolutionary era, Bukharin believed. Any relaxation of control, if it allowed oppositions to exist, would spawn rivals to the Bolsheviks for power and influence. Bukharin, like Lenin, was not a man to tolerate challengers to the power he coveted. Too great was his sense of insecurity. His brand of fanaticism, undiluted by any vision of compromise, was too fierce and too jealous to share power. Because of the harsh struggles of the underground revolutionary world out of which he emerged, Bukharin was skeptical as to the possibility of peaceful coexistence with rival forces. Persuaded utterly of his moral rightness, he insisted on the submission or destruction of all competing power. Outside the Communist party, Russian society was to have no rigidity.

There was to be no form of collective human activity or association which would not be dominated by the Party, the state. No other force in society would be allowed vitality or integrity. Only the Party was to have structure. All else was to be amorphous, unthinking, obedient mass.

And within the Party the same system was to apply. The majority of Party members might go through the motions of election, deliberation, decision, and action; but in these motions they were to be animated not by their own individual wills but by the overbrooding presence of the Party leadership.

Absolutism for its own sake, however, was not Bukharin's purpose. Doubtless he believed—and found it easy to believe—that the Party leadership alone knew what was good for society, and that they would accomplish good once their power was secure and unchallengeable. In justifying the search for that security, Bukharin was prepared to abandon all restraints and restrictions on the Party's methods. And until such time as security was achieved, he placed the comforts and happiness of the people entrusted to his care far down the scale of his priorities.

Any man has the right to believe that the world is his enemy; if he repeats the idea regularly enough, like some misanthrope's mantra, and makes it the background to his all conduct, he is bound eventually to be proved right.

At the start, Bukharin's book drifts into flights of Rousseauesque optimism about the future. Because socialist values are true, and everyone knows they are true, Bukharin concludes that there must come a time when these values will triumph. If only, he argues, the whole hateful business of property is eliminated, then society will be transformed. He starts to play all the old Proudhon gramophone records: "Property is the root of all evil . . ." Those who will build the future do not own things. This has a fine sound to it. And with this side of his nature Bukharin is not merely a reader of Rousseau, but also a decent individual; he believes that men will one day share his beliefs in community so that wars and floggings and tortures and exploitation and oppression of the poor must surely come to an end.

But only the blindest of Bukharin's readers could imagine that the buds on the Bolshevik tree really heralded the spring. Reading his words seventy years after they were written, we see a sort of tragedy in the fact that in Russia of all places, he felt that he could depend on the feelings of decency, not only in the general public, but in the government itself.

For in addition to the "dawnist" optimism of his study, there is another strand which is much more frightening. As a reader of Proudhon and de Maistre, he sees that power is of its essence violent, and that governments, capitalist or socialist, can only continue, whatever their complexion, by possessing the means to subdue their enemies with violence. To seize power and to retain it, it is necessary to love power. But love of power does not go with goodness but with the opposite qualities—pride, cunning, and cruelty. Here Bukharin skirts the difficulty of the socialist state; he is unable to face it squarely, and reverts, with tragic lack of foresight, to a justification of the Bolshevik monopoly on violence.

Bukharin justified the coercive measures of war communism and gave them theoretical expression. A new equilibrium is brought from revolutionary chaos by replacing the destroyed links in the process of production with new ones, by restructuring "in a new combination the dismantled social layers . . ."[28] This operation is undertaken by the proletarian state, which "statizes," militarizes, and mobilizes the productive forces of society. Similarity between this state of affairs and that which ruled under state capitalism is coincidental. As capitalist property was being transformed into "collective proletarian property,"[29] the two were "diametrically opposite in essence." "Surplus product," not "surplus profit" was being created. Exploitation was, therefore, "unthinkable." Labor conscription, which under capitalism was "enslavement of the working masses," became under socialism "nothing other than the self-organisation of the masses."[30] Socialism was the state and the state was socialism.

This agreeable person, conventionally dressed in tweeds and cloth cap, emerged as an uncompromising apostle of the necessity of violence. Man's progress toward perfection was being held back. Progress needed force and coercion. The spirit of revolt must be imposed:

> In the transition period, when one productive structure gives way to another, the mid-wife is revolutionary force. This revolutionary force must destroy the fetters on the development of society . . . the old state and the old type of productive relations. This revolutionary force, on the other side, must actively help in the formation of production relations, being a new form of "concentrated force," the state of the new class, which acts as the lever of economic revolution, altering the economic structure of society. Thus on one side force plays the role of a destructive factor; on the other, it is a force of cohesion, organisation, and construction. The greater this . . . power is . . . the less will be the "costs" of the transition period . . ."[31]

Bukharin argues that the massacres and brutalities of the civil war were, somehow, no single person's responsibility, but a historical necessity. They were the inevitable product of impersonal forces: mass need and, he often implies, justifiable retribution for the exploitations of the past. Revolutionary justice is swift, personal, satisfying; it meets the rage of the faithful. The overall effect is comforting to the revolutionary; Bukharin defends the scholarly normalization of evil.

Obviously the killing and imprisonment of tens of thousands in cold blood was the consequence of some sort of phobic condition brought on by both military crisis and the apocalyptic rhetoric of revolutionary conspiracy. For Bukharin there was also an element of armed sanitation about it, a logical consummation of Marx's jeremiads against the cloacal filth of the bourgeoisie. The trash to be disposed of comprised all of Marx's specified sources of contamination: aristocrats, moneylenders, venal priests. But the work of eliminating these human infections was not some generalized, indiscriminate mass mobilization. On the contrary, as Bukharin and Lenin argued, removals were the work of specific, identifiable state agencies.

Bukharin turned a blind eye to "proletarian coercion in all of its forms, beginning with shooting and ending with labour conscription," because it was "creating communist mankind out of the human materials of the capitalist epoch."[32] Any evil could be excused so long as it was progressive. Bukharin's ideas and the Central Committee's needs fitted together like sword and sheath.

From his ode to the state, Bukharin moved ineluctably to the heresy of undermining theoretical Marxism's applicability to post-capitalist society. The categories and economic laws discussed by Marx pertained only to capitalist production. "As soon as we take an organised social economy," Bukharin said,

> all the basic "problems" of political economy disappear: problems of value, price, profit, and the like. Here "relations between people" are not expressed in "relations between things," and social economy is regulated not by the blind forces of the market and competition but consciously by a . . . PLAN. Therefore here there can be a certain descriptive system on the one hand, a system of norms on the other. But there can be no place for a science studying "the blind laws of the market" since there will be no market. Thus the end of capitalist commodity society will be the end of political economy.[33]

Deftly, perhaps unconsciously, all Marxian proofs were swept away under Bukharin's broom. In their place he offered the state, ordering and imposing communism at its will. His theory of immediate socialist construction gave doctrinal legitimacy to Lenin's desire to eliminate opposition to the regime. What Stalin succeeded in doing a decade and a half later, Lenin and Bukharin already had in mind in 1920.

Under Bolshevism, Russia was at last changing. The state, source of all change, needed to be praised. For Bukharin it was like the moment, described so incomparably by Tolstoy in his novel *Resurrection,* when Nekhlyudov and Maslova, as very young people, emerge from the Easter liturgy in darkness and hear the sound of breaking ice coming to them upon the midnight air. Spring, dawn, and resurrection are in the sound.

4

֍ ֍

Visions of the Future
Vladimir Mayakovsky

In 1917 the false promise of communism and the fertile inventiveness of modern art mated, ever so briefly. For more than a millennium, Russia's Orthodox priests had indoctrinated illiterate peasants by using didactic icons. Aesthetically minded Leninists thought modern art might meet the challenge of training the skeptical masses in the new revolutionary faith. Changing the language of art in the name of revolution was thought to be akin to rebels seizing a television station today.

Lenin's abrupt triumph furnished the Russian avant-garde with their great artistic metaphor. Here, as the art critic Robert Hughes has written, "was process and transformation, the literal renewal of history: heroic materialism at work on the social plane, combining the fragments of an abolished reality into a new, collective pattern."[1] One artist of the revolutionary period, Natan Altman, went so far as to claim that "futurism" (his catch-all term for all radical art) was *the* form of "proletarian creation." "How terribly we need to fight against this pernicious intelligibility," he exclaimed, speaking of ordinary poster art—the muscular worker with a red flag. Instead,

> take any work of revolutionary, futurist art. People who are used to seeing a depiction of individual objects or phenomena in a picture are bewildered. You cannot make anything out. And indeed, if you take out any one part from a futurist picture, it then represents an absurdity. Because each part of a futurist picture acquires meaning only through the interaction of all the other parts, only in conjunction with them does it acquire the meaning in which the artist imbued it.
>
> A futurist picture lives a COLLECTIVE LIFE, by the same principle on which the proletariat's whole creation is constructed.[2]

An art of expectation was spawned. A future of equality and organized energy in which the arts would act as a transformer was envisioned.

The revolution had swept away the middle class. Art's lone patron was now to be the state. "Art is a powerful means of infecting those around us with ideas, feelings and moods," said Anatoly Lunacharsky, Lenin's first arts commissar. "Agitation and propaganda acquire particular acuity and effectiveness when they are clothed in the attractive and mighty forms of art."[3]

The art that the revolution gave birth to—Constructivism—was dialectics made concrete. Here was true modernity—rivets, celluloid, airplane wings. In place of static figures, the dynamic unfolding of historical forces. Art would be open to everyone instead of a few refined souls; old class distinctions between artist and artisan, architect and engineer, were to be fused and shaped by the state into a new concept of art as production. Still-lifes and portraits were reflections of private property and individuals, but "socialist art" would stop depicting ownable things. Sculpture would use common materials like iron and glass, comparable in their severity with the marble of antiquity. Such common materials would reveal a world of material "necessity" to parallel the one in which its supposed audience lived, the world of common manual work.

During this springtime of the revolution, the Central Committee entertained all kinds of demonstrations of devotion to the Communist state. For while Lenin, Trotsky, Bukharin, and the other Bolsheviks were, in the first instance, committed to the practical work of giving Russia new institutions of government and industry, the Central Committee also acted as a political theatre: the place where oratory and gesture, even on some occasions poetry and music, would dramatize the principles for which the revolution was supposed to stand. And since the Bolsheviks had repudiated historicity and precedent, those legitimating principles had, necessarily, to claim universal validity. In March 1918, for example, two convicts from Bulgaria made a formal appearance. Tsarist Russia had used its Siberian exile camps not just for its own criminals and dissidents but, on contract, for those of other states needing somewhere to dump their undesirables. The Bolsheviks had not yet taken action to abolish internal exile for the native population (and never would). But the Central Committee was eager to declare that it would no longer serve as the instrument of an ignoble "slavery" for European "bourgeois despotisms." Cheered by the committeemen and embraced by Zinoviev and Bukharin, the Bulgar convicts were paraded as heroes.

Such spectacles were more than acts in a revolutionary circus. They sustained the Bolshevik's self-belief and reassured them that their cause did not, after all, stand alone in the world but was part of some bigger, indefinitely extended family of the "oppressed"—who must now look to Russia for deliverance. Lenin, for one, found the whole thing risible. But as foolish as these occasions undoubtedly were, they corresponded to the equally sententious religion of proletarian brotherhood and amity being preached in official speech and text, not least by the poet Vladimir Mayakovsky.

Living in solitude, disillusionment, and a chronic, drug-blurred battle against insomnia, Mayakovsky produced a body of work around the central idea that if the revolution had created a new man—and it had—then art from the past was of no use. "We are shooting the old generals," he wrote soon after the October coup, "Why not Pushkin?"[4] Mayakovsky's alluring call for a "clean sweep" of Russian culture, for a "proletarian dictatorship" in the arts, seduced the imagination of leading Bolsheviks such as Bukharin. It stirred both their yearning hope for human progress as well as the nascent worship of the socialist state. Mayakovsky rejected the artistic ideal of individual expression as one hampering the development of proletarian man, although such freedom had allowed him to develop his art under the old regime. The art of Pushkin and Lermontov and Pasternak was merely a form of corruption. Displeasing people was a sign of integrity. Reason was itself suspect, for the revolution had been nearly aborted by men who wanted philosophy rather than the passions to be its guide.

Mayakovsky made an art form of confrontational ugliness, for which his personal appearance was ideally suited. His eyes were not quite aligned but they glittered blackly from out of a broad, flattened face. After the revolution he discarded the perfectly conventional attire he had previously worn for an appearance of ostentatious simplicity: bare-throated, unkempt black hair; an old ermine scarf sometimes thrown over his shoulders. It was not the attire of a true "prole," but it was a suitably theatrical costume for a friend of the people. He gloried in rudeness. Haunting Petrograd in June 1918, he burst into a dinner to harangue an editor he wanted to confront.

Essential to Mayakovsky's adoption of the personality of the revolutionary Jeremiah—dreamer, prophet, bringer of the apocalypse—was the challenge of martyrdom.[5] Like Trotsky and many other Bolsheviks, he was constantly offering to die rather than compromise his principles; to sacrifice his own person to the vengeance of the "liberticides." The fact that Mayakovsky took to his heels whenever danger actually closed in did not seem to tarnish this image of proffered self-immolation. He habitually carried a pistol—less, one suspects, to defend himself than as a stage prop.

The institutional machinery for artistic dictatorship which Mayakovsky advocated was quickly set in place by Lenin in the new Commissariat of Education. Here Mayakovsky and his "Futurist" colleagues, smarting from old critical wounds, set themselves up as the country's cultural arbiters, wielding a censor's stick to inculcate virtue. Mayakovsky thought of the revolution as a school but one in which knowledge would always be augmented by "social morality." Both, moreover, depended on state discipline. Terror and social virtue, he was fond of saying, were part of the same exercise of revolutionary improvement. Once the weight of the past had been cast off, it would be possible to begin this vast exercise of enrolling the entire nation in his school of the future.

For those Bolsheviks who shared Mayakovsky's vision, there were two necessary stages to this enterprise of social regeneration. First, the cultural anarchy unleashed by the revolution had to be channelled; second, it had to comport with an imposing, if disorderly, program of Communist edification. That program would leave no part of a citizen's life untouched. It would use music, open-air theatricals, and pageants; colossal public monuments; libraries, exhibitions, even sports competitions, to stimulate the new Communist virtues. The exaltation of the collective life would be in the strongest possible contrast to the acts of individual creation characteristic of the bourgeois age.

Poetry, Mayakovsky announced, must represent this ideal.

> I want the pen to be on par
> with the bayonet;
> And Stalin
> to deliver his Politburo
> reports
> about verse in the making
> as he would about pig iron
> and the smelting of steel.[6]

In 1919 his ode to anonymous millions who toiled in bitterness, "150,000,000," expressed this new communal art in a poem which he left unsigned, because he "wanted anyone at all to add to it and improve it."

> 150,000,000 is the name of the creator of this poem.
> Its rhythms—bullets,
> its rhymes—fires from building to building.

150,000,000 speak with my lips . . .
Who can tell the name
of the earth's creator—surely a genius?
And so
of this
my
poem
no one is the author.[7]

Mayakovsky's verse urged the creation of a cult of self-dispossession. Surrender of the self to the state became a demonstration of one's patriotic probity. Those who did not have creative works to give away could contribute to the hard-pressed coffers of the government through other kinds of donation. Former aristocrats, Mayakovsky argued, could demonstrate their loyalty by offering up their jewels. Socialism, he argued, must begin with acts of giving as well as acts of taking.

Devotion to the socialist state was supposed to be such that it superseded all previous allegiances—to job, union, province, social order, or confession—within the new extended family. But this militant inclusiveness by definition required outsiders in order to define its limits and to give insiders a sense of their own bonds. So all the images of incorporation presupposed counterimages of denial: obstinate men and women who, refusing to sink their differences within the revolutionary state, had to be extruded from it. Mayakovsky provided at least one such image: Woodrow Wilson, the defender of world capitalism in "150,000,000," who stands brandishing his pistols with four cocks and a sabre bent into seventy sharp blades. Wilson eats and grows fat, "adding one floor after another to his belly."[8] In the end he will be defeated by "Ivan," a thoroughly Russian champion of the poor and downtrodden.

All of these strains were brought together by Mayakovsky in his most ambitious political production: the revolutionary mystery play, *Mystery Bouffe,* presented on the first anniversary of the Bolshevik rising, and directed by V. E. Meyerhold. For Mayakovsky it was not just the officially instituted theatres that were now the ancien régime, but the entire manner of their art: stilted, artificial, academic, preposterously elitist, dedicated to frivolity and remote from the powerful universal truths that could, and ought to, be communicated by the theatre. No wonder Rousseau had thought the theatre incompatible with a virtuous society; no wonder that one of Trotsky's earliest acts was to commandeer the stages of Petrograd.

More completely than any other medium, theatrical works—or so

Mayakovsky believed—mirrored revolutionary life. Drama could leave the stage door and go into the street where, as in the Middle Ages, it could be produced by workingmen on wheeled platforms with different scenes drawn along in succession. Every mystery of the revolution, and its central tenet of salvation through submersion in the communal life of the state, could be made physical and concrete and be presented in terms of everyday life—irreverent, bloody, and bawdy. Revoltingly realistic scenes of torture could be made regular theatrical fare, as if a violent time bred enjoyment in violence. A capitalist slitting open the belly of a peasant woman to see if she is bearing a child could be portrayed with the aid of gory entrails, supplied by a loyal butcher, spilling from the victim. Such *schadenfreude* was not peculiar to Mayakovsky, but his was a dark variety indeed, which found its greatest expression in his play *Mystery Bouffe.*

For Mayakovsky's antennae always picked up whatever was in the air and he fixed unerringly on the destruction of the bourgeoisie as the subject of his play. All the fever and fecundity of the revolution he captured. Using more actors than any company in Moscow possessed, he went into the street for extras. The advertisement rang with revolutionary fervor:

> Comrade actors! You are under obligation to celebrate the great anniversary of the revolution with a revolutionary production. You must present the play *Mystery Bouffe,* a heroic epic, and satiric portrait of our era. . . . To work, everyone, time is precious.[9]

And he composed dialogue of tremendous complexity and exaggerated dissonance, with the cast to be divided at times against itself, shouting in bloodcurdling language as if to express the terror of the subject by terrifying the ear.

Rehearsals for the play took place in an atmosphere of uproar; everything was to be larger, noisier, more violent than life. Mayakovsky wanted the settings to express "something sinister about our time, a pride born of limitless power, a defiance . . . a new order lured out of chaos."[10] In a single act lasting three hours without interruption, he spared the audience's sensibilities nothing. Without overture or prelude, the curtain rose on a scene of devastation—the apocalypse, music thundering like the hammer of doom. Earth has been destroyed by flood. "Seven pairs of clean" and "seven pairs of unclean"[11] refugees struggle to survive at the North Pole. The clean are a variety of bourgeois types—Lloyd George, Clemenceau, a Russian speculator—who wear Saracen robes and grisly masks. At one point they run through the audience to pinch and frighten the spectators. The unclean are simple working folk: a miner, a carpenter, a laundry-woman. They are set upon and deceived by the clean, who throw them overboard from an ark. A system of weights and pulleys brings the unclean to hell, heaven, the clouds, and a new promised land. Angels and devils are made to appear magically through trapdoors; Hell opens and closes its monstrous mouth upon the clean. The unclean visit heaven with disgust, and return to earth to build the promised land of the communist paradise.

While such manifestations of the new revolutionary religion—the cult of a communal state—were theatrical and necessarily ephemeral, they were no less important for being that. In the emotive climate of 1918–1919, Mayakovsky made more of an impact through arresting spectacle than many of the institutional alterations on which the Bolsheviks concentrated. And it would be quite mistaken to see Mayakovsky's efforts as so much orchestrated mummery, staged at the behest of defensive politicians to disguise the frailty of their legitimacy. Mayakovsky's plays engaged large audiences in shared revolutionary enthusiasm. However repetitive and redundant these plays and ceremonies became, conscientious citizens never seemed to tire of embracing them, their individual identities fused into a single revolutionary will.

This is not merely a vindication of Bukharin's state-constructed socialism; it is vindication for a new religion of the state. When we look back at Bukharin, what we are most aware of is his sense that the creation of a socialist Leviathan was a necessary step for the creation of true socialism. Bukharin's primary concern was to build utopia. But Mayakovsky confused ends and means. For him the state, and nothing but the state, mattered. Utopia was already at hand; his duty was to protect and preserve it.

In his plays and poetry Mayakovsky roamed wildly. Beautifully, dangerously, his ideas rolled and billowed like storm clouds. He shared the leading Bolsheviks' rejection of the democratic idea of individual rights as hampering the state's ability to realize society's full capacity. He saw individual liberty as a ball and chain holding man back from his highest attainment. He saw the dominant weight of popular tastes, opinions, and moral prejudices as a slave morality. Society should live by a master morality above common precepts of good and evil. He preached "yes" to the promptings of state energy as good per se, regardless of conflict with conventional morality. Art and law and religion which discouraged such promptings frustrated man's progress. Limitation on the power of the socialist state was a sop for the weak, the meek, and the bourgeois. The state had no need of limits as it built utopia. It was a law unto itself.

Man must shake off the chains of tradition and history as the intolerable burden of the past. And Mayakovsky stated his creed, not in logical declarative language, but in a more emotionally charged prose poetry like the psalms, meandering and obscure, full of mountain tops and sunrises, the singing of birds and dancing of girls, carrying the new Leviathan state on its quest toward the perfection of human society. In a bedroom in Moscow, leaning against a pillow, staring at a new world out of sad lost eyes, Mayakovsky thought he was capturing the spirit of his age.

Not everyone endorsed him. Lenin hated his work. "Pushkin I understand and enjoy," he said, "Nekrasov I acknowledge, but Mayakovsky—excuse me. I can't understand him."[12] Lenin was into everything and alert to everything. Art, he announced in 1919, should represent the Ideal. He cited the educational effect of art upon the working class, who after a hard day could be lifted out of themselves by contemplation of beauty and the Ideal. Mayakovsky's art, he believed, was a messy and incomprehensible way to spread socialist virtue. Lenin's tastes were naturally conservative. He preferred to co-opt the "cultural heritage" as part of his relentless onslaught of socialist values. As Trotsky put it, "the Futurist break with the past is, after all, a tempest in the closed-in world of the intelligentsia which grew up on Pushkin. Fet . . . Balmont, and Blok . . . The Futurists have done well to push away from them. But it is not necessary to make a universal law of development out of the act of pushing away."[13]

It hardly needed spelling out to Mayakovsky that Lenin's criticism was a frontal attack on his methods and ideas. Mayakovsky's rejection of conventional artistic standards, which he intended as a stepping stone to a higher social and aesthetic ground, Bolshevik leaders saw as a command to roam the gutter. This made Mayakovsky and his friends seers of black, the black in men. If self-censorship did not work, then the state would have to intervene.

If art was to be wheeled into the state's service, it had to be comprehensible to the masses and not, as Karl Radek was to say of the writings of James Joyce, "A heap of dung teeming with worms." As Lenin knew so well, the majority of Russian people would never prefer the violent, dissonant, indecipherable pieces of Mayakovsky and his "clique" to the direct and commanding art of Tolstoy and Pushkin. Mayakovsky began to have trouble with the censors. *Mystery Bouffe,* he wrote in his autobiography, "was produced three times, then lambasted. Replaced by various Macbeths."[14]

Literature was no longer to be revolutionary. Enthusiasm for socialism persisted without any corresponding imaginative enthusiasm. The idea of culture was becoming more restricted. And Mayakovsky, for all his reaffirmations of socialism, his adoration of the state, appeared to the Communist leaders to be an ornament as decadent as anything from the bourgeois era. Instead of his work ingratiating himself with the Bolshevik Central Committee, it turned them against Mayakovsky and they began snapping at his heels.

Men like Bukharin were travelling away from the romanticism of the revolution, from the revolutionary enthusiasm and the emotional euphoria of 1917, and setting up the state as an exact, scientific mechanism for social construction. Where Bukharin embraced the state from a position of some detachment, in which the state was a question of need, Mayakovsky came to it from a sense of fierce partisanship, almost a religious need. It is no longer a question of socialism creating an all-powerful state, but of the state becoming socialism itself. Mayakovsky idealized the state, and to be idealized is to be overestimated.

Nothing was to be beyond the reach of the long arm and booming voice of political harangue. The degree of cultural mobilization envisioned by Lenin did not even respect the boundaries of privacy. Indeed privacy was itself suspect, being too close to the strategies of concealment that were said to be at the heart of bourgeois culture. So the test of socialist virtue did not even stop at the bedroom door. Newspapers enjoyed reporting or inventing stories of revolutionary Lysistratas who interrupted intercourse at critical moments to reprove their husbands for some lingering loyalty to the past. One stage further on in the conjugal life cycle of revolutionaries, the Central Committee ordered Mayakovsky's department in the Commissariat of Education to especially honor prolific mothers for their contribution to socialism.

All art was to be turned into an arm of patriotic propaganda, which was quite all right with Mayakovsky, in the abstract. The problem was that such art was to be straightforward; no invention, just editorializing, political preaching, and exemplary anecdotes designed to create not just a loyal but a morally alert audience. Back to the icons. Mayakovsky was ordered to produce instruments of conversion, poetry that would stiffen the doubts of waverers and inform those who had difficulty understanding the decrees of the Central Committee or the difference between "honest" and "feigned" patriots. It was in the official poetry coming from Mayakovsky's ministry that the rhetoric of conspiracy and denunciation against traitors within the country and without became most shrill.

But he had no hand in it. His state-sponsored god wanted nothing to do with his offerings. Ever smaller printings of his works ensued. A bizarre life, at once wretched and consoling, unfolded over the next decade. Characteristically, his circumstances were made worse by his own self-righteousness. Mayakovsky invariably believed everything he did and wrote to be in strict conformity with socialist principles. He sent his poetry to the censors, and it came back unopened, like a parcel nobody wants. *The Bedbug* and *The Bathhouse*, plays the increasingly depressed Mayakovsky wrote as Stalin consolidated his power—the former a satire of the socialist future in which flamboyant aesthetes like himself are treated as sideshow freaks, the latter a lampoon of the mushrooming bureaucracy that was progressively strangling him as a writer—were given only fleeting theatrical runs, and soon disappeared with his death. In a growing despair, Mayakovsky fell sick, lost much of his hair, grew thin and wasted. Darkness seemed to be closing around his life. He was resolved to be constant to his principles, even when socialism itself betrayed them, betrayed him.

The dilemma for successive Mayakovskys in Russia was that they owed their positions of influence to precisely the kind of individualism that made their continuing usefulness impossible. Socialism as insurrection would have been impossible without the lashings of verbal spleen and blood offered by the likes of Mayakovsky, but socialism as government was impossible unless judiciously, ruthlessly, managed.

Here was the first moment that revolutionary writers discovered the depressing dilemma that revolutionary socialism entailed revolutionary control of thought and deed, state control of minds as well as industry. And Mayakovsky would not be the last to break over its consequences.

In the last year of his life, "revolutionary fever" returned to Mayakovsky with all the force of delirium. He sat in his dingy rooms, his hair cropped, glaring at the walls. Periodically the black silence that descended upon him would be interrupted by a torrent of denunciation in half-intelligible revolutionary phrases. In the fiercest paroxysms of his dementia he would rage against "individualists." In February of 1930 a friend from the Commissariat of Education visited him. He left not knowing how mad Mayakovsky really was.

To some Bolsheviks, Mayakovsky became a source of amusement; to others, like Bukharin, a quaint kind of living museum of half-forgotten and embarrassing slogans. By spring 1930 he disappeared from the land of the living in all but biological fact. Sometimes he sat naked, angrily refusing a blanket to protect him against the cold. Periodically he was heard to mutter against those who would betray the revolution. Oblivious to all callers, concerned or callous, Mayakovsky lived entirely inside the revolution and the revolution inside him. Sympathy seems out of place here, for in some sense Mayakovsky's madness was a logical consequence of his compulsive worship of the socialist state. Discovering a person of almost sublime willingness, the revolution filled him up like a vessel. However many times his faith betrayed him, it would find Mayakovsky loyal to the spirit of 1917. Even his own suicide could be made into an offering. "Comrades . . . ," he wrote, "don't think me a coward. Really, it couldn't be helped. . . . In the desk drawer I have 2000 rubles. Use them to pay my taxes."[15] He signed and dated the note, April 1, 1930—April Fool's Day. Then he put a bullet in his brain.

Safely buried, Mayakovsky could be safely rehabilitated. But it was not his work that was retrieved, however, only his subservience to the new faith. In 1935, Lily Brik, long Mayakovsky's lover, complained in a brave letter to Stalin that bureaucrats were impeding her efforts to establish a Mayakovsky museum. Stalin, Robert Tucker informs us, soon "penned on her letter a note to Yezhov directing him to help Brik because 'Mayakovsky was and remains the most talented poet of our Soviet epoch. Indifference to his memory is a crime.' "[16] Monuments popped up to Mayakovsky's memory almost immediately. A Moscow metro station was named after him. Death—and Stalin's sanction—had washed him clean.

Mayakovsky left behind a testament of works, a perfume of revolt, but not a changed world. His art vanished too soon to have any lasting effect or influence. Besides, Lenin would have been foolhardy to commit scarce state resources to Mayakovsky's schemes, however edifying. So the drift from modern art into art as celebration of the state began before Lenin's death and burial; and Stalin soon made anything that was not mass art a state crime. In Stalin's eyes, Mayakovsky was but a bourgeois remnant—a speck of free imagination in the still ocean of his new Russia. After Mayakovsky, art, like socialism itself, became merely another tool to reinforce the narcissism of power.

5

⇨⟫ ⟪⇦

Stalin Identifies
Socialism with Violence

Nowadays, to look at Mayakovsky's work is to learn little of life during the first decade of Soviet socialism. In the world beyond his banal verse, hysteria and massacre ruled. Russia was almost continuously in a state of civil war throughout the 1920s. In the winter of 1928, men ate rats in the streets of Moscow; the Soviet economy was already nearly a wreck, though Stalin had barely laid hands upon it. But in Mayakovsky's work, as in the politically correct novels of Mikhail Sholokov, the signs of socialist progress are unending. Men demand paradises, however fictive, in times of trouble, and socialism always looked best on paper. The man—Stalin—who had seized supreme power in Russia, demanded scenes and words of hope to help disguise the long days of want and terror that he knew lurked in the years ahead.

For with the consolidation of revolutionary power in Stalin's hands alone, there were no longer to be debates over principles or programs. There was only recitation, enemies or comrades: harlequin politics. For Revolutionary Socialism was in the process of being killed off in the name of revolutionary government. Lenin died after a series of brain hemorrhages at Gorki, near Moscow, at 6:30 P.M. on January 21, 1924, at the age of fifty-three.

Winston Churchill subsequently claimed that Lenin might have saved Russia and socialism from the extremities and the violence that lay ahead: "He alone could have found the way back to the causeway. . . . The Russian people were left floundering in the bog. Their worst misfortune was his birth . . . their next worst—his death."[1]

It is a controversial point, never to be settled. Indeed, the only safe comment is the one that Lenin himself made so often when he quoted Napoleon: *"On s'engage et puis—on voit"* ("You commit yourself and then—you see"). Lenin committed not only himself but all of Russia. But he did not live to see.

*   *   *

The discussion of the transformation of the idea of socialism from utopian idea to actual centralized state power has now entered the period when Stalin's influence began to be the primary force shaping socialism. To understand Stalin's character and place in the socialist movement, it is necessary to grasp the great ethical debate that shivered the socialist religion almost from its very inception in the middle of the nineteenth century. This conflict arose from the friction between the utopian ideals of the movement's ends and the brutality of its means. At the beginning, the ideas that drove the majority of the revolutionaries were pure; yet as failures mounted, a suspicion gradually arose, which fermented almost into a mania, that the only path to realization of their goal was through acts of great cruelty. If you desire to save mankind, you cannot reckon the cost.

This willingness to sacrifice human lives on the altar of an abstract idea, to slaughter in the name of the future, was something from which one Russian radical, Alexander Herzen, recoiled. "If progress is the goal," he said,

> for whom are we working? Who is this Moloch who, as the toilers approach him, instead of rewarding them, draws back; and as a consolation to the exhausted and doomed multitudes, . . . can only give the . . . mocking answer that after their death all will be beautiful on earth. Do you truly wish to condemn the human beings alive today to the sad role . . . of wretched galley slaves who, up to their knees in mud, drag a barge . . . with . . . "progress in the future" upon its flag? . . . a goal which is infinitely remote is no goal, only . . . a deception; a goal must be closer—at the very least the labourer's wage, or pleasure in work performed.[2]

Others came to see the squeamishness of past revolutionaries as the primary source of their political failure. Only through wanton callousness toward the sacrifices necessary to bring on the revolution could a way be found to eliminate the ruthlessness and callousness practiced by the old regime against the mass of the people. A certain superior virtue and self-sacrifice was assumed for the employment of evil means to achieve worthy ends. The burden of guilt and sin was willingly accepted so that others might have the privilege of remaining guiltless as the world was made anew. A classic Dostoevskian dilemma.

It is possible to see the fate of socialism explained in terms of the movement's inability to cope with this dilemma. Those who called themselves Socialist Revolutionaries, for example, were carried away by a belief in the efficacy of personal terrorism. In deference to this belief, they assassinated literally thousands of people—over seven hundred in the year 1907 alone. That many of their incidental victims were innocent the terrorists would not for a moment deny.

Innocent blood as well as that of the guilty had to be shed so that the collective good could be served. In such minds, this added to their heroism. After all, it was (supposedly) harder to kill a child than to kill a police agent. Lenin and the Bolsheviks supposedly did not share this belief in personal terrorism. Assassination they rejected as a normal means of political struggle. Rejected, not because they thought it morally wrong, but because they considered it inopportune and inexpedient. Violence was to demolish a system, not individuals. This spurning of individual terrorism did not in any sense signify a repudiation of violence. Scarred by his brother's death on a Tsarist gallows, Lenin nevertheless accepted the need for violence in the overthrow of the propertied classes. He believed, to be sure, in using violence precisely to the extent that it was necessary to promote one's political ends. No particular lust for it, no sadism in his personality drove him to use violence as a political tool. Lenin simply viewed violence as a necessary political device. His feelings are perhaps best summed up by the sad observation he once made to the effect that one would like to stroke and caress human beings; but one dare not do so, because they bite.

One of the first moments when Lenin authorized violence for Party purposes was in the use of armed robbery to secure funds for the support of Party actions. It is revealing and symbolic that precisely at this time and in this connection, that Iossif Vissarionovich Djugashvili, a Georgian who used the pseudonym Josef Stalin, came to the Party's notice.

Before the abortive revolution of 1905, the Party had done well in getting money from upper-class sources—well-meaning people who salved pangs of conscience by donations to the struggling revolutionaries, unsuspecting that they might already be on the list of future victims.

When the disorders of the 1905 revolution made more evident what the revolutionaries were really up to, these benevolent patrons scurried away. In the following years the Party fractured over its response to this loss of funds. There were those in the Party who wished to meet the need for money by resorting to blackmail, extortion, and banditry, and those who wanted a ban on expropriations. Lenin opted for violence, and he found his greatest support in the Caucasus, where the ancient combination of corruption, racial rivalry, and vendetta fused with Marxism to produce an underworld of extreme volatility and commitment. In this netherworld where politics merged with crime, where fierce racial

and personal hatreds, intrigues, and plots ruled—Stalin had his origins
as a revolutionist.

The Bolshevik leaders were not a coherent group and never would be.
The dominant early leaders, in a pattern that would hold in all socialist
revolutions from China to Cuba to Nicaragua, were almost uniformly
from comfortable social backgrounds. They might profess open contempt for all bourgeois sentiments, but slavishly followed every middle-
class social restraint. Lenin, Bukharin, Trotsky, Litvinov, Radek: each
felt at ease in the myriad languages and cultures of Europe. For they
saw Marxism as the fulfillment of the European tradition, indeed of all
European history. They did not hunger for a working class base but
preferred instead to operate among their own kind, a scholastic regiment
of one or two hundred, aloof from the people—like Stalin—for whom
they supposedly toiled. Indeed, they had little use for them despite
paying constant lip service to the idea of the dictatorship of the proletariat. What was needed, Lenin argued, was a strong, no-nonsense
party and a business-like understanding of history's needs. Here was a
voice without a body.

Subservient to these effete Party leaders were those Russians who
had real gripes against the Tsar's regime, the peasant foot soldiers who
toiled underground in Russia. They lived outside the law and acquired
the mindset of outlaws, of men and women who regarded their breach
with society as irrevocable, and who sought vindication and vengeance
for the bitterness of their lives by glamorizing their struggle and despair.
These underground Bolsheviki—ever at the beck and call of the emigré
Bolsheviks to do the real dirty work of revolution—were the original
political street punks: a Clockwork Red, Alexi and his Droogs. Nowhere
were these qualities more pronounced, nowhere did they provide more
of a contrast to the mild intellectual sincerity of a Bukharin in exile,
than in the seething, savage underworld of the Caucasus, where Stalin
learned his trade.

Little contact took place between the two groups. Lenin and Bukharin
in press and pamphlet constructed marvelous paper models of the communist millenium; poured out hate and invective; issued trumpet calls
for action to incite the enemy's overthrow. And barely known to them,
in the lower depths of Russian society, lonely men were listening. They
heard echoes of the tirades and the trumpets, and caught an imaginary
glimpse of the shining millennium that promised them a life without
hunger and without a boss. Suddenly one of them, with a sense of injury
or a sense of mission, would rise up, go out, and kill or rob—and

sacrifice his own life on the altar of that only minimally understood communist idea.

Stalin was just one of the anonymous thugs who came to socialism from the warrens of the poor, where hunger and dirt prevailed, where consumptives coughed and the air was thick with the smell of latrines, boiling cabbage, and stale beer, where babies wailed and couples screamed in sudden quarrels, where roofs leaked and unmended windows let in the cold blasts of winter, where privacy was unimaginable, where men, women, and grandparents lived together, eating, sleeping, fornicating, defecating, sickening, and dying in one room, where a kettle served as a wash boiler between meals, old boxes served as chairs, heaps of foul straw as beds, and boards propped across two crates as tables, where sometimes not all the children in a family could go out at one time because there were not enough clothes to go around, where decent families lived among drunkards, wife-beaters, thieves, and prostitutes, where life was a seesaw of unemployment and endless toil, where a cigar maker and his wife earning the equivalent of 13 cents an hour worked seventeen hours a day seven days a week to support themselves and three children, where death was the only extravagance when the scraped savings of a lifetime would be squandered on a funeral coach with flowers and a parade of mourners to ensure against the anonymity and last ignominy of some potter's field.

Stalin was the son of this hell. He felt as a born peasant that he had nothing; and in reaction he wished—as though such a thing was possible—to become an agent of change, a kind of history man. An inability to put words to his feelings of disgust drove him forward. Feelings, uncontrolled by any thought but that of resentment, flowed into a search for something to believe in; committed Stalin to learning at an early age the basic commandments of Marx's redeeming missionary faith; concealed forever his motives, obscured his cause, hid himself from himself. Communism as religion would bury his real emotions of self-hate. He despised the world of his origins; he would work to uproot it. Every action in his overheated life would flow from this despair. Out of rage at the squalor of his childhood, his grandiose wish was to amount to something, anything, and he went out to set the world aright. That was the great task that Stalin fixed for himself from a very early age.[3]

For Stalin was born in Gori, Georgia, in 1879, to a peasant family which had saved enough money to buy freedom twenty years earlier, two years before the decree abolishing serfdom. With the great difference that Russia was scarcely yet an industrial country and indeed had hardly moved out of its medieval condition, Stalin's father had much in common with the classic, self-made, Victorian puritan. He was a fierce believer in self-help and the work ethic, a despot in the family, ruling his sons by beating them, saying—when his wife protested—that the same had been done to him and that it had made a man of him. Djugashvili *père*, the slave turned master, was a squat non-descript man with a grizzled beard and a glare in his eye, a man not to be argued with. All heads were lowered before him as he hectored his family on their duties.

Like the majority of houses in Georgia, Stalin's childhood home had a single story and a tin roof. There was no sanitation; the family had to go to bogs in a communal field. Where did the family sleep? Behind improvised screens in the living room. Stalin sometimes slept in a shed in the back. His father's tyranny extended, of course, to the religious life of his family, and here he had his most profound impact on his son's development. As a boy Stalin was packed off to a seminary for the training of priests of the Orthodox church. It was here, shortly before his graduation, that Stalin was expelled for having belonged, while a seminarian, to a secret Marxist discussion group.

Thirteen years were to elapse between the time of Stalin's being defrocked and his emergence, in 1912, into the Bolshevik hierarchy. The record of his actions during these years remains shrouded in secrecy. The vagueness, the omissions (deliberate and otherwise), the contradictions, the inconsistencies, the many shifts in the treatment of this subject by official Soviet historians at different periods; all suggest that the real record must contain items which neither Stalin nor his successors have wished to see exposed to the scrutiny of even tame Soviet scholarship.

To explain this state of affairs, three hypotheses have been advanced by Stalin's biographer, Robert Tucker. One is that Stalin sought to conceal his early obscurity in the Party. Another is that he was so closely involved in crimes that exposure of his youthful deeds would shatter the crafted image of the great leader and statesman. The third theory is that he was a paid informer, that his dealings with the Tsar's secret police were such that they would be impossible to explain or explain away. Perhaps all three theories contain shards of truth.

No matter which is true, Stalin moved throughout these years of obscurity in the Caucasus or its immediate neighborhood. It is likely that he joined the Party in 1904. It is also likely that he was expelled in 1907, by the local Menshevik majority, because of his participation in violent acts of banditry. Exiled three or four times from the Caucasus by the police, Stalin was always treated by them under strangely mild and lenient conditions. He attended three Party conferences outside the Caucasus: one in Finland, one in Stockholm, one in London's Whitechapel district. On the second of these occasions, in 1907, his credentials were disputed by the Mensheviki; and as we will see Lenin, who supported Stalin's admission to the Congress despite the weakness of his credentials, was forced to confess—or at least to claim—on the floor of the conference that he had no idea as to who the man was.

Ample evidence, quite apart from police documents that peg him as an informer, suggest that Stalin was known to his comrades as a troublemaker—a brute of a man fond of provoking quarrels and acts of violence, for getting his revenge on people who had in some manner offended him or stood in his path. Memoirs of the time depict him as rigid and moody, two characteristics that were to reappear. He despised regular work. He had none of the common vices, was too shy and awkward to have success with women. His passions were newspapers and talking politics. Outbursts of violent argument and denunciation alternated with moods of despondency. He gave reign to his hatreds—Jews, priests—without restraint.

During this formulative period of Stalin's socialism, his limited readings appear to have been as much Anarchist as Marxist, his major prophets Peirre Proudhon and Mikhail Bakunin as well as Karl Marx. Proudhon excoriated property in a passion of contempt, and Bakunin worshipped violent revolution—both useful doctrines to a young man like Stalin who robbed for an altruistic motive. Although both men's Anarchist sparks failed to ignite in the nineteenth century, their ideas took root in the Transcaucasus in a way that profoundly affected Stalin's outlook. Proudhon and Bakunin found a Russian offshoot in the Narodniki, or Populists, otherwise known as the Party of the People's Will, founded in 1879 to arouse the Russian masses. Because of communal use of land peculiar to the Russian peasant, reformers worshipped the peasant as a natural socialist who needed only the appearance of a Messiah to be awakened from his lethargy and impelled upon the march to revolution. The bomb was to be the Messiah. "Terrorist activity," stated the Narodniki program, "consisting in destroying the most harmful person in government, aims to undermine the prestige of the government and arouse in this manner the revolutionary spirit of the people and their confidence in the success of the cause."[4]

In 1881, two years after Stalin's birth, the Narodniki struck a blow that startled the world: they assassinated the Tsar, Alexander II. It was a triumphant coup, equal, they imagined, to the battering down of the

Bastille. It would shout aloud their protest, summon the oppressed, and terrorize the oppressors. Instead it unleashed retribution. The Tsar's ministers opened a campaign of savage repression, the public, abandoning all thoughts of reform, acquiesced, and the revolutionary movement, "broken and demoralised, withdrew into the conspirator's cellar."[5] Here Stalin's initiation into revolution and socialism began.

The failure of the Narodniki caused one part of the Russian underground to veer off, not toward the earth but toward the clouds. In the new period of revolutionary activity beginning in the nineties, their aims, always utopian, became ever more fanciful and their deeds less than ever connected with reality. They became impatient. They despised the puny efforts of trade unionists to achieve mere reform of working conditions.

In his seminarian's cell Stalin learned to hate and to rebel. He despised the rich whose immense possessions could, it seemed to him, only be explained as having been accumulated out of the pockets of the exploited masses. He read Proudhon's famous question and answer: "What is property?" asked Proudhon, "Property is theft." He also hated the peasants who existed in apathy, stupefied by poverty. Instead of turning to the gospels for comfort, as a good seminarian should, he turned instead to the great Anarchist prophets, the most prominent of whom was Prince Peter Kropotkin, by birth an aristocrat, by profession a geographer, and by conviction a revolutionist.

Kropotkin's faith in mankind, despite a life in the revolutionary underground of bitter hardship, was inexhaustible. He gave the impression, said the English journalist Henry Nevinson, who knew him well, of "longing to take all mankind to his bosom and keep it warm."[6] Kindliness shone from his bald and noble dome ringed with a low halo of bushy brown hair. An ample beard spread comfortably beneath his chin. He was very short, with hardly enough body to hold up his massive head. Descended from princes of Smolensk who, according to family tradition, belonged to the Rurik Dynasty, which had ruled Russia before the Romanovs, Kropotkin took his place in that long line of "conscience-stricken" Russian nobility who felt guilty for belonging to a class which had oppressed the people for centuries.

He was born in 1842. After service as an officer in Siberia, where he studied the geography of the region, he became secretary of the Geographical Society, for whom he explored the glaciers of Finland and Sweden in 1871. Meanwhile, his disgust with the Tsar led him to become a member of a secret revolutionary committee and on his being discovered, his arrest and imprisonment followed. After his escape from the grim fortress of St. Peter and St. Paul in 1876, he went to Switzerland, where he worked with Elisée Reclus, the French geographer and anarchist. With Reclus he founded the best-known Anarchist journal, *La Révolte*. His stream of convincing and passionate polemics, the vestige of his escape from the most dreaded Russian prison, his active work with the Swiss anarchists of the Jura—which caused his expulsion from Switzerland—all topped by his title of Prince, made him an irresistible hero to the young and impressionable Stalin.

From his wandering exile, Kropotkin wrote fiery paeans to violence which, through the secret circulation of *La Révolte*, found their way to the seminary at Tiflis. Man's progress toward perfection was being held back, Kropotkin wrote, by the "inertia of those who have a vested interest in existing conditions."[7] Progress needed a violent event "to hurl mankind out of its ruts into new roads."[8] The spirit of revolt must be awakened in the masses by repeated "propaganda of the deed."[9] Though never recommending murder in so many words, Kropotkin urged a "propaganda by speech and written word, by dagger, gun and dynamite."[10] He sounded an inspiring summons in the pages of *La Révolte* to "men of courage willing not only to speak but to act, pure characters who prefer prison, exile and death to a life that contradicts their principles, bold natures who know that in order to win one must dare."[11] Men such as these must form an advance guard of revolution long before the masses were ready, and in the midst of "talking, complaining, discussing," must do the "deed of mutiny."[12]

By Stalin, the seminarian-rebel of Tiflis, Kropotkin was secretly lauded as a seer, to be examined and discussed by his comrades in nightly vigils. Kropotkin's aphorisms were quoted by the young Stalin as if they were gospel verses. Because of his abuse of priests as vulgar, materialist, and philistine, Kropotkin was particularly welcomed by the poor seminarians who had to act as lackeys for the priests of the seminary. The sap of rebellion was rising in Stalin and he responded strongly to Kropotkin's call to violent overthrow. In Kropotkin's writings these were hedged about with a vast body of poetic suggestion and exploration, but taken crudely, as Stalin did, as positive precepts, they became both directive and justification. In a narrow cell in Tiflis, staring at the "dilapidation and ruin" of the Church of Ananour out of angry lost eyes, Stalin was bewitched by Kropotkin's verbal violence.

Not content merely with talking about the coming disappearance of the ruling class, Stalin became embroiled in practical attempts designed to overthrow it. This caused him to be suspected of "deviating" from holy orders and of leaning toward Marxism. Without a hearing, he was expelled from the seminary. From that point on, never discouraged, no matter how many of the deeds he midwifed were stillborn, Stalin was always on the verge of imprisonment, fresh from some dramatic escape or desperate adventure, forever an inner exile without a home or with hardly a room to call his own, always turning up, ready to renew the struggle. He assumed the natural philosophy of the doss-house. In the struggle to survive any trick or ruse, however unscrupulous, the use of any weapon or opportunity, however treacherous, are permissible. Stalin never trusted anyone; he never committed himself to anyone. He learned to lie with conviction and dissemble with candor. Distrust was matched by contempt. Men were moved by base impulses—fear, greed, lust, envy. Politics is the art of using these weaknesses for your own ends.

Stalin's suspicious eyes peering at the world around him found encouragement not in the exiled Marxist revolutionaries but in the bandits and anarchists who robbed and killed in the name of revolt. In the last years of the nineteenth century a two-year reign of dynamite, dagger, and gunshot erupted in the Caucasus, killing ordinary men as well as powerful ones, destroying property, banishing safety, and spreading terror, before it subsided. The small bandit cell which Stalin joined professed an extreme contempt for every bourgeois sentiment and social restraint, recognizing only the individual's right to life anarchistically, which included burglary and any other crime that served the need of the moment. They were interested in themselves, not in economic revolution. The unbridled operations of these miniature Borgias, usually ending in gun battles with the police and flaunted under the banner of revolution, added much to the fear and anger of the local Georgian peasants, who could not and did not distinguish between the aberrant and the revolutionary variety of violence.

So enchanting was the vision of a stateless society, without government, without law, without ownership of property, in which, corrupt institutions having been swept away, man would be free to be as nature intended him, that six heads of state were assassinated for its sake in the formative years of Stalin's revolutionary activities. He watched in wonder and envy as President Carnot of France in 1894, President Canovas of Spain in 1897, Empress Elisabeth of Austria in 1898, King Humbert of Italy in 1900, President William McKinley of the United States in 1901, and another Spaniard Premier Canalejas, fell in 1912. Not one could qualify as a bloody tyrant. Their deaths were the gestures of desperate and deluded men calling attention to the revolutionary idea. No single individual, Stalin knew, was the hero of the movement that swallowed up these lives. The idea itself was the hero. It was, as one historian of revolt has called it, "a daydream of desperate romantics."[13] To be sure, there was little of the romantic in Stalin's beliefs. This poor wretch, often half-starved, without a job, family or home, clung obstinately to a belief in violence for its ability to bolster up the inner claims of his own superiority. All his life Stalin was irritated by discussion. He would abuse opponents with a hysterical strain in his voice. Here was formed the pattern that would be displayed when he came to absolute power. This authoritarian strain developed with the love of violence, but it was there from the start, the instinct of tyranny.

Of the dual nature of revolution, half hatred of existing society, half love of humanity, Stalin was magnetically drawn to the first. It was the bombs and explosions, the gunshots and the daggers, that impressed him most. He cared little for the other side of revolution which hoped to lead humanity through the slough of violence to the Delectable Mountains. His image of Kropotkin was that of an evil genius of revolution. He did not trouble himself with the man whose philosophy and altruism caused him to deed houses he inherited to the tenants inhabiting them. As Stalin also knew little of Marxist writings, he could make little theoretical sense of the violent acts. They seemed impromptu, embittered, pure indulgence in bloodthirstiness for its own sake. The Russian press customarily referred to the revolutionaries as "wild beasts," "crypto-lunatics," degenerates, criminals, cowards, felons, "odious fanatics prompted by perverted intellect and morbid frenzy." They were Stalin's image of himself.

The increasing unrest of Stalin's apprentice years as a revolutionist encouraged him to believe that the time was ripening for open insurrection. The new Tsar, Nicholas II, who was that most dangerous of rulers, a weak autocrat, had marked his ascension in 1895 by flatly dismissing all pleas for a constitution as "nonsensical dreams,"[14] thereby causing moderates to despair and extremists like Stalin to exult. In the cities, strikes by newly industrialized workers followed one upon another. Over all, exerting a mysterious pull, like the moon upon the tides, loomed the moment of the turn of the century. There was that growing sense of end and a beginning.

All the discontented groups felt the need to prepare for the time of action, to gather their strength in parties and to state their program. But there was a conflict between the followers of Marxism, with its hard-bitten insistence on organizing and training, and the inheritors of the Narodniki tradition, who believed in spontaneous revolution brought on by some deed of terror. As a result, two traditions took shape in the years 1897 and 1898, the Marxist Social-Democratic party (including Lenin) on the one hand, and on the other, the Populist Socialist-Revolutionaries, whose various groups merged into a definitive party in 1901. Stalin's creed represents the fusion, and became the fulfillment of the two groups.

Like the Socialist-Revolutionaries, Stalin shared a belief that deeds of terror could precipitate revolution. Like them he saw violent revolution as a sunburst on the horizon under whose beams the future would come. Like the Marxists, however, he believed in planning and organizing. But his planning was not that of a theorist, such as Lenin. It was that of a master criminal who schemes and plots, and then leaves no witnesses alive.

In 1902 Stalin was moved by a line of Maxim Gorki's work *The Lower Depths*. Here Gorki portrays all the woe, the wretchedness and despair of Russia. "Man must live for something better!" cries a drunken card-sharp, "something better." Searching for words, for meaning, for a philosophy, he can only repeat the line, "something better."[15] Toward that end, in the years 1901–1903, the Terror Brigade of the Socialist-Revolutionaries assassinated the Minister of Education, Bogolepov; the Minister of Interior, Sipiagin, who directed the secret police; and the Governor of Ufa, Bogdanovitch, who had put down a miner's strike with particular brutality. On July 15, 1904, in the midst of the Russo-Japanese War, they disposed of a second Minister of Interior, Wenzel von Plehve, the most hated man in Russia. An ultra-reactionary, Plehve was if anything even firmer than the Tsar in the belief that autocracy must be kept unimpaired by the slightest concession to democratic processes. His sole policy was to smash every possible source of antipathy to the regime. He arrested revolutionaries, suppressed the orthodox "old believers,"[16] restricted the *zemstvos*, or village governments, victimized the Jews, forcibly Russified the Poles, Finns, and Armenians and, as a result, increased the enemies of Tsarism, and convinced them of the need for an irrevocable change.

In the ruthlessness of Plehve's methods, and the brutality of those opposed to him, Stalin found his idea for the practice of socialism. For Stalin, socialism was armed change. Every aspect of its program called for violence. Socialism without violence was not socialism at all.

In the decade between the aborted rising of 1905 and the outbreak of the Great War, the havoc wrought by bandit gangs became the major fact of life in the Caucasus. Armed toughs like Stalin became its sentinels, a part of society itself. They ate at society from within like Erysichthon, the "tearer up of earth," who, having destroyed the trees in the sacred grove of Demeter, was cursed by the goddess with an insatiable appetite and finally devoured himself attempting to satisfy his hunger.

In the half-lunatic world of the Romanov twilight, so darkened that it was never quite clear whether assassins were genuine revolutionaries or *agents provocateurs* of the police, Stalin formed a concept of socialism that had little to do with some future utopia. Years of failure and poverty had laid up a deep store of resentment in him, but had failed to weaken the conviction of his own superiority. The themes that would animate his career were fixed: Man of the People, Man of blood and steel. Years in the Caucasus criminal netherworld hardened him, taught him to be self-reliant, confirmed his belief in himself, toughened the power of his will. From there he emerged with a stock of fixed ideas and prejudices that were to alter little for the rest of his life: hatred of abstract ideals; contempt for weakness; a preference for authoritarian forms; and faith in the heroic virtues of violent change. For Stalin, socialism became subordinate to its means; violence became the end; the meaning of socialism succumbed to the crude triumph of brutality and force.

6

⤳⟫ ⟪⟨

Stalin Identifies
Socialism with Himself

In London in 1907, for reasons yet unclear, Stalin was lifted out of his mountain bandit's obscurity. At the Fifth Congress of the Russian Socialist-Democratic Workers Party, the last convened before the October revolution, Lenin proposed that the then twenty-seven years-old Georgian be granted a consultative delegate's status at the meeting. When queried by a Menshevik opponent as to who Stalin was and what were his credentials, Lenin could only meekly reply, "I really don't know . . . ."[1] Yet a mere five years later, in 1912 with the split between Bolsheviks and Mensheviks complete, Stalin became a member of the Central Committee of the Bolsheviks. Confused in the past, his relations to the party now became routine. He may or may not have continued as a part-time police informer, but with this turn the soft treatment he had received from the Okhrana came to a halt. In 1913 Stalin was exiled to eastern Siberia, where he remained until the revolution's outbreak.

When in 1917—having been liberated by the Tsar's removal in March, 1917—Stalin arrived in Petrograd and quickly resumed activity as a senior official of the Party, he had still had relatively little contact with the flashing cosmopolitan circle of Lenin, Trotsky, and Bukharin. To these literate men the thuggish Stalin was an unknown specter. N. N. Sukhanov, the Boswell of the revolution, referred to him in his memoirs as constituting in 1917 only a sort of "gray blur" in the background of events—a quip, incidentally, for which Sukhanov was later to pay with his life in one of Stalin's gulags. Unlike the intellectuals who made up the majority of Lenin's entourage, Stalin was merely a colorless drone in the Party's administrative offices. None of the usual reminiscences of friends and family or personal stories or saying accumulated around him; even as he grew in power he moved without attendant anecdotes, a man without a shadow. He didn't even speak proper Rus-

sian—at least he didn't speak with a proper accent—to say nothing of
the foreign tongues in which so many of the others were fluent. He was
without originality in the intellectual and literary spheres. He had no
personal charm, no oratorical gifts.

Half-gangster, half-bureaucrat, Stalin had no ideals; no ideological
notions of his own, save the elevation of violence into a sort of sacra-
ment. According to the composer Dmitri Shostakovich, Stalin wanted to
be attractive and tall, with powerful hands. The Kremlin court painter
Nalbandian satisfied this wish by fixing the angle of vision from below
and getting his master to fold his hands over his paunch; portrait painters who displeased Stalin were shot. Only five foot four inches tall,
Stalin was swarthy, and possessed a face that seemed to have been
formed by some volcanic eruption that had cooled into a crust of pumice;
pitted with dark holes, scabs, and craters. A Tsarist police description
noted that the second and third toes of his left foot were fused; a
boyhood accident had caused his left elbow to be stiff, with a withering
of the arm, the left hand thicker than the right. As Shostakovich said,
he kept hiding his right hand. Bukharin said that Stalin suffered from
these disabilities and from real or imagined incapacities. "This suffering
is probably the most human thing about him,"[2] Bukharin continued,
but it led Stalin to take revenge on anyone with higher capabilities:
"There is something diabolical and inhuman about his compulsion to
take vengeance for this same suffering on everybody. . . . This is a
small, vicious man; no, not a man, but a devil."[3] Stalin did not have
Lenin's theoretical appreciation of violence. Where Lenin saw violence
as a device to achieve socialism, which would cease to be necessary once
his dream had been achieved, Stalin saw violence as the continual
driving force of socialism itself. Without violence, socialism could not
exist. It was the engine of the movement. Socialist man could be shaped
only by force. Remove the threat of violence and man would lapse into
his bad old ways. Stalin thus offered a rationalization for unending state
terror. Not only would the state fail to wither away, but the violence
necessary to establish socialism would never wither away. Violence was
the hammer and anvil of permanent revolution. The emergence of Stalin as a dominant figure in the socialist movement changed the dynamic
of socialist brutality not in kind, but in degree and duration. Nonetheless, his arrival in a position of prominence is important because of the
sheer scale of the change. The arrests, the prisons, the camps, the
scope, the brutality and violence of his social engineering in the name of
socialism—nothing like it had ever been seen or even imagined before.

Compare these facts with what is known today of Stalin's character.

Insatiable vanity, a keen fear of inferiority, and jealousy of qualities in others which he did not possess; these traits pushed Stalin to love violence. He carried the characteristics of the Caucasian mountain people from which he sprang—inordinate touchiness, endless vindictiveness, inability ever to forgive or forget an insult, but great patience in selecting the moment to settle the score. He is said once to have observed that there was nothing sweeter in life than to bide the moment for revenge, to insert the knife, to turn it round, and to go home for a good night's sleep. At the same time, he was a man with the most extraordinary talent for tactics and intrigue, a consummate actor, dissimulator of genius, master not only of timing but of what communists call "dosage"—of measuring what the traffic would bear on any given occasion. He was a master at playing people and forces against each other. It was never he who would insert the knife; he found others to do his dirty work for him. Stalin merely looked on with benign detachment (or feigned shock), sometimes with grief and indignation.

Proud, bigoted, with a strong will and an uncommon power to discern the weakness of others, Stalin was perfectly suited to prosper in the chaotic world unleashed by the Bolshevik rising. His road to power lay in outwitting his better-educated but less cunning rivals, and he sought to do so by exploiting the young recruits who flowed into the Party on the flood tide of its victory. Thugs like himself, these newcomers (such as Molotov) felt little sense of kinship with the older Party intellectuals with their abstract theories and utopian ideals. For these young men on the make, socialism would be defined as Stalin defined it. Myths and dreams and memories, all the hopes of the hard, lonely days of exile outside Russia—the struggles, feuds, arguments, and intrigues of Geneva, Vienna, Berlin, and Crakow—were more than remote. They were meaningless, part of a history now in the dustbin.

And who was the enemy? All those like Bukharin who threw the dust of theory into the path of power, who sought to restrict by dogma the personal absolutism Stalin craved. These were his enemies and had to be rooted out—in good time. For Stalin understood that he had to be prudent in opposing them. Otherwise they would muster their loyalists at home and followers abroad in a counter-attack against him. Bukharin and his like were keepers of the communist gospel; they controlled the terms of the debate; they could brand Stalin a heretic if they chose. But in the secret war he would wage against them, Stalin was blessed with rare advantages: he had neither scruples nor inhibitions. He was a man without roots, with neither family nor friends; a man who admitted no loyalties, was bound by no traditions. Wary and secretive, he entertained a universal distrust. He would never let down his guard, or give himself away.

Of the grave danger posed by his more cultured rivals, Stalin was constantly aware. He would never forget it. After his primacy became unchallenged, indeed, he needed to maintain the fiction that the social-ist diaspora supported his regime unreservedly. Though ever holding a sword over his rivals' heads, Stalin never shed his insecurity. He never grasped how fully Lenin and Bukharin had already integrated his love of violence with the meaning of socialism. This was perhaps quite natural. Ideas and dogmas were not tools of rational communications but devices for manipulating men. Introduction of intellectual processes of criticism marked the intrusion of a hostile element that threatened the exercise of pure power.

All this leads up to the hideous brutality which Stalin perpetrated against the common people in the name of socialism: predominantly in the merciless process of collectivization, and also in some of his forced industrialization measures. The number of victims here—the number, that is, of those who actually lost their lives—runs into the millions. This is not to mention the shattered homes, twisted childhoods, millions of people half-killed: who survived only to linger in misery, with broken health and broken hearts.

Plainly, such excesses reached far beyond what was required for the protection of one man's personal position of authority. In part, they were the result of mental disturbance. But even to the extent that they represented rational action from the point of Stalin's personal interest, they coincided only in a limited way to the original theory of socialism. Yes, the state was almighty and the motor force for the establishment of the communist vision. Yes, violence and terror were sometimes neces-sary and certainly could be used to bring communism into being. But did this mean that violence was the only way to win the hearts and minds of men to socialism? Did worship of the socialist state have to come about only through fear?

To understand the changes in the meaning of socialism which Stalin brought about, a contrast between Stalin, as a socialist leader, and the man he succeeded in the position of supreme power in Russia, is useful. Differences are not easy to identify, for in many ways they were only of degree and motive. Lenin, too, was a master of internal Party intrigue. He, too, was capable of ruthless cruelty. In the elimination of people who seriously disagreed with him or seemed to stand in the path of the best interests of the Party, he, too, could be unpitying. Like Stalin, Lenin was implacably hostile to the bourgeois world and its values. He, too, based his politics on his ability to divide his rivals and play them off one another. Surprise was a favorite gambit of both men. In politics, diplomacy, war: each gauged the psychological impact of sudden hammer-blows in paralyzing their opponents. A regular device of both men was to place themselves on the defensive, to accuse those who opposed or obstructed them of aggression and malice, and to pass rapidly from a tone of outraged innocence to the full thunders of moral indignation. It was always the other side who were to blame, and in turn each denounced their antagonists of practicing an intolerable behavior which forced them to take drastic action in self-defense. At this, both men were consummate actors, with the actor's and orator's facility for absorbing himself in a role and convincing himself of the truth of what he was saying at the time he said it. In his early years Stalin was often awkward and unconvincing, but with practice the part became as second nature to him as it was to Lenin.

The gift of all great politicians for grasping the possibilities of a situation more swiftly than their opponents was pronounced in both Lenin and Stalin. Each saw, as their rivals often did not, how to play on the grievances and resentments of Party members. Stalin's insistence upon preserving the forms of Marxist-Leninist dogma in the struggle for absolute power showed a brilliant understanding of the way to disarm opposition, just as the way in which he undermined the political positions of his rivals showed his consummate grasp of the weaknesses and strengths of the Party's structure.

Behind all this, however, there were fundamental differences. No feelings of inferiority crippled Lenin. Well-born, well-educated, endowed with a fine, calculating mind, Lenin was no vulgar parvenu and knew himself to be the intellectual match for any man of any ideology. That terrible burden of personal insecurity that drove the emotionally crippled Stalin was spared Lenin. He never doubted the loyalty of his comrades to him, even when he heaped abuse on them. He ruled through the sort of love you find in the academy between great teachers and their pupils; Stalin ruled by fear alone. Thus Lenin ran the movement on the basis of what he assumed to be its needs, rarely troubling about his own. As the intellectual inventory of the Party was largely his creation, Lenin was relieved of Stalin's ignominious need to buttress his ideological views by constant resort to someone else's gospel. Having fashioned Leninism out of Marx's raw resources, Lenin had no fear of adaptation, of adjusting to events as circumstances dictated. Thus, his mind remained relatively open throughout his life—open, at least, to argument and suggestion from those who shared his core beliefs. Such men could talk to him, could find their thoughts honestly analyzed and accepted. They were not forced to fear, as they did under Stalin, that black, dangerous meanings would be read into whatever they might say, and that an innocent suggestion might mean their undoing.

Resentfully, Stalin was forced to placate a cult of Lenin throughout his career. The fact that he often quite willfully twisted Lenin's words and concepts does not matter: it was the effect, however grating, of continuity at which he aimed. He was indifferent to the ideas of anyone other than Lenin. The only idea that mattered was to be hard, and ruthlessness was the distinctive mark of such hardness. This belief cut him off from all human contacts, left him in a world of inhuman fantasy where the only thing that was real or mattered was his own will. In Lenin's era debate was thus much more colorful than under Stalin. Bukharin was able to develop his concept of the socialist Leviathan, which seemed to fly in the face of all that Marx had predicted, because Lenin saw the utility of such a theory and believed in adjusting dogma to the needs of the moment. Indeed, he could put Leviathan on hold during the time of the New Economic Policy (NEP), when the disintegration of the Soviet economy forced him to restore the ghosts of capitalism in a bid to save the country from starvation and financial ruin. Stalin's purpose, always, was to centralize and increase his power, and to that end he rigidified all theory. If Bukharin accepted the notion of an all-powerful state with its parallel postponement of the state's withering away, the matter was settled in his mind, and there was no going back on it, except as a temporary blip designed to undermine his rivals—precisely the reason he, for a short time, supported a slackening of socialist control after Lenin's death, he did so in order to damage Trotsky, not out of principle. For when Trotsky was weakened he immediately veered back into the camp of the state worshippers. In the change from Lenin to Stalin, the malleable theories of a revolutionary movement became the rigid defenses of a single man.

Voices of warning did ring out. Osip Mandelstam, for example, composed a sixteen-line epigram about Stalin, which soon earned him the gulag and a death sentence.

> We live, deaf to the land beneath us,
> Ten steps away no one hears our speeches,
>
> But where there's so much as half a conversation
> The Kremlin's mountaineer will get his mention.

His fingers are fat as grubs
And the words, final as lead weights, fall from his lips,

His cockroach whiskers leer
And his boot tops gleam.

Around him a rabble of thin-necked leaders—fawning
half-men for him to play with.

They whinny, purr or whine
As he prates and points a finger,

One by one forging his laws, to be flung
Like horseshoes at the head, the eye or the groin.

And every killing is a treat
For the broad-chested Ossete.

From mouth to mouth the verse secretly made the rounds in Moscow, until the day it reached the ears of the police. By then, it had acquired a new second stanza:

All we hear is of the Kremlin mountaineer,
The murderer and peasant-slayer.[4]

Mandelstam was immediately arrested. When Bukharin sought to intercede on the poet's behalf, the secret policeman Yagoda mincingly recited the epigram, word for word, by heart. Yagoda dared Bukharin to justify it. He could not.

As the terror encircled him, Mandelstram made a desperate bid, if not to save his own life, then that of his wife Nadezhda. He composed an Ode to Stalin. Being Mandelstam, however, he was unable to produce hack work. He waited for the axe to fall. Anna Akhmatova, Mandelstam's loyal friend throughout his ordeal, captured the doom that hung over his last years.

And the town stands locked in ice:
a paperweight of trees, walls, snow . . .
But in the room of the banished poet
Fear and the Muse stand watch by turn,
and the night is coming on,
which has no hope of dawn.[5]

Such socialist violence sanctified Stalin's inner rage—rage about himself, political rage: one was identical to the other. It made him able to conceive of, contemplate, and carry out great, bloody upheavals.

7

➤➤➤ ❰❰❰

Leviathan
Devours Bukharin

Stalin's burrowings in the dark recesses of the Party first became visible at the Tenth Party Congress in 1921, when Lenin convinced the Party to abdicate responsibility for itself. This surrender, which gave the Central Committee the right to pass death sentences on any party member (including members of the Central Committee), meant that Lenin had to hold an absolute two-thirds majority of the leadership to insure his own neck. It was Stalin who supplied it. The newly elected Committee included many already closely linked with him: Komarov, Mikhailov, Yaroslavsky, Ordzhonikidze, Voroshilov, Frunze, Molotov, Petrovsky, Tuntal, and candidate members such as Kirov, Kuibyshev, Chubar, and Gusev. These men formed the pliable legion Stalin recruited on Lenin's behalf—and his own! He was also extremely active in the new "Personal Chancery" or Party Secretariat, which began to grow almost as fast as the secret police, and for similar reasons. In May 1919, it had a staff of thirty; this had risen to 150 by the Ninth Party Congress of March 1920; and the next year, when Lenin killed democracy in the Party, it was swollen to 602, plus its own 140-strong staff of armed guards and messengers. Finally, at the Eleventh Party Congress, Lenin gave to Stalin formal possession of this lovingly assembled little private empire when he made Stalin General Secretary of the Party, with Stalin's henchmen Molotov and Kuibyshev as immediate lackeys. This was done in secret, hinted at only in a tiny, tucked-away *Pravda* article of April 4, 1922. One old Bolshevik, Evgenii Preobrazhenskii, protested vehemently against the concentration of power in Stalin's hands. Was it "thinkable," he asked, "that one man should be able to answer for the work of two commissariats as well as the work of the Politburo, the Orgburo and a dozen Party committees?"[1] Such protests went unheeded. For in order to rule efficiently Lenin needed Stalin as much as Stalin needed Lenin to facilitate his rise.

Two months later, Lenin had his first stroke. But his work was already completed. On the base bequeathed to him, Stalin constructed the most concentrated state machine the world had ever witnessed. The interests of the state, which Stalin interpreted as his own self-interest, were given absolute priority. In the old world, personal autocracies, except for brief periods, had been limited, or at least constrained and qualified, by other forces in society: a church, an aristocracy, an urban bourgeoisie, ancient charters and courts and assemblies. And there was, also, the restraint born of the idea of a Deity or Natural Law, an absolute system of morality. Stalin's new and murderous utopia had no such checks or balances or inhibitions. Every social institution that remained was controlled by the state, which meant by Stalin. All rights were vested in the state. Ever-growing as it was, every tendril of state power could be traced back to the hands of a minute group of men— ultimately to one man. There was, to be sure, an elaborate and pretentious structure of representation. By 1922 this system lost all meaning. You could search its echoing corridors in vain to find a spark of democratic life. How could it be otherwise? Lenin hated the essence of democracy; Stalin regarded its forms merely as a means to legitimize violence and oppression. In 1917, the year Lenin took power, he defined a democratic state as an "organization for the systematic use of violence by one class against another, by one part of the population against another."[2] Stalin followed and transcended this formula. Who was doing what to whom? Who was oppressing whom; exploiting or shooting whom? To a man who thought in such terms, a man incapable of thinking in any other terms, it was not possible to envisage a set of political arrangements except those of despotism, conducted by an autocrat and ruled by violence.

Stalin remained a revolutionary, because he strove to identify the organization of Russia with his will. The prophetic utopian claims of Marx and Lenin dissolved in those of the conqueror. The claims of a prophet are counsels of perfection, and perfection implies uniformity. But utopias are not achieved except through a process of levelling and dislocation which must erode all existing patterns of obligation. In Stalin the two great emotions of the revolution fused: the conqueror and the prophet, the quest for universality and for stability, for the peace of impotence and the peace of bliss. For Stalin's terror represented the abandonment of the old nineteenth-century dream of socialist revolution: that liberty and communism were not only reconcilable but mutually dependent. Accordingly, what had seemed the irrepressible features of the Russian Revolution—its political effervescence, its promises of hope—were trapped inside the vessel of dictatorship. Liberty had to end so that socialism might conquer: that was now the first commandment of communism, to be followed at all times and in all revolutions.

Left to his own devices, Lenin might have struggled back through the terror to the ideals that had first drawn him to socialism as a boy. But he was corrupted by the absolute power he forged for himself. The very process of violent revolution, and violent self-preservation thereafter, inevitably destroyed conscience and all other elements of idealism. The point had been well made a decade before, by the sad old Pole Joseph Conrad, in his novel about revolution, *Under Western Eyes:*

> In a real revolution, the best characters do not come to the front. A violent revolution falls into the hands of narrow-minded fanatics and of tyrannical hypocrites at first. Afterwards come the turn of all the pretentious intellectual failures of the time. Such are the chiefs and leaders. You will notice that I have left out the mere rogues. The scrupulous and the just, the noble, humane and devoted natures, the unselfish and the intelligent may begin a movement, but it passes away from them. They are not the leaders of a revolution, They are its victims: the victims of disgust, disenchantment—often of remorse. Hopes grotesquely betrayed, ideals caricatured—that is the definition of revolutionary success.[3]

Certainly Lenin never showed the slightest regret about his lifework, though in the last two years of his existence he was sick, angry, frustrated, and ultimately impotent. It is argued that, toward the end, he recognized Stalin as the emergent monster he undoubtedly was, and sought desperately to build up Trotsky's influence as a countervailing force. But he died too soon, bequeathing to Stalin all the justifications of a despotism in his gospel of the socialist state.

Bukharin's socialist Leviathan embodied the crudity of communism's worldview, and its shortcomings in the 1920s forced him to face its limitations. Bukharin understood capitalism as relying on sordid self-interest and the capacity for self-delusion that resulted; he rejoiced in communism's proud assertion of the human spirit's ability to throw off such degradation and oppression. However, he regarded these assaults on human dignity as exclusively the products of the capitalist class system rather than as impulses common to mankind and which should be expected to exhibit themselves in people of any class or any ideology. The dominant class of the capitalist era had never voluntarily done anything but rob the poor in the interest of its own well-being, so Bukharin believed; in his theory of the socialist Leviathan state

Bukharin assumed that the ruling class of the proletarian dictatorship would never dream of abusing its position. After witnessing the bloody brutalities of the civil war, however, Bukharin could never again believe in the absolute disinterest and objectivity of Party rule.

For the Party's ideological mindset was unsuited to a clear understanding of reality, and its structure prevented it from making adjustments to facts contrary to theory. The notion of democratic centralism degenerated into rote acceptance of a Party line. Those who counseled a patient interim in which peasants would be brought around to the advantages of socialized agriculture, for example, were derided as cowards. Indeed, once Stalin defeated Trotsky, he rounded against the appeasers of the agricultural bourgeoisie.

Infirm of purpose, Bukharin was temperamentally unsuited for battle. He was possessed of a soggy, tearful romanticism—even about the secret police. Trotsky is said to have spoken of him as "behaving in his customary manner, half hysterically, half childishly." It was not Stalin's ideas that irked Bukharin, as the fact that Stalin did not have any: "He changes his theories according to the need he has of getting rid of somebody at such-and-such a moment." Stalin, he argued, had concluded that the advance to socialism would only meet more and more popular resistance, and "that will mean a police state, but nothing will stop Stalin." As to the issue of the peasants, "the kulaks can be hunted down at will, but we must conciliate the middle peasants."[4] The speaker could well be Lenin.

The above conversation, with the then disgraced Lev Kamenev, was the worst of tactics on Bukharin's part. Kamenev noted the conversation and leaked it. More importantly, Stalin's position was already unassailable. At the end of 1928, Bukharin resigned from all his posts in the Party, in anger at Stalin's constant undermining of his position. For Stalin's purposes, Bukharin's departure came too soon, for Bukharin retained prestige among the rank-and-file party members who would begin to question his departure.

Immediately Stalin made some verbal concessions to Bukharin and passed a Politburo resolution that compromised with his rival's position. Attacks on Bukharin continued in secret. It would take time to destroy Bukharin's reputation.

In February 1929, Bukharin protested the forced collectivization and the disintegration of Party democracy: "We are against one-man decisions of questions of party leadership. We are against control by a collective being replaced by control of a person, even though an authoritative one."[5] Amidst jeers, Bukharin was charged with making a "direct slander of the Party, direct slander of Comrade Stalin, against whom they try to advance accusations of attempting the single-handed direction of the party."[6]

Bukharin pulled himself to his feet and spoke for a few moments as the hoots continued, the ghastly spectacle of a man knuckling under to ruin and knowing it. He repeated what he had been arguing for three years: that with patience the peasants would come around to socialism. He repeated time and again the conviction in which, publicly, he now stood alone: that inner Party debate was coming to an end; to let it do so would mean certain dictatorship. He paused. He knew his future was being decided. Stalin, who hated to listen to anyone for more than ten minutes consecutively, was making grunts of impatience and grimaces of disapproval. The moment of Bukharin's Gethsemane was at hand. He could either bow to a course he considered fatally wrong or he could stand by his moral convictions and leave the Party for good. Slowly, painfully, he stumbled toward his choice. Yes, it was true that collectivization was brutal and disruptive. True, centralization in the Party had gone beyond what he had once envisioned. But, on the whole, this was the Party's will. Of course, no single man could go against the Party . . .

Trotsky had made the same point in 1924, when he first faced an inquisitorial proceeding arranged by Stalin.

> None of us desires or is able to dispute the will of the Party. Clearly, the party is always right . . . We can only be right with and by the party, for history has provided no other way of being right. The English have a saying, "My country, right or wrong"; whether it is in the right or in the wrong, it is my country. We have much better historical justification in saying, whether it is right or wrong in certain individual cases, it is my party . . . and if the Party adopts a decision which one or the other of us thinks unjust, he will say, just or unjust, it is my party, and I shall support the consequences of the decision to the end.[7]

Disagreement or rebellion against the Party was, thus, psychologically impossible. The responsibility of power often requires resisting and redirecting a pervading condition, but as Trotsky and Bukharin demonstrate, Party leaders had been too firmly shaped by party ideology. Truly, they were the new machine-like men of Mayakovsky's vision, and thus succumbed to the worst of Stalin's schemes, and exhibited in the face of mounting and visible threats to their very lives, an unrelieved wooden-headedness.

For Bukharin—despite Stalin and his murders—still claimed the revolution as his own, seeing in any shift of the socialist movement the possibility and even the beginnings of another more beneficial turning. The revolution, though, had now turned against him. But revolutionaries have to be patient; and Bukharin had learnt patience during the long dull years of exile. He bore his disappointment of Stalin's regime stoically. For in his eyes two revolutions appeared to be flowing together, the revolution of Stalin, and what Bukharin saw as the true revolution of the people. And he kept them distinct—at least in his mind. All the crimes and failures were attributed to Stalin; this enabled Bukharin to keep his own faith pure.

Bukharin's faith in the Party as the embodiment of history continued even as he approached the scaffold. In 1936, a year before his own arrest, he remarked:

> It is difficult for us to live. And you, for example could not accustom yourself to it. Even for some of us, with our experiences during this decade, it is often impossible. But one is saved by a faith that development is always going forward. It is like a stream that is running to the shore. If one leans out of the stream, one is ejected completely. (Here Bukharin made a scissor-like gesture with two fingers.) The stream goes through the most difficult places. But it still goes forward in the direction in which it must. And the people grow, become stronger in it, and they build a new society.[8]

This is a plain and simple profession of faith. Stalin held in effect that his personal rule was essential on precisely the same grounds. This goes some way to explaining Bukharin's passivity as he watched Stalin consolidate his power, and the almost total failure of any party member to oppose Stalin even after his aims and methods were revealed.

To an ever-shrinking circle, Bukharin whispered his fears that the Stalinist state was something new, something eerily akin to Hitler's Reich. It represented, he knew, a nightmarish completion of his new Leviathan. Bukharin did not yet believe that the bureaucratic state was intrinsically evil. Yet he saw within it "the idea of violence, of coercion as a permanent method of exercising power over society, over individuals, over man's personality." This "terroristic dictatorship" was dependent upon "permanent coercion" and a "real gulf between . . . a small group of ruling exploiters and the exploited masses." Such a regime, "with all its organizational efforts, blind discipline, cult of Jesuitical obedience, and suppression of intellectual functions," created a "dehumanized populace." He applied this analysis to Hitler's Germany, but few who heard Bukharin doubted that his intent was also to damn the emerging cult of Stalin:

Fascism . . . has established an omnipotent "total state," which dehu-
manizes everything except the leaders and "supreme leaders." The dehumanization of the masters here is in direct proportion to the glorification
of the leader. . . . The great majority of people are thereby transformed
into simple functionaries bound by discipline imposed in all areas of
life. . . . Three ethical norms dominate everything: devotion to the nation
or to the state, loyalty to the leader, and the spirit of the barracks.[9]

Degeneration of *his* revolution into a new exploiting order horrified
Bukharin. Socialism, he believed, meant "a concern for all-round development, for a many-sided (prosperous material and spiritual) life." It
should spawn a society where "the machine is only a means to promote
the flowering of a rich, variegated, bright, and joyful life," where people's "needs, their growth, the broadening and enrichment of their life,
is the goal."[10]

Against the spectacle of Stalin's revolution from above, amidst the
agitprop displays that Bukharin saw as suggesting a new "military order," he sought to remind his Party that socialism's mission was the
creation of a new civilization, one which both preserved and transcended
the best achievements of the modern age. The socialist state now threatened to extinguish these values by its reliance on violence and contempt
for human achievement. He was reminding the Party that, despite all
the bloodshed, "a creative, happy, human society is for us an end in
itself."[11]

Most of all he feared the brutalizing impact of forced collectivization—"a mass annihilation of completely defenseless men, together with
their wives and children." Some communists remained aloof from this
bloodshed, some revolted, and some, including Stalin's own wife Nadezhda Alliluyeva, committed suicide in protest. Many, however, became acclimated and obedient to the rule of violence as *the* new socialist
norm, transformed into "cogs in some terrible machine . . ."[12] Advocacy of a benevolent socialist humanism was Bukharin's way of warning
against this pathology. He remained hopeful that party members who
behaved badly did so "not because they are bad, but because the situation is bad. They must be persuaded that the country is not against
them, but only that a change of policy was necessary." He was pleading,
against all the evidence of his eyes and ears, that a humane socialism
was the only means to "realize ideology in living practice." He was
pleading that his democratic socialism, not Stalinism, "become the ideological axis of our time."[13]

In Stalin he saw insatiable lust at work. Stalin, he explained, "is
wretched because he cannot convince everyone, not even himself, that

he is greater than everyone else . . . his wretchedness compels him to take revenge on people, all people, but especially those who are in some way superior . . . to him."[14] Bukharin was now a prime target of this wretchedness. Stalin's public conduct was occasionally friendly, as at a banquet in 1935 when he toasted "Nicolai Ivanovich Bukharin. We all know and love him, and whoever remembers the past—get out of my sight!"[15] But already Stalin's agents were concocting a secret dossier of Bukharin's past, something which Bukharin soon received warnings about. In Paris, on a mission to purchase archives of the destroyed German Social Democratic party, he said that he was "certain that he [Stalin] will devour us . . . he is only waiting for a more opportune moment."[16] "He is going to kill me,"[17] he told André Malraux.

No protection existed within the Party. There, Bukharin's influence was finished. He was removed from his editorship of *Pravda* and stripped of the chairman's post at the Comintern. On November 26, 1929, he was forced to recant his views, then stripped of his Politburo seat. After receiving this last news, Bukharin's young wife entered his study to find him slumped in a chair, looking utterly broken. Shocked, she asked, "What's the matter? Have we lost?"

"Yes," answered Bukharin, "the revolution is finished. That's the decision." He told her what had taken place. His wife said simply, "You should resign from the party."[18] Bukharin shook his head. He could not abandon the Party at this crucial hour, he said, for that would sow even more dissension and let the world know that the revolution could still fail. In the nakedness of lost dignity he wrapped himself in the cloak of party duty. A true Communist must carry out the Party's command, even against his own judgment, he said, and as a former member of the Politburo he could do no less. From that moment, Madame Bukharin ceased to believe in communism. But her husband persisted. It was a question of "My Party Right or Wrong." He returned to his office the next day to face the final humiliation of drafting a fresh recantation of his views. Kowtowing to Party dictates, none of Bukharin's supporters resigned.

Bukharin's submission was abdication, not in recognition of socialism as a failed idea but in recognition of political reality. Bukharin was a political animal to the core. His isolation within the Party was now patent, dragging down with him all notions of the gradualism he had come to support during the days of the N.E.P. As a true believer, Bukharin was not yet prepared to fight against the Party or to risk being branded a counterrevolutionary; he would not suffer such a humiliation. And so with craven words, he took himself out of the contest with

Stalin. In private, however, he saw the way ahead quite clearly, the building of socialism meant the progressive dehumanization of the Party.

Character is fate, as the Greeks believed. Bukharin had been schooled in the idea that the socialist state achieved its purposes by force, and was unschooled in notions of compromise and adjustment. He could not bring himself to go against the party-state's will even at the risk of his own life, and thus helped prepare his own harsh fate. Before his fall, however, Bukharin published a final article "Routes of History: Thoughts Aloud," which appeared to many readers as a final testament. Its theme was the true direction of events under Stalin's rule. "Everyone is talking about the Stalin constitution," he said, but the thing of real importance was the "consolidation" of Stalin's regime and the impending destruction of all resistance to it. Lest anyone mistake his analysis of fascism's "beastly, bullying oppression, violence, and war,"[19] as applying only to Germany, Bukharin pointed out: "An intricate network of decorative deceit (in words and deeds) is an extremely essential characteristic of fascist regimes of all kinds and complexions."[20] No one could doubt that he was pointing an accusing finger at Stalin.

Regimes of Stalin's sort, Bukharin predicted, were doomed by a "paradox of history." They were based on an "ideology of hatred toward the masses . . . for them the masses are . . . subhumans, inferiors. . . . The masses, however, have already entered the historical arena, and there is no way they can be driven completely underground." Such regimes must therefore "create the illusion of mass participation in power. . . . But it would be extremely shortsighted not to see the historical limits of this organized deception. . . . Sooner or later this deception must be exposed."[21] The revolution had laid the "basis of socialism." Despite Stalin, ordinary people were ceasing to be "mere *instrumenta vocalia* (tools with a voice, as Roman slaves were called)" and becoming "a conscious mass of conscious personalities."[22] This guaranteed socialism's future. Or so he hoped. On the eve of his own destruction, having drawn up and then dissected the state that was preparing to execute him, Bukharin retained his faith in the people and in history.

Bukharin was now almost absolutely isolated. Throughout the years 1930 to 1936 he was, on the whole, left unmolested, provided he behaved in a correct and inconspicuous manner. (Nevertheless, even this passivity would be used against him when he came to trial, for Stalin's allies would label this period "Bukharin's conspiracy of silence.") Old comrades treated him with formality mingled with a public indifference to his fate, which both irritated and amused Bukharin. As a man who had spent his entire adult life in a ferment of intellectual and political activity, Bukharin found these years of ideological and personal isolation inhumanly cold. The sense of ostracism and inner exile was brought home to him even more sharply by the great irony that it was Stalin who paraded himself as Bukharin's protector from the Party's just and growing rage.

Yet in this vacuum Bukharin did recover, physically and spiritually, from the nightmare of his fall. Distance from the events of Stalin's murderous program created a certain feeling of tranquillity, which at times spawned a sense of stagnation that demoralized and embittered, but which also freed Bukharin from his feelings of complicity in fostering the conditions that allowed Stalin to come into control of the revolution.

Poverty and something like squalor were added factors in desiccating Bukharin's never entirely romantic view of the socialist cause. He retired almost entirely into the narrow circle composed of his young wife Anna Larina, and a few intimate friends also fallen from Stalin's favor. Bukharin's dislike of the society he had helped to shape became more and more acute as personal contact with individual members of it became more and more difficult. His mode of life, to be sure, had scarcely changed from his heyday as a revolutionary. He rose at seven, drank several cups of black coffee, and then retired to his study where he read and wrote until two in the afternoon. After hurrying through his midday meal he worked again until dinner, which he ate with his wife. After that he sometimes took an evening walk, or returned to his study, where he worked until midnight.

As the purges and terrors of collectivization mounted, Bukharin fell into one of his rare moods of deep melancholy, almost of despair, very different from the cloud of anger and activity in which he usually lived. He suddenly became overwhelmed by the sense of his own isolation, and the hopelessness of individual endeavor in the face of Stalin's power. Indeed, Stalin's absolute sway over the Party brought Bukharin an implicit understanding of his own personal failure, and inspired some erosion of faith in the power of men to achieve their own emancipation. He slumped into a cautious, almost cynical quietism which he knew to be an admission of defeat and a complete nullification of a life spent in revolutionary warfare. This mounting despair should have brought on the final collapse of his faith in that ideal communist world, in the construction of which he had invested everything he possessed, and much that belonged to others. But it did not. Bukharin's faith in the

ultimate victory of his vision was not destroyed. Insulated as he was
from the bloody consequences of Stalin's bloody deeds, Bukharin could
not and did not break with his socialist creed. He still saw the world in
terms of black and white; those who were not with socialism were
damned, those who followed Marx's creed were ultimately saved—even
Stalin. He knew upon whose side he stood, his life had been spent in
fighting for the cause, he knew that his vision must ultimately triumph.
No crisis of faith assailed him. He looked upon such doubts in others as
so many signs of bourgeois degeneracy which took the form of morbid
attention to private emotional yearnings, irresponsible self-indulgence
in an age when the greatest battle in human history was being fought.
Bukharin displayed uncompromising sternness toward personal introspection, an almost religious insistence on self-deluding discipline. For
Stalin was, perhaps wrongheadedly and monstrously, nevertheless pursuing the great goals that Bukharin had consistently advocated all his
life. Bukharin, however, refused to accept Stalin as a logical consequence of his socialist beliefs. As a result, his response to Stalin was
ever tepid. Time after time he issued vague appeasing statements that
acknowledged mistakes in his thinking. By repudiating all deviations
from the Party line he hoped to be saved, and perhaps politically res-
urrected. More than that, he hoped that through his collaboration socialism would save itself, that the "contradictions" of Stalin's rule would
prove to be mere digressions in the forward march of history.

For Bukharin, history was by its nature a violent drama. Terrible
tribulations occur, collisions, battles, destruction, appalling suffering;
but the story has, it must have, a happy ending—the radiance of a
static, conflict-free world in which men are rational, cooperative, virtuous, and happy. This vision was the source of Bukharin's feeble
attempt to justify his continuing loyalty to the Party: to allow for and
accept genocidal violence as inevitable, believing it both unavoidable and
a temporary way-station on the path to total self-fulfillment for all of
mankind.

Doubts gnawed at him, and yet he continued in the faith. Such is the
disturbing heritage of his total belief in socialism despite his own fore-
bodings of approaching doom. The horrifying picture of a frictionless
society where differences between men are eliminated and the flow of
life reduced to utter uniformity, which Bukharin had intuited in his
look into the capitalist Leviathan, and now witnessed in real life as
Stalin maimed and crushed in the name of the perfect communist
dream, did not destroy his own faith. No evidence could do that. For
Bukharin, what mattered in socialism was not the reality but the vision.

No matter the overwhelming weight of facts, he could not imagine socialism as some gray, corpse-like affair devoid of life, art, and simple humanity. He had a craving for unity, for the recovery of man's lost innocence and harmony, the return from a fragmented existence to the all-embracing whole. It was an infantile and dangerous delusion, but Bukharin never saw that to crush all diversity and conflict in the name of uniformity was to crush life itself.

Never did Bukharin understand that his doctrines of liberty and absolute harmony were innately incompatible. They are, indeed, ancient antagonists. But Bukharin yearned for a final solution; it could be achieved; by revolution it would surely come. If this was possible, then no price was too heavy to pay for it; no amount of cruelty, oppression, coercion would be too high, if each sacrifice was the price of salvation for all mankind. Bukharin did not believe this doctrine to be a delusion, and he did not disagree with Stalin's brutal methods because they were morally wrong. He merely believed that the Soviet people were paying a price that did not have to be paid; that other policies would bring about utopia. Stalin's killings were mindless killings. There was no justification for them. It was Bukharin's great moral corruption to believe that killings on such a scale could, if necessary, be justified. To be exempted from moral condemnation they need only be absolutely essential to socialism's triumph. The great irony of Bukharin's life is that Stalin would one day deem Bukharin's killing absolutely necessary to both his own well-being and triumph, and to the survival of socialism.

At nine o'clock on the morning of March 2, 1938, the greatest of Stalin's purge trials convened before a handpicked audience in the Kremlin. At the tribunal, next to the Presiding Magistrate V. V. Ulrikh (who was the hanging judge at Zinoviev's show trial in 1936), sat André Vyshinsky, the Chief Prosecutor, his yellow, lined face as expressionless as always. Dignitaries, officers in uniform and more than fifty foreign journalists filled the packed rows behind the defendants. When Ulrikh was seated a cry went out, "Bring in the accused!"[23]

At once every voice was stilled, every mouth closed, people seemed to hold their breath as with one movement every head in the audience turned toward a small door in the wall on the right. Every gaze fastened on it with a sort of shrinking awe as if fearful to look upon a parade of ghosts. For the men on trial were ghosts, whom few had laid eyes on for over a year, whom some in the audience had never seen at all. Since the execution of Zinoviev the accused had been present in all their minds, not as men but as ideas; now Nicolai Bukharin and Alexei Rykov and the secret policeman Genrikh Yagoda were going to walk through the door and each would seem to look like Lazarus. A minute passed and then another while the waiting people were gripped in silence.

The door at last opened, six armed militiamen in uniform were seen; between them came forward a shuffling line of prisoners. The last to come out was a thin, worn, desiccated figure, a strange shred of humanity, seeming neither young nor old, with a shrunken face and dried-out skin, and a body looking almost hollowed out but holding itself erect as if not to falter in the last few yards between the door and the dock. Only the beard familiar from pictures and posters of the revolution had not suffered. A moment of horror and pity filled some of the European journalists watching, and the look of rage bent on Bukharin by Vyshinsky was so intense that it could be felt by people in between.

After his arrest, Bukharin hardly spoke or heard a friendly word. Illness, sleeplessness, day and night interrogations, periods of chains and brutality when the frenzy in the Kremlin was reflected in his jailers, enfeebled him physically if not mentally. In conversation, he spoke only slowly and at first seemed to only vaguely understand what was said to him. Mounting the steps to the tribune he staggered momentarily, straightened himself, stood with impenetrable face. For some minutes he remained a statue. He knew little or nothing of the charges against his fellow defendants, the bloodletting in the Lubyanka, the rigged confessions and testimony; nothing of the charges against former members of Lenin's Politburo, Rykov and Nikolai Krestinsky. Rigidly determined to allow nothing to show that would appeal to pity, Bukharin soon antagonized many who came prepared to pity by the darting quickness of his responses.

In the end it was not the impression Bukharin made that determined the outcome any more than it was he who made the Moscow show trials an international spectacle: it was the dilemma Stalin had formulated long ago and it was Stalin himself, never visible to the galleries, for he watched the proceedings through smoky glass high above the courtroom, who dominated the trial.

The scope of the charges against Bukharin drew world attention to his trial and gave it the proportions of heroic drama. That one of the most senior Bolsheviks could be accused of plotting to murder Lenin and of being in league with the capitalists in fomenting a coup against Stalin was scarcely believable. When the trial opened Bukharin was conscious of that audience. He would play to it. "The scene is Moscow; the theatre is the world," said the exiled Trotsky. The trial of Bukharin transformed Stalin's purges from the local to the universal.

Despite objections and jeers, truth did advance. Before the trial, during three months of torture, including threats against his wife and infant son, Bukharin had broken and written to Stalin, offering "if it is necessary for the party, . . . to go to trial as you wish." To save his wife's life, he confessed to all the charges, including that of having planned to murder Lenin.[24]

When, two days later, on reading the confession as amended and corrected by Stalin personally, he was so stunned that he withdrew the whole thing. The threats and interrogations began once more, and Bukharin agreed to testify at the trial, refusing only to confess to plotting Lenin's assassination. So new charges were invented, including that of espionage. But Bukharin was to learn of them only when in court.

Verbal dexterity marked his defense. His confession avoided any admission of direct complicity in any of the most heinous acts. It accepted only a general responsibility. Anything less in the way of admitting guilt would have meant immediate execution for his wife and himself without the pretense of a trial. But as Bukharin proceeded along these lines, Vyshinksy threatened to halt the proceedings. For Stalin intended to milk the proceedings for all they were worth. Nothing must remain of Bukharin's reputation.

Before Vyshinsky could act, Bukharin asked for permission to present his case "freely," and began by making his meticulously crafted acceptance of guilt:

> I plead guilty to being one of the outstanding leaders of this bloc of Rights and Trotskyites. Consequently, I plead guilty to what directly follows from this, the sum total of crimes committed by this counter-revolutionary organisation, irrespective of whether or not I knew of, whether or not I took part in, any particular act.[25]

He admitted planning the overthrow of Soviet power, and "with the help of a war which prognostically was in prospect,"[26] relied on the help of foreign states who, in return, would receive territorial concessions.

The questioning shifted to the charge of attempting to murder Lenin. Bukharin admitted that there had, indeed, been a plan in 1918 to arrest Lenin, but asserted that there was no intention of murdering him, and pointed out that Feliks Dzerzhinsky₁ himself had been arrested at the time by the Socialist-Revolutionaries and that no harm had come to him. Balked in his purpose, Vyshinksy turned to the question of espionage:

Vyshinsky: . . . Why was it so easy for you to join a bloc which was engaged in espionage work?

Bukharin: Concerning espionage . . . I know absolutely nothing.
Vyshinsky: What do you mean, you don't know?
Bukharin: Just that.
Vyshinsky: And what was the bloc engaged in?
Bukharin: Two people testified here about espionage. Sharangovich and Ivanov, that is to say two *agents provocateurs.*[27]

Bukharin's manner was resolute and his eyes had the peculiarly piercing gaze expressive of inner conviction. For with this argument he spoke volumes in a sentence. In the Bolshevik mind, no lower form of life existed than that of an *agent provocateur* in a revolutionary movement. The testimony of paid stooges was worthless automatically. Bukharin was also implying that the two men were still following their old line of work, but for a different master.

Vyshinsky soon lost his composure, and Bukharin was able to calmly mock him: "There is nothing for you to gesticulate about." Stunned, Ulrikh called Bukharin to order, and Vyshinsky exploded: "I will be compelled to cut the interrogation short because you are apparently following definite tactics and do not want to tell the truth, hiding behind a flood of words, pettifogging, making digressions into the sphere of politics, of philosophy, theory and so forth . . ."

"I am answering your questions," Bukharin replied, and went on to deny any connection to British spies. Vyshinsky, enraged, claimed that Bukharin was "obviously a spy." And Bukharin took him up on this point:

Bukharin: During the year I was in prison I was not once asked about it.
Vyshinsky: We are asking you here . . . in this court before the whole world.
Bukharin: But you did not ask me this before.
Vyshinsky: I am asking you again, on the basis of the testimony which was here given against you: do you choose to admit . . . by what intelligence service you were enlisted . . . ?
Bukharin: None.
Vyshinsky: I have no more questions to put to Bukharin.[28]

Faced with this extraordinary filibuster, the trial judges fell into discord. Court adjourned. Vyshinsky continued in a frenzy.

Bukharin knew that he was facing certain death and that socialism, as he believed in it, was doomed. His defense has a coolness and realism which suggest that he could no longer call upon his faith in the Party to redeem him. The blinders of ideology are off. No longer is his rhetoric the passionate and grandiose speech of 1917. With more than a little courage and insight, Bukharin was able to analyze and puncture the rigged charges levelled against him. His defense is like a summing-up of the socialist state's betrayals of the socialist ideal. There are moments in his presentation that amount to grandeur.

But it was to no effect. He accepted group responsibility but denied that the group existed:

> Citizen the Prosecutor explained in the speech for the prosecution that the members of a gang of brigands might commit robberies in different places, but that they would nevertheless be responsible for each other. That is true, but in order to be a gang the members of the gang of brigands must know each other and be in more or less close contact with each other. Yet I first learned the name of Sharangovich from the indictment, and I first saw him here in court. It was here that I first learnt of the existence of Maximov, I have never been acquainted with Pletnev, I have never been acquainted with Kazakov, I have never spoken of counter-revolutionary matters with Rosengolts. I have never spoken about it to Zelensky, I have never in my life spoken to Bulanov, and so on. . . . Even the Prosecutor did not ask me a single question about these people. . . . Consequently, the accused in the dock are not a group.[29]

The bloc had supposedly been formed in 1928, long before Hitler's rise to power, so "how then can it be asserted that the bloc was organized on the instruction of fascist intelligence services?"[30]

Complicity in plots to assassinate leading Bolsheviks he categorically denied. He denied being a spy. He denounced his own confession, saying it was the result of "a medieval principle of jurisprudence." He admitted the charges in general, but demolished them in particular. He had, indeed, sunk into "the stinking underground life." He had "degenerated" into an enemy of socialism. He attacked Western commentators who suggested that the confessions were coerced. He was guilty of treason, the organization of kulak uprisings, the preparation of unspecified terrorist acts. He hoped that his execution would be "the last severe lesson" to those who had wavered in their support of the USSR and its leadership.[31]

The final act followed logically. By fulfilling only the minimum requirements of a confession, Bukharin's attitude in court assured him of execution. The judges retired early on the morning of March 12 and returned late the following afternoon to announce the decision reached before the trial even began. Bukharin was found guilty on all charges. A sentence of death followed.

Before he died, Bukharin was given a final opportunity to meet with his wife. He was ready for death, he said. He gave his wife a last

testament which she was to memorize, then destroy. Bukharin's last
letter appeals to the future and denounces the "pathological suspicious-
ness" of Stalin. The Party had betrayed or was about to betray nearly all
the political ideals that had brought it to power. That "hellish machine"
could now cheerfully transform any party member into a "terrorist" or
a "spy."[32] He was guilty of nothing. He would have died willingly for
Lenin; he had never raised his hand against Stalin. He had no connections with underground struggles designed to bring down socialism. He
still believed.

But Bukharin's last testament did not reach the outside world for
thirty years. Soon after their meeting Anna Larina, his wife, was arrested. She spent six months in a dark cell, ankle-deep in water. Later
she was exiled to a labor camp for eighteen years. Bukharin's son was
raised by his sister-in-law and for twenty years knew nothing of his
father. Only in 1988 would the testament be published in Moscow. For
decades, merely to mention Bukharin's name in Russia meant certain
imprisonment.

Part
Two

8

>>> <<<

The Decline of the
Revolutionary Ideal

Bukharin's last testament shows that up to the very end he could still dissemble and self-delude. He reaped what he (no less than Stalin's other co-conspirators turned victims) had sown—a state power unbounded.

To cement his victory, Stalin lashed out at every group in Soviet society. In 1937 alone he killed three thousand senior secret policemen, and 90 percent of the public prosecutors in the provinces and constituent republics. Following the execution of Marshall Tukhachevsky in June 1937, perhaps as many as thirty thousand Red Army officers went to their graves. Most were shot within hours of their arrest. In every group under attack, the aim was to kill the most senior members, especially those who had fought in the revolution or who had known the Party before Stalin owned it. The purge within the Party was the most severe. In Leningrad only two out of the city's 150 delegates to the Seventeenth Party Congress were allowed to live. Equal losses took place in Moscow. In all, at least one million party members were executed during the 1930s.[1]

Refugee Communists in Moscow were also murdered, and in large numbers. Béla Kun and leaders of Hungary's aborted Communist regime of 1919, nearly all the top Polish Communists; all the Yugoslav Party brass save for the young Tito, all the Koreans; many Indians and Chinese, and communist leaders from everywhere in Europe and North America—Stalin had them all murdered. Hardest hit were Germans who had fled Hitler, only to be tortured by the NKVD. European communists were, in fact, safer in their homelands than in the socialist mother country.

During these years something like 10 percent of the Soviet Union's vast population passed through Stalin's penitential machinery. Famous

Tsarist prisons, such as the Lefortovskaia, which the Bolsheviks had turned into museums and peopled with waxwork figures, were put into service again, the wax replaced by flesh and blood. Churches, hotels, even bathhouses and stables were turned into jails. Dozens of new ones were built. Within these establishments, torture was used on a scale which even the Nazis later found difficult to match. Men and women were mutilated, eyes gouged out, eardrums perforated; they were encased in "nail boxes" and other medieval devices. Victims were often tortured in front of their families. The wife of Nestor Lakoba chose death under torture as her son watched, rather than accuse her husband. As recorded by Medvedev, NKVD recruits were "taken to torture chambers, like medical students to laboratories to watch dissections."[2]

Blanketed by the propaganda of Stalin's Comintern agents, partisans and Communist front groups in the West knew little or nothing of these conditions. They shut their eyes. They duped themselves. Lincoln Steffens set the tone: "Treason to the Tsar wasn't a sin, treason to communism is,"[3] he declared. George Bernard Shaw argued that, "We cannot afford to give ourselves moral airs when our most enterprising neighbour . . . humanely and judiciously liquidates a handful of exploiters and speculators to make the world safe for honest men."[4] André Malraux argued that "just as the Inquisition did not affect the fundamental dignity of Christianity, so the Moscow trials have not diminished the fundamental dignity of communism."[5] Many intellectuals, including some who knew what totalitarian justice truly meant, defended the trials. Bertolt Brecht said: "Even in the opinion of the bitterest enemies of the Soviet Union and of her government, the trials have clearly demonstrated the existence of active conspiracies against the regime," a "quagmire of infamous crimes" committed by "All the scum, domestic and foreign, all the vermin, the professional criminals and informers . . . this rabble . . . I am convinced this is the truth."[6] "The more innocent they are," Brecht added, "the more they deserve to be shot."[7] Lion Feuchtwanger, a spectator at the early trials, wrote an instant apology for them which declared that "there was no justification of any sort for imagining that there was anything manufactured or artificial about the trial proceedings."[8] So craven was his line that Stalin immediately had the book translated into Russian and promoted its sale personally. Proofs of the book were pressed on the wretched Bukharin on the very eve of his own trial, to complete his despair.

Refusal to draw inferences from negative signs was a form of moral blindness endemic to Communist sympathizers. As the chariot of a new and higher order of life, communism demanded of its supporters a suspension of critical judgment. The goal gave an excitement, a meaning, a glow to their lives which many of them substituted for the usual drives of personal ambition, profit, and intellectual rigour. Party militants, they knew, worked for nothing. Since there was no money in the movement, there could be no corruption. Since it could offer no livelihood or gain, its leaders must be idealists. Here was the religious strain that infuses belief in Marxism's mission. For it infused a passion which could be understood across the barriers of language and culture, and above the barrier of mere facts. The revolution appealed more to intellectuals who had no doubt of their capacity to manage society than it did to the working class.

Attempts by Western intellectuals to defend Stalin's state socialism involved them in a process of self-corruption which transferred to them, and so to their countries which their writings helped to shape, some of the moral decay inherent in totalitarianism itself, especially its denial of individual responsibility for good or ill. Lionel Trilling shrewdly observed of the Stalinists of the West that they repudiated politics, or at least the politics of "vigilance and effort":

> In an imposed monolithic government they saw the promise of rest from the particular acts of will which are needed to meet the many, often clashing, requirements of democratic society. . . . they cherished the idea of revolution as the final, all embracing act of will which would forever end the exertions of individual wills.[9]

Only gradually, and with more than a little reluctance, did a few Communist sympizers come to see enemies on the Left as well as on the Right. Outrage at socialism's resort to purges and judicial murder was a common inner revulsion; but to protest against such brutality was seen as a sure-fire way of undermining the common goal. This queasy feeling, regularly stimulated by Stalin's repression and horror, became chronic. The dilemma for some of the socialist-minded seemed insoluble. They yearned for a cause which seemed wholly just. But they also believed in reason, the rights of the individual, freedom of speech, of association, of opinion, the liberty of groups and races and nations, above all in the rule of law and justice. They could admire Lenin and Trotsky and Bukharin and even Stalin for selfless dedication and seeming purity of motive. Nevertheless they feared the losses induced by state socialism's terrorist methods might be irreparable, and greater than any possible gain. Some were horrified by the fanaticism and barbarism of the Stalinists, by the USSR's open contempt for the only culture that they knew, that of the free and capitalist West.

Gradually, some sympathizers with socialism could not bring themselves to contemplate, still less to sanction, the destruction of much that seemed of universal value. Caught between a Right they loathed and a Left that disappointed, many simply mumbled mild and rational words with little hope of being heard. This was in some way a product of guilt: they believed in the goals of Soviet socialism but, spurned by Stalinists as soft-hearted, began to question, as self-critical and open-minded men do, the validity of their own positions. They doubted, they wondered, they felt tempted to jettison their principles and find peace by complete conversion to the revolutionary faith, by submission to the domination of the state. To stretch out on a bed of dogma would, after all, save them from being plagued by uncertainties, from the terrible suspicion that the simple solutions of the Stalinists might, in the end, be more repressive than the free-for-all capitalism of the Right. Yet somehow the Left seemed to stand for a more human faith than the frozen, bureaucratic, heartless politics of the Right, if only because it was better to be with the false defenders of the exploited than with the exploiters themselves.

But there was one conviction which could not be abandoned: evil means destroy good ends. To extinguish existing liberties, civilized habits, rational behavior, to abolish them today in the belief that they could arise like a phoenix in a more pure form tomorrow, was to fall into utter delusion. Mikhail Bakunin had declared on the part of the nineteenth-century socialists that "one must first clear the ground: then we shall see." This seemed to his friend Herzen to stink of the Dark Ages. "If progress is the goal, for whom are we working? Who is this Moloch who, as the toilers approach him, instead of rewarding them, draws back; and as a consolation to the exhausted and doomed multitudes, shouting 'moriturite salutant,' can only give the . . . mocking answer that after their death all will be beautiful on earth. Do you truly wish to condemn human beings alive today to the sad role . . . of wretched galley slaves who, up to their knees in mud, drag a barge . . . with . . . 'progress in the future' upon its flag? . . . A goal which is infinitely remote is no goal, only . . . a deception."[10]

In this Herzen prefigured the liberal-minded men of the 1930s who first supported but then came to doubt the cause of soviet communism. Three of those men—André Gide, Arthur Koestler, and Ignazio Silone—whom we will now examine were first tempted by the siren call of state socialism, only to come round to the position first advocated by Potugin in Turgenev's novel *Smoke*, when he says "I am devoted to . . . civilisation . . . this word is pure and holy, while the other words, 'fold,' for example, or . . . yes, or 'glory,' smell of blood."[11] Like Turgenev's hero, their condemnation of socialist absolutism became categorical when they came together to contribute to Richard Crossman's epochal study of communism's heretics, *The God That Failed,* published in 1950.

But their change of heart came only with agony. To be sure, to support the Left in its excesses went against the civilized grain; but to go against it, to remain indifferent to its fate, seemed somehow even more unthinkable. They hoped against hope that the malignant power of the socialist state in the hands of Stalin was a passing excess of immaturity, and that it would vanish once the pressures of establishing socialism were removed. Each tried at first to explain and explain away the violent language and the ever-more-violent acts. For a time they could, but in the end they could not.

The similarity with Turgenev is instructive. For decades, Turgenev's name lay under a shadow in his native land. His artistic reputation was not in doubt; it was as a social thinker and critic that he remained a figure of dispute. The situation he diagnosed in novel after novel, the painful predicament of believers in liberal values who found themselves trapped between the violence of the oppressors and the fanaticism of the oppressed, a predicament once seen to be peculiarly Russian, came to be seen in the 1930s as universal. So, too, his oscillating, uncertain position, his horror of reactionaries, his fear of barbarous radicals. Even more familiar was his inability to cross over to either side in the conflict of ideas. The figure of the well-meaning, troubled, self-questioning witness to complex truth, which Turgenev invented as a literary type, became in the age of Stalin a common reality.

9

➔➔➔ ⬅⬅⬅

The Decline of the
Revolutionary Ideal

André Gide

I n 1937, as the Great Purge Trials raged in Moscow, a strange recruit alighted on the communist movement, like an exotic butterfly who soon flew off. The publication of *Retour de l'U.R.S.S.* marked the end of communist infatuation for the French novelist and future Nobel laureate André Gide.

Among all his other creative qualities Gide had, like Mayakovsky before him, an abiding capacity to irritate friends and readers. Doubtless it was a capacity which produced its own curious inner satisfactions. But much more than his capacity to irritate, he had a power to disturb, to unsettle, to upset. Although his targets were most often his own contemporaries—the French Third Republic, the Vatican, the middle class, the literary establishment of his youth, together with experts and intellectuals of all types, medics, barristers, scientists, and theologians—he also possessed a prophetic knack. Gide expressed opinions about the human condition which remain capable of getting under people's skin and making them angry. In no area of his writing was this more evident than in his study of the Soviet Union under Stalin.

That Gide's brooding look at Soviet communism shocked the fellow travellers should not have been surprising. All his novels had been rebellions, or, rather, a series of guerrilla ambushes from a lapsed Protestant point of view. Gide was certainly at variance with the dominant Catholic traditions of France. His religion—as we see it in his novels— has the egocentricity and aggression ever-present in non-conformity, though it finds more to savor in failure than success. God is his misadventure and, for this reason, perhaps he was always a religious man, that is, he did not expect to get anything but conflict and pain out of faith. Gide wishes to have an adulterer's, a gambler's, or a spy's relation with God, finding far more merit in despair than in the laborious connivings at goodness the ordinary hypocrite goes in for. Yet a man like Lafcadio, in *The Vatican Swindle,* can hardly rank with the great sinners; he lacks the pride. His muddles and illegalities rate official damnation but there is still God's mercy. Gide's world—as he said repeatedly in his *Journals*—is the revolutionary's world of desire and illusion. His way is the primrose path of nostalgia, sensual pessimism, and self-love. The famous irony is the artful weapon of the bookish man who won't grow up, who tastes life and history. They are a gourmet's dish, sweetened by the senses, salted by horror. Beginning as a dreamer, a faun-like comedian of museums and libraries, he ends in moral nihilism. Sometimes Gide can seem like the evil Passavant of *The Counterfeiters,* a short-term man, buying and selling fast on the moral market.

Gide's novels were not escapes from ordinary life, but painful journeys into it: the hero, hunted or hunter, is unveiled. In this manner Gide could transcend his perverse and morbid tendencies to present whole and memorable human beings; this wholeness is exceptional, for Gide was generally an impressionist, a cutter of mosaics. We expect from incisive talents some kind of diagnosis, some instinctive knowledge of the human situation to which we have not attended; this Gide seemed to have. But there is cause to doubt. One does not pity men until one understands their dignity. To learn of Gide's life is to build a picture of a man shut up in a daydream world, protected by all the authority of a superb culture, tortured by self-pity and not by pity for mankind. To fall, eventually, for the socialist dream was almost natural. His novels reveal a man who wants to exploit the pleasure, the terrors, and the final anarchy of a personal solitude. This is not a cold complacency; it is the complacency of the daydream; it is the Bukharin-like complacency that allows one to experiment with all mankind.

As a novelist Gide was less a creator of character than a compressor of them. He squeezed them out of books, as wine drips out of the press. His naive priests and fanatics, his thugs and his sluts, his always bedable boys and girls, his politicians gulled by their own corruption are the fantasies of the library, jocosely removed from the treadmill of life. There is scathing diagnosis. There is art. But we can at times fail to take them seriously. They have wine instead of blood; sex but not vitality. The anarchism in *The Vatican Swindle,* the deceits of *The Counterfeiters,* do not frighten except as theories. For Gide was as blasé about the idea of violence as Stalin was to its practice. Surely something has been left out. Surely it is perverse to personify the Anarchist violence of the late nineteenth century in a narrow prig like Lafcadio and to treat the murders and bombings as an outburst of mere self-righteousness or to isolate it as a clinical instance of insanity. Is it enough to regard, say, the Anarchist killers of the Haymarket merely as one of the frenzies of human nature? Was it not in some ways inevitable and therefore tragic? Is it not an insult to those men jolting in a cart toward gallows or guillotine to give them the pathos of marionettes, to treat them as a cat treats a mouse, to use them as a psychiatrist's anecdote? The sadism and pity of André Gide are certainly powerful and unrelenting; but, in the end, one comes to regard them as a piece of erotica.

Gide's subject was modern loneliness, ugliness, and transience. Hatred of these conditions drew him, in time, to communism. We despise the ugliness of our civilization without recognizing that, for some reason, we *need* to make it ugly. Behind the ugliness is loneliness and betrayal. Nearly all Gide's characters are marked by the loneliness of modern life, and on the simplest level—Lafcadio's, for example—they are merely self-pitying. They fail to communicate. They hate talking to their lovers for fear that it will incite yet another scene. His people wish to be alone; yet when they are alone, sad dialogues of nostalgia, conscience, and betrayal begin in the mind; and presently each character breaks in two: pursuer and pursued, watcher and watched, hunter and hunted. The relationship with God is the same. One moment it is God who will have no mercy; next it is Lafcadio who is torturing God. Loneliness, the failure to communicate in love, or rather to sustain communication, is the cause, and behind that is the first cause, the breakdown in understanding among men that industrial capitalism supposedly caused. In Gide's rendering of the world, we are now anonymous. We are bleak, observable people in streets, on staircases, in Roman boardinghouses, hotel rooms, cafés, police stations—free, but disheartened and "wanted." As with Lenin, there is little that is humane in Gide's vision. Gide misses the sight of individual human dignity. For his irony trivializes horror. You see it through a keyhole. Even a mystic like Blake did not think of the Terror as chiefly an example of the savor of human cruelty.

Gide's failure to rise to the fullness of a great theme is curious from a brain and taste so gifted. That failure may have been the result of his lack of some comprehensive and energizing philosophy of life, which goes some way to explaining his attraction to communism when an old man. Bourgeois culture over time became for him static and self-contained. Gide wrote enough about himself—and very honestly, too—to show that he was essentially a timid and egotistical writer; and one can understand how the Great War and Russian Revolution must have crystallized his dreams by showing him History out on the hunt and with a purpose in its eye. But a writer can not have a comprehensive view about mankind just for the asking. And when he went out among the socialists in search of a philosophy of life it was with the avidity of a connoisseur for his collection. In his hunt, Gide's delusion was that he could preserve bourgeois civilities while throwing over the irksome conventions that protected them.

Gide's masterly power of evoking the shabby scene, whether it is the Quartier Latin or the Vatican, the Congo or Neuilly, reveals a vision true to its misanthropy and quickness of eye; but it also owes something to his sense of being an accomplice. We are guilty transients leaving our counterfeits and our litter. There is an odd and frequent suggestion that romantic literature misled us—a premonition of his later disillusion with communism. Rome, Africa, the world ought not to have looked like this. And as he sought to change it, he became a true accomplice in communism's crimes.

André Gide was born to a prosperous Huguenot family during a thunderstorm on November 22, 1869, at the time Pope Pius IX was preparing the document that would declare him infallible. Gide died on February 19, 1951, days before Stalin took to his deathbed. It was almost as if Gide was cocooned between the two doctrinal revolutions embodied by these men. Both shaped the pattern and texture of his life.[1]

Gide's childhood and early years as an adult were punctuated by a series of false starts. Independence of mind makes it almost impossible to enjoy school. Nonetheless, Gide did quite well. He won prizes, and he was indebted to his teachers for giving him a thorough grounding in the classics. He grew to love, as a schoolboy, the plays of Molière and Racine. Gide left school eager to see the world, but with no sure idea of his place in it. While the unfortunate truth was brought home to him that he was not actually the heir to a huge fortune, he had a sufficient private income to thrash about for ideas, wildly veering from one extreme to another in his notion of who he was and what he ought to be, both politically and sexually.

Gide's relation with his own life, like so many other French intellectuals of his generation, was profoundly altered by the onset of the Dreyfus affair. Until then, Gide had sentiently been only an artist, concerned with no revolution except the ceaseless one of literary invention—his first book, *The Journal of André Walter,* had been published to critical acclaim—and dissociated from any rising threats or hopes in European politics. When friends talked of politics, he would sit sullen and silent, or perhaps stamp out of a café in a huff. Sometimes he would leave them in the street with no explanation of his disappearance except the tacit one that his mind was on something else. Upon the outbreak of the "Affair," however, he was doubly roused—first, as a romantic, and then as an immediate and ardent champion of Captain Dreyfus througout the trial.

Gide returned to Paris from Tunisia two weeks before the discovery of the notorious *bordereau*, the flimsy piece of paper which appeared to be a disclosure of French military secrets to the German attaché in Paris. The *bordereau*, as was later confirmed, was a fake. But, at the time, the blame for the supposed espionage was placed firmly on an officer named Alfred Dreyfus, who was court-martialled and sentenced to exile on Devil's Island, a leper settlement on a crag off the Guiana coast.

L'Affaire, which began as an ill-considered blunder on the part of a few intelligence officers, in 1894 erupted into a tempest which shook France for over a decade, revealing the extraordinary divisions between Republican and Royalist, Catholic and Free-thinker, Right and Left which existed in the Third Republic. The first and most obvious thing it showed, however, was the extent to which all Jews were detested and feared in all ranks of French society.

Throughout his life Gide's enemies could point to his disastrous habit of backing the wrong horse, in political terms. This may indeed be true. But it must also be conceded that, whatever horse he backed, he did so with unfailing loyalty and gusto, never wavering in his support, when more faint-hearted or rational men would have changed their allegiance.

The first symptom of this tendency in Gide can be seen at the close of 1898, when he set out to acquaint himself more fully with the details of the Dreyfus case. By then, it was becoming apparent to most reasonable people that Captain Dreyfus had been sentenced to exile for an offense of which he was completely innocent. Colonel Henry, the officer responsible for this condemnation, had been so sincere in his belief that Dreyfus was guilty, that he had forged the evidence against him. The notorious *bordereau*, giving a list of secret documents which its author was willing to sell to the Germans, had been penned not by Dreyfus but by Major Esterhazy, who was initially acquitted of the offense by a more than biased court martial. These events came to light in the course of 1898, largely because of the publicity given to the case by Emile Zola's famous "J'Accuse" letter in *L'Aurore*. Zola, who was sued for defamation, was obliged to leave France. The lone occasion when Gide attended the trial was the day a gunman wounded Dreyfus' counsel, screaming as he fled, "I have killed the Dreyfus. I have killed the Dreyfus."[2] The cause had become an abstraction.

Like Zola, Clemenceau, and Labori—Dreyfus' primary defenders—Gide saw grave danger in abstractions that, with a single cry, provoke men to slaughter. These were new idols at whose altars blood would be shed as stupidly as at any time in the past. Gide delighted in variety, the free play of temperaments. He desired the richest development of character, valued spontaneity, pride, and passion; he detested conformism, cowardice, submission to the tyranny of brute force or pressure of opinion, arbitrary violence, and anxious submissiveness. As a homosexual who had personally witnessed the degradation of Oscar Wilde in his French exile, Gide hated the worship of power, blind reverence for tradition, for institutions, for taboos and myths; the humiliation of the weak by the strong, sectarianism, philistinism, the resentment and envy of majorities, the brutal arrogance of minorities. He merely desired social justice, economic prosperity, political stability, but these must always remain secondary to the need for protecting human dignity, the upholding of civilized values, the protection of the weak from aggression, the preservation of genius from individual or institutional bullying. Any society which failed to prevent such invasions of liberty, and opened the door to insult and grovelling, Gide rejected with the same moral fury as that with which Ivan Karamazov spurned the promise of eternal happiness bought at the cost of the torture of one innocent child: more prosaicly, as George Painter has pointed out, Gide's "sense of encroaching old age, the waning of the desires of the flesh," catalyzed his budding altruism, for "lost desires leave the way open for moralizing."[3]

Beyond skepticism of abstract ideas, Gide saw something even more disquieting, a haunting sense of the ever-widening and unbridgeable gulf between the humane values of the relatively free and civilized elites (to which he knew himself to belong) and the actual needs, desires, and wants of the vast voiceless mass of mankind. The old world at the turn of the century was crumbling visibly, and it deserved to fall. It would be destroyed by its victims—the slaves who cared nothing for the art and science of their masters. Indeed, Gide asked, why should they care? Was this world not erected on their suffering and degradation? Filled with a just hatred of a world built on their father's bones, the new barbarians would raise to the ground the monuments of their oppressors. Such a cataclysm, Gide reckoned, might not only be inevitable but justified, since civilization, noble and valuable to its beneficiaries, had offered nothing but suffering, life without meaning, to the vast majority of men. Yet Gide does not pretend that this makes the prospect, to those who, like him, have tasted the fruits of civilization, any less dreadful.

It has often been asserted that Gide allied himself with the Communists after the Russian Revolution because he was a passionate, even a utopian idealist, and that only the excesses of Stalinism brought about his disillusion and a new, more pessimistic realism. This is not supported by the evidence. Even in 1917, the skeptics note, in particular his pessimism about the degree to which human beings can be transformed, and the still deeper pessimism about whether such changes, even if brought about by fearless and intelligent revolutionaries (ideal images of whom floated before the eyes of his radical friends in Paris), would in fact lead to a more just order, or on the contrary to the rule of new masters over new slaves—that ominous note was with Gide from his youth. Yet, despite this, he became a convinced, ultimately optimistic revolutionary. The spectacle of the trial of Dreyfus haunted Gide all his life. His early novels are masterpieces of revolutionary writing. So, too, are his journalistic sketches of the personalities involved in French politics which he contributed to the *Nouvelle Revue Française* and other literary periodicals. Gide became a rebel despite himself.

Yet Gide was not blind to the crimes of the revolutionaries. The rash of anarchist bombings and shootings in the 1890s that claimed the lives of Sadi Carnot, President McKinley, and the dowager Empress of Austria, seemed to him frivolous, a kind of political *gaminerie*. Formulas grow into terrible weapons in the hands of fanatics who seek to bind them on human beings. Gide was constant in his denunciations of those who, for the sake of some absolute ideal kill and torture because they know that they and they alone hold the solution to all social and political ills.

If History, the Marxist god, has an inexorable direction, Gide cannot discern it. Thus it is criminal to justify the oppression and cruelty, the imposition of one's arbitrary will upon many thousands of human beings, in the name of hollow abstractions—the demands of history or of historical destiny, of national security or the logic of facts. Abstractions are for Gide merely attempts to evade facts. "Do not sacrifice to idols," Gide once declared, and it is ironic that he made that clear sighted démarche at the very moment when he had "temporarily mistaken" the communist idol "for a true god."[4]

Then there are those who cry "progress" and are prepared to sacrifice the present for the future, to make men suffer today in order that their remote descendants might one fine day be happy. For them, Gide reserved his most violent contempt and ridicule. For Gide the purpose of life is life itself, the purpose of the fight for liberty is the liberty here, today, of living individuals, each with his own ends, for the sake of which they work and fight and suffer. To crush their freedom, put a stop to their pursuits, to ruin their ends for the sake of the future, is morally blind, because that future is too uncertain, and vicious.

Why, then, is liberty worth pursuing? Only for what it is in and of itself, Gide believes, because liberty is what it is, not because the majority desires freedom. Indeed, Gide believed that men in general do not seek freedom, and that most of them do not like liberators. They would rather bear the ancient yokes than take the risks of building a new life. Men prefer (Gide said again and again) even the hideous cost of the present, muttering all the while that modern life is at least better than feudalism or barbarism.

Man wants to live in his own day. His morality cannot be derived from the laws of history (which do not exist). Moral ends are what people want for their own sakes. As with the amoral Lafcadio, the "truly free man creates his own morality."[5]

Nature, personal relations, quality of feeling—these are what Gide understood best, not politics. These, and their expression in art. He loved every manifestation of art and beauty as deeply as anyone at any time. The use of art for extraneous ends—ideological, didactic, or utilitarian, and especially as a weapon in the class war—was detested by Gide. He was often portrayed as a pure aesthete and a believer in art for art's sake, and was accused by the French Left of escapism and lack of civic sense—then, as now, regarded by Marxists as gross self-indulgence. Gide's writing was not as passionately committed as, say, that of his future editor André Malraux, or of the late Tolstoy, but it was consistently concerned with social analysis so that both revolutionaries and their critics could draw ammunition from them. Clemenceau, who admired Gide's early work, ended by looking upon him as a *bête noire*.

In this Gide was typical of his time and class. More sensitive and scrupulous, less obsessed and intolerant than the great tormented moralists of his age, he reacted just as bitterly against the horrors of inequality and exploitation. The society which Gide depicted in his novels was one distorted by bullying, conformity, and obsequiousness. Gide saw a world in which men of independence or originality or character had scarcely an outlet for normal development.

This may account for the genesis in his novels of the "superfluous person," of heroes such as Lafcadio who are unable to find a place in their native lands. Each escapes into fantasies and illusions, cynicism or despair, and ends life in self-destruction or surrender. He faithfully described them all—the talkers, the idealists, the fighters, the cowards, the reactionaries, and the radicals, sometimes, as in *The Counterfeiters*—with biting polemical irony, but, as a rule, so scrupulously, and with so much understanding that he angered almost everyone at once.

Those who think of Gide as an uncommitted artist, raised above pitched ideological battles, should be surprised to learn that few writers in the history of French literature have been so ferociously and continuously attacked—from the Right and the Left—as Gide. Malraux and Céline held far more violent views, but they were formidable figures, angry prophets treated with jittery respect even by opponents. He seemed to embody no clear principles, advocated no set doctrine. In a country in which readers look to writers for moral direction, Gide (for the first two-thirds of his life) refused to preach. He was aware of the price of reticence. He knew that readers wanted to be told what to believe and how to live, expected to be provided with heroes distinguishable from villains. When the author did not provide this, Gide wrote, the reader was dissatisfied and blamed the writer, since he found it irritating to make his own way. And it is true that Malraux never leaves you in doubt about whom he favors and whom he condemns; Mauriac, Sartre, and Camus do not conceal what they regard as the path to salvation. Among these great, tormented Laocoöns Gide tried to remain cautious and skeptical; his readers kept in suspense, in a state of doubt: central problems are raised, and for the most part left—it seemed to some a trifle complacently—unanswered.

After the Russian Revolution of 1917 French society demanded more of its authors. Gide was accused of vacillation, temporizing, infirmity of purpose, of speaking with too many voices. His major works are preoccupied by weakness—the failure of men of generous heart, who remain impotent and surrender to the forces of stagnation. Lafcadio talks well and fascinates his listeners, but is made of paper. He crumples and collapses. As in all Gide's novels, the reader is left without guidance.

Les Caves du Vatican (The Vatican Swindle), however, was a novel which the radicals of the Left could use. A few Communists saw Lafcadio as a positive hero: for he was ready to give his life in the fight against the Church. We too want destruction, revolution, new foundations of life; nothing else will destroy the reign of darkness, members of the French Communist party argued. This, for French Communists, was the clear implication of Gide's novel. But he, evidently, was too craven to see it.

Gide was upset and frightened by this interpretation. He tried to get the review that made it withdrawn. He said that he would not know where to run. Nevertheless, Gide was fascinated by the new radicals. He loathed their gloomy puritanism, and could not bear their fanatical rejection of all that he held dear. But they were young, brave, ready to die. Gide wished, in spite of everything, to be liked and respected by them. He tried to flirt with the communist writer Ilya Ehrenburg. He was a celebrated charmer; he did his best to woo the grim young man. It was of no use; when Ehrenburg saw Gide approach he stared at the ceiling or left the room. This was worthy of Lenin. Nobody had ever treated Gide like this. He was deeply wounded.

For a while he persisted, but faced with implacable hostility, gave up. Througout the 1920s the political atmosphere in Paris grew more stormy. Violently worded manifestos in support of the Bolsheviks were submitted for publication in the *NRF*. Their brutal mockery of French civilization seemed to Gide mere vandalism, and as a member of the editorial board he was ever inclined to spurn them. Nevertheless he felt that something new was rising—a vast social mutation of some kind. He was repelled and also fascinated. A new regime was coming into existence. And Gide's curiosity was always stronger than his fears: he wanted, above all, to understand the new Jacobins. They were crude, fanatical, hostile, and insulting. They were also undemoralized, self-confident, and, in some narrow but genuine sense, rational and disinterested. He could not turn his back on them. They seemed to him part of a new, clear-eyed generation, undeluded by old myths. Above all, they were young, the future lay in their hands. Gide did not wish to be cut off from anything that seemed alive, passionate, and disturbing. After all, the evils that they sought to fight were real evils; their enemies were his enemies, too. Young Communists might be wrong-headed, barbarous, and contemptuous of liberals like himself, but they were also fighters and wanna-be martyrs in the war against exploitation. Gide was intrigued, horrified, and dazzled. From the 1920s onwards he was obsessed by a desire to explain himself to them, and perhaps them to himself.

In 1925 Gide set out for a year's sojourn in Africa, an expedition which would yield two travel books—*Voyage au Congo* and *Retour du Tchad*. But the immediate reward of his African journey was a sharpening of his social awareness. Gide was disgusted by the exploitation of blacks in French Equatorial Africa, and when he came home said, "Henceforth an immense lamentation abides in me."[6] This change of mind was verified in a letter to his friend Charles du Bos:

I would like not only to attain happiness myself but to make others reach it as well. I consider that it consists in the surrender of self. That is why to feel happy is nothing; happiness consists in making others happy.[7]

This new model Gide was a champion of the underdog and dispossessed—criminals for whom he demanded humane treatment; women for whom he demanded equality (particularly spiritual equality); colonial subjects whose cause went unheeded even by the liberals and Socialists; and the socially outcast. In 1935, when he was an active supporter of the Communist party, he would say of this period that he had been a Communist supporter without knowing it. What he admired in the new Soviet regime was the abolition of that abominable formula: "Thou shalt earn MY bread in the sweat of THY brow!"[8]

Humanity had always been Gide's subject, but the personal sense of liberty expressed at the turn of the century in *Les Nourritures terrestres* now gave way to what he called "la liberté serviable mais no servile."[9] His play of 1931, *Oedipe*, shows the total destruction that comes to a man who can think of nothing greater than himself and values personal liberty above all other things. Oedipus begins adult life with normal Gidean detachment, joyous in his freedom from family and tradition. But he is defeated by his determination to be self-sufficient. For Gide a man without God is doomed to despair unless he can substitute some idea or cause for God. Oedipus, in the end, realizes this and substitutes a faith in man for a faith in God. Thus is Gide revealed as someone for whom liberty is no longer sufficient in and of itself; that it actually destroys the self unless it is linked to something beyond mere egotism, to some duty even.

Yearning for that wrenching sense of moral obligation, Gide turned to communism. With its ideal of service, its discipline, he thought he would find an acceptable form of liberty. "The triumph of the individual," he said in denying his old faith in individualisms, "is in the renunciation of individualism." And in *Les Nouvelles Nourritures terrestres*, written in 1935, Gide says, "Each human being who has only himself for an aim suffers from a horrible void."[10]

His conversion was complete. "I feel myself the brother only of those who have come to Communism through love,"[11] he wrote in his *Journal*. For "what leads me to communism is not Marx but the Gospel."[12] And again: "I would like to cry aloud my sympathy for the Soviet Union and hope that my cry might be heard and have effect. I would like to live long enough to witness the triumph of that tremendous effort which I hope from the bottom of my heart will succeed and for which I would like to work."[13] He was ready for the individual to willingly sacrifice some of his autonomy so that communism should work, but he did not think it essential in all cases, and certainly did not suspect that the state should compel it in the name of communism. "I remain a convinced individualist," he said,

> but I consider a grave error the contrast which some people try to establish between Communism and the individual. To believe firmly that one can be—indeed must be—at the same time a Communist and an individualist, does not prevent one from condemning privileges, the favouritism of inheritance and the whole procession of errors of capitalism to which our western world is still attached and which are dragging it headlong to its ruin. Why do I long for Communism? Because I believe it to be equitable and because I suffer on account of the injustices which I feel more strongly than ever when it is I myself who am favoured. . . .
>
> Why do I long for Communism? Because I believe that through it we shall be able to reach the highest culture and because it is Communism which can—indeed must—promote a new and better form of civilisation.[14]

Communism, properly understood, would need to encourage the values of individuals in order to get the best out of them. And yet always at the back of his mind was the stark realization that "conversion . . . implies submission to dogma, recognition of an orthodoxy—and to me all orthodoxies are suspect."[15]

By 1935 Gide's shortcomings had been forgiven by the Left. Moments of weakness, continual attempts to justify himself to Communist leaders, all these sins appeared to be forgiven. He praises the sycophantic Congress of Soviet Writers in 1935. He is asked to speak at Communist rallies. Gide's charm, his evident sympathy for the persons and convictions of individual revolutionaries, his reputation for honesty and standing as a writer, were seen as useful by Party leaders, as they began that in-house period of collaboration among communists and democratic leftists known as the Popular Front. No illusions were harbored about the moderation of Gide's views and his habit of taking cover when a battle grew hot. And he went on telling them that their ideas were in many ways mistaken. When the old has lost authority and the new works badly, what is needed is patience, cunning, and ingenuity. Gide said over and over again at Popular Front rallies of the time that he loathed revolution, violence, barbarism. Indeed, it is not Marx which brought Gide to communism—he "made strenuous efforts to read him, but in vain; I persevere, but it is certainly not his theory which won me over." It is characteristic of Russians to "pick up an old, worn-out shoe which long, long ago fell from the foot of a Saint-Simon or a Fourier, and, placing it reverently on one's head, to treat it as a sacred object."[16] Still the Communists were young, the party of the have-nots, of those in pain or at least in distress; he could not refuse them his sympathy, his help, his love, even while at the same time looking over his shoulder guiltily at his society friends to whom he tried again and again to minimize his unceasing flirtation with the Left. At Party rallies he tried to charm young radicals with reminiscences of Jaurès and Dreyfus, but they tended to become bored and resentful. Even those who liked or admired him felt a gulf dividing them. It was the gulf between those who wanted to destroy the old world root and branch, and those who, like Gide, wished to save it, because in a new world created by fanaticism and violence, there might be little worth living for.

He seemed to enjoy his doubts, and this some Party leaders found intolerable. Maurice Thorez, the French CP's General Secretary, who welcomed Gide's adherence in 1935 to the Bolshevik cause, soon came to look upon him as a shallow, cosmopolitan poseur. Even his friend and editor André Malraux thought him a gifted and truthful writer but a moral weakling, blind to the deep, agonizing spiritual problems facing man. The one step Gide refused to take under attack was to seek an alibi in the doctrine of art for art's sake. He did not say, as he might easily have done, "I am an artist, not a pamphleteer; I write fiction, which must not be judged by social or political criteria; my opinions are my private affair; you don't drag Flaubert or Stendhal before your ideological tribunals—why don't you leave me alone?" He never sought to deny the social responsibility of a writer, and it was this that broke the reserve of the most skeptical Communist. They knew that Gide was genuinely at ease only with friends of his own class, but because he admired them he could be useful to the Leftists. What few friends Gide made among the Communists became so because he was responsive to them as individuals and did not treat them as representatives of parties or outlooks. This was paradoxical, for it was precisely such individual characteristics that, in in theory, these men tried to ignore.

This was the very attitude from which Gide recoiled. Acts, ideas, art, literature were expressions of individuals, not of objective forces of which the actors or thinkers were merely the embodiment. The reduction of men to the function of carriers was deeply repellent to him. Thus he observed, "the Soviet Union owes it to herself to prove to us that the Communist ideal is not—as her enemies are always pleased to claim—an ant-hill Utopia." He continued:

Her duty is to inaugurate in art and literature a Communist individualism. . . . No doubt a period of mass affirmation was necessary (after the
revolution) but the Soviet Union has now passed beyond that stage and
Communism can prevail only by taking into account the particular idiosyncrasies of each individual. A society in which each resembled all is not
to be desired . . . how much more a literature. Each artist is of necessity
an individualist—however strong may be his Communist convictions. . . .
It is only thus that he can do valuable work and serve society. I consider
foolish and dangerous that fear which only the impotent experience, of
being absorbed in the mass. Communism has need of strong personalities,
in the same way as these find in Communism their justification and
strength.[17]

To be treated with so much sympathy and understanding, and indeed
affection, as human beings and not primarily as spokesmen for their
ideology, was a rare experience, a kind of luxury, for many young
Communists in the French Party. This alone goes some way to account
for the fact that Gide, even after his break with the Party, continued to
be regarded by some—Aragon for one—with affection.

Gide was determined, then, to see for himself what the Soviet experiment was like, and to learn all he could. He set off in the summer
of 1936 hoping that the Soviet Union would reveal itself as producing a
new civilization, one without the need, as Enid Starkie has written, of
"reducing to serfdom a single class."[18] Sacrifice, Gide knew, would be
necessary. Artistic standards might be lowered for a time. "It is perhaps
right," he said, "for achieving that end [the good society] to sacrifice
even a few works of art."[19] But he was soon convinced that the price was
too high.

The book Gide wrote about his journey is one of the very few excellent books of travel written about the Soviet Union. He is exact and
prophetic in his own restricted way as the extraordinary and very different de Tocqueville was in his as a travel writer. This ought not to
surprise us: great artists are often far-seeing. They avoid the stumbling
blocks of fact. They rely on their own simplicity and vision. Fact-
fetishism had by 1936 produced scores and scores of books on Soviet life,
the works of sociologists, anthropologists, topical "problem" hunters,
working parties, and statisticians, which had none of the impact of
Gide. He succeeded because he rejected official information. He was all
the information he required.

Gide yearned for a personal involvement with the cause to which he had allied himself. A celebrity, he was fêted everywhere. (But not without some awkward explanations. *Pravda*, in announcing Gide's arrival in Moscow on June 19, 1936, took pains to mention that the writer was born in 1869 to "an aristocratic Protestant French family."[20] Such an odd reference can be explained only by understanding that in Russian transliteration, Gide's family name is rendered as *Zhid*, the Russian word for "Yid" or "Kike." *Pravda* was warning its readers not to rush to judgment: this new and welcome comrade from France was no *zhid*!)

Moscow excited in him a mixture of fear and delight. In the first July days, he suffered from indigestion, stayed too long in a windowless bedroom, and met mainly Russian writers. One day he was taken, for some reason, to a shooting gallery. Gide detached himself from his hosts and went about the city on his own. Within hours, he was picking up interesting friends on the street. "I was able to enjoy moments of deep joy. Nowhere are human relations as easily formed as in the Soviet Union, nor as warm or deep. Friendships are quickly made—often a mere glance suffices—and strong bonds of sympathy are instantly forged."[21]

Gide was a traveller, that is to say, a story-seeker to the marrow. His novels themselves are conscious journeys into the interior. The Soviet Union roused in him the same passions that stirred him as a novelist. Thus, he could not limit himself to the world introduced to him by Gorki. He would either sink or be raised by the challenge Russia posed. Gide ignored the obvious news. He saw that his subject was not shock and that he was not in Russia to advertise or boost the obvious. His subject was how the consciousness of a half-converted socialist would be affected, and what inner meanings and sensibilities he could offer in return. Guilt there would be, but distaste: nostalgia for what was being destroyed, but a feeling for the drama; he knew that he would have to be both personal and analytical. He became a seeker, open to the full bewilderment of his situation. André Malraux later described the book as a prose poem; an excellent description. Generously evocative and labyrinthine in its tact, it also shows a man struggling with love and menace.

On Stalin's brutality, however, he did not mince words. Perhaps the reason was that he was trying to hoe the true Party line. "Was I mistaken?" he asked within five days of his arrival.

> Those who have followed developments in the U.S.S.R. . . . . will decide whether it is I who have changed or the U.S.S.R., and by U.S.S.R. I mean the man who rules it . . . . Dictatorship of the proletariat, we are promised. We are a long way from it. Dictatorship, yes, of course; but

dictatorship of a man, not of the united proletariat, not of the Soviets. It is as well not to be deceived; let there be no mistake about it: it is not this we wanted. Another step and we might even say that it is exactly what we did not want.[22]

His chief complaint was about the depersonalization of the individual. Economics and social reorganization Gide leaves to the experts. He was quite ready to forgive the inequality of incomes in the "classless" society. His department was the spirit. Gide had hoped to find in the Soviet Union a mankind liberated from servility and conformity, a people that held its head high and spoke its mind freely. But he doubted whether "in any other country today, be it in Hitler's Germany even, the mind is less free, more servile, more fear-ridden, more vassalised."[23] Was this the land of revolution—"his patrie d'élection, his guide and model"?[24]

A number of instances illustrate for Gide that "deformation" of the temper under Stalin's rule. When, at a gathering shortly after his arrival in Moscow, Gide made some sly comments on the Spanish Civil War, everyone looked uncomfortable, everyone seemed to look to his neighbor for a cue. The Party line on Spain had not been announced. "No one knew what to think on the question."[25] Several days later the Politburo took its stand, and Gide's words were greeted with general enthusiasm. In the USSR a great deal was made of "self-criticism." Gide when in Paris admired it and dreamed of the results it must have.

> But I grasped that apart from denunciations and remonstrances (the soup in the refectory is not cooked enough, or the reading club hall is not swept properly) this self-criticism consisted in wondering whether this or that were or were not "within the line." The line itself is not discussed. What is discussed is whether such a work, such an act, such a theory is consistent with this sacred line. And woe to him who tries to push on farther.[26]

Again and again, Gide remarks on the pathos of a civilization so exuberantly on the move, but is bewildered that everything about it seems so tawdry and temporary. Of the new collectives he writes:

> I wish I could give some conception of the uniformly depressing impression which is communicated by each of the dwellings, that of a total absence of individuality. In each there are the same ugly pieces of furniture, the same picture of Stalin, and absolutely nothing else—not the smallest vestige of ornament or individual belonging. Any house could be exchanged for any other without the tenant being aware of the alteration.[27]

They live in a world in which

> their homes are only . . . lairs to sleep in; the whole interest of their lives
> is centered in the club. Doubtless the happiness of all can most easily be
> achieved by the sacrifice of the individuality of each, through conformity.
> But can it be called progress, this loss of individuality, this uniformity,
> towards which everything in Russia is now tending? I cannot believe that
> it is. In the Soviet Union it is accepted . . . that . . . there can only be
> one opinion, the right one.[28]

And so each morning

> *Pravda* tells the people what they need to know, and must believe and
> think.[29]

Even thought has been collectivized:

> . . . Each time you speak with one Russian it is as if you had spoken
> with all.[30]

This inability to communicate was felt not as a loss to society, but
rather as a gain; they had become true Communists. Gide, the chatty
European traveller, had put his finger on what most often dismayed
during casual contacts with Soviet citizens: the Communist chill.

Other than Maxim Gorki, Gide was starved of two things in the
USSR: conversation—for all that was offered was "recitation"—and
privacy. Everywhere there are watchers. "It is essential to recognise
this and not to allow oneself to be bamboozled. This is not what was
hoped for."[31] No longer do workers even have the privacy to elect their
own representatives to defend their "threatened interests."

> Free ballot—open or secret—is a derision and a sham; the voters have
> merely the right of electing those who have been chosen for them before-
> hand. The workers are cheated, muzzled and bound hand and foot. . . .[32]

So the best way to get ahead is

> to become an informer; that puts you on good terms with the dangerous
> police which protects you while using you. Once you have started on that
> easy, slippery slope no question of friendship or loyalty can intervene to
> hold you back; on every occasion you are forced to advance, sliding fur-
> ther into the abyss of shame. The result is that everyone is suspicious of
> everyone else and the most innocent remarks—even of children—can
> bring destruction, so that everyone is on his guard and no one lets him-
> self go.[33]

The Soviet Union was becoming hateful to him. He felt no interest in the self-conscious literary milieu in which Gorki moved. So he fled Moscow.

Between Tiflis and Batum the Gide party paused at Gori, the little town where Stalin was born. It occurred to Gide that it might be courteous to wire a word of thanks to the ruler of Russia for all the hospitality that had been shown him and his friends. He drew up the message: "Passing through Gori in the course of our wonderful journey I cannot refrain from addressing to you . . ." But that was as far as he got. The translator was scandalized. One could not say just "you" to Stalin. It would not be decent. One must add a flourish of some sort: "you, the leader of the workers," or "you, master of peoples."[34] There was nothing to do but submit.

But there was more than just fault-finding within the book. On any number of subjects Gide was enthusiastic. "My conviction remains whole and unshaken," he said in concluding his preface, "that the USSR will conquer the grave errors which I am pointing out and—more important—that the mistakes of one country cannot possibly compromise the genuineness of a cause which is international and world-wide."[35]

In the middle of Gide's visit, Maxim Gorki died. At the funeral in Red Square, Gide was asked by the Union of Soviet Writers to speak in honor of Gorki. These literary meetings in honor of great writers who had died often became under Stalin an occasion for the pronouncement of some great words, *ex cathedra*, by the writer selected to make the chief speech. Gorki had made a great speech at the funeral of Mayakovsky some years before. Gorki's funeral was to be another similarly public occasion, with speeches made about the state of literature and the benefits of communism in Russia. Workers and peasants would stand up and urge Soviet writers to equal the achievements of Soviet industry and agriculture. Of course, none of them realized that in writers like Mikhail Sholokov, they had found literary equivalents to Soviet industry—junk.

Yagoda was at this time Stalin's chief henchman. When he came to hear that Gide was planning to speak at the Gorki commemoration, he drafted a memorandum in which he denounced the author of *The Counterfeiters*. There was an effort made to rescind the invitation to Gide, but someone—Stalin, it was supposed by Gide at the time—allowed his speech to go on. Whoever made the decision, if not Stalin, would not have lived to regret it. Gide let them have it.

He spoke of the "new problems which the very success of the Revolution had provoked." He continued:

> As the future of civilisation is closely linked with whatever solution is found for them in Russia, it seems to me profitable to raise them again here. The majority, even when it compromises the best elements, never appreciates what is new or difficult in a work of art, but only what can readily be recognised—that is to say what is most commonplace. It must be remembered that there are revolutionary as well as bourgeois commonplaces and cliches. It is essential to realise that what gives quality to a work of art . . . is never what comes from the revolution nor what reflects its doctrine. . . . A work of art will survive only by what its truly original in it, by the new questions it asks or anticipates, and by the answers that it gives to questions that have not yet been formulated. I greatly fear that many of the works of art impregnated with the purest Marxist doctrine . . . will, for posterity, smack only of the laboratory. Now that the Revolution is triumphant . . . art is in danger of becoming an orthodoxy. What triumphant revolutions need to grant, above all else, to the artist is freedom. Without complete freedom art loses all its significance and worth. . . . I often ask myself anxiously whether a Keats, a Baudelaire or a Rimbaud may not languish unknown today in the Soviet Union . . . by reason of their originality. You may argue that we do not need nowadays a Keats, a Baudelaire or a Rimbaud . . . you may say, if they cannot prevail, so much the worse for them and so much the better for us, since we have nothing to learn from their like and the writers who teach us something today are those who, in the new society, feel perfectly at home—in other words, those who approve and flatter the regime. . . . It is precisely the works which flatter . . . which are of poor educational value and that a culture, if it is to progress, must ignore them. . . . To remain in constant self-contemplation and self-admiration may be one stage in the development of a young society, but it would be . . . tragic if this first stage were to remain the final and only one.[36]

Gide believed that great art was used and useful in its own right, and the gradual disclosure of its usefulness would be an invaluable accompaniment to the Soviet experiment:

> As long as man is oppressed and downtrodden, as long as the compulsion of social injustice keeps him in subjection, we [must] hope for much . . . from . . . the fallow classes. Instead, I see a new bourgeoisie developing in the Soviet Union from these untried masses, with exactly the same faults and vices as ours. . . . They may well be members of the Communist Party, but they are no longer Communists at heart. I blame the Soviet Union not for having failed to achieve more—I see now that nothing better could have been accomplished in that time, the country had started

from too low—what I complain of is the extent of their bluff, that they boasted that the situation in the Soviet Union was desirable and enviable—this from the country of my hopes and trust was painful to me. . . . It is time that the workers . . . realise that they have been bamboozled and led astray by the Communist Party.[37]

The Soviet Union is acting senselessly, Gide tells the assembly, moving toward the very thing "that has destruction within it." Hisses and shouts come from the crowd. A Party official intervenes to say that Gide is speaking "windy nonsense." In the fury of the seer ignored, Gide grabs the microphone and shouts back in anger.

I would have remained silent if I could have been assured of any faint progress towards something better. It is because I have reached a firm conviction that the Soviet Union is sliding down the slope that I hoped to see it ascend, and because it has abandoned, one after another—and for the most specious reasons—the liberties gained by the great Revolution after so much hardship and bloodshed. It is because I see it dragging in its wake to irreparable chaos the Communist Parties of other countries that I consider it my duty to speak openly. . . . For I place the truth above Party. I know well that in Marxist doctrine there is no such thing as truth—at least not in any absolute sense—there is only relative truth. I believe, however, that in so serious a matter it is criminal to lead others astray, and urgent to see matters as they are, not as we would wish them to be—or had hoped they might be. The Soviet Union has deceived our fondest hopes and shown us tragically in what treacherous quicksand an honest revolution can founder. The same old capitalist society has been reestablished, a new and terrible despotism crushing and exploiting man, with all the abject and servile mentality of serfdom. Russia . . . has failed to become a God and she will never now arise from the fires of the Soviet ordeal.[38]

A decision to ban Gide from other public engagements was taken immediately. That came as no surprise. No great public speaker, Gide was probably not even particularly disappointed that the Communist authorities stopped his mouth. They could not do the same to his pen.

Writing with a speed almost unknown to Gide, *Retour de l'U.R.S.S.* was ready for publication six weeks after Gide's return to Paris from Moscow. It was an immediate success, selling over 150,000 copies in two weeks, and thus becoming the best-selling book at Gallimard since the release of André Malraux's *La Condition humaine* (Man's Fate) four years before. Gide's work appeared as an exciting, invigorating piece of heresy. While all over Europe intellectuals were agonizing about whether or not they should support Stalin's policy in the Spanish Civil

War, which was then raging, Gide was tabling a much more fundamental question—is Soviet communism any less evil than fascism? If it
is not, then we are required to acknowledge that fact. With one book,
the shape of the battleground over communism was altered. Stalin himself had been for the first time indicted by someone more than sympathetic to the cause of communism. And Gide remained so. As Chesterton
had once said about Christianity: communism had not been tried and
found wanting. It had never been tried.

Gide wanted to try still. That is one of the inescapable conclusions of
Retour de l'U.R.S.S. Gide could no longer believe in socialism; he only
could hope. He was too much of an egotist and rationalist to submit to
the lies and disciplines of Stalinist ideology. It was little more than
twenty years since Lenin had declared the infallibility of the Communist party. In Gide, in the autumn of 1937, a heresy was raised against
the power of the socialist state. All that was lacking, Gide himself
acknowledged, was a devotee ardent enough to take the heresy to the
world. Gide was too timid to play the part. When a congress of
communist-minded writers meeting in Madrid at the height of the Spanish Civil War denounced Gide as a "fascist monster," instead of defending himself, he went into hiding.

"I do not like your lips," Oscar Wilde once said to the young Gide
when they first met in Paris, "they are quite straight, like the lips of one
who has never told a lie."[39] In his old age Gide's lips were still like a
long, truthful line ruled across his face to which experience had given
that look of dominance and seduction sometimes found in the saint, the
confessor, and the actor. But the penitents of this confessor were those
who had committed the sin with which he himself had at times either
struggled or ironically philandered: the sin of faith. Gide was, in the
Socratic sense, a corrupter, one who liberated only to impose an infinitely arduous pursuit of virtue, and this made him a hard moralist as
all true puritans are. For most moralists—Goethe and Montaigne are
two exceptions who come quickly to mind—have the attraction of working in a fixed climate from which there is no escape; they write us into
an algebra which is a pleasure in itself, and give us the relief of a sort
of fatalism. But Gide's imaginative world was changeable; spring is
defeated but spring returns; the moral frontier, like the year, is open,
exposed and dangerous. This calls for courage, the loveliest of the virtues; but, alas, also for diligence, the grimmest of them.

Gide belonged to an essentially non-political generation, and when he
fell into the trap of the social problem, he found that he had sacrificed

his art and integrity—"since these began to encumber my head and heart, I have written nothing of value."[40] His dejection was that of the open, civilized mind in agitation, trapped in political defeat. As always, Gide was a resistance movement in and of himself, and the lasting impression his infatuation with communism leaves is of a man who was working at a technique for freedom:

> I am reproached for my oblique gait—but who does not know that when the wind is contrary, one is obliged to tack? It is easy to criticise for you who let yourselves be carried by the wind. I take my bearing on the rudder.[41]

Tacking was always Gide's method, for he was most alive when there was an opposing force and he drew as close to it as he could. The charge of vacillation was unjust. Conscience was the instrument by which he lived and worked; and the hypnotic effect of his disillusion with communism is that sense that we are watching not a free man but a technician or tester of freedom.

The papacy of the Counter-Reformation was immeasurably strengthened by the energies of St. Ignatius of Loyola. The very gospel of Christ might never have been preached beyond the bounds of Jewry had it not been for the fervor of Paul of Tarsus. Anti-communism after Gide awaited its archpriest. And in civil war Spain this penitent-prophet was learning of his vocation.

10

>>> <<<

The Decline of the
Revolutionary Ideal

Arthur Koestler

André Gide's hopes for the future had their analogues in the savage
prophecies of Bukharin and Mayakovsky, who gleefully predicted
the doom of the bourgeoisie in death and lava and of the birth of a new
civilization. In Gide there was always squeamish fascination at the
prospect of vast destructive powers unleashed, a movable holocaust of
innocents and fools, unsuspecting of their fate. For even when damning
Stalin's USSR, Gide continued to be seduced by the dream of socialism,
reasoning that anything that could be studied and written up was also
subject to adjustment and correction. One of the unintended consequences of *Retour de l'U.R.S.S.* was the conclusion—drawn by a few of
his readers if not consciously by Gide himself—that such reasonable
reform was beyond the reach of the socialist state. The nature of the
beast was revealed.

Why didn't Gide's revelations cause a wave of revulsion against Stalinist socialism? Gide's timidity was one factor; ill-luck was another. It was
one of Gide's misfortunes that the publication of his book coincided with
the bloody highpoint of the Spanish Civil War. In April 1937, as galleys
of Gide's book began to circulate in Paris, forty-three aircraft of Hitler's
Condor Legion bombed the historic Basque town of Guernica, whose
famous oak tree had shaded the first Basque parliament. One thousand
people were killed and 70 percent of the city's buildings destroyed. For
Stalin's propagandists—the best in' the world—it was a stroke of un-
covenanted good fortune, and they turned it into the most celebrated
episode of the entire war. Picasso, who had already been asked to do a
large painting for the Spanish pavilion at the Paris World Fair, leapt at
the subject. His painting helped to push a whole segment of Western

114

opinion toward the Communists after its revelation that summer, ten days after the publication of *Retour de l'U.R.S.S.*

Throughout the Spanish war, Stalin was assisted not only by such public relations coups, but by the naiveté, gullibility, and it must also be said, the mendacity and corruption of Western intellectuals, especially their willingness to overlook what W. H. Auden called "the necessary murder" in his infamous poem "Spain, 1937." The majority of intellectuals of the Left did not want to know the truths revealed by Gide; they were unwilling for their illusions to be shattered. They were overwhelmed by the glamour and excitement of the cause and few had the intellectual determination of Gide to uphold absolute standards of morality, or the experience of the horrors that occurred when relative measures of morality took their place. Many treated the Party with craven subservience. Thus Cecil Day-Lewis, who became a Communist in 1936, apologized for not having done so earlier, priggishly confessing to a "refinement of bourgeois subjectivism by which I was unwilling to join the party till I was making enough money to be able to assure myself that I was joining from disinterested motives, not as one of the lean and hungry who would personally profit by revolution."[1] He felt he had to ask the party's permission even before he accepted an invitation to join the selection committee of London's Book Society.[2]

In the course of the war the Spanish Republic became the prisoner of its friends—the Communists and fellow travellers and all the antifascist groups who made its defense the rallying cry of their own causes. Caught in the trap of their commitment, the cause of Spain became synonymous with that of communism. Spain, like communism, became a fort to be defended against all criticism.

Resistance to criticism was grounded in the belief that to reveal flaws in Soviet society or policy was to discredit the Left and a discredited Left could not fight fascism. Revelations by men such as Gide destroyed confidence in the Soviet Union as a bulwark against Hitler and Mussolini and Franco. It was this fear of what would happen if Stalin was weakened by distrust that intimidated writers such as Hemingway and Spender and turned old friends such as André Malraux against Gide. Communism was their supposed guarantor of liberty. By casting doubt on the infallibility of the USSR Gide committed sacrilege, and anyone who supported him or his ideas was pro-fascist if not an outright traitor.

Heresies, however, have their own dynamics, which tend to help them to propagate. The fear and disgust heresy engenders are enough to keep it going. For Gide, communism's moral authority drowned in the evasions and the cowardice he witnessed in Moscow. For Arthur Koes-

tler it ended as a silent loss of faith. While Gide was comfortably sitting
out in his apartment near the Palais Royale the abuse heaped upon him
by Communists, Koestler was shivering in a prison cell in Spain, awaiting execution at the hands of Franco's forces after his arrest and conviction as a Soviet spy.

The charge was true but the sentence was rescinded at nearly the last
moment and by the time Gide was retreating to the safety of his villa on
the Riviera, Koestler was on his way to England, deported from Spain as
part of deal struck between Franco and the British government of Stanley Baldwin.

In their own persons, Gide and Koestler embodied the split personality of revolutionary communism. For while it is commonplace to recognize that the Russian Revolution gave birth to a new political world,
it is less often understood that that world was the product of two irreconcilable interests—the creation of a potent state and the creation of a
community of equal citizens. The fiction, begun with Marx and abetted
by Bukharin, was to imagine that each might be served without damaging the other, and the history of the Soviet Union since the revolution
amounts to the bitter realization of that impossibility. Gide and Koestler, indeed, personify the two tempers—rhetorical and rational, vis-
ceral and cerebral, sentimental and brutal—from whose imperfect union
Communist politics was born. Both men shared a sympathy for socialism
and its founders; both also saw little to gain from the replacement of one
class of despotism with another. Neither man believed in the innate
virtue of workers. Gide, however, faced life as if wearing a hairshirt,
whereas Koestler (whether in his pro-or anti-Communist phases) could
easily sail off into the happy realm of incendiary phrasemaking with all
the gusto of the adolescent and essentially frivolous.

Koestler's interest in communism, like Gide's own, stemmed from his
passionate interest in the self. But the self in which he took the most
interest happened to be his own. Koestler saw his own personality not
only as a labyrinthine mystery but also as the anarchically heaped material for a great work of history. An irrepressible agitator, a philosopher
and a hack, thin-limbed and thin-nosed like Don Quixote, Koestler saw
monstrous windmills to charge in every political storm. The prime objective of his life was to define his identity and in so doing to shape it:
to make himself into a being fit to bear the name of Arthur Koestler.

For Koestler this process of remaking himself involved inhabiting a
hall of mirrors. It was impossible for him merely to be. He had to be in
relation to others. Whatever he thought or did must be observed from
outside and the observation must be reflected back. It hardly mattered

whether the outside observer was another person or another part of his own nature. When he poured his self-analysis and self-observation onto paper, he was addressing that part of his own personality which could stand aside and watch with detachment as the panting, sweating, involved self pushed on through thicket after thicket.

Koestler's thirst for self-observation was matched by his need to measure himself against others. He was, in that sense, one of nature's parasites, living from one intense commitment to the next and always drawing a great deal of energy from the host. His dog-like hero worship and his equally dog-like sexual promiscuity were opposite sides of the same coin. Whether he was coupling his mind with that of some comrade, or coupling his body with that of some attractive young girl, he felt a relief from the intolerable burden of the unmitigated self, and in this sense his whole life was one long act of copulation.

For Koestler life was a seduction, a ceaseless campaign. And when people are at war, no code, no manner, can contain the experience. Thus Koestler's combative personality became an asset for his writings. In Koestler, unlike in Gide, the tragedy of Soviet communism is not passive; it lies not only in what is done to a man but in what he himself does and in what happens to him inside. When we compare these things with the sentiment of Gide and the harsh satire of Orwell we see that these authors are propagandists (of a sort) concerned with society. The freshness of their documents is deceptive. They describe Soviet ways with wonderful verisimilitude; but the stories appear disconnected from life, like painfully digested hearsay. They are propagandists with an uncommonly delicate ear. They write to warn opinion in the domestic parlor beyond the shop.

Compared with Gide and Orwell, Koestler does not appear at first to know his mind. He is all over the place. He is the confused public. It is typical of *Spanish Testament*, for example, that its purest picture of Communist intoxication is of rumor and news being spread at night in the streets. The emotion of the street catches him. He is not intoxicated with ideology but he does not deny the message of the pennants and the flags in the street. He is the innocent who goes out into the street and loses his head. As with Bukharin and Mayakovsky before him, he feels the herd instinct. We may suspect Koestler's idea that out of this a sort of terrible beauty is born; it sounds like the cracked bugle and slack drum of propaganda. Yet, the loquacious Koestler is right. It is the bewildering thing in all his work, that this dressed-up egotist with all the air of a ham actor, is always half-right when he is most dubious. He is the newspaperman who reflects the ambiguous brute quality of public feeling. His virtue is that he begins on the pavement and that, like the streets, he has no shame and no style. Excitement and incantation take the place of them.

Such emotions mark the attitude of so many intellectuals toward the Soviet Union. Gide approached communism as a follower, not a leader. Koestler writes most surely when he lets his sense of anonymity dominate. (Odd that this huge and often so flaccid egotist should be able to puff himself large enough until he can identify with all the masses and become lost in them: it is his paradox.) It is his paradox, too, that purple prose and the real thing traipse along together like the blind leading the blind, unable to see, unable to stop.

The infection is common. The people of Koestler's novels are notable not for their ideological commitment but for their gregariousness. They run in crowds. If they plan a crime or betrayal, they tell everyone. They are missionaries in mass-morbidity, mass-guilt, and mass-confession. When alone they are not absolutely alone; they have at least two selves. You hear not the private groan but the public lamentation. It is not surprising then that in the late 1930s and early 1940s Koestler found that he had prophetic warnings to issue to a Europe which was becoming a mass of broken pride, vengeance, humiliation, and remorse. As a novelist he had a profound instinct for the character of groups of people, their ideas and the common hungers that delude and bind.

Sensationalist that he was, Koestler also gave the impression of realism and sanity. Koestler knew the world from behind the scenes. The accent was decisive. The voice bristled with satire and a capacious humor, for he had the satirist's satanic genius: his sneers a true expression of his nature. Koestler at his best wrote like a hunted man who, for a moment, had fooled the bloodhounds and thus had time to confess and to laugh with scorn before the baying drove him on again. He was laughing hotly from the midst of experience. He did not laugh in order to forget. He scoffed, but not for humor. Once a believer, he was as obsessed with his faith as only a fallen believer can be. Koestler could see the terrors of men's double natures, the fever in which inner ghosts encounter each other. It is frightful that we have so many selves and that the unconscious may wreck us; on the other hand there is something bizarre, something comic, something pitiable, in this squabbling assembly that has somehow got into one once well-tailored pair of trousers. For Koestler pushed things to extremes where other people went only half-way. And despite his great appetites, there was, in his single-mindedness and obsession, something like purity, and it was this quality that made him an anti-Communist prophet.

Koestler was concerned not only with spiritual headlines; he was also content to bring the laconic daily news. Like Balzac, he plundered society. So gregarious and populated is the Koestlerian unconscious, that in the dreams of his characters crowds of people may appear. Sinister fingers point at the condemned men in horror during the purge trials of *Darkness at Noon*. In this novel it has been suggested that Koestler parodied himself—it was written after *Spanish Testament*, his autobiographical account of terror in fascist Spain—and certainly all Koestler's ideas are there: the double, the unconscious, the fantasies, dreams, persecutions, suspicions, shames, and exchanges of personality. But this polemical masterpiece carries its own underworld along with it, stands on its own feet. In the first place the growth of the accused's sense of guilt from a vague irritation of mind and health into definite consciousness is described with wonderful passion and suspense. The value of psychological analysis to the novel lay, for Koestler, in its latent dramatic quality. Psychology was dramatic; it becomes a metaphor for explanation. Koestler can push things to extremes, because unlike Gide, at his extremity there is pity for human nature. Half-way, where other writers might leave his kind of story, lie the conventions of melodrama and intellectual comedy; and, mad though the story of the purge trials is, it is full of the madness history has injected into the lives of the Soviet people. The madness is the madness of communism, not the madness of the mind. No one will ever accuse Koestler of failing to complicate a situation, and the novel is certainly a succession of complications. The unconscious, Koestler believed, gave probability to the most bizarre situations and turned coincidence to fate.

Communism, with its dirty inquisitorial figures, was Koestler's fate. It has a sense of history which Koestler's Mitteleuropean imagination made theatrical. Koestler seems to have turned the Hungarian exile's natural preoccupation with nationality, history, defeat, and unavailing struggle, from his own country to the Communist party. Even he recognized its irrational element:

A faith is not acquired by reasoning. One does not fall in love with a woman, or enter the womb of a church, as a result of logical persuasion. Reason may defend an act of faith—but only after the act has been committed, and the man committed to the act. Persuasion may play a part in a man's conversion; but only the part of bringing to its full and conscious climax a process which has been maturing in regions where no persuasion can penetrate. A faith is not acquired; it grows like a tree. Its crown points to the sky; its roots grow downward into the past and are nourished by the dark sap of the ancestral humus.[3]

Koestler, as both enemies and friends testify, dedicated his life to communism because of his faith in liberty. He fought for it in action and in words. He stood for ceaseless rebellion against despotism, for unending protest in the name of the oppressed. His power of destructive argument was extraordinary, and made him a potent propagandist for whatever cause he fronted. His onslaughts remain a model of polemical prose. With talent and high spirits he carried on the militant tradition of the violent and polemical poetry of Vladimir Mayakovsky. He shared its buoyancy but also its weakness, and his doctrines, as with Mayakovsky, became mere strings of ringing commonplaces rather than a coherent structure of ideas. In the most uncritical manner of the revolutionary propagandists of 1917, Koestler poured together all the virtues into one vast undifferentiated lump: justice, humanity, goodness, freedom, equality ("the liberty of each for the liberty of all" was one of his favorite empty incantations), science, art, reason, good sense, hatred of privilege and of monopoly, hatred of oppression and exploitation, of stupidity and poverty, of weakness, inequality, injustice, snobbery— all these he represented as forming one lucid ideal.

Once launched on waves of romantic patter, one knows only too well what to expect. Liberty becomes reciprocity. I am free and human only so far as others are such. My freedom is limitless because the freedom of others is so. Our liberties mirror one another. So long as there is a single slave, I am not free. Liberty is not a physical or social condition; it is a mental one. It consists of universal recognition of the individual's liberties: slavery is a state of mind; the slaveholder is as much a slave as his chattels.

Koestler's thought is simple, sometimes shallow, always clear; the language passionate, direct yet imprecise, riding from climax to climax of rhetorical evidence, sometimes expository, more often polemical, usually ironic, constantly related to the facts of his life. Liberty—the idea occurs ceaselessly. Sometimes Koestler speaks of it in exalted terms, declaring the instinct to mutiny—defiance—one of the basic "moments" in the development of Man. In this he sounds like Milton's Lucifer, the first rebel, the true friend of freedom. In such moods, Koestler saw brigands and desperadoes as the only truly revolutionary figures—a throwback to Stalin's ideal revolutionary. Having nothing to lose, such men might destroy the old world to make room for the new. As a young man he placed his hopes in all who drown their sorrows in violent outbursts against their confinements. He might sometimes speak of the need for an "iron dictatorship" during the transition from the vicious society of today to the stateless society of tomorrow. At other times he believed that all tyrannies tended to perpetuate themselves, and that the dictatorship of the worker would become just one more brute rule of once class over another. Few of the optimistic confusions of the Romantics fail to take a bow somewhere in his work. After one day proclaiming the right—the duty—to mutiny, and the necessity for the overthrow of the state, he would the next happily proclaim belief in absolute historical determinism. Our environment shapes us entirely. Yet we must fight for independence, not of the laws of nature, but of laws imposed by other men. No matter his politics, that remained throughout his life Koestler's definition of liberty. The meaning of the phrase is for anyone to seek. Koestler hated the imposition of restraints upon anyone at anytime under any conditions. Lift restraints, and all will be set right. The search for something less philosophically muddled in Koestler's work is unrewarding. He used words not to describe but to inflame, and became a master at it.

Koestler belonged to that class he described in his book *The Scum of the Earth*, the human wreckage of the Left which fascism scattered over Europe. He was born a displaced person; half-Austrian, half-Hungarian, all-Jewish, Koestler was educated in Vienna, worked with Zionists in Palestine and for communists in Germany, lived in France in both freedom and an internment camp, escaped to England, where he ended his life in an elegant townhouse in a Knightsbridge square. Koestler seems to have been created to wander the earth without the mundane private allegiances that bind most men to people and place. His allegiances were always with the world of ideas or myth; and when these failed, to the world of random physical events. The eccentric, the crank, and the thorn in the flesh were sorts of people who turned up regularly in the socialist diaspora. Koestler was all three at once. Guilt and self-pity were the price he paid for his wanderings.

Arthur Koestler grew up in extraordinarily exciting times in the history of his native Hungary. Within intellectual circles the march of progress was keenly and optimistically felt, in spite of the many repressive measures of the Hapsburgs. Whatever the Emperor and his advisors may have wanted, Hungary was on its way to being a fully separate country, open to all the cultural and ideological conflicts sweeping Europe in the run-up to the Great War. If the generation of Lassalle had brought back liberal books and ideas as though they were some kind of guilty contraband (in the way that a modern Hungarian citizen once used to smuggle home blue jeans after a trip to Paris or New York), members of Koestler's generation were less self-consciously borrowers and more surely partakers of the European political and intellectual inheritance. The future became a vast and free expanse which men could assume as a field for innovation.

Koestler, then, belonged to the first generation in Hungary to have been born into a full, vigorous literary and intellectual inheritance; to have been born into a Hungary which not only received Western intellectual writings as well as novels and poems, but which also now produced such writings themselves, writings of a kind that could stand next to their Western equivalents. And with the dismemberment of the Hapsburg Empire after World War I, he was also part of the first generation to be able to say they were Hungarian.[4]

On one level, then, bliss was it in that dawn to be young and alive. But there was a drawback. In Central Europe, for intellectuals, there has always been a drawback.

Neither Emperor Franz Joseph, to put it mildly, nor his postwar successors as rulers of independent Hungary—the Communist Béla Kun or the conservative Admiral Horthy—were intellectuals and their reaction to all that imaginative renaissance in their midst was characteristically decisive. Writers and playwrights and journalists suffered exile or imprisonment. Only during the brief, liberal regime of Count Michael Karolyi in 1918 were the arts given free play.

This, then was the climate in which Koestler grew up: a renaissance such as had never been seen in Hungary before and, in reaction to it, as the euphoria of independence cooled, a time of upheaval and censorship which vigorously suppressed signs of independent life among poets, journalists, and novelists. It is rather as though the government of Louis XIV, instead of persecuting Huguenots, had turned its attentions on Corneille and Racine; or as though Elizabeth I, not content with making Catholic martyrs, had sent Shakespeare and Marlowe and Spenser to jail. At the Technische Hoschule in Vienna (a technical college), which Koestler attended between 1922 and 1926, he first became aware of this intellectual ferment. Not by the lectures themselves. Koestler's father paid high fees for his son's attendance, and his son lived a smart student life, frequenting fraternities and duelling societies. The secrecy and comradeship of fraternity life played well with Koestler's budding love for conspiracy. Koestler's friendships, at least initially, were not enlightened. He chose his friends because of their looks and social contacts. He would rather ride in a carriage wrapped up in a rug with some attractive young girl than discuss how to set the world to rights. Late nights were devoted to drinking and wenching, not to the niceties of philosophical argument. Only the Zionist ferment really grabbed him, so much so that he went to work on a kibbutz in 1920. Political engagements, as opposed to unspecified discontent, would not have dawned on Koestler at university unless there was a considerable politicized student movement. And this there was. Thus Koestler was

> ripe for the shock of learning that wheat was burnt, fruit artificially spoilt and pigs were drowned . . . to keep prices up and enable fat capitalists to chant to the sound of harps; while Europe trembled under the torn boots of hunger marchers and my father hid his frayed cuffs under the table. The frayed cuffs and drowned pigs blended into one emotional explosion as the fuse . . . was touched off. We sang the "Internationale," but the words might well have been the older ones: "Woe to the shepherds who feed themselves, but feed not their flocks."[6]

Bitter, crafty, unable to contain himself, after graduation Koestler spent the years 1926–1931 as a correspondent for the Ullstein chain of newspapers, which he joined after becoming disillusioned with kibbutz life—first in Palestine and the Middle East, then in Paris. He became science editor for the firm's Berlin flagship newspaper, *Vossische Zeitung*, in September 1931, just at the moment when German discontent came to a head in the first electoral triumphs for Hitler's Nazi party. In the spring of that year the Weimar leaders discovered that they had drained the cup of public confidence by their inability to control inflation or end it.

Germany was caught in the contagion of lawlessness which the Depression had spread upon the Continent. Great War soldiers had for a decade formed small freebooting bands to live by robbery, or as strong-arm gangs for political parties such as the Nazis and Communists. Corruption and instability in the Weimar Republic were by 1931 old complaints common to many Germans, but they were sharpened by the continuing economic slide. As elsewhere in Europe, there was a deep craving to restore lost order. In Adolf Hitler the political and spiritual strains of German despair met and were fused into a philosophy and program.

Koestler was terrified. His employers, the Ullstein brothers, were "like the original Rothschild brothers," liberal and democratic, who conducted their "House in the Kochstrasse as more of a Ministry than an editorial office."[7] They were an early Nazi target. Koestler did his job, "writing about electrons, chromosomes, rocket-ships, Neanderthal men, spiral nebulae and the universe at large; but the pressure of events increased."[8] Not prepared to be swept along as a "passive victim" to nazism, it "became imperative" for him "to take sides."

The Socialists pursued a policy of opportunist compromise. Even by a process of pure elimination the Communists, with the might of the Soviet Union behind them, seemed the only force capable of resisting the onrush of the primitive horde with its swastika totem."[9]

But it was not by a process of elimination that Koestler became a Communist. He began "for the first time to read Marx, Engels and Lenin in earnest. By the time I had finished . . . something had clicked in my brain which shook me like a mental explosion."[10] He was born again:

> To say that one had seen the light is a poor description of the mental rapture which only the convert knows. . . . The new light seems to pour out from all directions across the stray pieces of a jig-saw puzzle assembled by magic at one stroke. There is now an answer to every question; doubts and conflict are a matter for the tortured past—a past already remote, when one lived in dismal ignorance in the tasteless, colourless world of those who *don't know*. Nothing can disturb . . . except the occasional fear of losing faith again, losing thereby what alone makes life worth living, and falling back into the outer darkness, where there is wailing and gnashing of teeth.[11]

Koestler applied for Party membership on December 31, 1931. His "new life was to start with the calender year."[12] Like a schoolboy in search of his first job, he sent off his résumé and a brief biographical sketch which highlighted his family's poverty during and after the Great War, not the elegant bourgeois life he had known as a child. His meeting with the Party's vetting officers does not appear to have been entirely successful—even at this early stage they seem to have had some doubts about that lively, erratic streak in the young man—but they were delighted by his vigor and intelligence. They accepted him as a disciple, knowing that his job with the Ullsteins was "an important asset for the Party."[13] They gave him the cover-name Ivan Steinberg.

The sensational rise in electoral support for the Nazis added to the sense of Weimar's crumbling authority. As Communists, the German Party saw its best opportunity in conspiracy, not in votes, and began to move underground. Koestler went with it. He found himself "plunged into a strange world," like a "deep-sea aquarium with its phosphorescent light and fleeting elusive shapes." For him,

> It was a world populated by Christian names only—Edgars and Paulas and Ivans—without surname or address. . . . It was a paradoxical atmosphere—a blend of fraternal comradeship and mutual distrust. Its motto might have been: Love your comrade, but don't trust him an inch—both

in your own interest, for he may betray you, and in his, because the less he is tempted to betray, the better for him.[14]

Koestler's frame of mind was heartily conspiratorial: he felt a sense of "fraternal collaboration" when revealing stories he had "picked up in the House of Ullstein."[15] There was nothing about the workings and opportunities of the Party's netherworld that he did not grasp. Intelligent and energetic, he felt frustration at the need for "conspiratorial vigilance."[16] His female "minder" would "never accept a drink or refreshment: when we met in a café, she insisted on paying for herself; the first time I showed her where to wash, I caught her look of sulky disapproval at my dressing-gown."[17] He was "running after the Party, thirsting to throw myself completely into her arms, and the more breathlessly I struggled to possess and be possessed by her, the more elusive and unattainable she became."[18] Koestler "racked" his "brain for gifts to make her smile and soften her stony heart."[19] He recruited the aristocratic son of an ex-Ambassador to Turkey, and through him was able to provide "diplomatic gossip, military titbits about rearmament, and information about the complicated and suicidal intrigues between the German parties"[20] in the last year of the Weimar Republic. One incident stuck in his mind:

> One day I learnt, off the record, from Reinger, the diplomatic correspondent of the *Vossische Zeitung*, that the Prussian police were to carry out a surprise raid at S.A. headquarters the next morning at 6 A.M., seize their arms and archives, and impose a ban on the wearing of the Nazi uniform. I hurriedly passed on the news   The action was carried out according to plan; but while Berlin feverishly discussed the chances of immediate civil war between Nazis and Socialists, our Communist *Rote Fahne* came out with its usual streamer headline sneer about the Social-Democratic government's tolerance of the Nazis, thus making a complete fool of itself. I asked . . . why my warning had been discarded; [it was] explained that the Party's attitude was a set, long-term policy which could not be reversed by a small incident. "But every word on the front-page is contradicted by the facts," I objected.[21]

He then received a dialectical interpretation of the facts:

> The action of the police was merely a feint to cover up their complicity; even if some Socialist leaders were subjectively anti-Fascist in their outlook, objectively the Socialist Party was a tool of Nazism; in fact the Socialists were the main enemy, for they had split the working class.[22]

But wasn't it the CP, after all, that had broken with the Socialists in 1919?

"That's the mechanistic outlook again," Koestler was told. "Formally we were in the minority, but it was we who embodied the revolutionary movement of the proletariat; by refusing to follow our lead, the Socialist leaders split the working class and became lackeys of the reaction."[23]

Understanding that the Socialists were necessary to beat back the Nazis was not lacking; the trouble was that Communist tactics did not allow alliance with the democratic Left an essential place. The reason was a mixture of contempt for the Socialists and fear for communism's primacy on the Left. By 1932 the hope that Nazi streetfighting might provoke a revolution gave any desire for a left-wing alliance a short life. After a brief period during which negotiations with the Socialists took place, the Communist International insisted that any agreements be revoked, fearing that the Socialists would gain support from the working-class members of the Party. The Communists were caught in that common irony of human endeavor when one self-interest cancels out another.

Like a shark in a net, Koestler thrashed about in his ideological commitments. He learned to "distrust" his "mechanistic preoccupation with facts."[24] Ignorance was bliss:

> Once you had assimilated the technique you were no longer disturbed by facts; they automatically took on the proper colour and fell into their proper place. Both morally and logically, the Party was infallible: morally, because its aims were right . . . and these aims justified all means; logically, because the Party was the vanguard of the proletariat, and the proletariat the embodiment of the active principle in History.[25]

Renegades from the Party were "lost souls, fallen out of grace; to argue with them, even to listen to them, meant trafficking with the powers of Evil."[26] What the Party offered Koestler was salvation, which was reached only through Party rituals and with the permission of its ordained priests, the commissars. Like the Catholic church of the Middle Ages, *Extra eccelesiam nulla salus* (No salvation outside the Church) was the rule.

A mystic in faith, Koestler was rational in practice. He distrusted the devotional excesses of the Party's mystics and visionaries. As a Communist, he was both conformist and non-conformist. Humane in ideas, he opposed the Party's condemnations of the Socialists. This was not because he was a closet liberal, but because he understood the need for allies in the fight against Adolf Hitler.

> As far as I was concerned, I was quite prepared to become one; I was one of those half-virgins of the Revolution who could be had by the S.S.S.

(Silent Soviet Services), body and soul, for the asking. The Comintern and O.G.P.U.A. carried on a white-slave service whose victims were young idealists flirting with violence.[27]

But his questioning meant that he was "not drawn into the vortex to become a full-fledged 'apparatchik.' "

It was not Koestler's conscience that threw his Party career off course, but that of his aristocratic mole, who reported his conversations with Koestler to the authorities. No arrest followed, but the Ullsteins sacked Koestler. It was, he said, "the end of my connexion with the Apparat. Having lost my usefulness for them—in a manner which proved my total unfitness for intelligence work—they dropped me without ceremony."[28] Only contacts in his cell on Berlin's Bonner Platz remained, and he threw himself into the life of the cell "body and soul."[29]

News sheets flooded forth, carrying banner headlines proclaiming peace. And as their titles warned, they were full of rage. Exactly how much of the cell's broadsheets were suggested by Koestler cannot be established. But it seems reasonable to suppose that he, one of the liveliest and most creative people of his cell, would have played a central part in this zestful enterprise. The premier edition began with an article by Dr. Wilhelm Reich, who argued that "sexual frustration of the proletariat caused a thwarting of its political consciousness; only through a full, uninhibited release of the sexual urge could the working class realize its revolutionary potential,"[30] quite agreeable dogma to the lecherous young Koestler.

These broadsides are an important element in Koestler's thought. On the score of length alone, and even allowing for the uncertainty as to how much he actually wrote, they amount to well over a half a million words. To compose so much, and so fast, was necessarily to put on journalistic muscle. It is said that Koestler's practice was to shut himself in his room, alone except for the printer's devil who ran between him and the waiting compositor. But at no time of Koestler's life, either then or later, did rapid composition mean thin or ill-considered work. It was simply a reflection of his powers of concentration.

Not only his thinking, but his entire "vocabulary was reconditioned. Certain words were taboo—for instance, 'lesser evil' or 'spontaneous'; the latter, because spontaneous manifestations of the revolutionary class consciousness were part of Trotsky's theory of the Permanent Revolution."[31] Other words became

favourite stocks-in-trade. I mean not only the obvious words of Communist jargon like "the toiling masses," but words like "concrete" or "sectarian" (you must put your question into a more concrete form, comrade; you are adopting a left-sectarian attitude, comrade). . . . According to the vocabulary . . . you could smell out at once people with Trotskyite, Reformist, Brandlerite, Blanquist and other deviations. . . . Communists betrayed themselves by their vocabulary to the police, and later to the Gestapo."[32]

To be immersed in the actual process of political decision fascinated Koestler. The young enthusiast soon learned that doctrinal purity, rigid adherence to a line, and an inflexible refusal to dilute one's ideological brew were not always and everywhere the virtues he once took them to be. Spokesmen for his own side sometimes lose their wings and harp, those on the opposite sometimes their horns and tails. Of course, an impatient man will come away from such an experience still impatient. Charles Dickens, for example, was a Parliamentary reporter in his youth, and it certainly left him with a contempt for the confusion and leisureliness of democratic assemblies. But while Dickens was a gallery reporter, Koestler was an underground pamphleteer. The task was one that continually drove his mind back to political principle. How shall a society govern itself? What is the degree of community, of liberty, that best produces happiness? What are a man's rights and what are his duties? These questions were steadily before him. He emerged from the experience more skeptical, more suspicious of utopian views.

No Communist dictate was more severely doubted by Koestler than rulings on sex. Promiscuity had once flourished in the Party, until Lenin made his puritanically Marxist pronouncement against the Glass of Water Theory (that is, "against the popular maxim that the sexual act was of no more consequence than the quenching of thirst by a glass of water").[33] Bourgeois morality was a bad thing. "But promiscuity was an equally Bad Thing, and the only correct, concrete attitude towards the sexual urge was Proletarian Morality," says Koestler in portraying the Leninist position on sex.

This consisted in getting married, being faithful to one's spouse, and producing proletarian babies. But then, was this not the same thing as bourgeois morality? The question, comrade, shows that you are thinking in mechanistic, not in dialectical, terms. What is the difference between a gun in the hands of a policeman and a gun in the hands of a member of the revolutionary working class? The difference is . . . that the policeman is a lackey . . . and his gun an instrument of repression, whereas the same gun in the hands of a member of the revolutionary working class is an instrument of the liberation of the oppressed masses. . . . The same is true of the difference between so-called bourgeois morality and Proletarian Morality. The institution of marriage, which in capitalist society is an aspect of bourgeois decay, is dialectically transformed in a healthy proletarian society. Have you understood, comrade, or shall I repeat my answer in more concrete terms?[34]

Such silliness was accepted without open demur. Koestler suffered "the deep, instinctive resistance of the political dope addicts to the cure."[35] His mind, Koestler later said, had been equipped with "such elaborate shock-absorbing buffers and elastic defenses that everything seen and heard became automatically transformed to fit the preconceived pattern." The unexamined life, said Socrates, is not worth living. To this, Koestler has added a corollary: the underground life cannot be examined if it is to be maintained.[36]

Picture what then happened to Koestler. When the Comintern sends him to civil war Spain in 1936 the fiction cracks. Koestler is swimming in his natural element, or rather, in one of his natural elements: anarchy and disillusion. His eyes are skinned for every incident. The entire Koestler lexicon is present in his memoirs of the Spanish Civil War, *The Spanish Testament*. There are the twisted, internalized portraits of the faithful Party cadres; the stabbings, the penetrations of secret agents; the Aeschylean furies; all of which aspire to the condition of forensic documents. Here is the outer limit of human experience, symptoms of ideological addiction: Koestler's characters are symbols of the alienation through which the bland willingness of communists to betray and to tolerate suffering has reduced the human character. The collective psyche of the socialist faithful is imploding, leaving only blurred individuals hideously generalized. Even the landscape becomes corrupted. We see the sullen sky over Vigo harbor glowing "under an evil spell."[37] It is the Koestler spell. We are in for melodrama. "The constriction in the throat that affects a whole town, a whole population, like an epidemic,"[38] comes upon him. Betrayal, anger, and raw humor let the wind out of his hysterical faith.

The report is alive; it is packed with human beings; it is resilient, almost buoyant. Koestler sees himself not as some sort of literary expressionist but as a realist who nevertheless stakes the outcome of his art on a magnetic opposition between intelligent understanding and gut sensation. His characters do not merely tell their stories of murder and disillusion; they seize hold of the reader's nervous system and offer sensation without conveying real-life terror. For the peculiarity of his style is that he manages to be both precise and ungraspable. Communism destroys by a sort of moral slippage: men and women are mentally and emotionally smeared as though they had endured some terminal rearrangement by massage. Their basic human instincts can retain an obstinate integrity, for Koestler breaks the chain of pessimistic expectation by taking his characters beyond themselves into grandeur. They command us to focus and look, to know their ideologically incited crimes for exactly what they are.

Koestler documents the political prisons and torture houses established by both Fascists and Communists alike. And they are alike, in their essential inhumanity. Certainly the hellish little automatons scuttling through these party classrooms are fantastic, but they are, Koestler says, the real inhabitants of a land gripped by ideological hysteria. Relying on direct observation, fixed by incessant note-taking, Koestler's genius was to leave his readers feeling that such monsters *may* very well be chatting to one another, in darkness or sunlight, just around the corner. To cage these goblins in the white sunlight of the printed page was to have power over them; it was to have something like dominion, once more, over himself.

How much in this book (as in all Koestler's writings) is true personal experience and how much is intense imaginative identification is not important; only his identification with the tortured and not the torturers is what truly matters. It is passionate because it is moral: it is complex because it is at once theatrical and always self-consciously aware of itself. Having endured and survived a nightmare, Koestler reconstructs the madhouse of his experience of the Spanish Civil War. The message is one of cumulative despair. Hysteria, evil, cruelty, and irrationality are not just waste products of socialism, they are its very fiber. Only awareness can possibly stop these Furies from spinning and snipping the thread of life. Moderation, understanding, debate will not tame them. They are virulent presences, and the socialist diaspora is thick with them. They are as pervasive as demons were to the medieval mind; their total destruction is the only possible remedy. Koestler was politically trained and liked to be politically bespattered. But as he witnessed the brutalities of Stalin's agents in Spain, he had to overthrow his long held illusions. Socialism's message was that human nature was naturally good but deformed by a corrupt system which imprisons all humanity in the sterile equations of profit and loss. Man is born free, but he is everywhere in chains. Koestler's warning, after he left Spain, was different. New chains were being attached somewhere deep inside humanity: they were being forged in the name of socialist liberation.

In the end, when the curtain falls on *Spanish Testament*, much of Koestler's intended audience remained not entirely convinced. Perhaps this was because they were overconvinced. Few Communists and Socialists wanted to face the fact that communism had become merely a dogma to justify absolute power. Yet this may not be the only explanation. The source of the problem many be literary; Koestler had a voice, an urgent voice, vital, voluble, and lively, above all never boring—a voice, but an arid and mechanical style. On the face of it this is an unkind criticism to level at a displaced person who is not writing in his own tongue (*Spanish Testament* was written in English), who has to make shift to write in a new language and does master the grammar, if not the poetry, of it. But we suspect that no language is an inconvenience to him; language is a machine; not even in his own language, we feel, has he any love of words or any sense of their precision and grace. The professional propagandist's contempt for language lingers—it is a device to convince or confuse. Here, for example, is a passage from *The Yogi and the Commissar.* The manner itself forbids total belief in the argument, and leaves us with the sensation that Koestler himself would only half-believe in it if he could express it simply, for it is only half-true:

> The law of the novel-perspective prescribes that it is not enough for the
> author to create "real life," he must also locate its geometrical place in
> the co-ordinate system, the axes of which are represented by the dominat-
> ing facts, ideas and tendencies of his time; he must fix its position in an
> N-dimensional space-time continuum . . .[39]

Koestler used words as thought saving gadgets from some sort of ironmonger's counter, and drew especially on the vocabulary of science and economics which are paralyzed by patents. Like the Latin tag, they may appeal to the vanity; and the Central European mind appeared to be susceptible to all that technical coagulation, but neither exactitude nor true illumination issued from them. Love of jargon suggested Koestler's lingering lack of aesthetic instinct or sense, his deaf and arbitrary nature.

The deficiency is more damaging to Koestler's reporting than to his early fiction. Shaky as some of the passages in his novel *The Gladiators* are—though originally written in German, it was his first novel published in English—they are reasonably free of his vices of style. His warnings ring clear and true. The jargon of Marx, Freud, and Einstein would have been grotesque in a story of ancient Rome and the Spartacus revolt. We are captured at once in this novel by the sardonic vivacity of the author, the raciness of his reporting, his light mastery of the novelist's and historian's material, even by his boyish humor. No personal hatred, no extraneous obsession with persecution or guilt, clutters the flow of the narrative, or impedes the growth of his argument: for though the matter of the Trotsky-Stalin blood feud is implicit in the central crisis of the book, Koestler has not yet projected himself into the Moscow trials. Success destroys: that is his message. Revolutions that fail preserve their myth; and to Koestler faith and myth are everything.

The subject of *The Gladiators* is the rising of the slaves under Spartacus; their race to triumph; the tragic split between Spartacus and Crixus; and the final defeat of the slave army. On the one hand the laxity and shamelessness, the experience and corruption of Rome are comically and diversely rendered with a ribaldry and a talker's scholarship. Koestler's Roman portraits are plump and impudent medallions, cheerfully unclassical; they are the footnotes of Gibbon turned into scabrous propaganda cartoons. Indeed, Koestler takes us back to the classical past, not for its marbles, but for its sacrifices. For beyond the classisim there is the raw, rushing, high-voiced rebellion, tearing down all roads, laughing, shouting, guzzling, raping, killing. The wings of the traditional humane ideal of fraternity raise riot above its own lusts; a brotherhood of the camp makes the spirit flesh. Here is the spirit of fraternity that has energized socialism since its birth. There is pity for the mindless hopes and follies of simple people: this is the only book of Koestler's to show us the lowly material of revolution in the mass, the simple man who, even in his excess, does not wish to die, and whose last look, as he falls, is of utter surprise. In Koestler's later books, the dying of revolutionary leaders loses all human quality; the deaths are mere transactions of policy. But Koestler's experiences in Spain awakened him. The masses, as portrayed in *The Gladiators*, are incapable of salvation, and between the Gadarene downward rush which Crixus will lead, and the slow, painful political course for which the brain of Spartacus is pathetically groping, they chose the mindless exaltation of the former. He who cannot stand the screams of his own prisoners, is overwhelmed by the seeming necessity to be a tyrant. Spartacus parts company with half his horde; "objectively" he ought to have killed them.

Night, dawn, noon, the spell: the symbols in *The Gladiators* are always theatrical. Spartacus fails, but the dawn of a new age has come nevertheless; we are moving toward the success of Noon, the darkness at Noon which is the corruption of success. This is an ancient and haunting Jewish theme. The race, by numberless pronouncements of Jehovah, has been fated to be destroyed in success, to be searching forever.

*   *   *

Darkness at Noon is a *tour de force*, a book terrifying and claustropho-
bic, an intellectual thriller where ideology is the killer. Where Gide's
language, which seemed precise, had a way of leaving indistinct impressions, Koestler's words confront us with the undeniable fact that
socialism demands the construction of a tyranny far more oppressive
than the one it was designed to replace. No just and noble world follows
the establishment of the socialist order: communist idealists are wiped
out as surely as the opponents of socialism, and the masses are reduced
to a slavery far worse than their original position under the old regime.
We are with the apocalyptic rhetoric of Bukharin and Mayakovsky once
again, but it is no longer the fat and comfortable bourgeoisie that is
being annihilated. Workers and revolutionists themselves go to the gallows.

Here in *Darkness at Noon* is the story of a man arguing his way (or
being argued) toward the confession of crimes he has not committed, an
interpretation of the Moscow show trials, a dramatized examination of
the problem of ends and means. As a novelist, Koestler has a superb gift
for the handling of argument in a living way; he knows when to break
off, when to slip into the personal or the small incident, when to digress
into the minor character, where to tighten the screw. Rubashov, the
accused, makes the pace all through the story; he is an alert, intelligent
man, a live-wire brain where Spartacus was passive. And occasionally,
like a sudden fragment of sunlight in this grey, horrifying book, horrifying in its grim pistol-muzzle logic, glimmers of human illumination
occur in Rubashov. They are truly moving. Yet, and here Koestler
focuses on the dehumanizing demands of the socialist vision, Rubashov
and Gletkin are a sad pair of Jesuits consumed and dulled as human
beings by their casuistry. The Communists have taken over the doctrine
of original sin from the Roman Catholic church, and have tacked the
Calvinist doctrine of Predestination on to it; but they have dispelled the
visionary and emotional quality of these dogmas, with the dull acrimony
of the makers of company bylaws. An irredeemable dreariness surrounds the lives of Rubashov and Gletkin. They are not "great"; they are
merely, like Bukharin as he silently accepted his doom, sterile committee men or faceless chess players.

The book is not tragedy. Yet to be destroyed by your own church or
by your own deeply held beliefs ought to be tragedy. It is surely tragic
for the young to destroy the old. There were (if Koestler had not been
so gifted in the art of making a case) tragic springs in Rubashov's
history. Somewhere in the tale, Ivanov (one of the Inquisitors who is

drugging himself with drink) remarks that the murders of Raskolnikov were trivial because they served, or failed to serve, private ends; had they served the ends of the collective morality, they would have been significant. But in *Darkness at Noon* Koestler shows that no act, official killings like that of Rubashov most of all, can reach this high standard. It is a police act, not a tragedy, the closing of a case. Koestler argues that the casuistry of Gletkin and Company, the socialist state itself, had destroyed the concept of tragedy on the collective plane. Everything is ends and means. Rubashov, who has betrayed so many people in the name of "objectivity," has destroyed himself in advance, and is simply getting what is coming to him. By inference, the same will happen to Gletkin. The two rascals are agreed. Wolf, as the Tsarist officer says, eats wolf. Great ideas are in conflict, but in the socialist world order they cannot be embodied in great men.

We have to turn to the greatest of all novels about the revolutionary, Dostoevsky's *The Possessed*, to see that *Darkness at Noon* is a powerful book, but not an imaginative work of the highest kind. It has the intensity of obsession, the precision of surgery, but no largeness. Listen to Koestler's description of what made Stalin tick, it has all the insight of an article in *Psychology Today*:

> What went on in No. 1's brain. . . . What went on in the inflated grey whorls? One knew everything about the far away spiral nebulae, but about them nothing. That was probably the reason that history was more of an oracle than a science. Perhaps later, much later, it would be taught by means of tables of statistics, supplemented by such anatomical sections. The teacher would draw on the blackboard an algebraic formula representing the conditions of life of the masses of a particular nation at a particular period: "Here, citizens, you see the objective factors which conditioned this historical process." And, pointing with his ruler to a grey foggy landscape between the second and third lobes of No. 1's brain: "Now here you to see the subjective reflection of these factors. It was this which in the second quarter of the twentieth century led to the triumph of the totalitarian principle in the East of Europe." Until this stage was reached, politics would remain bloody dilettantism, mere superstition and black magic . . .[40]

The Soviet cult of Lenin's brain is accurately parodied, but of Stalin's hidden motives we learn nothing.

Darkness at Noon is like that. It is a document, pulled up by the roots from a native soil. A few old Bolsheviks may have confessed from Rubashov-like motives; but for the great tormented majority of Stalin's real life victims, one survivor tells us, *Darkness at Noon*, "would have been the subject of gay mockery."[41] The revolutionaries of Dostoevsky's novel are all living people with ample biographies, and they are set among and feed upon other living people. Russia breathes in *The Possessed*, its landscapes, its cities and towns, its rough climate, its murderous history, and grants the characters a sort of pardon of time and place. The Russians are as Dostoevsky drew them; a people living by wont in a natural atmosphere of suspicion and paranoid mistrust, and consumed by fantasies. *The Possessed* is soaked in its own people, grows out of Russian soil. It is truly felt.

Compared with *The Possessed*, *Darkness at Noon* grows out of nowhere. It is like the allegory of communism itself, a prophecy of the inevitable and remorseless future. The Party is the same in all countries, and the problem of ends and means is decided not by moralists, but by inflexible laws of history. Koestler states only a case, the novel understates its field of human, psychological, and historical reference. He wishes to undermine the argument for socialism, unlike Gide who still hoped to save it, somehow. Kostler's own mind was like a prison, with its logical corridors, its dazzling but monotonous lighting, the ingenious disposition of its control towers, its traverses and its walls. And there are also the judas slots through which we are led to observe the sudden, shocking, physical revelation; those cells where the dingy human being stands in his daydream; and, outside, the courtyard where the man circles, dragging his shame on his scraping feet. Koestler's images of scowling commissars and deluded prisoners coming to their senses, at long last through meditation, punctured the Stalinist fantasy: its obsession is with trance, death, and the link between socialist faith and cruelty—the dungeon beneath the courtroom, the Grand Inquisitor's icy hands on the cattle prod. The death-haunted visages of his soon-to-be martyrs force the faithful (or so he hopes) to think about their own voluntary human dissolution. Pathos, energy, despair, exhaustion, orgasmic pleasure: every shade of meaning, all the sensations that socialism plays upon, find their way into his tale. There is relentless autophagy: the cannibalizing, bit by bit, of his own life story of doubt and disillusion, in numerous variations. *Darkness at Noon* is as much about the condition of secular despair, bad faith, and the uprooting of the self—a vast and almost illegibly complex dirge that touches now and then on the language of Dante's *Inferno*—as it is about damnation. Koestler cannot, as Dostoevsky did, discern the psychic causes for converting to the revolutionary faith. Yet the sense of strain and rupture speak more eloquently of dislocation and frustration than anything Gide ever wrote.

No selfless emotion, no love above all, can be felt within the party, but only self-love and self-hatred. And Koestler, who once occupied this spiritual prison through his own faith in socialism, is like some new and enterprising prison warden, humane enough, but more and more attached to the place and infected with the growing belief that the guilty are ourselves, the free, the people who remain always outside the socialist allure. This is a position he shared with Gide and other disenchanted Communist intellectuals of his generation. Their habit of hypnotizing and magnetizing a subject by the incantations of repetitive argument, so that it becomes rigid, is his. Like his youthful propaganda, Koestler intended *Darkness at Noon* as an act of literary hypnosis. But the argument was so successful and complete that readers began ceasing to believe in its human application the moment they put the book down.

For Koestler, after *Darkness at Noon*, there was an almost inevitable decline. Disillusion brought his powers to a climax. He descended into nihilism. *Arrival and Departure*, his next book, was an assault upon belief itself. The book was Koestler's attack upon himself for his membership in the Party, and justifies his new isolation. With the cause thrown over, humanity must go with it. Koestler had a theatrical view of his faith; it was a vision, not a bond. He is like Ivanov in *Darkness at Noon*, who said that ever since the invention of the steam engine, there has been no normality, only war. A remark that is deeply untrue. There is always normality. But for Koestler, after the invention of the socialist state, man was irredeemably cursed, perhaps damned. Communism was like the second coming of original sin. People are debased by the inevitable half-truths and power plays. It is the price they must pay for trying to make the world anew.

The novels of Koestler are, however, skeletal. They are like the steel frameworks of a modern skyscraper before the pre-fab walls go in. Up there, shaking all over with the vibration of the thing, is Koestler furiously concentrating on his pneumatic riveter. A guilty figure, he wants to warn us of that which he has helped to build. So guilty does he feel that presently he stops work, harangues the crowd below, and attempts to sabotage the building materials. The building must never be completed, for it remains a stimulus, an incitement to others, a threatening outline against the sky.

All of the ideas to be found in Koestler were, of course, not new to him. Under Stalin a shadow Russian culture was clearing illusions away. Mikhail Bulgakov, in his novel *The Master and Margarita*, portrays a satanic Moscow where truth, creativity, and love are crushed. The novel's action takes place, in part, in Jerusalem on the day of Christ's interrogation before Pilate. Yeshua (Christ) is the victim of a rigged denunciation. Pilate fears that he will be undone if he does not affirm a death sentence. Careless words at any time may lead to death. Anna Akhmatova, Russia's greatest poet in the twentieth century, whose husband was condemned to death on rigged charges in 1921 and whose son was arrested in 1935, also wrote about a time when:

> The stars of death shone high above
> As innocent *Rus'* writhed
> Under bloody boots
> And the wheels of black ravens.

The poem, *The Requiem*, is not merely about Stalin's victims, the disappeared and tortured, the gulag inmates. It is about the cowering masses in the USSR who live on after a loved one has been taken away, who wait night and day for the knock at the door:

> I have learned how faces fall to bone
> how under the eyelids terror lurks
> how suffering inscribes on cheeks
> the hard lines of its cuneiform texts,
> how glossy black or ash-fair locks
> turn overnight to tarnished silver,
> how smiles fade on submissive lips,
> and fear quavers in a dry titter.
> And I pray not for myself alone
> but for all who stood outside the jail,
> in bitter cold or summer's blaze,
> and me under that blinded red wall.

She ends, yearning to be buried,

> here, where I spent three hundred hours
> in line before the implacable iron bars.
> because even in blessed death I fear
> to miss the rumbling of the black ravens
> and the old woman's howling like a wounded beast.[42]

Whatever his errors, the unsystematic and wayward Koestler displayed unique powers in identifying and unmasking for all the world the revelations of Mandelstam's, Bulgakov's, and Akhmatova's forcibly invisible writings.

11

⇢≫ ≪⇠

The Decline of the
Revolutionary Ideal

Ignazio Silone

More obsessed than either Koestler or Gide, with a passion nothing could assuage, was the Italian writer Ignazio Silone. For Silone was, Arthur Koestler once wrote, a "natural communist . . . the only one among us," meaning that he came to communism almost organically, not as part of some moral transformation or ideological rebirth.[1]

In Gide and Koestler we saw what Communist politics on the ground were all about; both men spoke with the air of stage conspirators uttering deadly secrets aloud. Where Gide stated his belief in communism, put down on the page the desire for faith, Koestler broke his beliefs down into their phases, as though acts of belief and unbelief were fates, unsought sufferings that have been thrust upon us. Koestler was able to catch the process of believing in communism as it first stirs the entrails, as it breaks down the unity of personality: for his characters have all a dramatic propensity for turning into the opposites of what they themselves desire. You believe in their believing because, like the comic characters of Dickens, they live in the manias of human solitude. Such maniacal inner solitariness is all the more convincing because of the gregariousness of his people. Each character enters with his soul on his sleeve, and can be almost heard blatantly proclaiming his craving for faith, and later the shattering emotional upheaval of its loss. Not only is this solid, raw, and touching, but it is frightening, too: Koestler knew the faithful's nightmare dread of unbelief, the fanatical isolation of ostracism from the Party. He brings to us the sense that faith in communism is overpowering, full of a darkness which only he can illumine; that to follow Marx and Lenin is to live on the point of Judgment Day and dissolution. As a novelist he was like some face on the screen which

138

gets larger and larger, coming closer and closer to us, until frightened, exalted, and perhaps a little disgusted, we are engulfed by that spongy unhealthy face, laugh when it laughs, and are submerged in its nightmares which must shortly come to seem our own.

For both Gide and Koestler, part of the human personality was made a casualty by communism, in that injury was the desire that cannot be realized. Their terrors, their pains, their guilt, their punishments, their melancholy itself, are inflations and energies of the soul. They are not presented as maladies to be cured and both men in some ways do not wish to lose them. They feel romantically larger and more powerful because of their disillusion, as if their suffering were a gift and a privilege. Koestler was perfectly able to live his isolated life regardless of the community of hate swirling about him. A loquacious and throbbing pride enabled him to do so; his sorrow ran a pipeline to the eternal. Gide lacked this aggressiveness. Pain was self-inflicted. He was a cipher of passivity—as, indeed, the ordinary man is among the political horrors and farces, the double-faced institutions of communism, where persecutors and persecuted change places with the nullity of papers in a file. It is pure speculation but, if his youthful literary talent could have been reborn after his return from the USSR, one imagines Gide writing novels not about the victims of communism, but about the morbid psychology of Stalin's inquisitors and torturers and their suppressed inner guilt; simply because that was the dominant and energetic aspect of contemporary pain. The modern inquisitor has his romantic wish for power: what price has he paid for it?

But Gide and Koestler had little direct knowledge of this subject. Among novelists who succumbed to the socialist temptation only the Italian writer Ignazio Silone experienced this wish for power first-hand, saw it as the nourishment of leading Communists and, like some zoological keeper, he showed them to us at their feeding stations.

Unlike the bourgeois Gide and Koestler, Ignazio Silone (who was baptized Secondo Tranquilli) came from a true peasant family of Italy's impoverished Abruzzi region. Within Silone were locked generations of grief and rage. He was born on labor's holy day, May 1, in 1900. A scorned and lonely youth spent wandering from place to place, sometimes starving, sometimes finding odd jobs, was natural food for an animus against society, the natural breeding ground of communism. In Silone this animus sprouted with the energy of a weed. So great a rage left no room for private life, the play of simpler emotions. "I was a child—just five years old—" he said, when, one Sunday, while crossing the little square of my native village my mother leading by the hand, I witnessed the cruel, stupid spectacle of one of the local gentry setting his great dog at a poor woman, a seamstress, who was just coming out of church. The wretched woman was flung to the ground, badly mauled, and her dress torn to ribbons. Indignation in the village was general, but silent. I have never understood how the poor woman ever got the unhappy idea of taking proceedings against the squire; but the only result was to add a mockery of justice to the harm done already . . . the unfortunate woman could not find a single witness prepared to give evidence before the magistrate, nor a lawyer to conduct the prosecution; on the other hand the squire's supposedly Left Wing lawyer turned up punctually, and so did a number of bribed witnesses [who gave] a grotesque version of what had happened . . . accusing the woman of having provoked the dog. . . . The magistrate acquitted the squire and condemned the poor woman to pay the costs.[2]

The effect of this incident upon Silone was decisive. From a very young age on he was a rebel. It is easy to imagine how he strikes out against authority, even against his parish priest. During a catechism class there is a skit where the devil is searching for a child. The children are to learn not to lie:

Not even to the devil? . . . A lie is always a sin, the priest replied. . . . And he began to explain the doctrine about truth and lies in general in the most elegant language. But that day the question of lies in general was of no interest to us; we wanted to know "Ought we have told the devil where the child was hiding, yes or no?"

"That's not the point," the poor priest kept repeating. . . . "A lie is always a lie . . . it's always a sin. . . ."

To end it, I put forward an objection of unheard-of perfidy, and, considering my age, considerable precocity: "If it had been a priest instead of a child," I asked, "what ought we to have replied to the devil?" . . . as punishment for my impertinence, [the priest] made me spend the rest of the lesson on my knees. . . . "Are you sorry?" he asked. . . . "Of course," I replied. "If the devil asks for your address, I'll give it to him at once."[3]

By age seventeen Silone was a practiced revolutionary, acting as secretary of a peasant movement organized by Syndicalists in his native Abruzzi. In a room furnished with only a table and two chairs, he lived and worked, dressed invariably in a workman's long dark blouse, surrounded by pamphlets and newspapers, all the ascetic clutter of a revolutionary. It was a monkish life that was not at all at odds with Silone's inherited Catholic faith; indeed, part of the attraction of socialism for Silone was the sense of continuity it had with the beliefs he received from his devout father. But his choice to join the radicals, Michael Walzer has written, "required . . . uprooting."[4] "Who can describe," Silone later wrote, "the private dismay of an underfed youth living in a squalid bedroom . . . when he has given up forever his belief in the . . . immortality of the soul."[5]

Silone's followers, who were the body of the peasant movement, never formed a coherent party but associated only in the small, localized clubs and groups. Such formations existed not only in Abruzzi, but in most of the rural regions and small towns of Italy. As the firebrand of the movement, Silone carried the flame to others. Bony, a face lined with pain, with eyes that stared out from their caves, Silone seemed to be ever in search of new indignations to combat. Indeed, he looked like a romantic bandit who might have befriended the Count of Monte Cristo.

The problem Silone had with his supporters in the Abruzzi was that many of them were, at heart, anarchists. They professed extreme contempt for every bourgeois sentiment and social restraint, recognizing only the individual's right to "live anarchistically," which included burglary and any other crimes that served the need of the moment. They were interested in themselves, not in revolution.

Not content merely with talking about the coming disappearance of the state, Silone became embroiled in practical attempts to help it disappear. This caused him to be suspected of deviating from "pure" union activity and even of leaning toward Marxism. On one occasion he was shot at by a comrade from the extreme *anti-organizzatori* wing of the movement. Here terror was added to the anarchist vision. The end—the destruction of organized social life in any form—justified all things, including the murder of friends.

Indeed, in 1919 a series of devastating fires swept through the wooden buildings of Abruzzi and other regions, and these may well have been the work of anarchist incendiarists. A bomb which killed fourteen nuns was but one incident in a spate of bomb-throwing. There sprouted up subterranean schools where weapons were made and the arts of detonating bombs were demonstrated to beginners, usually illiterate peasant boys. The anarchists of Abruzzi now became professional terrorists, poor embittered men who lived in a world of passionate idealism and passionate hate. Violence begets violence in a vicious and never-ending circle, and because they lacked any program, the anarchists were destroying the only chance to better the lives of the peasants—or so Silone was coming to believe.

For Silone this amounted to "a new religion without procedure, without ceremony and without a church," and he rebelled. "Not even its faith was formed,"[6] he declared in 1940, recalling his flight from Abruzzi to Rome, where he settled after 1921. In the capital, then seething in a frenzy of Left and Right, for Benito Mussolini was reaching for supreme power in Italy, Silone fell in with a variety of conspiratorial groups. Most had not yet become associated with a political party, and they had no hierarchy of officials, no settled meeting places, and no established creeds. Silone found this state of affairs to be as unsatisfactory as the revolutionary scrum of the Abruzzi, for he had come to understand that without some unifying creed, there could be no prospect of united action. "Each man," he said, "works underground, illegally, and in place of a constructive programme there is a confused belief in idealistic terrorism for its own sake."[7]

For Silone to join the Communists was no simple matter; "it meant . . . a complete dedication." He explained:

My own internal world, the "Middle Ages" which I had inherited and which were rooted in my soul, and from which I had . . . derived my . . . aspiration to revolt, were shaken to their foundations, as though by an earthquake. Everything was thrown into the melting-pot, everything became a problem. Life, death, love, good, evil, truth, all changed their meaning or lost it altogether. It is easy enough to court danger when one is no longer alone; but who can describe the dismay of once and for all renouncing one's faith in the . . . immortality of the soul? It was too serious for me to be able to discuss it with anyone; my Party comrades would have found it a subject for mockery, and I no longer had any other friends. So, unknown to anyone, the whole world took on a different aspect. How men are to be pitied."[9]

Life in the Communist underground during the Mussolini years was, of course, harsh and dangerous. For the true believer, however, there was a sort of spiritual satisfaction in this, because an outlaw status "provided an opportunity to create a type of organisation which was in no way incompatible with the Communist mentality."[9] So Silone adapted himself "to living like a foreigner in my own country. One had to change one's name, abandon every . . . link with family and friends, and live a false life to remove any suspicion of conspiratorial activity. The Party became family, school, church, barracks; the world that lay beyond it was to be destroyed and built anew."[10] His cause made his world complete, left no room for doubt, supplied explanations for everything. No part of him was private, no part untouched by his cause. Secondo Tranquilli was dead: Ignazio Silone was born.

The years 1922–23—the time Mussolini consolidated his Fascist movement—see the beginning of the end of all this; the first major

Communist figure dominates the Italian radical scene. Antonio Gramsci occupies a strangely muted place in Communist history. It was not surprising that later on the Italian Communist party, as it sought to disown its past and to undermine the democratic traditions of Italy's other parties in the 1940s, should have distorted and suppressed his reputation—they did that with nearly everyone—but even in the books written by his contemporaries Gramsci continues to be an uneasy ghost. There is a colorlessness about him; he occupies a place which can be compared not too fancifully to that of the Venerable Bede in English literature; he is acknowledged as the pioneer, the founder figure, but with a kind of perfunctory reverence, like that afforded the unfortunate Bede as he lurks, a pale shade under the eminence of Chaucer.[11]

Yet Gramsci was not only the founder of the Italian Communist movement: he dominated it until his imprisonment by the fascists in 1925, and was the reason for Silone attaching himself to the Communist cause. He enlisted Silone to co-edit the Party's newspaper with him, and for years Silone never dreamed of challenging his intellectual superiority. He sat at Gramsci's feet, eager to pay homage and to learn. It was upon Gramsci's ideas that Silone fed.[12]

Silone was exalted in his new world. Solidly built palazzi and cooling squares met him at every street corner; compared with the Abruzzi, how spacious, seemly, and grand. More wonderful than any of these things to Silone was the society which Gramsci provided. Here were groups of young men like himself whose principal object was to apply Marxism systematically to the Italian scene. There had never been anything like this in Abruzzi. He was overwhelmed by their intelligence, and by the affection and warmth with which they received him. Most of these young revolutionaries came from Italy's cities, but they were delighted by the agrarian Silone as a man. Within the Italian Communist party—as in the Russian Communist movement—there was a debate as to whether the revolution could take place only as a workingman's revolution or whether Italy must have a capitalist and industrial phase throughout the country before the revolution could occur. Silone held that Italy could proceed directly from serfdom to socialism. Here was a vision born not of ideology, but from sweat and sorrow. As Silone's friend Nicola Chiaromonte wrote, Silone's socialism lay "wholly in the memory of the . . . warp and weft of peasant life and the fact that the need for justice is an integral and daily part of that life . . . Silone is bound up with this need and this hope, and by comparison nothing else matters to him."[13]

All his life Silone had the power of attracting strong affection from

friends of both sexes, which is evident from his ability to persuade
hardened urban Communists to, at the very least, accept the validity of
his views. Throughout these early years of the 1920s the strongest
documentary evidence of Silone's opinions and the workings of his mind
comes from the pamphlets and editorials which he wrote on moving to
Rome. They show him as a harsh, combative figure, often grotesquely
funny, but at the same time bullying, arrogant, self-centered, and tortuous. Yet a man's public self, the self he reveals to his readers, is very
often a distortion of what he is like in private conversation. The testimony of Silone's friends suggests a different man from the author of the
more scabrous assaults on his political adversaries.

So it was, then, that Silone, who had failed to find intellectual companionship in the Abruzzi, and who despised the nihilism of the local
terrorists, found himself happily a member of the Roman Communist
set. With Gramsci presiding over his court, Silone could see the triumph of at least some of his ideas. In his writings he urged that terrorism was a secondary weapon; the main object was to set up a
Communist organization among the workers and peasants, to train agitators, to stimulate urban and rural strikes and demonstrations, and to
spread Marxist ideas through the illegal printing press. Soon small
groups of Gramsci's followers were organized by Silone in the principal
cities of northern Italy. The Italian Communist party was born.

Through all these years the Italian Communists were relatively small
fry in the sea of Italian politics. Mussolini's Fascists dominated the
country and seemed to many to be the wave of the future. Yet Gramsci
and Silone, the General Secretary and Deputy Leader of the Party,
continued to gain supporters, especially in the cities of Milan, Turin,
and Bologna. The brutality of *il Duce* no doubt helped their cause, and
the Party's underground cells continued to steadily expand in number.

Training was the essential task that dwarfed every other for the Party
hierarchy. To create through training an underground that could com-
pete with Mussolini's black-shirted bullyboys was the central effort of
the Party during the 1920s. It was essential to find men who would not
run away, which could only be assured by training. Without training,
Silone mused, the Party would be little more than a "rabble."

Thus between 1921 and 1927 Silone had "repeated occasions" to go to
Moscow and take part in schools organized by the Communist International. Like a bone fracture that cannot be seen by an X-ray, Silone's
doubts now began. "What struck me most about the Russian Communists, even in such really exceptional personalities as Lenin and Trotsky,

was their utter incapacity to be fair in discussing opinions that conflicted with their own. The adversary, simply for daring to contradict, at once became a traitor, an opportunist, a hireling."[14] Such intolerance shivered his respect for Lenin. "Whenever he came into a hall," Silone says of Lenin, "the atmosphere changed, became electric. It was a physical, almost palpable phenomenon. He generated contagious enthusiasm, the way the faithful in St. Peter's, when they crowd around the Seida, emanate a fervor that spreads like a wave throughout the basilica. But to see him, to speak with him face-to-face—to observe his cutting, disdainful judgments, his ability to synthesize, the peremptory tone of his decisions—created impressions of a very different kind that overrode any suggestion of mysticism. I remember how some of his terse remarks which I happened to hear during that 1921 Moscow visit struck me with the force of a physical blow."[15] So Silone soon learned that the notion of a loyal opposition was inconceivable to the Soviets. "If you happen to read in the papers that Lenin has had me arrested for stealing the silver spoons in the Kremlin," Alexandra Kollontaj told him, "that simply means that I'm not entirely in agreement with him about some little problem of agricultural or industrial policy."[16]

Liberty, Silone believed, was "the possibility of doubting, the possibility of making a mistake, the possibility of searching and experimenting, the possibility of saying no to any authority."[17] But that, for most Communists, was the active definition of counterrevolution.

Silone's most disquieting visit to Moscow came in 1927, the moment when Stalin's bid for absolute power came to a head. An enlarged executive for the Communist International had been assembled, with Silone and Palmiro Togliatti (who headed the Italian Party's Central Committee) acting as the representatives of the Italian communists. Immediately on arrival, the two men found themselves in the midst of "wrath and crisis" surrounding the struggle between Trotsky and Stalin. The meeting—"ostensibly summoned for an urgent discussion of what direction should be given to the Communist Parties in the struggle 'against the imminent imperialist war'—was actually designed to begin the 'liquidation' of Trotsky and Zinovieff . . ."[18]

As was the practice, the meeting of the Comintern was preceded by a session of the so-called Senior-convent, a group that consisted of the leaders of the most important national delegations. Here the Italians were well-equipped. Through the hard school of the Italian political underworld, Togliatti had learned to keep his thoughts to himself, so that he was accused quite often of being subtle and secret. That may account for his shrewd understanding of Stalin. Sensing the double-game afoot in the meeting, Togliatti refused to attend on his own, insisting that Silone accompany him. After some debate, this was agreed.

At the first session the time had come for Stalin to lay his cards on the table, and he wasted no time. A proposal by which the Comintern would condemn Trotsky was read aloud. The charges stemmed from a document which Trotsky had written in denunciation of Stalin's failed policy in China. (This would later be published under the title *Problems of the Chinese Revolution*, which upbraided Stalin for his naive assessment of Chiang Kai-shek.) There was no debate. The Finnish delegate called for harsher wording. Stalin, Rykhov, Manuilsky, and Bukharin smiled. Silone, however, wondered if he might see the document which had earned Trotsky such condemnation.

There was a bitter reaction. No one had seen the document. Silone repeated his point: "It may very well be true," he said, "that Trotsky's document should be condemned, but obviously I cannot condemn it before I've read it."[19] In a brief speech Stalin claimed that it was impossible for the Political Office of the Party to release the document, "because there are various allusions in it to the policy of the Soviet State."[20] Unconvinced, Silone mounted the tiger. "I do not contest the right of the Political Office of the Russian Communist Party to keep any document secret," he said. "But I do not understand how others can be asked to condemn an unknown document."[21] The debate that followed bordered on lunacy. Every statement by Silone or Togliatti was interrupted by howls, catcalls, and jeers. "It's unheard of . . . that we still have such petty bourgeois in the fortress of the world revolution."[22] The Finnish delegate put his finger in his mouth and whistled as though at a wrestling match. A recess was called.

Remaining calm, Stalin stretched out in his chair and once pretended to sleep. Silone and Togliatti held on against the hoots and jeers as the gathering broke up. Before they scattered, Stalin spoke. "If a single delegate is against the proposed resolution, it should not be presented." Then he added: "Perhaps our Italian comrades are not fully aware of our internal situation. I propose that the sitting can be suspended until tomorrow and that one of those present should be assigned the task of spending the evening with our Italian comrades and explaining our internal situation to them."[23] That thankless task fell to the Bulgarian delegate, Vasil Kolarov.

Kolarov carried out his task with "tact and good humour," Silone recalled, years later:

He invited us to have a glass of tea that evening in his room at the Hotel Lux. And he faced up to the thorny subject without much preamble. "Let's be frank," he said to us with a smile. "Do you think I've read the document? No, I haven't. To tell you the whole truth, I can add that that document doesn't even interest me. Shall I go further? Even if Trotsky sent me a copy here, secretly, I'd refuse to read it. My dear Italian friends, this isn't a question of documents. I know that Italy is the classic country of academies, but we aren't in an academy here. Here we are in the thick of a struggle for power between two rival groups of the Russian central directorate. Which of the two groups do we want to line up with? That's the point. Documents don't come in to it. It's not a question of finding the historic truth about an unsuccessful Chinese revolution. It's a question of a struggle for power between two hostile, irreconcilable groups. One's got to choose. I, for my part, have already chosen. I'm for the majority group. Whatever the minority says or does, whatever document it draws up against the majority, I repeat to you that I am for the majority. Documents don't interest me. We aren't in an academy here." He refilled our glasses with tea and scrutinized us with the air of a schoolmaster obliged to deal with two unruly youngsters. "Do I make myself clear?"[24]

This was the first moment that Silone sensed what loomed ahead for Russia. He refused to give in. "And why not?" the jittery Kolarov asked. "I should have to explain to you," Silone said, "why I'm against Fascism?" Stunned, frightened, unable to contain himself, Kolarov sprang to his feet. "You are still too young," he shouted. "You haven't yet understood what politics are all about!"[25]

Next morning, Stalin conducted one of his political master classes. "An unusual atmosphere of nervousness pervaded the little room into which a dozen of us were packed,"[26] Silone recalled. A vote was to be taken. But voting is a procedure from which there can be no turning back without acknowledging defeat. This was the self-laid trap into which Stalin walked. His position in the Party remained such, however, that a condemnation of Trotsky could not be undertaken without a solemn statement of justification, a sort of political statement equivalent to the medieval concept "just war." However false and specious the justification might well be, and usually was, a legalism of the kind served to state the case and automatically enlarge the prosecutor with enhanced powers.

But Stalin was forced to do without his declaration. "Have you explained the situation to our Italian comrades?" he asked the hapless Kolarov. "Fully," came the nervous reply. "If a single delegate," Stalin reiterated, "is against the proposed resolution, it cannot be presented to the full session. A resolution against Trotsky can only be taken unanimously. Are our Italian comrades favourable to the proposed resolution?"[27]

A more experienced man than Silone would not have answered. Togliatti, to be sure, avoided implicating himself in the hope of not arousing Stalin's ire. But Silone steamed ahead. "Before taking the resolution into consideration, we must see the document concerned."[28] No one else, however, stated their doubts publicly. Stalin, they all knew, wanted his policies ratified, not questioned. Disconcerted at being opposed, Stalin fell into silence. A general uproar ensued. It was broken only by Stalin's sudden climbdown: "The proposed resolution is withdrawn,"[29] he muttered.

Recrimination followed. The German delegate Thaelmann argued that Silone's "scandalous" attitude indicated that the Italian Party's entire program to counter fascism in Italy was probably in grave error. As Silone said, "if Fascism was still so firmly entrenched in Italy it must be our fault." Thaelmann demanded that the Italian Party be subjected to a general review of its conduct. "This was done," Silone recalled, "and as a reprisal for our 'impertinent' conduct those fanatical censors discovered that the fundamental guiding lines of our activity, traced in the course of the previous years by Antonio Gramsci, were seriously contaminated by a petty bourgeois spirit."[30] Temperamentally an appeaser, Togliatti was predisposed to accept the rebuke. He did not like confrontation and thought it would be dangerous to confront Stalin once again. Silone persisted. A statement of principle was at stake.

Togliatti surrendered, and addressed a letter to the Political Office of the Russian Party which, though it defended the Italian position, lacked Silone's bite. No Communist, the letter said in effect, would presume to question the historical pre-eminence of the Russians within the International. This dominance, however, imposed special duties on the Soviets. They could not apply their rights in a dictatorial manner. Bukharin received the letter and, says Silone.

> sent for us at once . . . to withdraw it so as not to worsen our already appalling political position.
>
> Days of sombre discouragement followed for me. I asked myself: have we sunk to this? Those who are dead, those who are dying in prison, have sacrificed themselves for this? The vagabond, lonely, perilous lives that we ourselves are leading, strangers in our own countries—is it all for this? My depression soon reached that extreme stage when the will is paralysed and physical resistance suddenly gives way.[31]

This showdown with Stalin was no prelude to action in the only way that mattered, a vote against the dictator, but merely a sterile intellectual exercise concerning "Communist ethics." In the end, the belief that the leader knows best prevailed. There was no room for heretics. Subservience was part of the completeness of the faith. Allow one doubt to stand, and everything was threatened; everything might start to unravel. On his way back to Italy, during a brief stopover in Berlin, Silone learned of the Comintern's unanimous vote to condemn the Trotsky document. "Has the mysterious document finally been produced, then?" he asked his German host. "No," came the firm answer, "but I hope the example [of the vote for condemnation] . . . has shown you what Communist discipline means." Here was a complete expression of the critical vacuum demanded by the Party: the ordinary cadres, full of anger, with no ideas of their own, rejecting rejection. Silone was taken back. "These things," he recorded, "were said with no hint of irony, but indeed with a dismal seriousness that befitted the nightmare reality to which they referred."[32]

On his return to Italy the chief concern of Silone was to get some coherence of thought into the Italian Communist party, which was essentially a scattered and uneven organization. Principles had to be laid down—the written creed of the new religion—and tactics agreed upon. But how to meet so that members could talk freely without danger of arrest? That was the question that daily confronted Silone, for he had become Gramsci's envoy to the leaders of the regional parties. Everywhere he went he heard rumors that Fascist spies might be listening to his conversation and that his life was in danger from Mussolini's secret police. Probably there was some truth behind all this cloak-and-dagger stuff. Silone quite plainly was a Communist who was also a fine journalist, a cultivated talker, and inoffensive, handsome, and charming, too. These were very bad attributes from the point of view of the Fascists who would have liked all Italians to think of the Communists as veritable devils, poised to murder their priests and burn down their churches. Certainly there were real threats to Silone's life. They did not stop him, however, from going round and organizing new Communist cells, such as in Naples in June 1928, and even in Syracuse later that year. In terms of sheer numbers, the Italian Communist party remained very weak, but Silone's organizational skills had helped to transform it into something more than just isolated bands of outlaws; it became an influential, if underground, part of the political scene.

One starts to see here the beginnings of Silone's future disenchant-

ment with communism, and of his rivalry with Gramsci. Gramsci, sick-
ened at the Duce's popularity, was beginning to doubt that the struggle
could be conducted in a less ruthless way. Silone disagreed emphatically
with him. That cleavage became apparent to other members of the
Party, and however blurred and confused it was at every step of the way,
it served to drive almost every Party member toward either Silone or
Gramsci. Silone in a general sort of way wanted to come out from the
underground and fight the Party's battles out in the open. Gramsci
remained implacably opposed to these ideas. He wanted to continue the
underground life of the Party, and its struggle, a struggle which he
insisted had to be controlled by a small group of professional revolutionaries at the top. He did not believe that any good would come from
fighting Mussolini in the open, because Mussolini was strong and would
inevitably arrest or deport any opponent who posed a threat to his rule.

Events proved Gramsci at least partly right, but his imprisonment
prevented him from benefiting from this affirmation. In 1929 Silone had
to flee to Switzerland to escape Mussolini's police. Silone suffered from
the demoralization of exile almost from the start: the ennui and frustration of never being on his native soil, of watching the years of Mussolini's rule go by and little or nothing happening to oppose him.

For a forced emigré, the daily evil of life is isolation. He has lost the
main ground of the moral life: that we do not live until we live in others.
The temptations that faced Silone, like those that faced Koestler, are embittering to any man capable of reflection: you can live in the past; you can
become an uprooted dilettante; you can adapt, in Silone's words, to ever
living underground, there to "remain until we have cleared the surface
of the earth of you [the police] and your masters."[33] Crime may come
nearer to his fingers and, with less obstruction, to his imagination than
it does to rooted people. Most emigrés evade and alleviate their sense of
persecution by living in the past and keeping their nostalgias and their
rancors alive in the mind. But these force upon the isolated man the emigré's addiction. He becomes preeminently a conscience.

Isolation and conscience are the dominant motifs in the novels of
Silone and they arose during his period of exile. He was forced to
confront the central questions of belief in communism—what was his
attitude to treachery and what are the moral consequences of belief in
revolution?

In isolation, Silone lived life second-hand, constantly talking about
the Italy he could not see and the revolution that had not happened,
endlessly reading newspapers and awaiting word from Rome. But Rome
receded.

It was the old loneliness and ineffectiveness of the outsider, and the coming of Mussolini's attacks on Albania and Abyssinia made Silone triply an outsider since he had no country of his own, no patriotism and no political following of any consequence. Throughout the early 1930s we find him wandering aimlessly about. He involves himself in the small affairs of the Swiss Communist movement. He goes roaming in the woods of the Ticino, camping out under pine trees, sending a comrade to Lugano for the newspapers and such news of his comrades as he could pick up in the city. There was a sudden alarm in March 1930; Silone heard that the cantonal police had accepted an Italian warrant for his arrest, and with a guide he bolted hastily across the Alps to France. The next year is a story of restless movement: visits to Spain, England, Stockholm, and Moscow, and back to Switzerland again. Once Silone found himself giving lectures at Gorky's school in Moscow, but neither there nor anywhere else was he able to find supporters.

Silone's continuous movements from country to country during this period reminds us of the movements of his mind, too. His foreign travels of 1930 are more pregnant with the future than his earlier trips to Russia, because they aroused such profound reflections upon his past. His confinement to a TB sanatorium in Switzerland tore him back to the lost arcadia of his childhood; and successive encounters with unthinking Stalinist agents remind him of a yet-more-remote lost Eden — Italy before the Great War, when aristocratic, free-thinking men had, or might think they had, the King's ear. Hunted or confined, Silone had time to reflect upon the unjust way in which the world was ordered, but with the Communist solution he was losing sympathy.

Doubtless there were many reasons for this, but the imaginative ones are clear. He was not a fanatical Communist for the simple reason that he did not believe that society was all that existed. This had always been true, but the cynical schemes of the Comintern and his isolation abroad confirmed it. Exile made him long to settle openly in Italy, and in particular into the countryside, with its immediate, local difficulties and problems. He looked back with a growing distaste upon his affiliation with the secret world to which Gramsci and Togliatti had introduced him. (As Nicola Chiaromonte has brilliantly observed, all this rejected side of Silone's own nature became embodied, when it became time for him to write his novels, in the Communists of his stories; each, with their uncertainties and moral scruples, are in many ways quite different from the actual men he met in the movement.)[34]

Silone's ambivalence was soon apparent to his comrades, and it produced conflicts, some comic, some touching, some prophetic. Silone was not sure where he was or who he was.

In Geneva, he found that he had been appointed, *in absentia*, as a sort of justice, with special responsibility for enforcing Party discipline. The innocent outsider might suppose that it was a strange honor to have conferred upon a foreigner who was not very popular with the local cells and whose thinking was becoming increasingly undisciplined—at least by Party standards. But consider the nature of his task. The local Communist hierarchy had already made representations to the Comintern that the traditional procedures for discipline were no longer effective because of the influx of exiled Communists from Italy and Austria (which was then under the dictatorship of Dollfuss). The exiles refused to accept the commands of local Party leaders. A system of redress and discipline was needed. It was to be Silone's job as an arbiter to intervene and make sure that justice and discipline were done.

Is it any wonder that the Comintern gave the uncongenial task of arbiter to a young man in exile? Anyone doing the job was bound to make enemies, so why not entrust it to a young man whom the locals and exiles regarded with suspicion and awe. His ability to speak of personal conversations with Lenin would command respect; his distance from the local cells would insure his loyalty. The fact that Silone was offered the job is a tribute not to his powers of leadership, but to his already observable social and political isolation.

There were many cases such as the one of an Austrian journalist who wanted to leave the Party on the grounds that he had joined as a follower of Trotsky, and since Trotsky's imprisonment in Alma-Ata, he no longer felt bound to party discipline. Silone as arbiter ruled that the man should be given his complete freedom, and also three months' wages to compensate for the time he was wrongly held by his cell against his will. When the Austrian Communists-in-exile appealed to the Comintern, which was of course filled with their own kind, Silone's decision was overruled.

Though the Comintern had thought Silone's appointment would have the advantage of increasing Party discipline, it only infuriated the local Communist leaders in Switzerland. Silone was this funny mixture. They knew that he had travelled widely and picked up a lot of ideas. But they did not suspect that someone who had once held Lenin's confidence would side against them. The Comintern in Moscow reversed nearly all his decisions.

The Comintern began to regard Silone as a dangerous heretic, which he was; much more potentially dangerous than either they or he then realized. Disillusion was beginning to disturb the minds of other Communists figures, and Silone became their voice. Seen through the telescope of history, he was, next to Trotsky, the significant dissenter of the time. The tyranny of the Stalinists within the Comintern and the subservience to Soviet needs were by 1931 old complaints common to Party members througout Europe and America, and they sharpened as Stalin's one-man-rule became more apparent. There was also a deep craving among some Communists to restore the moral imperative to Communist ideology by clearing away all the crimes and compromises of the years since Lenin's death. In Silone, the political and moral strains of dissenting communism met and were fussed into a philosophy if not a program.

His critique went beyond politics. On the issue of authority and discipline, he carried on the dangerous thoughts of Trotsky and found himself a champion of the struggle against the supremacy of Stalin's rule. When he returned, in secret, to Italy in October 1931, Silone metaphorically nailed his thesis to the door.

Silone's realization that he had, in fact, broken with the Party came only slowly. "The day I left the Party was a very sad one for me, it was like a day of deep mourning, the longing for my lost youth." It was not easy for him to free himself from the intense connections life in the Communist underground had brought to him. "Something of it remains and leaves a mark on the character which lasts all one's life," he later declared. "One can, in fact, notice how recognisable the ex-Communists are. They constitute a category apart, like ex-priests and ex-regular officers." The final struggle, he joked with Togliatti (who remained on good terms with Silone), "will be between the Communists and the ex-Communists."[35]

Faith in socialism, however, remained "more alive than ever"[36] in Silone. It became a dominant theme of his novels, the writing of which dominated the remainder of his life. In a sense he returned to the pure impulse that had animated his youthful revolt: "a refusal to admit the existence of destiny, . . . a need for effective brotherhood, an affirmation of the superiority of the human person over all the economic and social mechanisms that oppress him."[37]

Like nearly all men who have wanted to establish a kingdom of peace and love on this earth, Silone had an ambivalent attitude toward the human race. Sometimes he was able to disguise his misanthropy as a scheme of universal improvement (as when he was a Communist) and sometimes not. In moods of self-awareness he knew that he was a much less simple character than his guru-like poses seemed to allow. However much he wanted to be a secular priest, a self-made saint, he knew that he was (because he was so much more complicated) in fact much weaker than the men who continued to subscribe to Party discipline and upon whom he looked down with such condescension.

It was such somber thoughts which inspired Silone's novels. Silone is the novelist of those who expose themselves and take sides. The failed ascetics of his fictions are brilliantly lurid self-projections of Silone himself. Into each is poured Silone's everlasting war with faith—religious and ideological. For he writes with the gentleness, the irony, the anxiety and love of one who has passed through a deep personal crisis. And there are also the insidious pleasures of framing himself for a religious role to which he now knew he was actually unsuited. There is also always the dream of martyrdom at the hands of the authorities, exile, and a life of genuine simplicity and obscurity.

Silone's typical heroes are workers for the cause of Marxist revolution. He was obsessed with the relation of the dedicated revolutionary to the people whom he is supposed to serve. When the Party line loses touch with the people, as it so often did in his Communist career, he concludes that something is amiss with communism itself. His protagonists, such as Pietro Spina in the novel *Pane e Vino* (Bread and Wine), may never weary of his efforts to connect the peasantry to the Party, but his continuing failure to do so releases him, at the expense of his Marxist faith, to see the peasants' points of view. Pietro Spina, impatient of the netherworld into which the Fascist Blackshirts have driven him, returns, in the guise of a humble priest, to his native Abruzzi mountains in an attempt to rouse the peasants against Mussolini and thus build a revolutionary movement. At every turn, however, he is thwarted by the primitive vision of the peasants, who see the world through medieval eyes: sins, pardons, saints, miracles, prayers, and sacrificial rites. Here is a world of innumerable secret meanings and contacts. Contact, a connection, comes about not by an appeal to class consciousness, but because of his evident sympathy for them. His sobriety, asceticism, and and spiritual candor are things the peasants recognize and to which they respond.

Spina is no whiskey-priest in the manner of the runaway cleric of Graham Greene's *The Power and the Glory*. In Silone's novel there is meaning, not fear-fantasy; Spina is taken from depth to depth in physical suffering and spiritual humiliation. The climax comes when he finds that he is at peace with the villagers and outcasts from whom he need not hide his identity, and that he is in danger only from conventional piety. They look to him for forgiveness and guidance. They believe he has the power to heal. Transfigured, he begins to preach as a militant disciple of Christ. No longer is he a lone outside agitator. This message is not introduced as mere pious starch into the narrative, but is native to it. Silone drew close to the concept of primitive Christianity as he sought to fuse the ideals of socialism with those of Christ. His grave manner removes the sickliness from piety and restores to it the strength of nature.

There is always a danger in Silone's novels that the stress on anonymity and disguise will turn into typecasting and that he will forget that the loneliness of people, on whatever level, is only an aspect of them. In his honesty, he is sometimes too eager to see evil doing its stuff. In *Bread and Wine*, however, by quickness of cinematic cutting, by turning everything he sees to the advantage of action, he makes circles round our doubts. There is no overt resentment. There are no innuendoes. Trailing his coat in order to provoke mercy, Silone has the subtle and compassionate intelligence of unvoiced pain. He is free of the novelist's vice of explanation; we see a soul grow and recover lost dignity. And the dialogue between religious and ideological faith is a true dialogue; it is not a confrontation of views, but of lives. Spina thinks. It is a constant feature of Silone's fiction that his heroes are political Hamlets, tortured by the guilt of being outsiders, of always keeping an escape route open. Guilt sharpens even as it perverts observation.

"In the modern drama," Silone has written,

> a new element has appeared as a protagonist: the proletarian. Not new in the sense of not already having existed in antiquity, but because his or deal and destiny were not then considered suitable subjects for history, thought and art. If to us moderns the situation of this character seems the nearest to the human truth, it is because, in the last analysis, between the ancients and us there has been Jesus.[38]

This quotation served as the introduction to Silone's play, *Ed Egli Si Nascose* (And He did Hide Himself), which revives the themes of *Bread and Wine*, but finds Silone in a worse temper. The title is taken from the Gospel of John, Chapter 12. The play develops, on a larger scale with different implications, one of the incidents in *Bread and Wine*. In that novel a young man from the country has gone to Rome to study. In the city he falls in love with a girl who is an underground anti-Fascist, who introduces him to the cell. When the cache of funds that is to pay for his studies runs out, he begins to inform on his comrades for pay. An informer's secret torments are sharply evoked. No one so powerfully burns a guilty scene on the mind as Silone. Rome is a city run by faceless

Blackshirts and part-time crooks in sunglasses. In the context of secret betrayals, beatings, and dejected plotting, in which both Fascists and anti-Fascists have brutal and dedicated parts, the student and his lover conduct their private sexual comedy. They are nervous of discovery. It is an affair constantly on edge because of the nagging torments that possess him—Silone is always on the *qui vive* for the ironies of impotence and desire. And, of course, of betrayal. Treachery is always one of Silone's central preoccupations as a moralist. The boy betrays for love and money; and the irony is that the stout-hearted girl would do the same. In all the meetings of his characters there is a watchful, instinctive, animal awareness of other people; fear and love are his constant subjects. This fits admirably with Silone's gift for creating suspense.

The student is cool enough as an informer, but he is a born destroyer of his own and his mistress's happiness. So he flees Rome. When caught by rural police who have stumbled on him and who believe him to be an uncorrupted revolutionary, the boy submits to execution. No protest is voiced. Death becomes an expiation. In Silone's account of it and of the funeral, there are echoes of the Last Supper, the Passion, and the Crucifixion.

In the play, Silone has the young man redeem himself through a far more positive gesture. He prints and distributes a proletarian manifesto. And his murder at the hands of the Fascist militia proves to be the catalyst—where Spina failed—of an awakening by the people, who unite in opposition. The death ends the play with sort of liturgical drama, which has its Joseph and Mary, its Mary Magdalene, its John the Baptist, and its Holy Eucharist, all worked out in a deliberate parallel. Indeed, in his foreword to the play, Silone explained his belief that "the revolution of our epoch, which has been promoted by politicians and economists," presents

> the appearance of a "sacred mystery," in which the very fate of man is at stake.
> In the scared history of man on earth, we are as yet, alas, only at Good Friday. The men who "hunger and thirst after righteousness" are still being derided and persecuted and put to death. The spirit is still forced to hide in order to save itself.[39]

Structurally and in content, the story of *And He did Hide Himself* is unsustaining. *Bread and Wine* as a chronicle of Spina's adventures and disillusions, with its procession of Italian characters, had something of the energy of a great picaresque panorama, such as *Huckleberry Finn* or *Dead Souls*. In that novel his portraits of party hacks have the flowering malice of Proust, the historical reflections are wise, dyed with experience. The play shows that Silone lacks a dramatic sense comparable to his narrative one. Only what the student sees, the accidental detail of his experiences, is impressive. Here he grows. And his talk carries us along for a while. This is particularly enthralling during a post-mortem discussion of Communist psychology in the years before World War II. "The underground character of the movement," the young renegade explains,

> offers to the weak man the important and deceptive advantage of secrecy. He lives in sacrilege and shudders at it, but this is all concealed from the world. He is outside the hateful and terrifying law, but the guardians of the law do not know it. His denial of the established order remains an intimate and secret thing, as if it took place in a dream, and precisely on that account is likely to run to ideas that are drastic, catastrophic and bloody; but his external behaviour remains unchanged. In his habitual relations this kind of weak man remains as timid, silly and nervous as before. He conspires against the government in the same way that he may be in the habit of dreaming that he is strangling his father, with whom he will sit down to breakfast in the morning.[40]

There is an equally merciless passage on revolutionary work as a drug. The Communist's life is so dangerous and hard, one underground worker explains, that the only way to accomplish anything is to eliminate the strain on your nerves, and to do this is to induce a narcosis. "But," one of the women objects,

> excuse me if I ask a stupid question. How can we be true and brave fighters for the revolution and be drugged at the same time? Shall we turn into a movement of sleepwalkers? . . . If we come to the revolutionary cause precisely through our sensibility—because our senses have been wounded by the savagery, the injustice, the brutality which we have found in today's society? If we neutralise our sensibility, aren't we destroying in ourselves the very feelings that have brought us to the revolution?[41]

The narcotized revolutionary may become unscrupulous and cruel and lose sight of the ends that he set out to serve; the weak man who loves concealment may find it easy to betray the underground movement and to keep this betrayal concealed. When young Murica turns stool pigeon for the Fascists, he begins to be tortured by the notion that, if no one finds him out, he will never be punished for his treason. It is a horror of the idea that good and bad may be mere matters of practical expediency which drives him, in moral protest, to do something that will get him into trouble.

Silone is grappling with the problem of justification for human morality at a moment when religions have lost their force. Man, he says, is alone on earth, and thus must decide what should and what should not be done. The situation of Soviet Communists under Stalin was precisely that of young Murica: why worry about moral principles if you are never to face a day of judgment?—and, unlike Silone's young student, they could never see that they did have to worry.

Silone, confronting this question, reverted to the Christian religion in a special non-ecclesiastical way, a version which one may find it easier to sympathize with than the formal official versions of Catholic converts of the time, such as Evelyn Waugh, Graham Greene, and Malcolm Muggeridge. His point of view is curious. He makes one of his characters speak of "the new idea of good and evil" of "those who do not believe in the death and resurrection of Jesus but do believe in his agony," and he explained that he did not accept what he called "the mythology of Christianity," that the liturgical form of his play and analogies with the Gospels came to him in the most natural way, as a result of having known in his childhood no literature except the Bible and no drama except the Mass. Yet certainly the life of Jesus had mystical meaning for him, and he claimed to be among those "God-seekers" of whom "St. Bernard speaks, those whom God pursues, and whom, when He overtakes them, He tears to pieces and chews and swallows."[42]

The argument at the heart of Silone's work is the search for meaning and value: but meaning and value for Silone lie in the rendering of life itself. This central preoccupation of Silone's is personal and egotistical: uprooted from his own class, gifted, ambitious but without means or rank, bearing the scars of class resentment in his nature, Silone began life from an imaginary blank sheet to find out what a "superior man" could make of himself in a world hostile to high feeling. And so all of his novels, like his politics (and those of Gide and Koestler), have the critical tone of experiments in self-creation. They are lives for possible selves. And the lessons he learns are not about politics, but about life. He does not end by acquiring ever more sound political beliefs. His one abiding political belief is the love of man, and he ends up giving up his commitment to politics altogether, forsaking faith in history for a faith in god. It was necessary for him to make this break because under communism he saw close up the dehumanization of man. Communism was not only brutal, it was meaningless. It wanted to remake life without knowing of or caring about that which makes life really worth living.

Human beings, Silone knew, have a right to their tragedies; they have the right to be incurable.

So the loss of faith comes like this: men awakened to a bitter knowledge that the world cannot be made to conform to their private visions, that men and the world cannot be created anew. For Gide, Koestler, and Silone, the inner rage—the rage of true believers no longer able to believe—becomes absolute and comprehensive. Only one weapon is left to them, one act of vengeance: open denunciation. To damn the abandoned faith becomes something of an act of penance. But it also serves their grief and feelings of betrayal. Thus the socialist faith, with its own personal roots, converts and converts again, feeding other private distresses. And word of its false promises must be spread, as a sort of good news.

Now, having followed the breakdown of the revolutionary ideal to its disintegration in the novels of Ignazio Silone, it is time to turn to the Communist *apparat*, to watch as the infection of doubt reaches into, and begins to rot, the socialist state itself.

**Part
Three**

12

⇢⟫⟫ ⟪⟪⟸

Enemies of the People

Once the absolute certainty of doctrine has been questioned, there can be no return to perfect faith.

It was no ordinary loss of faith over which Gide, Koestler, and Silone despaired; there was more than a loss of certainty in their sorrow. There was guilt and dismay. Afterwards, the mourners were haunted not only by a dead system of belief, but by themselves. If we set aside the skill of their arguments—and we ought not really to do this, because part of their gift to politics was the teaching and example of conscious artists—there is more than expert dissection of disillusion and doubt; there is a sustained enacting, in conditions amounting almost to claustrophobia, of universal human pains.

Gide, Koestler, and Silone show us that communist intoxication was not the result of indifference to religious questions. On the contrary, it resulted from man's anguish at his inability to answer religious questions positively, which incites a feeling of cosmic homelessness. This was a central theme of literature from Kafka to Camus: the lonely existential plight of modern man, convinced of God's death, yet not exulting in it as Nietzsche had done. Instead, there is only resignation at lives that must be led without transcendent meaning, but ever aware of the need for it. "We are the dispossessed," Koestler once declared. ". . . the dispossessed of faith; the physically or spiritually homeless."[1] To search for God is to find only pain, to search for faith in history is to find only crimes. This dilemma finds almost perfect expression in Kafka's *The Castle*, with its antihero "K" trying to establish telephonic communications with the Lord up there on the hill, but never succeeding. K finds God alternately remote, cruel, incommensurable with the human mind, and perhaps non-existent. He dies without ever receiving confirmation from Castle bureaucrats of his appointment as a land surveyor in his village down below.

In no small way did this craving for faith contribute to the state of

163

mind demanded of communism's supporters. It was George Orwell more than anyone else who exposed this fact of communism. "The very concept of objective truth is fading out of the world,"[2] he said in 1942 in witness to the triumph of dogma over documented facts in the minds of communist true believers. His novel *1984* portrayed a world in which a party elite determines what is to pass for truth, re-writes history to conform with that invented truth, and communicates its truths to the waiting masses by means of Newspeak. Discourse and debate are unwanted; faith comes about only through blind acceptance and obedience:

> The intention was to make speech, and especially speech on any subject not ideologically neutral, as nearly as possible independent of consciousness. For the purposes of everyday life it was no doubt necessary, or sometimes necessary, to reflect before speaking, but a Party member called upon to make a political or ethical judgement should be able to spray forth the correct opinions as automatically as a machine gun spraying forth bullets. . . . From the foregoing account it will be seen that in Newspeak the expression of unorthodox opinions, above a very low level, was well-nigh impossible.[3]

It was this sort of calculated irrationalism of which Sir Isaiah Berlin was thinking when he observed the "great gap"[4] between nineteenth-century philosophy and twentieth-century religious-cum-political thinking.

In their newfound unbelief, Gide, Koestler, and Silone began the assault on communism's irrationalism, a war soon joined by Orwell and others who had dabbled with the Left. As the struggle intensified, the Viennese Karl Popper published his own "war effort,"[5] *The Open Society and Its Enemies,* which does read like a war book, though it begins benignly with Plato and scatters shots among Marxists, fascists, and contemporary social scientists such as Pareto. Popper attacked communism for its surrender of the use of reason, its elevation of economic faith into a science, which betrayed communists into thinking that they had discovered *the* laws of history which all men must obey. To pretend to prophesy the course of history and thus plan the future for whole societies was the fanatical arrogance of a true believer. There was nothing scientific about it. Scientific knowledge, he said, is hypothetical and tentative, subject to elimination by trial and error. Popper saw the closest connection between this critical or rational attitude, generated by true science, and the maintenance of an "open" or free society.

Popper's *Open Society* was distinguished from the closed embryonic utopias of communism by its recognition that no perfect society can ever exist, but that it is nonetheless possible to search out and combat by rational means the greatest evils of a society. An open society recognizes that freedom is more important than equality, and that attempts to enforce true equality require the elimination of freedom. Democracy alone provides the institutional framework for a process of continuous reform without violence. Only an open democratic society demands the use of reason in its politics, and freedom of thought and the progress of science. Truth for Popper meant quite simply correspondence to the facts as ascertained by science. Such knowledge was always growing and must be allowed to grow. It was the search for truth, not faith in truth revealed, that ennobled man and brought stability to an unstable world.

Orwell and Popper thus set upon communism with a ferocity utterly foreign to Gide, Koestler, and Silone. In the course of their vivisecting socialism, they exposed its essential assumptions as fraudulent. To communists who lauded socialist equality, Orwell and Popper answered that it amounted to little more than state slavery. To communists who talked about dialectical inevitability, Orwell and Popper pointed out that death, too, is inevitable. But that does not mean that it should be worshipped.

Like an ice floe cracking, the socialist world's split was revealed by the defections of Gide, Koestler, and Silone, and as the Second World War came and went, leaving Stalin as master of half of Europe, the two halves spread wider and wider apart. Former comrades passed each other on the street in silence. It is said that when Sydney Hook took the opposite side from an old Communist friend and college classmate, they shunned each other without communication for decades. When Koestler's *Darkness at Noon* began to circulate in Paris in its French translation, two Communist journalist friends of André Malraux tried to persuade him to denounce the book. They failed, for Malraux had become a Gaullist. Throughout the 1930s, Malraux had worked tirelessly for the advance of socialism. After Spain and communist treachery in the French Resistance the word "communist" became for Malraux a synonym for "assassin." Socialism had debased *la Condition humaine.*

All the strength, except truth, however, was on the side of the believers. Each time a Gide or Koestler brought forward new evidence which they were certain must force a re-thinking of allegiance to communism, it was denounced, suppressed, or matched by new fabrications supported by the USSR and the screams and thunders of the Communist and fellow traveller's press. Walter Duranty, the longtime Moscow correspondent of the *New York Times,* built a disgraceful career on misleading American opinion. As Malcolm Muggeridge wrote, "There was something vigorous, vivacious, preposterous about his unscrupulousness, which made his persistent lying somehow absorbing." Duranty's favorite expression was "I put my money on Stalin."[6]

Swept into this tide of apologists for Stalin was Edmund Wilson. In the winter of 1930–1931, *The New Republic* was without a vision to confront the Great Depression, and as its most dominant writer Wilson proposed socialism as the antidote to economic collapse. Capitalism had broken down, he argued. Americans must "put their idealism and their genius for organization behind a radical social experiment."[7] He equated Stalin's first five-year-plan with the patriotic boosterism of the Liberty Loan drives of World War I. Communists were correct to insist that "the impoverished public has no choice but to take over the basic industries and run them for the common benefit."[8] So naively enthusiastic was Wilson that, when he visited the USSR for his study *Travels in Two Democracies* (an almost obscene comparison between America and Stalin's Soviet Union in which the Soviets usually come out on top), he claimed: "You feel in the Soviet Union that you are at the moral top of the world where the light never really goes out."[9]

Approached by Arthur Koestler on the theory that he would relish the challenge to prove communism a lie, Jean-Paul Sartre had been cordial but was dissuaded from the cause by the proposition that evidence about Stalin's crimes and labor camps should be ignored, even if true, on the grounds that otherwise the French proletariat might be thrown into despair. Why the labor-camp populace should be sacrificed for the benefit of the French working class was something Sartre never bothered to make clear. Sartre was typical of the kind of ideologically minded journalist whose capacity for mischief was unfettered by truth: the more deluded his convictions, the more brilliant and scathing his pen. A constitutional "anti," a Grand Inquisitor without knowing it, Sartre combined in his person almost every tendency, no matter how contradictory, of the fellow traveller. He was deaf to disaffection, blind to the alternative ideas it gave rise to, blandly impervious to challenges to his faith, unconcerned at the Communist party's misconduct and the rising evidence of its crimes, fixed in refusal to change, almost stupidly stubborn in maintaining belief in a corrupt system. The effects of Stalinism took a long time to sink in. He rejected them, indeed, until they were admitted by the dictator's successors. Evidence which would have been sufficient to damn any other regime was rejected—a phenomenon ludicrously illustrated by Sartre's introduction to Henri Alleg's book about torture in Algeria. Sartre said that we now know of the existence of torture in Communist countries as well, because of Khrushchev's admissions in 1956 and the evidence given at the trial of the Hungarian Police Minister Farkas. That is to say, evidence of Alleg's sort, mere first-hand accounts, was to be admitted to damn French actions in Algeria, but revelations like those of Gide and Koestler were of no import in judging communism. Sartre could not change his opinions about communism because he was part of it, grew out of it, depended on it.

What happens to a communist convert when he does renounce the faith? Gide never worked in the inner Party hierarchy; his personality was never fully molded into the life of the Party. His withdrawal, though agonizing, did not permanently distort his nature. Koestler and Silone, on the other hand, could never completely escape from communism. Their lives were always shadowed by its dialectic, and their struggle against Stalin and the USSR always a reflection of a burning inner struggle. The true ex-communist can never be a whole personality. In the case of Koestler, for example, this inner conflict was the wellspring of his work. The Yogi peers into the looking glass, sees the Commissar, and shatters the glass in rage. His writing is not an act of purification that brings tranquillity, but a merciless interrogation of himself—and the movements in the world that reflect it—by another self, indifferent to suffering. Silone, by moving full circle back to the Christian ethic from which he started, achieved a moral poise which gave him a certain distance from the conflict. For Silone was only joking when he said to Togliatti that the final battle for the souls of men would be between the communists and the ex-communists, but he hit upon an essential truth. The fury of the ex-communists' revulsion became something characteristic of the time, and their embittered doubts slowly spread into the heart of the communist world itself.

13

→» «←

Enemies of the People
Milovan Djilas

All centrally controlled movements based on zealotry and doctrine
eventually pay a price for their success in fragmentation. As Christianity straddled the known world, the Roman Pontiff's hold on distant
churches gradually broke down. Schisms erupted. Rival centers of authority, independent of Rome, arose to challenge the Vatican's primacy.
Islam too, as it expanded, split into feuding caliphates. Understanding
to his marrow the nature of dictatorial and doctrinal power, and its
structural limits, Stalin was well aware of the divisive danger posed by
having communists come to power in areas beyond the long reach of the
Red Army; for the very existence of any Communist state outside Stalin's grip was all too likely to one day incite a challenge to his absolute
authority, providing communist faithful the world over with an alternative altar at which to worship. Unperceived by most, here was the
catalyst of socialism's internal division and decay.

Schism, indeed, became an issue at that very moment, the summer of
1947, when it was almost impossible to travel in Eastern Europe and
avoid socialist revolution. As it was in the Bolshevik coup of 1917, there
were few points of agreement between what happened in postwar Europe and what had been predicted in *The Communist Manifesto*. Here
was revolution by military occupation, not an uprising of workers. This
period of Communist consolidation behind the marching Red Army
went unquestioned among Communist leaders until Stalin's attempts to
subjugate Yugoslavia roused the latent doubts of Milovan Djilas.

For Stalin evidently decided to put his European empire in order in
1947, shortly after the Marshall Plan was announced. He held the
initial meeting of the newly organized Cominform (the successor to the
Comintern, which had disbanded to appease Britain and America in
World War II) in Belgrade, Yugoslavia, to demonstrate that that Balkan

land was an integral member of his system. But Stalin's hidden objective was to replace local communists who might prove independent with men who owed everything, including their lives, to him. The coup in Czechoslovakia of February 1948 was a prelude to this process. Stalin also planned to destroy Marshall Broz Tito. The same month as he was murdering the Czech leadership, Stalin summoned to Moscow Dmitrov, the Bulgarian Communist leader, whom he consistently humiliated, and Edward Kardelj and Milovan Djilas from Yugoslavia, one of whom, if pliable enough, he intended to make Tito's replacement. He ordered them to knock Yugoslavia and Bulgaria into an economic federation along the lines of the Benelux countries, which he thought consisted solely of Belgium and Luxembourg. Told that it also included the Netherlands, he denied it and shouted angrily, "When I say no it means no!" Then, switching to bribery, he offered to Yugoslavia the bait of Mussolini's little victim: "We agree to Yugoslavia swallowing Albania,"[1] he said, sucking the forefinger of his right hand.

When Tito got Djilas' report of the meeting he smelled a putsch against himself. Like Stalin, Marshall Tito was a consummate political gangster familiar with the rules of survival. During the partisan war of 1941–1945, for example, Tito husbanded his resources, often shielding them from battle. But if his leadership was questioned, he told Djilas, "Shoot anyone—even a member of the provincial leadership—if he wavers or shows any lack of discipline."[2] Thus Tito's first response to the threat posed by Stalin was to cut off information from Yugoslavia's inner Party organs, police, and army to their counterparts in Moscow. On March 1 he brought the crisis to the boil by having his Central Committee throw out Stalin's proposed treaty. In the subsequent theological dispute, which began on March 27, Tito was accused of anti-Sovietism, of being undemocratic, unself-critical, lacking in class-consciousness, of having secret links with the West, of engaging in anti-Soviet espionage; and eventually the whole Yugoslav Party was branded as "Menshevist, Bukharinist and Trotskyist," the accusation culminating in a crude threat to Tito's life: "I will shake my little finger—and there will be no more Tito."[3]

Milovan Djilas was never a suitable quisling for Stalin's manipulations. However skeptical he might have been of Tito's program, Djilas did not intend to bear the brunt of wrecking it in the name of Stalinist orthodoxy. Like God in the British national anthem, Djilas was ready to confound the politics and frustrate the knavish tricks of Yugoslavia's enemies. He was ruthless, sometimes cruel, always resourceful. His piercing eyes, his unrelenting drive, his magnetism could get anything he wanted out of anybody.[4] Wherever Stalin's minions were plotting, Djilas was listening and, like a dog who can hear high-pitched sounds that never reach the human ear, Djilas could hear intrigues hatching. Capitulation to Stalin was a prelude to suicide. Yet the clamor for it was rising as from a lynch mob. In the mob were the Moscow indoctrinated cadres who had been carefully groomed to pin their faith on the Kremlin's central control of the worldwide Communist movement. Djilas trembled as he listened to this clamor. The issue was being fought out daily in secret sessions of the Yugoslav Politburo. Tito was preparing his defenses in feverish haste. As Tito's dauphin, Milovan Djilas was the second-most powerful figure in Yugoslavia during these years of struggle with Stalin. It would have required great gifts of prescience, as Djilas worked to defend Tito's position, to know that he was to become the greatest communist heretic since Trotsky. For in the pressure and paranoia of the battle between Tito and Stalin, Djilas' faith in communism itself was shattered.

Djilas was the only son of a prosperous merchant of Montenegro, a land where, "from time immemorial, ideas found consummation in sheer violence."[5] He was born on June 12, 1911, and so was nearly twenty years younger than Tito. Young Milovan was an active, driving, sharp-witted boy who climbed rooftops, drowned rabbits in the horse trough, and exceedingly disliked Sunday services which he was often required to attend three times in the day. Active church membership was the necessary step to public importance in Djilas' native village of Polja, near Kolasin. Djilas' father rose to the official rank of "merchant of the third guild," which dated from the eighteenth century when the kingdom, mimicking Tsarist Russia, created an official class system. Through his rank Djilas *père* could claim an important honorary connection with the police. He became a proud figure in official local processions, wearing a top hat with the other local dignitaries, who lived very much in one another's pockets. If the mountain villages lived by trade, their habits were oiled by bribery.[6]

Acceptance to the university at Belgrade was the goal handed from father to son, and young Milovan plunged with characteristic intensity into the endeavor of gaining admission. On the application form Djilas senior lightly penciled in the blanks before allowing his son to copy them over in ink. At the ordeal of the qualifying examinations Milovan thought he had failed in mathematics, but when the names of those failing to qualify were mercilessly read aloud, he found, to his surprise, that he had passed.

Once enrolled, Djilas found "normal" student behavior appealing but not reasonable. The drinking, the debates, the debaucheries; it was too easy. Like some blameless clown, he preferred the difficulty, the busyness of trying all the wrong roads first. With communism outlawed, he stumbled down its path.

The Communist underground which Djilas entered was not a movement of national sentiment, which had been sated by the creation of Yugoslavia itself at the Versailles Conference of 1919, nor of true political ideology. Although the Yugoslav communists partook initially of the general conflict of communist versus capitalist erupting out of the triumph of the Bolsheviks in Russia, the motivating sentiment in Belgrade was hatred of domestic tyranny. Forces and events in the Yugoslav underground were a turmoil of infighting among sects and cells, of deals and overtures to the Comintern, of mounting oppression by the Yugoslav throne that catalyzed the students' hatred to a frenzy and, in a deeply fragmented state like Yugoslavia, linked the fragments of dissent together in a common will for change.

With so many student friends swept into prison by the royal secret police, Djilas adopted communism with an intensity as stern as that of Scottish Protestantism under John Knox. When the proctors of the university forbade even the discussion of reform or public speaking by student leaders, the prohibitions lit a fire of indignant protests and active resistance. A petition to the university's overseers to cancel the edicts only confirmed the government to tear the idea of revolt out by the roots and erect in its place a pillar of authority based on a firm foundation of royal absolutism. But it takes two—one to impose and one to acquiesce—to make authority function. Djilas and the other student activists were not prepared for the latter role. When their petition went unanswered, they went on a rampage of desecration, smashing images of the despised royal regime. The student underground reflected an unusual fusion of people from every Yugoslav province, although they clung as ever to national cultures and languages. Unrest at the university ignited agitation in the towns and among small sectors of the peasantry, raising hints of a truly national rising to come.

No plan for reformation, but simple brutality, met this boiling distress. As Djilas had risen by the early 1930s to a post in "the highest echelon of the underground Party organization" he became a primary target for the secret police.[7] In the fall of 1933 he was "hauled off to the penitentiary." Here a new rite of Party initiation awaited. Djilas was given the job of "passing along through the sewer system Party literature and light reading material as well as food sent by families or else purchased from the outside."[8] The stench assailed him, "solitary confinement" and "wearisome fantasizing" tested his faith. Yet his "spirits soared" in the presence of comrades who were to him "living legends," despite the fact that they had handed him the "slop bucket chore."[9] "After all," Djilas later wrote, "wasn't this communication link through the sewers as exalted in its own way as spiritual creativity? Did it not help bind the wounds of tortured, hungry, resentful fellow warriors?" For all tasks when in the service of his faith, he realized, "were alike— pure, exalted, and urgent. I became convinced that no job was dirty, low or inconsequential where the idea was concerned."[10] By day Djilas "studied the Marxist-Leninist holy scriptures"; by night, "we discussed, probed, and clarified what we had learned."[11] Like so many others, jail did not break Djilas of his communist faith. Instead, it completed his conversion.

More than asceticism and discipline was needed to secure the victory of the revolution. Throughout the 1930s Djilas engaged in impetuous and reckless expeditions against the royal authorities. When each plot or assault was broken and Djilas' friends captured or killed, leadership of the movement passed into the hands of true peasants such as Broz Tito.

The son of Croat peasants, Josip Broz had been converted to communism through his experiences in the Great War. A conscript in the Austro-Hungarian army, he was taken prisoner by the Russians and so witnessed their revolution. He returned to Yugoslavia as a union organizer in Zagreb. Imprisonment for five years brought him to a position of leadership within the Party. He was sent to Paris in 1936 to organize Yugoslav recruits for the International Brigades in Spain. When the Nazis occupied his country, he quickly emerged as leader of the Communist partisans.

Such leadership, Djilas discovered, infused the movement with will and eliminated class suspicions. But it took the Nazi invasion and conquest of Yugoslavia to fan the spark of revolution into a flame. For the German answer to any insurrectionary outbreak was to compel obedience by a reign of terror. The Nazi method was massacre in the towns and forced labor in the countryside. Peasants who were leaders of the partisans were publicly tortured and killed. Farms were confiscated, scores fled the country. To make sure that they made everyone of all classes an insurgent, the German Gauleiters imposed high taxes on every sale and income. The hated taxes did more to spur revolt than all the atrocities.

In 1944–1945 Yugoslavia only nominally underwent the sort of Communist revolution designed by Marx, and became a Communist state under the dictatorship of the proletariat—again nominally. For Yugoslavia was predominantly a country of peasants and mountaineers. Djilas understood that the movement that liberated the country from within and gained control of it at the end of World War II, the movement that Tito and he led, was a movement of peasants and mountaineers inspired by patriotic rather than proletarian zeal. This dichotomy was the first source of doubt for Djilas.[12]

The fact that nationalism was the motive which brought a Communist regime to power in Belgrade was a guarantee that the Party could not for long make the country subservient to the national interests of Russia. Initially, ideological intoxication had its effect even on Djilas. Although he knew that his movement was obliged for its success more to the British than to the Soviets, he turned with ideological passion against the capitalist West and made his obedience to what he still considered as the shrine of Marxism-Leninism in Moscow. He faithfully submitted himself to the will of the Kremlin.

Stalin, however, was reluctant to transfer his wartime support of the anti-Communist resistance group commanded by General Mihailovich to the rival group commanded by Marshall Tito. The Red Army had imposed Communist regimes on Poland, Hungary, Romania, and Bulgaria, and was to do the same in Czechoslovakia. Such a procedure was not needed in Yugoslavia, because the local communities had done the job themselves. If Stalin had been a pure ideologist, intent on the spread of communism to embrace the world, he should have rejoiced at this as representing the fulfillment of Marx's prophecy and of Lenin's—the delayed consummation of the predictions of worldwide revolution with which Lenin had been so deeply disappointed when, after his seizure of power, the revolution failed to take place elsewhere. As a practitioner of realpolitik, however, it troubled Stalin; for the implications of self-liberation, as opposed to liberation by Moscow, were independence. When the Red Army liberated a country from control by the Axis it simultaneously brought that country under Soviet control. There was no assurance that native liberators would do the same. Add to this that Yugoslavia was separated from the Soviet Union by the width of Hungary and Romania, so that it was not so vulnerable to the pressure of the Red Army.[13]

Immediately after the war Stalin gave great thought to the problem of how he could bring Yugoslavia under his firm control, despite the fact that Winston Churchill, in his "naughty document," had promised the dictator only fifty percent of the country as part of his sphere of influence.[14] Because of his renown as an idealogist, Djilas was looked at as a possible Kremlin factotum. But when his doubts about the nature of the revolution in his country took hold, his belief that a true communist revolution was not yet possible because Yugoslavia lacked the necessary proletarian foundation, he balked at assisting in Stalin's plans. He refused to even transmit Stalin's order to Tito that Yugoslavia form a federal union with Bulgaria. What Stalin had in mind, Djilas surmised, was that, through Soviet control of Bulgaria, Stalin would be able to control the new, unified Bulgar-Yugoslav state because the Red Army in Bulgaria would stand on its borders. Certainly Stalin intended to vet all foreign activities of Communist states. In a meeting of February 1948 Stalin scolded Vice President Edvard Kardelj of Yugoslavia, demanding that the Communist insurrection in Greece, which Tito was supporting, be brought to an end. Djilas, who accompanied Kardelj, reported Stalin as saying: "What, do you think that Great Britain and the United States—the United States, the most powerful state in the world—will permit you to break their line of communication in the Mediterranean? Nonsense. And we have no navy. The uprising in Greece must be stopped, and as quickly as possible."[15]

Only vaguely aware of Stalin's domestic terror, it was this betrayal of the ideal of global revolution that brought Djilas' doubts to the surface. Throughout his life he had believed in the morally purifying power of revolution. That was why he had gone underground as a young man, not really comprehending on what possible basis of either morality or theory a vanguard elite without a proletariat could stand. Stalin's use of revolution merely to extend his power, or not extend it for the moment, as in the case of Greece, shook his belief in the absolute historical correctness of communism, for Stalin revealed the morally base ways in which power could be abused. Worse still was the supine compromise many members of the Yugoslav Party were willing to make with Stalin's dictates.

A contest was under way which became a test of Moscow's power to enforce upon Tito the unquestioning conformity that, in Stalin's conception, ideological purity and the exigencies of the emerging Cold War alike required of the Communist movement. "I'm absolutely sure," Khrushchev later wrote, "that if the Soviet Union had a common border with Yugoslavia, Stalin would have intervened militarily."[16]

The outcome of this contest confirmed for Djilas the principle that real circumstances must ultimately prevail over ideology where the two conflict. Although devout, Djilas was a Yugoslav federalist first. Having to deal with the actual events of Yugoslav life, rather than with the mythical society of the ideologists like Bukharin, he was bound to find Moscow's directives frequently irrelevant. And he had reason to lose his naive faith in the supreme wisdom and moral elevation of Stalin when, confronting the dictator face-to-face, he found that, so far from being cut in a heroic mold, Stalin was petty, brutal, and uncomprehending.[17] Since real circumstances made Djilas and Tito independent of Moscow, they could hardly fail to defend their society against the alien Russians who, while nominally representing Marxist-Leninist authority, were in their "barbaric crudeness"[18] far from representing any innate superiority, intellectual or moral.

On June 28, 1948, the Yugoslavs were expelled from the Cominform, and communists in Yugoslavia were invited to rid themselves of their delinquent leadership if it persisted in the error of its ways. A communist Cold War was declared against Tito. Economic boycotts, internal subversion, incitements to assassination, public denunciations, and threats of military action were used. Tito and Djilas held their own and at last brought humiliation on the Russian Goliath who could not overcome them.

For Djilas, Tito's successful defiance of Stalin had fateful significance in the weakening of his faith. The proletariat, Marx had declared, knew no country. Nation-states and nationalism were devices of the proletariat's class enemies. After the worldwide revolution, what had been Russia, Yugoslavia, Hungary, Germany, etc. would become all one fraternal community as communists assumed power in each. Tito's rejection of Stalin was rejection of the international proletarian cause. That cause, Djilas realized, had been transformed into an arm of Russian power, and local Communist parties were merely to be fifth columns of the socialist fatherland. Intellectuals and workers who placed themselves under Communist discipline were expected to give all their allegiance to that fatherland, rather than to their own countries.

In the days when Lenin and Bukharin ostensibly represented the interests of the masses in all countries, and stood opposed to the interests of any nation-state as such, Moscow laid claim to the allegiance of socialist-minded men everywhere. This was the basis on which the young Djilas gave his loyalty to the original Bolsheviks and their successors. It was another matter, however, to demand that communists outside Russia prefer the interests of the Russian nation to those of their own. What Tito's defiance represented was the disintegration of Marx's world vision.

Realization that there was a direct relationship between the centralizing of power in the hands of the state which Djilas accepted from Bukharin, and Stalin's bloody attempt to centralize all world communism in his hands, shattered the moral basis of the movement for Djilas.

No longer did he see this lust for power as peculiar to Stalin. It was an invention of 1917, not 1945. Stalin's rule was merely 1917 with a higher body count. For Djilas it was now apparent that absolute dictatorship was not just an unfortunate if necessary tool from the use of which it was necessary to avert your eyes; it was communism's source of energy. It was what made the Revolution revolutionary.

No one grasped this dismaying fact more immediately than Djilas. The fact that Tito withstood Stalin only by the application of greater power was itself alarming evidence of communism's corruption.[19]

The failure of Stalin's agents to remove Tito allowed for the consolidation of Party power in Yugoslavia along the lines established by Bukharin in 1918. Tito argued that the conspiracy against him had been organized from abroad and led by traitors. No public trials were held, but Tito carefully selected for publication a small list of ringleaders, their deaths never to be announced but implied. Hundreds, perhaps thousands, were murdered after the conspiracy was crushed, though the details will probably never be known: the episode has been entombed by official Yugoslav historiography beneath a massive pyramid of lies.[20]

Once dissent was crushed, Tito determined he would no longer tolerate any form of political opposition. Secret policemen moved to arrest communist and non-communist foes alike; the summer of 1949 marked the extinction of visible political opposition in Tito's state. He had given non-communists the choice that Lenin had offered them little more than thirty years earlier: acquiescent silence, prison, or exile.

At the same time, Party membership became essential to the holding of any position of importance in the state or economy. From 1950 on, Tito began a systematic effort to screen Party members (a central "verification" committee was set up, with Djilas a member), expel those lacking in zeal or loyalty, subservience or connections, and turn the Party into a valuable social privilege, to be earned.

Mimicking the hated Stalinist system, Tito adhered to the most important single characteristic of a Communist totalitarian state: the pyramid of organs of control, beginning with a Politburo and working down to village councils and factory watchdog committees. The vanguard elite of the partisan war against Hitler was transformed into a vanguard of perpetual rule, the Party becoming and always to remain, the leading and directing force of society. "The so-called socialist ownership," said Djilas, "is a disguise for the real ownership by the political bureaucracy."[21]

A new ruling class displaced the old. And this New Class, as Djilas was to call it, enjoyed privileges and administrative authority but would never share power. The exercise of power was the sole right of an inner vanguard, a largely secret elite. For Djilas, one of the most depressing features of Tito's regime was the almost conscious reproduction of the very worst features of the monarchy against which he had rebelled as a student. The King, too, had experimented with responsible government, a cabinet system representative of the people's will and the constituent nationalities of the Yugoslav federation. But the fusion of autocracy with bureaucracy wrecked the reforms in all instances. Where the whiff of Divine Right was too strong in the King's nostrils, the scent of History was too strong for Tito. When it came to the point, Tito did not want a government representative of his people, because he did not want any kind of legal, constitutional, or democratic checks on his decisions.

"Under the Communist systems," Djilas wrote,

> the people realize quickly what they are and what they are not permitted to do. Laws and regulations do not have an essential importance for them. The actual and unwritten rules concerning the relationship between the government and its subjects do. Regardless of laws, everyone knows that the government is in the hands of the party committees and the secret police. Nowhere is the "directing role" of the party prescribed, but its authority is established in all organizations and sectors. No law provides that the secret police has the right to control citizens, but the police is all powerful. No law prescribes that the judiciary and prosecutors should be controlled by the secret police and the party committee, but they are. . . . Everyone knows what can and cannot be done, and what depends on whom. People adjust to the environment and to actual conditions, turning to party forums or to organs under the party's control in all important matters.[22]

Such were the dire conditions of Yugoslav life at the start of this process that Djilas foresaw that a purge and centralization of authority were necessary for the revolution to be preserved. The newborn people's republic could not long survive isolation from both the communist and capitalist worlds and endless contention within its ruling establishment. But what kind of revolution was it that merited preservation, Djilas wondered silently? One in which law had prostrated itself before the crudest form of bullying; one in which elected representatives of the nations of the republic could be humiliated and driven from responsibility by the armed minority of Tito's government?

There was, Djilas knew, a grim truth to this miserable episode of

threat and surrender. The Yugoslav Revolution had been made possible
by force of arms, by violence and riot. At each stage of its progress those
who had profited from its force sought to disarm those who had put them
in power. And Tito had no intention of becoming a prisoner of insurrectionary power, rather than its beneficiary. This threat would continue so long as any group could oppose him, possibly by resort to arms.
It is probably not too much to say that, even had Stalin not challenged
him, Tito would not have tolerated a state of affairs that allowed for
opposition. Like Bukharin in the midst of the Russian civil war, it was
essential in Tito's eyes that the power and violence that had been liberated by the revolution be returned to and concentrated in the revolutionary state.[23]

Gradually, however, Djilas discovered that absolute centralism meant
absolute rigidity, with Tito increasingly withdrawn from contacts outside
his inner circle, trusting no one but himself, and thusly ignorant of conditions in the country. In the Byzantine atmosphere of Tito's court, no
one was anxious to inform the Marshall of any deteriorating realities, and
the worse these became, the less he was told by lower Party organs. This
stemmed not merely from fear or servility, but from the basic need of the
new class of bureaucrats to preserve appearances. Maintenance of privileges newly won was their interest. The result was to leave the Party
hierarchy in ignorance and fatuous complacency, making it almost impossible to convince Tito and his cronies of the need for change or reform.

Djilas saw Tito's government resting upon a medieval-minded demi-
aristocratic clique, a new mandarin class grown slack and inefficient
through its many privileges. The Politburo dispensed goodies to Party
cadres according to rank and loyalty, and Party members scrambled for
them. When foreign investors appeared, graft was demanded; nepotism
proliferated, asserting by its very presence the permanence of Party rule;
managerial positions were assumed because of favoritism and loyalty to
high Party officials, causing a decline in industrial production. The Party
enveloped the country, but sapped its will and capacity for growth.

Increasingly complacent and conservative, the new Communist ruling class shared the point of view toward the working class of any
privileged class of the past, seeing them as the "little people"—the
populo minuto, as the Renaissance Italians called them—and were not
shy about saying so. "This new class," says Djilas,

> has all the characteristics of earlier ones as well as some new characteris-
> tics of its own. . . . Other classes, too, obtained their strength and power
> by the revolutionary path, destroying the political, social, and other orders
> they met in their way. However, almost without exception, these classes

obtained power *after* new economic patterns had taken shape in the old society. The case was the reverse with the new classes in the Communist systems. It [the new class] did not come to power to complete a new economic order, but to establish its own and, in so doing, to establish its power over society.

In earlier epochs, the coming to power of some class, some part of a class, or of some party, was the final event resulting from its formation and development. . . . The new class was definitely formed after it attained power. . . . The promise of an ideal world increased the faith in the ranks of the new class and sowed illusions among the masses. At the same time it inspired gigantic physical undertakings.[24]

The belief of this new ruling class—like that of all old aristocracies, who fussed about protocol and precedence, was that they alone were qualified for the task of governance, whereas the unqualified and mean proletariat should have nothing to do with government or administration which must be served by the ideologically correct. Too open in their contempt for the workers in whose name they ruled, local Communist satraps made themselves hated, with the result that in Djilas' home province of Montenegro three village leaders appointed by Belgrade were torn to pieces by a lynch mob in 1952, when the peasants, suffering the fury of having their crops commandeered, believed the local officials responsible for failing to prevent it. The murders were a strange paradox of workers exacting their vengeance against the workers' state, and one year later the state exacted its revenge with show trials and hangings.

Political voice was confined to the Communist party. Because the socialist state was supposed to be the fulfillment of all the proletariat's needs, there would be no popular vote. The political system allowed for a nominal recognition of the different nationalities within Yugoslavia—Serbs, Slovenes, Croats, Montenegrans, Macedonians, Albanians—that made up the Yugoslav federation. But all policy was fixed by Tito and his henchmen on the Central Committee. The regional governments of the constituent republics were under the thumb of this group. All local decisions had to be vetted by the Party chain of command. Autonomy for factories ended at the gate. The result in delay and inertia was another sacrifice made in the name of Party dictatorship.

Though a tight and narrow organization, the Communist government was so restricted by its method of administration as to be as impotent as Gulliver tied down by the strings of the Lilliputians. Tito seemed so afraid of any opponent gaining power that he preferred an almost ridiculous system of precaution to the dangers of independence and efficiency.

By 1952 Djilas felt a noticeable decline in ideological enthusiasm, it being replaced in the hearts of Party members by a passion for comfort. Party officials were all literally thieves or money grubbers. Greed for possessions and privileges was as "intense as anywhere in the imperialist countries." Members of the Party became "sunk in ease, devoted to the pursuits of gain, afraid of taking any decision except those that benefit them directly."[25] Pride in the sense of revolutionary purpose withered. Industries were bogged down in waste and ignorance. The size of the bureaucracy was swollen, spreading Party patronage ever wider. Beggars and the homeless appeared in the street. Instead of being given assistance, they were hauled off to prison.

Startled by this rampant corruption, Djilas caused a sensation in the Central Committee in 1951 by a speech denouncing Party privileges, and proposing the election of local Party leaders to relieve the administration of the burden of the corrupt. Djilas had always been a revolutionary hothead, and at this point he thought that the socialist state could still be purified, that there was no need for it to be junked. He actually believed in collective ownership, equal distribution, and shared responsibility. And he foolishly supposed that his comrades, in their hearts, did so as well. But as each of his proposals was ignored, his attacks spread into an indictment of the entire regime. He asked for the election of the Central Committee by secret ballot, instead of a show of hands at mass meetings; and free campaigning by the rival candidates. He denounced all existing communist structures as unrepresentative. He called for freedom of speech and of the press for workers, peasants, socialist parties, for free trade unions, freedom of assembly, the formation of peasants' unions, the freeing of all political prisoners and anyone imprisoned in connection with workers' and peasants' movements, the setting up of a commission to review the cases of all those in prison or concentration camps, the abolition of political departments in the army and in industry, since no one party should receive privileges for the propagation of its ideas and receive money from the state for this purpose. Lastly, he demanded the right of peasants to do what they please with the land. What Djilas was objecting to, in short, was virtually everything Tito and communism had accomplished since coming to power, "the pragmatist['s] vulgarization of Marxism."[26] He was naive, to put it mildly, to assume that any one of his demands would be granted except over the barrel of a gun or, indeed, over Tito's dead body.

By vesting all power—political, economic, intellectual, and moral—in the hands of the state, communism's founders had committed a fundamental error: to assume that men with unbounded power would administer justly and disinterestedly was to deny a central fact of human nature. The laws of history as determined by Marx had not repealed the fundamental laws of man's character: though men must make every effort to overcome their weaknesses, they must also not deny the existence of their flaws and treacheries and lusts. Communist idealism and communist will-to-power spawned a system at war with itself. For although it claimed to be building heaven on earth, communism in practice recognized no theory or structure or social instrument beyond arbitrary force. This did not mean that Djilas thought communists incapable of governing wisely or well, for his hope still outshone his reason. But to assume that such governance was inevitable after a successful revolution was to ignore the inherent corruptions of men.

What Djilas concluded from his time at the top of Yugoslavia's communist hierarchy was that Party leadership had alternate strains of altruism and corruption. There was no such thing as scientific management of society; the "ripe fruits" of privilege were too tempting to be ignored always. The old politics of the bourgeois world had no relation to economic realities; the new politics of socialism had no understanding of human nature. The dictatorship of Tito was as remote from the true needs of society as the dictatorship of kings. Tito, like all Communist leaders, assumed that the essence of society was economics, whereas society's actual objects were a fusion of history, physical wants, and myths. For Party leaders to extract personal benefits from their posts was merely to follow communism's potted understanding of the laws of history; the things of this world were all that mattered. The concern of communist administrators became not socialist construction but personal benefit, absolute obedience by the weak to the strong. Djilas knew that the socialist state, to be loyal to its purpose, needed an absence of overriding personal ambition together with shrewd common sense. But the theorists of the socialist state, most particularly Nicolai Bukharin, just assumed such moderation on the part of the state's administrators, and so failed to understand the terrors of power. The beneficiaries of the revolution were not prepared to accept any limits on the exercise of their fiat. They were determined to rule and, even if lightly endowed for the tasks assigned to them, were rich in the capacity to learn nothing and forget nothing.

Limit the sway of the Party, then; limit the posts open to Party patronage, and the length of the terms for administrators; finally return the primary voice in government to the people. For the new socialist society should not be organized on the brute lines of the old, but according to merit and public consent. This was Djilas' idealistic and impractical (for he had no plan to get it across to the nation) program, in summary. The Party's primary responsibility must be emotive, to supply a vision of what the socialist society must look like, and to transmit that vision in a form compatible to the majority. The privileges of Party members were by law and an independent judiciary to be strictly monitored and limited. Abuses, of course, must be punished.

In his book, *The New Class,* Djilas both damned and delivered a new version of the socialist utopia. He still believed that the Party, his party, could be made to understand that an improvement in its methods of governance would mean an honest pursuit of the true communist vision; the apparatchiks must be made to understand that boundaries on their power are in the interest of socialist construction. Why not trust the people? Djilas asks. They are the intended beneficiaries of socialism, after all; if correctly presented to them, they will work for socialism voluntarily. Coercion would become unnecessary.

But these hopes were not in keeping with the spirit of the time. And Djilas knew it. For the communists were

> no longer capable of seeing contemporary reality. The world which they see is not the one that really exists. It is either the one that used to exist or the one that they would wish to have exist. Holding on to obsolete dogmas, the Communist leaders thought that all the rest of the world would stagnate and destroy itself in conflict and struggles. . . . The opposite happened. . . . [Thusly] they spend more time defending themselves from world reality and attacking it than they do in getting accustomed to it. Their adherence to obsolete dogmas incites them to senseless actions, from which, on more mature thoughts, they constantly retreat, but with bloody heads.[27]

When he launched his protest, Djilas imagined that he was engaged in a war for Tito's soul. He did not see, or failed to recognize, Tito's unwillingness to accept criticism in any form. Criticism was, for Tito, inevitably seen as a Stalinist plot. In 1953, Djilas was forced out of the Party.

Three years later Djilas was imprisoned. Books he wrote in confinement had to be smuggled out of the country and published in the West. Yet despite all this, Djilas still believed everything that he argued to be in strict conformity with his youthful ideals and principles. For even though purged and imprisoned, he told himself that it was not his faith that had betrayed him, rather the cutthroats who had hijacked the socialist dream were the true heretics. Here Djilas faced and succumbed to the last temptation of socialism: an almost sublime willingness to practice "perfect faith in an imperfect idea."[28] This surrender made him a loyal socialist still, not a counterrevolutionary traitor. "In the eyes of my former comrades," Djilas said, "I was a renegade; in my own, I remained a believer. . . ."[29] As Djilas seemed publicly determined to behave like a counterrevolutionary, Tito was determined to treat him like one. Djilas was confined to Mitrovica prison for a decade. His name was quietly removed from all the official histories.

14

⇢⇢〉 〈⟵⟵

Enemies of the People

Imre Nagy and the Hungarian Revolution

While the persecution of Milovan Djilas smoldered in secret, a more importunate flame began to burn in the open. History chose the moment of Djilas' disgrace to return Imre Nagy to power in Hungary.

In his way, too, Nagy was an apostle and redeemer, not a Messiah like Djilas, but rather a Luther, intent upon a reformation, incorruptible and sure of purpose, mandated by himself if not by his party to sweep away the iniquities and greeds that Djilas had revealed, and thus redeem the moral standing of communist politics. Reform was what the times demanded, and reform was the device on Nagy's banner. With him he brought to the Central Committee in Budapest other devotees of a new-model Marxism. Yet Nagy, in the bloody duel with his party's unrepentant Stalinists (under the leadership of Mátyás Rákosi), that was to follow, could not suppress his lingering admiration for his rival's icy nerve and implacable resolve.

The persecution of Djilas, a reform communist like himself, occurring simultaneously with his own rise to power, brushed Nagy almost too closely and shocked him inexpressibly. It should not have, since hardly an opponent of Marshall Tito had failed to be locked away or die a violent death, but Nagy felt Djilas's ouster and imprisonment like a brother's, though they had never met. Perhaps some prophetic sense that Djilas' disgrace would one day be his own added to Nagy's fears and indignation. From the moment he assumed office in June–July 1953, shortly after Stalin's death, Nagy proclaimed a far-reaching program of reforms, including the abolition of prison camps, the protection of personal freedom and safety, the development of a consumer goods industry, the freedom for farmers to leave the collective farms, and a tolerant policy toward the intelligentsia.[1] Nagy was determined that the Communist party must rule with the consent of the governed and that it had devolved—somehow—upon him to accomplish this goal.

That he found himself in a position of power was something of a fluke. With a deadlock in the debate over a successor to Rákosi, Nagy was nominated at the strong suggestion of the Soviets, particularly Georgi Malenkov.[2] As the virtues of this reform-minded, austere, but otherwise somewhat neglected figure were extolled, the party rank and file came to see him as the Soviets did—a benign rather shadowy figure, loyal to the party, and yet no Stalinist in the manner of Rákosi and his henchmen.[3]

Engrossed in the paranoid drama of the succession crisis, Stalin's successors abetted the rise of the relatively liberal Nagy. Hungarian reformers, encouraged by Nagy's reputation for decency and tolerance, became hopeful of change. They drew up programs and lists of long-discarded party rules that needed to be enforced in order to cleanse the bureaucracy of Stalinist terror and corruption. For hatred of the Soviets and their Hungarian satraps was swelling. The party's rulers, hand-picked by Stalin at the end of World War II, had ruled with the contempt of colonial governors for backward natives. Hatred of everything communist now pervaded all of Hungarian life. For "the indigenous problems" of the satellite states "hardly seemed to interest" the Soviets, as they treated the basic problems caused by national, cultural, and social differences and antagonisms as trivial. "They believed that the crisis caused by the violation of a whole national way of life . . . was nothing but a passing discontent and could be resolved by political expedients and various, very necessary, economic reforms."[4]

Nagy was to be the agent of this limited change. And here a fundamental misunderstanding, one which was to help incite the Hungarian revolution three years later, came to pass. Stalin's successors in the Kremlin saw Nagy a useful tool in their struggle to remove Stalinists, such as Rákosi, from positions of influence from which they might compromise the Kremlin's modest reforms. But among certain Hungarian communists, Nagy's rise was interpreted as a far more liberating gesture. They were being set free to build socialism in their own more liberal image. From all this confusion, the Hungarian Revolution would arise.[5]

During a food scarcity in the USSR that winter (1953–1954), when the Soviets insisted on the export of Hungarian grain to Moscow, anti-Soviet passions reached a point of belligerence. Rákosi's terrorist rule was fatally discredited. Popular sentiment was so aroused that the Party moved to appease national feelings. It was this desire that brought Nagy to the forefront, but he was an individual destined to be the catalyst of a new calamity.

Amiable, seemingly indecisive, subject to stronger-minded comrades for much of his career, Nagy was a contrast to Rákosi in every way except in equally undermining the legitimacy of Communist rule in Hungary—in his case by omission and unexpected strength of character. And he made his intent to reform clear from the start. The disrepute of the Party throughout the country was a scandal, and he implored his colleagues to banish corruption and abuse of power from their lives and, as a sacred duty, to set a positive example through socialist regeneration. His audience, however, was even then deaf to his plea. No one, not even the more liberal-minded, was prepared to separate personal power from Party office. When Nagy suggested a fixed tenure for all Party and civil posts, he met only sullen resistance.

Nagy issued rules to prohibit the joint holding of Party and state offices, the practice which had first catalyzed Milovan Djilas. He sought to appoint only qualified Party members to government positions and to limit each to one, on the innovative theory that positions should be supplied with people, not people with positions. At each effort, he was told that he would only demoralize and weaken the Party if he pressed on with his reforms. This is the same web in which Djilas had been caught and which fixed the terms of the struggle between Nagy and the Stalinists. The system, he soon became aware, was too strong to be dislodged from within.

That the impulse to reform should come from a man like Imre Nagy was a surprise to communists and non-communists alike. Nagy was not one of the Western-educated group of Hungarian Reds who had returned home after the liberation in 1945, nor was he Soviet oriented. Rather the contrary occurred during his exile in Moscow after the Russian Revolution. A close look at Stalin made him an early anti-Stalinist.

Large and stocky, with a huge head and heavy coarse features, Nagy with his walrus moustache looked more akin to the cozy American trade unionist Samuel Gompers than to some revolutionary firebrand. Born in 1896 into a three-room cottage in the village of Ötvöskony, near Kaposvár and brought up with four adults and seven children in those rooms, where somehow his mother taught him to read and write, he went to work as a factory-hand at the age of ten. In this he was following the pattern of his father's life, for his father was a peasant who had abandoned the land to make his way as an electrical fitter and later as a postal inspector.[6]

Although Nagy held down many jobs, none paid enough to keep his family from misery. Accordingly, he is rumored to have taken to illegal supplements, but with a certain fierce pride of principle. Robbery of the rich was the right of the poor. Ever in want, Nagy pondered the lessons of poverty. His understanding, like his hate, became generalized, and directed toward the destruction of the "existing class rule" by "relentless revolutionary action."[7] Captured by the Russians during the Great War, imprisonment in revolutionary Russia fed his hate. He joined the Red Army, fought against Kolchak as well as the Czech Legion, and joined the Russian Communist party in 1918.[8]

Nagy joined the Hungarian Communist party during the short, euphoric, and bloody rule in Hungary of Béla Kun, one of those wandering minstrels of socialist revolution who used the chaos unleashed by the collapse of the Austro-Hungarian throne to briefly seize power in Budapest. Under Kun's sway, the city buzzed with manifestos, claims, and counterclaims. Kun and his gang enticed the urban poor and mobs of demobilized soldiers, back from conditions of near starvation on the Galician and Italian fronts, with parades and propaganda characterized by dynamism and simplification of the truth. Like Koestler in Berlin and Silone in Rome, Nagy caught the infection. As a Party operative he moved in the Budapest mafia world that controlled various rackets as well as the Hungarian version of ward politics. A professed Marxist who had read almost nothing of Marx, and appeared to know even less, Nagy played his role in this upheaval by organizing rent strikes and anti-landlord demonstrations. He was a lighthouse of idealistic vitality.

But Béla Kun's regime was doomed. In the city of Szeged a rival "White" government was established. Admiral Miklós Horthy, commander of the Austro-Hungarian navy at the close of the Great War, organized insurgent forces and, aided by Romania, Britain, and France, marched on Budapest. A purge of the Left followed, with three thousand Marxists hunted down and 200 killed.[9] The Hungarian Revolution of 1919 turned from Red to Right. Kun's revolution lasted a mere four months. The Admiral forced the National Assembly to proclaim him temporary Regent until a new King could be chosen. None ever was, and he ruled his country until 1944.[10] Horthy's coup was both turning point and point of no return for Imre Nagy. Like Béla Kun, he fled for his life to the Soviet Union. (But unlike his former leader, who was murdered during the purges of the 1930s, Nagy would survive Stalin's protection.)

In the following decade Nagy appeared and disappeared as a Comintern agent, sometimes taking part in Communist International agitprop campaigns in his homeland, sometimes working within the Soviet Party itself. But his work did not connect him with the murderous forced industrializations Stalin was then undertaking, the forerunners of his collectivization campaigns. Instead, Nagy was a commissar assigned to the social reform movement launched by Stalin in 1927 to take people's minds off the brutalities. This assured his survival, for hundreds of Hungarian communists (including Béla Kun) were executed by Stalin.[11] Directed toward the improvement of behavior, manners, social service, cleanliness, honesty, and the elimination of drunkenness and graft, it represented the Marxist-Leninist spirit of "right conduct," and as such had meaning for the young Nagy, who approached Party membership with the zeal of a circuit preacher. To a Western mind not native to the phenomenon, admonitions against spitting and noisy eating and exhortations to "Be Prompt," "Correct your posture," "Kill rats and flies" seemed frivolous at a time when millions were being killed to create the communist utopia.

As a Comintern agent, Nagy lived in a world of fantasy. He brushed aside reports of Stalin's atrocities. To acknowledge the terror was not convenient to his faith. Out of sympathy with the Soviet cause Nagy concentrated on the regime's admirable aspects and left unmentioned flaws and failures. An idealized image of the USSR came through in his correspondence home. As a result of the USSR taking him in while on the run, Nagy felt a responsibility for it as strong as that which he felt for his native land. Once committed to Stalin's perfection, he regarded any suggestion of blemish as inadmissible. Nagy assisted in the illusion that the killings already taking place were justified, and extended only to criminals and traitors and collaborators with the White regime. He did so because it was the Party line, and in any case such upheavals were merely a stage on the way to the eventual goal of communism. This willful ignorance Nagy maintained for the rest of his life; indeed, at the ceremonies in Budapest marking the death of Stalin, it was Nagy who was chosen to give the official eulogy.

The isolation of the USSR shaped Nagy's view of Stalin and the fervent syllogism at its core: communism was threatened by the capitalist enemy; the Soviet Union was under economic attack by capitalist countries; therefore the Soviet Union *was* communism and her battle was the battle of world communism. To a man of goodwill such as Nagy, this appeared self-evident, and to criticize Stalin not in communism's self-interest. Strategically this was valid, if not ideologically. But strategy is most attractive when dressed in ideology and people on "our side" are considered to be moral regardless of political experience. Nagy found it difficult to imagine that Stalin was any more bloodthirsty than his incompetent hero Béla Kun. [12]

This habit of mind was revealing of Nagy's future rule in Hungary. Nagy was a man of values and feelings, not merely of action or theory. Nagy was the authentic communist, not in doctrine, but in the essence of the idea and the cause. He believed that man was good, that society could be made good and the struggle to make it so was to be fought daily, by available means and with realistic expectations. He fought for it wherever it appeared: in strikes, demonstrations, petitions. His communism did not stem merely from Marx; it was the product of history, of endless and timeless sufferings. Nagy's idea of revolution was rather of taking over than of overthrowing the state. His communism was fluid: he was a Hungarian patriot as much as an internationalist, and believed in individual liberty no less strongly than in collectivism.

His faith had the strength of an engine. To Nagy's speeches Clemenceau's critique of Jean Jaurès might easily be applied. "Do you know how to spot an article by Jaurès?" asked Clemenceau. "Very simple; all the verbs are in the future tense." [13] Nevertheless, of all the Communist leaders who came to power in the wake of the Red Army's conquest of Central Europe, Nagy was the most pragmatic, never a doctrinaire, always a man of action. He lived by doing, which meant advance and retreat, adaptation, give and take. A formal dogma that might have closed off some avenue of action was almost imbecilic to him. He was always the bridge, between men as between ideas. He was a working idealist.

This was Nagy's peculiar strength as well as his weakness. Conscious of the purity of his own motives, he unwaveringly pursued and supported what he believed was right, regardless of the cost. The Communist party consolidated its power with absolute disregard for obstacles and with Nagy's unquestioning public aid. (In private, however, Nagy was expressing some doubts early on. Indeed, in 1945 he thought that collectivization would take at least twenty years.) [14] In October, 1945, the Smallholders party received an absolute majority in free parliamentary elections. Dr. Zoltán Tildy and Dr. Ferenc Nagy (no relation), both members of the Smallholders, became respectively president and prime minister of the new Hungarian republic that was declared on February 1, 1946. Having experienced the bloody chaos of Béla Kun, both Hungarians and western diplomats hoped that the country would shun a similar communist experiment. [15] In that election the communists received a paltry 7 percent of the vote. But the Soviets were Hungary's occupying power. No government could be formed without their consent. Nagy and his comrades were ordered by the Kremlin to block the Smallholders from establishing a government of their own. With a Soviet Marshall at his side, it is said that Nagy went directly to the Ministry of the Interior and took control of it, which meant that the communists now oversaw the police and the security services. An Hungarian version of the Cheka was immediately established, and began its work of exterminating all political rivals to the communists, a process the presence of eight hundred thousand Soviet troops made much easier. As Hugh Thomas has written, "The 'Liberation' of Hungary by the Russian army, and the ferocious seven-week siege of Budapest of the winter of 1944–45, had left all democrats with their wills frozen in the face of a determined Communist drive to power, and of the memory of the barbarism committed by the Red Army."[16] With Stalin's army at his back, Nagy manipulated the most powerful instrument in Hungary, and he was ruthless—as ruthless as any other Communist. The Smallholders were progressively outlawed, and orders went out for the arrest of its leaders, including men such as Béla Kovács, who had fought equally as hard as the Communists to defeat the Nazis, and was amenable to the idea of socialism—but not to socialism of the Stalinist sort, socialism imposed by terror.[17]

Defenders of Nagy's acceptance of terror credit him with following a conscious policy based on the firmly held conviction that in order for the Party to exercise its authority, it had to achieve absolute control of all aspects of society. Here is the persuasive argument of realpolitik, which, as the history of socialism demonstrates, has a corollary: that the process of gaining power employs means that degrade and brutalize the seeker, who wakes to find that power has been possessed at the price of virtue— and moral purpose—lost.

But Nagy was not to be swerved. The continued existence of private property remained for Nagy a political sin, a golden calf around whom backsliding Hungarians were bowed in worship, an idol which he, bidden by a voice from some inner Sinai, must smash. In 1948, land and capital were nationalized, with Nagy's interior ministry seeing to it that confiscations were carried out on the spot, despite Nagy's private doubts. All this left the country gasping for breath, but the shock was as nothing compared to that which rocked the Party when terror was turned on the terrorists themselves. For Communists were not safe from persecution. The breach between the Soviets and Tito in the summer of 1948 was followed by a campaign against "nationalist deviation." In Hungary the chosen victim was Nagy's old friend, Laszlo Rajk. Whether or not Rajk had in fact close connections with Tito is doubtful. Certainly Rajk had never spent time in Moscow, and thus was not beholden to Stalin. At his trial he confessed to innumerable faked charges, and was soon hanged. Of all the postwar treason trials in Central Europe, Rajk's show trial most closely resembled that of Bukharin's in 1938.

Rajk's execution was the prelude to a purge, about which Nagy raised not a whisper of dissent. The victims included old Communists and new. Among the victims was Janos Kadar and the renegade socialist Gyorgy Marosan, both of whom were to reappear in sinister roles in 1956. In two years, half the membership of the Central Committee was removed.[18]

With Rajk's judicial murder, Nagy's loyalty cracked. The strongest prop until now, the most hardheaded, the manager of the Communists' seizure of power, lost faith in the totalitarian system and from this point on Nagy lost influence with Rákosi, the Party's leader. When during a Central Committee meeting he said nationalization of land, besides failing to increase crop yields, was destroying the countryside, his comrades stared at him in uncomfortable silence. Reformers within the Party waited, yearning for Nagy's disavowal of the Party's bloody purges and abuse of power, but it did not come. Loyal to the government game, Nagy, like Bukharin in Moscow during the 1930s, continued to help preside over a strategy he believed to be futile and wrong. To do otherwise, each man would have said, would be to show disbelief, giving comfort to the enemy. The question remains where duty lies: to loyalty and ideology, or to truth? Taking a position somewhere in between, Nagy did not last long. By 1950 he was stripped of his leadership posts, but not of his Party membership. At his departure from office, Nagy was discreet and well-behaved.[19]

By this time Rákosi's pursuit of the Stalinist model of communism was on the defensive. Everywhere the economy was failing. When objective evidence disproves strongly held beliefs, what occurs, according to theorists of "cognitive dissonance," is not rejection of the beliefs but rigidifying, accompanied by attempts to rationalize the disproof. The result is "cognitive rigidity"; in lay language, the knots of ideological blindness draw tighter. So it was with Rákosi's pursuit of state communism. The more punitive and economically disruptive it became, the more it foreclosed his ability to seek more moderate options.

Instead, the train of totalitarianism gathered speed. Catholicism, that ancient opiate of the people, was denounced and religious instruction eliminated from the schools. Churches were allowed to perform religious ceremonies, but were banned from participating in any social activities. Nationalization of the church schools brought the conflict into the open. Cardinal Mindzenty balked at the act, was arrested, charged with treason, tortured for five weeks, then brought to trial. He confessed to the charges made against him, and was condemned to life imprisonment. Soon the other leading Catholic bishop—Archbishop Grösz of Kalocsa—was also arrested and jailed.*[20]

Nagy's purpose in taking office in 1953 was to halt this drift to mindless tyranny. He saw the brilliant hopes of revolutionary Marxism overcast by the Leviathan state and the energy for progress absorbed in the growth of the military and police. The state having failed to bring about pure communism, and showing no signs of withering away, Nagy sought a new philosophy of communist government, one in which the "Bonapartism" and "Fuhrerism" practiced by Rákosi could no longer flourish. Here Nagy adopted the virulent language endemic to party discourse. To bring about moderation, "the Party's leading cadres had to be exterminated."[21] But though Nagy's language was poisoned by ideology, his diagnosis was not. Under Hungary's new regime "most of the workers have come to believe that they are at the mercy of illegalities and abuses, that there are no laws that protect their rights as human beings and citizens. Thus a sinister understanding of socialism was spreading: "A People's Democracy is synonymous with the anarchy of law and order." For under communism "the number of persons imprisoned is greater than ever before. . . . But the most alarming fact is that the majority of those convicted come from the ranks of the working class, the industrial workers."[22]

Nagy fixed on the state stranglehold of the economy as the crux of the matter. He saw that it wasted human resources and included in that waste the idle Party bureaucrats.

Something, he knew, was terribly wrong with the communist system. Somehow its material and social promises were being twisted out of shape. Excessive state intervention was the chief cause of trouble and he began to see state ownership not as a socialist burden nobly and disinterestedly shouldered, but as a new hunger for dictatorship. What Hungary needed, Nagy decided, was socialism without Lenin or dictatorship—a modern, gradual, practical socialism powered by modest men attentive to detail and what really works. This socialism included the dissolution of some collective farms, increased attention to the produc-

* Grösz would later be rehabilitated. Janos Kadar sought to use him to divide Hungary's Catholics between those loyal to Cardinal Mindzenty, who was trapped in the U.S. embassy, and the more pliable Grösz.

tion of consumer goods, and a return to the trade unions of some degree of their independence.[23]

Nagy's notions had some strong roots within the Hungarian Communist party. For Georg Lukács in his *History and Class Consciousness* (published in 1923) had sought to return socialism to some sort of humanist foundation. Lukács, like Lenin, stressed the role of consciousness in making history. But it was the consciousness of *all* the proletariat, not just some self-selected Party elite. And the achievement of a classless society was not the sole end of history; it was not pre-ordained, for it depended for its accomplishment not on inexorable laws and ruthless determination, but on human reason and flexibility. To be sure, Lukács came under attack within the Party. Bukharin himself denounced him at the Fifth Congress of International Communism in 1924, and Lukács soon recanted—under pressure.[24] But his ideas did not die. They helped to shape Nagy's own alternative to the Stalinist model.

In Nagy's mind, as in Bukharin's before his execution and in Silone's when he bolted the Italian Communist party to later establish his postwar Socialist party, there was but one adversary. The absolute centralism established by Lenin and codified by the young Bukharin had to be abolished. Out of power, Nagy had preached against Rákosi's Stalinist authoritarianism. What was essential to his vision of communism was a notion that the socialist state ought to derive its authority from the people themselves instead of being able to dictate from on high, and that industries and peasants ought to be able to govern their enterprises through democratic procedures. But Nagy was no gifted theorist, and his notions and his actual practice when in power during the 1940s presented his opponents a vista of so many inconsistencies that it was more than easy for Rákosi and his cronies to ridicule them with telling effect when they set out to discredit him. They pointed out that his ideas were not the product of any democratic consensus, but were solitary musings, and such solitary thought from a political leader prefigured a sort of mental dictatorship by a single man.

Nagy was as yet no blind lover of democracy or free-ish enterprise, but he knew that it was folly to crush individual initiative entirely. The sensible thing was to manage it, to find ways of working with those of business acumen while at the same time putting through a program of social reform.[25] As opposition from Rákosi's supporters in the Party swelled, Nagy handled it coolly and well. Nothing could shake him. His was the sort of loyalty that makes for ruthlessness; drawing on the only model of government he knew, Nagy acquiesced in the establishment of tribunals that promised to put opponents of reform into prison, so that he could embark resolutely on his program, which concentrated on agriculture.[26]

Briefly, his plan was to make it possible for peasants to own their own land outright, instead of sharing it with others on the new collective farms. Immediately as he restored private ownership, there was an improvement; men began to take a pride in their farms and worked hard to buy more land and to increase the yield. In a certain sense, Hungary was transformed by Nagy's work, and the Prime Minister, ever a realist, saw danger in this, the danger that the revolutionary spirit might die among the peasants as they prospered.

Biding his time for a coup, Rákosi saw these reforms as nothing less than counterrevolution. An ultra-Leninist, Rákosi was if anything even firmer than Stalin in the belief that state control must be kept unimpaired by the slightest concession to democratic and liberal practices. His sole policy was to smash every possible source of antipathy to communism. A method favored for undermining Nagy was supposedly expressed by a colleague of the Jewish Rákosi in the words, "We must drown the reforms in Jewish blood." Here the anti-Semitism practiced by Stalin found its Hungarian equivalent. Stirred by his agents, watched tolerantly by the secret police, Rákosi's henchmen at Passover in 1955 burst into a frenzy of violence against the eternal scapegoat, desecrating synagogues, tearing the sacred Torah from the arms of a white-bearded rabbi who had survived the Nazi camps but who, in his horror at seeing his Torah defiled by the same communists he had yearned to come to power, died of an abrupt heart attack. The "Rákosi" pogrom, as Nagy later called it, resounded throughout the country, and when Nagy voiced support for the Jews, it succeeded in compromising his government in the eyes of rank-and-file Party members.[27]

Refusing to give up the principle of class dictatorship, Rákosi, through his control of the Party's machinery, rallied the Party against Nagy. Rákosi and a majority of the Party's members could not and would not nerve themselves to cut the umbilical cord to Lenin. Rákosi made some efforts to close the rift with Nagy and his revisions, and proposed that both men sponsor a Party resolution stating it to be "indispensable" to have only one policy for the development of socialism. Left unstated was that that policy was the one founded by Lenin and Bukharin so long ago. All who claimed the name of communist must work for unity in the interest of the working classes, to whom they were responsible.[28]

In his struggle with the hardline *apparat*, Nagy was ambivalent. Common sense told him that he did not want to continue in office under the existing conditions of enmity with the Rákosi controlled Party machine, yet at the same time he did not want to forsake his program and tried his best to adhere to it. His sense of responsibility to his country was strong. The facts of economic life were making a necessity of reform whether the Party liked it or not. But Party discipline remained a stronger lure. He knew that Rákosi's patched-up formula left the underlying antagonisms resolved in Rákosi's favor, but he did not continue the fight. Like Bukharin in the early 1930s, he was ousted on April 18, 1955, deceiving himself that he could not be right against the Party's will.

Nagy's reforms, however, though a botched affair, did something to harden antagonism to Marxist dictatorship, to invigorate resistance and give ordinary citizens a will they had been lacking before. Rákosi's re-introduction of collective farms and all the panoply of communist repression precipitated the most serious threat to the rule of any Communist government since the Russian civil war of 1919–1920. Eleven months of dictatorship revisited broke the morale of Hungarian farmers, and in the cities civilians were sick of working at pressure and in miserable conditions for an ideology they did not support or understand.[29]

Like Napoleon at Elba, Nagy in his internal exile awaited his moment of return. Sacked from his post within the Central Committee, stripped of his chair in agriculture at the university, Nagy had time on his hands. From the summer of 1955 until the beginning of 1956, Nagy worked on a draft dissertation he intended to present to the entire Party membership at the next Party congress. He knew that all the forces of reform had focused on him, and that if he failed socialism in Hungary was doomed. The stakes were high. he would either break the Party of the tyranny by which society had become paralyzed, or he would be destroyed in the effort.

Marxism's development, Nagy argued, was being obstructed by two recurring flaws: first, "dogmatism, exegetic Talmudisms," a rigid adherence to theory come what may: and secondly, the "monopolization . . . of explaining Marxism-Leninism . . . the crippling of courageous and pioneering theoretical work, the disregarding of the particular characteristics of the particular countries—and the applying of the old, sometimes antiquated scholastic theories." Every view that diverged from dogma was deemed "anti-Marxist, anti-Leninist, anti-Party deviation."[30] And to hold such views was to be a criminal.

Nagy saw socialism's promise being debased by the "degeneration of power": "Power is increasingly being torn away from the people and turned sharply against them." The people's democracy promised by the Party was being replaced by a Party dictatorship, which does not rely on Party membership, but relies on a personal dictatorship and attempts to make the Party apparatus, and through it the Party membership, into a mere tool of the dictatorship. Its power is not permeated by the spirit of socialism or democratism, but by a Bonapartist spirit of minority dictatorship. Its aims are not determined by Marxism, the teachings of scientific socialism, but by autocratic views that are maintained at any cost and by any means.[31]

Nagy makes the Party's pretensions evaporate before our eyes. The old sport of craving for office, the old game of stealing the fruits of someone else's labor, have returned in all their glory; with Nagy's memorandum we see the conflict of appetites that was leading the idea of socialism to ruin. We might be listening to Marx denounce the carnival empire of Napoleon III in *The Eighteenth Brumaire of Louis Napoleon.*

For Nagy now prophesied two paths for socialism. One was "Bonapartism, individual dictatorship, and the employment of force; this had brought about a situation where the standard of social and Party morals and ethics has slumped lower than ever before." And the other, Nagy's dream, a "constitutional, legal system of the people's democracy, with its legislature and government, with the democracy of our entire state and social life." Socialism, he argued, could only be developed on a foundation of "constitutional law and order and legality."[32] Otherwise, it is the same old oppression as before.

Both the secret police and Nagy's wing of the Party saw trouble coming, and each in its way tried to head it off. Time and again Nagy sought to meet privately with Rákosi to urge reforms upon the government, only to be met with a blank, uncompromising no. The Party, Rákosi repeated, must remain inviolate. He indicated, however, that he himself had plans for certain new political laws which he would introduce in his own good time. It was a promise of a sort but something more than promises was needed.[33]

In the growing relaxation that followed Stalin's death, there was a general ferment in Central Europe from which Hungary was not immune. Popular forces threatened to rise up and sweep the despotic regimes that had been imposed upon them away. In Poland the anti-Stalinist reaction brought to power a man who had long ago established his identity as a Polish Tito. Wladyslaw Gomulka had, years earlier, been deposed as First Secretary of the Party and imprisoned for "nationalist deviation." With Stalin's death he was released and in 1956 rehabilitated. After an uprising he was returned to Party membership. The popularity of the Titoist reformist views associated with him, his own astuteness, and his consequent political strength, were such that he resumed prominence like a cork released below water.

Essentially, the same sort of crisis brought Nagy back to power in Budapest. But whereas Gomulka was able to keep Polish reforms within limits the Soviets could accept and live with, Nagy in Hungary was unable to prevent events from getting out of control. At first, Nagy on his recall did not devise a grand new scheme of government but rather hoped to resume the correction of abuses that marked his previous incarnation in office. Long exasperated by the tyranny of Rákosi and his successor Ernö Gerö and sensing opportunity, the mobs in the street would not be satisfied with limited measures. They seized upon Rákosi's demise to try to impose some form of constitutional control on the Party.[34]

At a critical moment for Nagy, public rage offered him an added weapon against Party hard-liners, which he seized in a fatal choice that was to lose him the support of Moscow. At his instigation, the offices of Rákosi's supporters were made the targets of roving bands of street toughs. They were sacked and destroyed. Breaking into one building, a mob cornered one communist figure inside. On his knees before his "class enemies," he was forced to take an oath to disown Moscow and swear loyalty to a fully independent Hungary.

Yet there was still nothing here that really amounted to counterrevolution. Revolt was in the air, but no one yet seemed to be able to give it any practical expression. It hovered over Budapest like a threatening thunderstorm.

But the thunderclap never seemed to come. Instead, revolution insinuated itself, as it were, into the capital, and for days Nagy waited, not believing what was happening before his eyes. The everyday things of life went on and got mixed up in the oddest way with street brawls. A milkman's van was seen trundling down a narrow street at the very moment when the secret police were getting ready to fire on a crowd; and when the firing did start groups of women typists could be seen looking down from upper windows as though some kind of parade was going on, a ceremony for some visiting dignitary. And it was difficult to know who started the revolt or just what forces were behind it.[35] If Nagy was engineering things behind the scenes in an effort to cow the hard-line communists and take full control of the government, it certainly did not appear so on the streets. The mob was in the streets, and the truth was that the Hungarian Revolution, like so many risings in the past, was not directly provoked by its leaders, least of all by Nagy. In the beginning it was a movement of the people themselves. For weeks and months, even for years, an outburst of some sort had been expected, and many different groups were ready to take advantage of it once it happened. But quite plainly, at the start, the Hungarian Revolution was a boiling over of mass discontent, no less an authority than the leader of the Hungarian freedom-fighters, Major General Béla Király, tells us.[36] The workers and peasants of Hungary were sick of communism. Their food was rationed, they were cold in winter, and they were furious at the bureaucrats who determined every aspect of their lives.

Nagy at first did not know what he was going to do or what he was supposed to do: he simply felt the need to support public protests. But then, as more and more men poured into the streets, he took confidence from the numbers and found with astonishment and exhilaration how he was not alone in wanting to dismantle the totalitarian apparatus: not just a reckless few supported the idea, but a host of comrades in a fighting mood. And the crowds gradually accepted his leadership as they went along. In the absence of personal enemies, they attacked symbols. The policeman in his uniform was a symbol. So was the communist bureaucrat in his car. So was the statue of Stalin. So was the communist flag, and the hammer-and-sickle symbol was soon cut out from the center—a prelude to the Romanian revolt of 1989. All were symbols of corrupt and hated authority and they were attacked.

Compromised by disorder and destruction, Nagy mounted the tiger. A bid to severely limit communism in Hungary was now in the open. It might have been a twentieth-century Runnymede if the challengers had been as powerful and cohesive as the English barons of 1215, but they were weak and soon split into factions.

Driven by popular clamor at the Soviet invasion of October 30, Nagy found himself constrained to announce, on November 1, 1956, the severance of Hungary's alliance with the USSR and the nation's claim to be regarded, from that moment, as a neutral state—like Switzerland or Sweden. Only by going along with such populist notions could Nagy remain in touch with his country, uniting it behind him. In Budapest, after the declaration, the question everyone asked Nagy was, what will the Russians do? Nagy, hearty with false courage, had for days worked to convince himself and everyone else around him that the USSR might not intervene after all.

Nagy's ongoing naiveté about Soviet motives sounded more frivolous than it was. For behind the hopeful chatter—as Béla Király has written, "one of the most poignant and melancholy aspects [to Nagy's declaration of Hungary's independence from the Warsaw Pact] . . . was the unequivocal friendship that it offered to the Soviet people."[37] The coherence that guided him, in a phrase used by his daughter, was "his sense of the future,"[38] and he could not believe that the Soviet Union he so loved would willingly throw away the future of communism in his country. Nagy's dominant characteristic at this dark hour was his feeling of confidence—overconfidence as some like Kiraly thought—perhaps the result of the Soviets twice sanctioning his coming to power in Budapest, which may have left him with a sense that there was no dispute with the Kremlin that could not be solved. What motivated Nagy in his decision-making was faith, not strategy. He was not concerned with making some historic choice, for that decision had been made in favor of socialism. He was concerned with preserving his idealized socialist vision—a fantasy, and not a harmless one. It allowed him to rest his government on a collapsible base.

On October 28, defending the decision to withdraw from the Warsaw Pact before the Communist party's Central Committee, he argued all the reasons why the Soviets would not intervene. He was like a boy who, aghast at having opened a dam, tries to tell himself the water will somehow not rush through.

For six days Nagy wrestled with himself as the Soviets prepared. He told one aide that he felt as if the world had suddenly reversed itself and was now going from west to east instead of east to west, and that he could not get his balance. He insisted that he would not allow any further Hungarian provocation to lead to war if it could possibly be avoided. Nagy said that the Hungarian people would not believe that Russia was hostile to them "unless and until we are obliged to believe it." Such an obligation was already on the march.

At dawn on November 4, 1956, a fusillade of shots cracked through the suburbs of Budapest. During the night ten divisions of the Red Army had invested the city. Red flags still decked the streets refracting the sun through their fabric as Soviet tanks assumed their positions. The Red Army had come, said Russian radio, to "smash the sinister forces of reaction . . ."[39]

At last Nagy brought himself to face his political commitments. In circumstances of the utmost confusion, with impromptu meetings going on in safe buildings throughout the city, Nagy began to hammer out a new socialist program which, if the truth be told, was very little like Marxist socialism at all.[40] Pale-faced, impassioned, his eyes blazing, he rushed from place to place, now arguing with the Hungarian Communist party's Central Committee, now with members of the street militias, now pausing to harangue a crowd. The mobs greeted him with cheers: he appeared to be the very embodiment of the revolution at this moment.

To a meeting of the Party's Central Committee on October 30, 1956, Nagy's speech cast a veneer of socialist conformity onto a policy that was heretical. In substance this address was a sharpened repetition of the arguments and proposals Nagy had been advancing for some years, but it was more precise and dogmatic. The dictatorship of the proletariat, as embodied by the rule of the Communist party, must be replaced by a democratic republic.[41] All power must be handed over to freely elected representatives. Communism, however, was to be overthrown. In the place of the communist state-run economy there was to be a free market, private ownership of banks and the means of production, and the return of all farmland to farmers, though the big estates would be distributed to their tenants. The police, army, and bureaucracy were to be made independent of each other and all political parties, and the Communist party's private militia was to be disarmed.

Many of the Communist leaders heard these views with open hostility. After a confused and angry debate, the meeting closed without any decision being reached about Nagy or his entire program. Outwardly, Nagy still professed to remain a loyal communist. In his speeches and private conversations he kept hammering away at his critics with his old persistence, and it is only from the recollections of his family and friends that one learns of his secret misgivings about remaining a communist in any form. They recall his nostalgia for his underground days, for the black-and-white world of the conspirator. His was the voice of the man of faith who seeks to construct heaven on earth, only to find that he is building another form of hell.[42]

For twelve days in the cobbled streets of Budapest, Hannah Arendt's profoundly pessimistic theory of totalitarian invincibility (expounded in *The Origins of Totalitarianism*) was wounded by fact. Hungary threw its unconquered spirit into the face of the Leviathan state.[43] The ideological indoctrination which Arendt and Orwell dreaded had, in fact, left the majority of the Hungarian people untainted. Characteristically quickly, Miss Arendt rejoiced in this refutation of her hypothesis. She wrote: "The voices from Eastern Europe, speaking so plainly and simply of freedom and truth, sounded like an ultimate affirmation that human nature is unchangeable, that nihilism will be futile, that even in the absence of all teaching and in the presence of overwhelming indoctrination, a yearning for freedom and truth will rise out of man's heart and mind forever."[44]

The striking fact of the Hungarian Revolution was that Nagy's leadership was not fundamental. The revolt was unique in history in that the Hungarian revolution had no leaders. It was not organized, it was not centrally directed. The will for freedom was the moving force in every action. Marx's proletariat was on the move at last, but against the Communist party.

Protest by the people against the Party seemed for a moment to be irresistible. Workers' soviets were organized to combat the tanks of the Soviet Union. Railway, telegraph, and telephone strikes paralyzed the whole life of Hungary. For when the call came, the worker, whom Marx had declared to have no fatherland, identified with country, not class. He turned out to be a member of the Hungarian national family like anyone else. The force of his antagonism which was supposed to be trained on capitalism found a better target in the Communist.[45]

The Hungarian Revolution lasted little more than a week. Soviet Ambassador Yuri Andropov gave orders to bombard the city. The Hungarian freedom fighters of General Béla Király who were not torn to bits in the shelling were slaughtered on capture. Snipers stood up to the Soviets for nine days, at the end of which they were crushed by Soviet troops turning their artillery not merely on the barricades and the re-sisters, but on the people's houses. By mid-November the Soviets had slaughtered a thousand, executed hundreds more, and arrested fifty thousand.

Nagy was now an anti-communist in all but name. The massacre of innocents was the deciding factor upon him. It was the last drop that emptied his cup of faith.

There were other factors, more long-term factors, too, not least the persistent failure of the Leviathan state to create a prosperous and happy society. Probably the nearest one can come to understanding what moved Nagy into active anti-communism is to say that a combination of events brought him to a point where he had no alternative but to renounce his faith. He was in the grip of events.

The kick that shattered his faith was the invasion. It was a betrayal of the very notion of socialist fraternity; it was a perversion of history. It awoke that part of Nagy that had been hesitant or blinded before. It transformed doubt into intense hostility, and in one day accomplished a change in sentiment that might have required many more years to be accomplished. It was not an argument or a theory but an unmistakable gesture that anyone could understand. It was the Soviet boot planted firmly upon his face.

The Communist victory over Nagy was celebrated in the usual way. Through the battered city, almost an aspect of Budapest's death, came a huge, solemn parade of mandatory marchers, strutting past the litter and rubble and hopelessness. Once again, people were supposed to be deceived by the poetry of red flags and revolution. And Imre Nagy, who had taken refuge in the Yugoslav embassy, remained a Soviet target. A pledge by the Soviet quisling Janos Kadar not to arrest lured Nagy and his colleagues into forsaking asylum. It was a worthless promise, as Nagy should have suspected. Immediately, they were arrested. For one-and-a-half years they were imprisoned in Romania. On June 16, 1958, Nagy and his comrades were brought back to Budapest and put on trial behind closed doors. Convicted, he was executed in secret, then sent to an unmarked grave. Thus the Soviets passed sentence on the idea of reform.[46]

In the history of the decline and fall of the socialist idea, Nagy's defection was seemingly but a minor loss. In the lives of European communists who turned away in horror from the USSR in the wake of the invasion of Hungary and the judicial murder of Nagy, his defection represented the end of ideological innocence.

15

※≫ ≪※

Enemies of the People
Khrushchev's Secret Speech

T he Hungarian Revolution was a pivotal event in shattering the
socialist vision. We have seen how famines manufactured by Stalin
in Georgia and Ukraine and the slave labor used in gargantuan industrial schemes pushed Nicolai Bukharin into a malaise that bordered on
despair; how a few short months among Stalin's agents in Spain so filled
Arthur Koestler with hatred that he devoted the remainder of his life to
denouncing communist ideology; how Milovan Djilas saw that communism in power was inherently corrupting. For a historical movement
that claimed to be the vanguard of the working class triumphant, revolution against the Communist party by Hungary's workers stripped the
socialist idea of any claims to political and moral legitimacy. Like those
Soviet historians and propagandists who studied the Bolshevik triumph
of 1917 for augeries of the future, some reformers and heretics took
heart from the suppression of liberated Budapest. They studied and
celebrated it, as the Irish celebrate the failed Easter rising of 1916. In
the exercise yard of his prison, Milovan Djilas whispered to other inmates the story of the aborted rising in Hungary.

Unknown to the world outside, inchoate heresy as personified by
Djilas and Nagy had entered full maturity ten months before the Hungarian Revolution, when Nikita Khrushchev presented his "Secret
Speech" to the Twentieth Congress of the Soviet Communist party in
January 1956. It was only after Soviet tanks rolled over Hungary, however, that Khrushchev's stunning revelations of Stalin's crimes seeped
into the socialist world at large.

For Nikita Khrushchev, despite being the man to give the go-ahead to
the invasion of Hungary, was not the type of might-makes-right communist his most famous phrase ("We will bury you!") has left him
reputed to be.[1] To be sure, Khrushchev wanted greater power, greater
prestige, and above all a greater say over the world's affairs for the

USSR. He preferred, however, to obtain them by frightening rather than by fighting. He wanted a gladiator's reward but without giving battle. When Khrushchev startled America with his boast, he was not so much brutally affirming the inevitability of a communist-capitalist clash as expressing a braggart's dismay that the two systems were locked in unending combat. For no one wanted to avoid a bloody invasion of Hungary more than the squat, volatile Khrushchev, so cunning and crude behind his round double chin and that bulge at the back of the neck that Emerson called the mark of the beast. Well-meaning but erratic, inclined to trim when convictions were at stake, Khrushchev, it was said, if he ever sat across a treaty table with the capitalists, would play his hand so clumsily that he would be lucky to come away with Moscow.

Nikita Khrushchev was, indeed, one of those gambler's for whom the wheel of fortune turned too late. Ignored and degraded after his fall from power in 1964, he declared, with only the slightest hint of self-pity, indeed confident in his blistering vanity, that the wheel would turn again twenty-five years after his death. And in fact, in little more than twenty years, he had his revenge, with an unequivocal condemnation of his usurpers by Mikhail Gorbachev.

Khrushchev, indeed, has been so blackened and discredited by Soviet propaganda in the twenty-five years since his overthrow by Leonid Brezhnev that it is almost impossible to see him any more. Like Richard III of Plantagenet England, or Italy's Cesare Borgia, he is portrayed as all villain, the pure quintessence of bullying wickedness, a monster with the cunning of Iago and the brutishness of Caliban. In such officially fabricated profiles nothing is good about him; he seldom washed and he supposedly smelled vilely; at table he would plunge his greedy hands into his favorite fish stew, and he was the kind of drunkard who smashes the furniture. He was blasphemous about Lenin, vicious and obscene, and his temper had a barbaric mongol quality that made him more like a beast than a human being.

Without denying a word of all this one still feels that the picture is incomplete; one still needs to know, for example, how such a demon got to the top of the Communist party and remained there cherished and honored, almost able to plunge the world into nuclear annihilation during the Cuban Missile Crisis of October 1962. It is not enough to say that after Stalin the Communist party remained fatally attracted to monsters; Khrushchev had serious and far more menacing rivals in the struggle for the succession. The Party leadership thought they discerned something superhuman in this unreconstructed peasant, something that lifted him up above the other survivors of Stalin's inner circle and put him in touch with bolshevism's primal forces. And in fact the more you learn about Khrushchev the more you realize that he was not at all bogus. According to his own code he was entirely consistent; he never recanted anything, he had no practiced mumbo jumbo of mystical speeches like Lenin or Trotsky, no horde of obsequious disciples in some Stalinist cult of personality. As leader of the Communist party he merely did exactly as he said he was going to do—and that led him into heresy.

In the eyes of the Party his real crime, of course, was that he broke the conventions, he told some of the truth as to how Bukharin's benevolent Leviathan had mutated into Stalin's bloody national tomb.

The puzzle of Khrushchev's motive in revealing the monstrousness of Stalin's crimes remains. One widely favored explanation argues that Khrushchev acted less from humanity and a scrupulous fidelity to the truth than from a keen instinct for self-promotion and self-preservation. In the dark space of Stalinist history Khrushchev turned like a ball with mirrored facets, immediately casting back whatever light brushed against him. He had the gift of survival in dangerous times. Under Stalin his chosen role was that of factotum and toady; he ingratiated, licked at his leader's heels. By goading into action his leader's adversaries whom he depicted as traitors, conspirators, and backsliding poltroons, Khrushchev could pose as Stalin's champion. He made an art form of this kind of confrontational abuse. Subservience he projected as integrity. He gloried in rudeness. His eyes were the eyes of Stalinist surveillance. Nothing escaped them. And in the complicated intrigues set off by Stalin's death, Khrushchev was thus well prepared to assure his own personal survival.

For the succession was a situation which had a perverse attraction for Nikita Khrushchev, and he made the most of it. He was the consummate ward boss, gross, hard, yet good-tempered, with his tendrils everywhere, and in place of faith possessed an instinctive understanding of the weaknesses of human nature. In that hushed and conspiratorial air that enveloped the Kremlin after Stalin's death, he was in his element.* Even in a place with so lurid a reputation as Stalin's Kremlin it would be difficult to imagine a stranger group of competing men. There is a dramatic quality about Khrushchev and his key rivals—Malenkov, Be-

---

*So nimble was Khrushchev that he successfully rummaged in the Kremlin files and purged documents that implicated him in Stalin's crimes. For this and other details of Khrushchev at this time see: Dmitri Volkongonov, *Stalin: Triumph and Tragedy* (New York, 1991).

ria, Molotov, Mikoyan—a wild and dated theatricality, which is familiar and yet quite unreal. One tends to see them in terms of a gangster movie, half documentary and half extravagant make-believe, and it would be very easy to dismiss them to that convenient limbo that surrounds most political adventurers, had they not, at the instant of Stalin's death, had such power over so many millions of men and women.

Cabals and intrigues, arrests and assassinations, marked the internal struggle for control after Stalin's death. There must have been immense anxieties in the breast of each individual in the Kremlin leadership over the succession. In Russia's Byzantine tradition, exemplified by the struggle for mastery after Lenin's death, the man who won the struggle for mastery sought death for all who might remain his rivals. Only the winner survived. Inevitably, then, on Stalin's death a deadly minuet among Malenkov, Beria, Khrushchev, Molotov, Kaganovich, the Red Army's Marshalls, and others began. "Each," Louis J. Halle has written, "had come through the most extreme personal dangers only by a vigilant mistrustfulness of everyone, by conspiratorial skill, and by sheer nerve."[2] At first, there must have been some sort of comrade's agreement on the rules of the game, perhaps made in secret in advance of Stalin's death—in any case, before its announcement. Initially, an element of solidarity would have existed among them—if not as a matter of criminal acts shared, then because of the threat to the state that the death of Stalin must, in their view, incite. It is reasonably clear, for example, that they agreed on the principle of collective leadership, and on a corresponding rejection of what, in that period after Stalin's death, they were to denounce repeatedly as the "cult of personality." They had also agreed on a complete reorganization of the top commands of the government and Party, including the posts to be held by each, so that they were able to shape the new government simultaneously with the announcement of Stalin's demise.

By virtue of the fear and hate he inspired, one member of the new Politburo caused all the others to huddle in a common front against him. For, said Khrushchev, as soon as Stalin died, [Laventi] Beria was radiant.

> He was regenerated and rejuvenated. To put it crudely, he had a housewarming over Stalin's corpse before it was even put in its coffin. Beria was sure that the moment he had long been waiting for had finally arrived. There was no power on earth that could hold him back now. Nothing could get in his way. You could see these triumphant thoughts in his face. . . . I considered him a treacherous opportunist who would stop at nothing to get what he wanted. Ideologically, I didn't recognize his position as a Communist one. He was a butcher and an assassin.[3]

But that, Khrushchev should have known, was the prototype of the communist true believer.

Even well before Stalin's death Laventi Beria had been increasing the sinister hold on society which his control of the secret police gave to him. If the invention of the doctor's plot (one of Stalin's anti-Semitic rantings that proclaimed a conspiracy among Jewish doctors to murder him) had been designed to discredit him, then Stalin himself had been planning Beria's destruction. Stalin would hardly have been unconcerned by the steady growth of the secret police under Beria until they had come, at last, to number one-and-a-half million men. In addition, Beria had under his command a militia of three hundred thousand men, and through his control of the labor camps nearly one-fifth of the entire labor force in the Soviet Union was under his personal rule. No other member of the collective leadership at the time of Stalin's death was as powerful. He had, in effect, his own praetorian guard. Fear that he might use his power to make himself absolute dictator in the manner of Stalin drew the others together in the kind of comradeship that only a great common danger makes possible. A struggle for power between Beria and the others began in the spring of 1953. By inserting his own men into key positions, Beria tried to gain personal control of the Party apparat. He sought to make himself supreme in his native Georgia. A trap was set for him, however, and was sprung on June 27, when tanks and soldiers were seen moving through the streets of Moscow. Two weeks later the world was informed of Beria's arrest as "an enemy of the Communist Party and the Soviet people."[4]

According to the official announcement, Beria was executed with six of his cronies in December 1953, after he had, in a secret trial, been found guilty of high treason.*

From this point on, the struggle among the members of the collective leadership took a more civilized form and, proceeding slowly, was not fully resolved until 1957, when Nikita Khrushchev expelled his rivals from their commanding positions in the Party and the government on the grounds that they constituted an "anti-party group."[5]

The odd thing, of course, was that Khrushchev should have survived to come to power at all, that a position of supreme responsibility should have reached him, and that he would use that position to undermine

---

*Khrushchev had another version of the tale of Beria's demise. He told an Italian communist leader that Beria was in fact murdered immediately on his arrest: while reaching for a gun, Beria was seized and strangled. See Robert Payne, *The Rise and Fall of Stalin* (London, 1968), pp. 718–719.

forty years of socialist history, indeed the very meaning of socialism. Nikita Sergeievich Khrushchev was not a member of that rising mandarin class which had nurtured Lenin and Trotsky and Bukharin in resentment and hate. Shrewd and ruthless, yet retaining a vibrant sense of humor, Khrushchev was a "pugnacious figure with a peasant background and no formal education."[6] Like Stalin, he began his life in squalor, and he never really made much of an outward show of acquiring further refinement. Certainly he never overcame his exceedingly gruff rural accent, for he felt little personal sense of insecurity and hence slight need to compensate by remaking his image. He was extremely vain, but it was a special kind of vanity which was overlaid by an air of shyness and modesty, and his reckless bravery throughout his career was offset by an appearance so cool and unhurried, that some of his early rivals thought him half asleep on the job. As he climbed the Party ladder he exhibited this same distinction of manner, so that no disaster ever appeared to flurry him, and no decision, however important, caused him more than a few moment's hesitation. Even his ambition was disguised by a certain ease with which he moved among people who belonged to a much more cultivated society than his own. With this fluency and this charm it was no small wonder that, years later, European diplomats in Moscow made so much of him; here was the socialist ideal in real life, an unassuming young hero. All this was a most effective cover for the innate cunning, the shallowness and the squalor that lay beneath.[7]

Khrushchev was born in the village of Kalinovka, near the Russian-Ukrainian border, in 1894. Khrushchev's father had been born a serf, and though formally freed of his master's control had never escaped the agrarian anthill. Nikita's school record was poor, for he was sent out to work at a very early age—first as a shepherd for the family's flock of goats, and then down into the coal pits at age sixteen. The more hungry and exhausted he was, the more he was forced for food and diversion to draw on his own mind and imagination. In the bleak and disease-ridden tunnels he built up his political vision of the world. In this way he seems to have ideal socialist origins; for with his black lung-ridden colleagues Khrushchev formed warm friendships and shared dreams of revenge. A thinning mop of black hair on his head, with hairy hands and a crookedly buttoned coat, Khrushchev soon acquired the air of a man used to commanding the respect of others. His movements were clumsy but increasingly self-assured. His manners defied the accepted conventions of working-class docility, were haughty and almost deliberately contemptuous of his superiors. His voice with them was harsh, and he spoke of men and things in tones that would brook scant contradiction, which seemed to express his own firm conviction of his mission to sway men's minds.

With other workers young Khrushchev had a generous, extravagant, wildly impulsive character, a rich, chaotic, unbridled imagination, a passion for the violent, the immense, the sublime, a hatred of enforced discipline, total lack of all sense of personal property, and, above all, a savage and overwhelming desire to annihilate the rigid society of his time, in which, like Gulliver in Lilliput, he saw the human individual as suffocating for want of room to realize his faculties. He became a gifted mob orator, consumed with a genuine hatred of injustice and a burning sense of his personal mission to rouse mankind to some act of magnificent collective heroism which would set it free forever; and he exercised a personal fascination over other men, blinding them to his irresponsibility and opportunism, his mendacity, his bouts of frivolity, by means of the overwhelming revolutionary enthusiasm that he communicated. Indeed, when the civil war in Russia broke out in 1919, he was chosen by acclaim to lead a band of ill-trained metalworkers against a troop of Cossacks. Without any military training, he led his men to victory. This is not to imply that Khrushchev was blessed with originality and deep strategic or tactical insight; but he readily absorbed the ideas of others and was an inspired teacher. Although his entire creed amounted to little more than a passionate egalitarian belief in the need for the destruction of authority and the freeing of the oppressed, mingled with a deep nativism, he built on this a political career that would bring him supreme leadership of the Communist movement.

Backed by the Cheka, Khrushchev enrolled in a miners' school in 1921. His pride and Party loyalty marked him for advancement, which was also aided by his willingness to inform. It was in a manner characteristically resourceful that he married his first wife, a young primary schoolteacher named Nina Petrovna Kukharchuk, who helped secure for her new husband a post with the Ukrainian Party boss Lazar Kaganovich. Sometime around 1927 he followed his patron to Moscow.

Exuberant, energetic, his hooded peasant's eyes bespeaking a practiced servility, Khrushchev rose fast to become a member of Stalin's inner circle. In those frenzied years of the late 1920s and early 1930s, to question Stalin's actions was to invite self-destruction. To stay alive, you went along. Making himself a crude comic figure wherever he went, impulsive, voluble, and jovial, with a folksy manner and wit, Khrushchev developed all the attributes of a populist demagogue such as Huey Long, rather than of his sullen master Stalin. Like Long, he climbed the ranks through his opportunism, his quickness and his energy, his daring and his capacity to cajole. All the while he was protected as Stalin's fool. As Moscow's Communist party chief Khrushchev took part in the bloody purges and collectivizations, but one suspects that there was little or no joy in it for him. In 1938 he was sent to Kiev as Stalin's personal agent, there to wipe out any lingering resistance among the Ukrainian peasants. Through the ruined nation he left his own defiled path. Early in World War II, he followed the Red Army as it occupied the eastern third of Poland, Stalin's spoils from the Molotov-Ribbentrop Pact. Khrushchev treated the region as just another part of the USSR; he immediately enforced the communist system. When Hitler invaded Russia in the spring of 1941, Khrushchev retreated with the Red Army. He helped to plan the disastrous assault on Kharkov, but his loyalty to Stalin protected him from retribution. At the time of the Battle of Stalingrad he was Political Commissar for the triumphant Red Army, and stole as much of the glory as prudence would allow. After the war, Khrushchev returned to his post as head of the Party in the city of Moscow, and in 1949 he joined the Central Committee as Secretary. These were the years of Stalin's most malignant paranoia, when anyone close to him became suspect. Yet Khrushchev prospered.

His actions represent the primacy of survival in the dangerous career he was making for himself under Stalin. Add to this that he was a rapid improvisor of great daring rather than a man of deep and patient calculation. He would, one supposes, have made a first-rate robber baron in the Gilded Age. He had only a crude and superficial knowledge of Marxian dialectics, and like all practical operators of his type he had little respect for abstract theoretical considerations. This left him free to be the more flexible in his opportunism. For his talent was not ideological but political, exercised through a mastery of balance between factions and plots so that he was sometimes referred to as being like a billiken, a weighted doll that cannot be knocked over. A virtuoso in political improvisation, Khrushchev knew how to advance boldly, and how to retreat when one would have thought he had burned his bridges behind him.

But Khrushchev must also be credited with an instinctive tolerance, with impulses in the direction of decency. Even as he served as a Stalinist tool he was revolted by the murders and mistreatment of people, by the torture and death meted out to men for whom he may well have had great respect.[8] This was expressed with a sort of personal passion that could not have been altogether affected in his talks denouncing Stalin after his own coming to supreme power.

It is easy to imagine that Khrushchev's rise to dominance after Stalin's death was in large part attributable to this very human streak, to the fact that his rivals in the collective leadership could feel a confidence in him that they could not feel in one another. He was so personally compromised as to seem unthreatening. Far from having the qualities of a dictator like Stalin, Khrushchev preferred to consult and to act on the basis of consensus. He was not a misanthrope who, achieving power, would be highly disposed to use it with Stalin's ruthless cruelty. And he had a self-deprecating quality which made it clear that he did not fancy himself in the role of dictator. Those who were moved by revulsion against what Stalin represented would quite naturally be drawn to Khrushchev.

The collective leaders surely appreciated this. They were determined that a Caligula should not succeed a Caligula. The principle of moderation had enough credit among them, and they had enough respect for orderly procedures, so that they were unwilling to settle their differences and rivalries by assassination or to mete out death to the losers as Stalin had done. The death of Beria, since it was the product of a secret trial on essentially political charges, must be accounted an exception; but what is to be noted is the fact that it was so. When Khrushchev, in successive maneuvers, defeated Malenkov, Molotov, Kaganovich, Bulganin, and Marshall Zhukov, he simply sent them into comfortable retirement. And when he himself was overthrown in 1964, like consideration was shown to him. This represented a marked improvement on the Byzantine tradition that Stalin had embodied, though few outside observers credited it at the time.

But after Stalin, what? In his famous telegram from Moscow, of February 22, 1946, the American ambassador in the Kremlin George F. Kennan had written:

> It has to be demonstrated that [the Soviet system] can survive supreme test of successive transfer of power from one individual or group to another. Lenin's death was first such transfer, and its effects wracked Soviet state for 15 years after. Stalin's death or retirement will be second.[9]

In the days and months after Stalin's burial the very question of whether or not the USSR would survive must have been as lively a topic for discussion in the Kremlin as it was in the West, where only the inhibition against "wishful thinking" held in check the hope that the Soviet state, unable to resolve the question of the succession, would fall into confusion and helplessness with Stalin's removal from the scene. And this might have happened. In the absence of effective constitutional provisions establishing the procedures for an orderly transition—provisions that cannot exist in connection with a system of absolute one-man rule—the door was open to anarchy. Beria, overthrown in Moscow, might have found refuge in Georgia, which he had been converting into his personal fief: and civil war might have ensued. Or he might have seized power in Moscow and found that he could maintain it only by the practice of such terrorism as would itself have spelled chaos. Or the Red Army might have moved against the Party, or against the secret police, with incalculable consequences. Anarchy tends to propagate itself. In the USSR, no doubt, anarchy would have been like a fire spreading in a dry forest.

To take into account these political possibilities, as Nikita Khrushchev did (as revealed in his memoirs), one is bound to begin to question the very system that could give rise to such potential disruptions. As power became concentrated in his hands, Khrushchev came to realize that absolute state control had been rendered increasingly obsolete. Soviet society was outgrowing the inherited barbarism that had made such rule, if bloody, practical under Stalin. But with the rapid, forced industrialization a relatively sophisticated class of managers and technicians had been rising, and their loyalty lay outside the sway of the Party. These men, whose role was indispensable, could not function under the conditions that for forty years had kept the Russian people in a state of servitude akin to that of barnyard beasts. They were no longer illiterate peasants or assembly-line proles. Their roles and their willingness to perform them required greater freedom of debate and decision. And their training made them as apt to question political authority as to accept it. Scientists and scholars, upon whom a modern Russia would depend more and more, had the same needs, if in a greater degree. All this meant to Khrushchev that the days when Russia could be ruled by an Ivan the Terrible or a Stalin were at an end. For,

> with Stalin's death an ambiguous situation had arisen. Stalin was dead and buried, but . . . Stalinist policies were still in force. Business went on as usual. No one thought to rehabilitate the people who had gone to their graves branded as enemies of the people or to release the prisoners from the camps. . . . We were unable to lift the curtain and see what had been hidden from us about the arrests, the trials, the arbitrary rule, the executions and everything else that had happened during Stalin's reign. It was as though we were enchained by our own activities under Stalin's leadership and couldn't free ourselves from his control even after he was dead. . . . For a while . . . we blamed everything on Beria. He was a convenient figure. We did everything we could to shield Stalin, not

yet fully realizing that we were harboring a criminal, an assassin, a mass murderer! I repeat: Not until 1956 did we set ourselves free . . .[10]

Khrushchev's first years in power revealed that the imperial lusts of the USSR also discredited socialism. The West was united in hostility. Yugoslavia was alienated. Stalin had blundered in Korea. In a world of nuclear weapons, Stalin's conduct of foreign policy had raised international tensions to a point of extreme danger for the USSR. Khrushchev, although he could not expect to disengage from the Cold War and so bring it to an end in the immediate future, this being beyond the bounds of political possibility, showed himself anxious to relax international tensions and to retrench the over-extended empire where it could be retrenched without much danger. Here was a recognition of limits, something which had eluded Soviet leaders since Bukharin's creation of Leviathan.[11]

The fundamental change that all this represented was not recognized at the time by Khrushchev, let alone by his adversary, the United States. No one in Washington dared accept at face value the new attitudes voiced by the demonic enemy. McCarthyism, beginning at the end of 1949, had only in the mid-1950s achieved the heights of its supremacy, and anyone who suggested that Stalin's death might diminish the menace of the communist conspiracy was likely to find himself branded suspect. He would, in any case, be silenced by the flood of opinion against him. Everyone agreed that no one must allow himself to be misled by the smiles of the new Communist leadership. Everyone felt impelled to make it clear how little Khrushchev, in any case, was in danger of being duped by them.

Khrushchev, indeed, was not about to be deceived. In some ways he was being converted. He thought of himself as belonging to the second generation of communists who recognized the necessity of responding to the rising challenge of running a modern economy. Yet bred as he was in class antagonism he could not, when issues came to a test, range himself on the side of those who advocated a return to private property and a restoration of the financial mechanisms of capitalism. When he had first joined the Party and began to rise in its leadership, he worked with men who had supported Lenin's loose-construction socialism during the NEP, because, he said, they were the men who ran his local Party machine and slackening socialism was the ruling idea. But the choice indicated a point of view. The NEP supporters were gadflies of the belief that the declining power of capitalism could be harnessed in partnership with socialism. Khrushchev now set about following a similar line—a project comparable to restoring virginity.

Whether or not Khrushchev was truly persuaded of his convincingly phrased argument is a subject of some considerable doubt. In the 1930s he stood four-square behind Stalin's absolutist five-year plans, a position which he may have adopted through conviction, but seems as likely to have been voiced for simple self-preservation. Sometimes Khrushchev's sycophancy left his comrades aghast. "He is the best that humanity possesses," Khrushchev said of Stalin in 1937, "for Stalin is hope, he is expectation; he is the beacon that guides all progressive mankind. Stalin is our banner! Stalin is our will! Stalin is our victory!"[12] At a late-night banquet—one of Stalin's specialties—Khrushchev was ordered to dance the *gopak* (a Russian folk dance) for the amusement of his leader and his guests.

Enormity of the stakes induced Khrushchev's self-hypnosis of that time. To question Stalin's policies would have meant certain imprisonment, and possibly death. To question his leadership would also have given incalculable encouragement to communism's enemies everywhere. Like Bukharin during his purge trials, Khrushchev believed that to offer any alternatives to Stalin's program while Stalin lived was to open a self-destructive debate. He was as sure of this as nearly as anyone can be certain of anything. No one is more sure of his premises than the man who knows too much.[13]

In the abstract Khrushchev believed in orthodox socialism and of state control of all economic life, but not at the cost of economic breakdown or inefficiency. Here was the fundamental difficulty of reforming communism. Its advocates thought it possible to meet the demands of economic change and modernization while at the same time preserving intact the citadel of central control of all aspects of national life. Khrushchev was groping for a philosophy of government that would allow for a decentralized economy and yet not betray the cause of the revolution. The state was losing touch with the engines of economic growth. Even in the darkest days of the 1930s he continued from time to time to suggest that communism might need to make "detours and stops" on the way to utopia. But when it came to specific acts of amelioration, as suggested by Bukharin, he was not enthusiastic or deeply concerned. The fact that Stalin remained undisturbed by Khrushchev's early association with NEP communism and that confidence between them remained unclouded, or at least as clear as was possible with Stalin, suggests that there was a basic identity of belief stronger than the difference.

Khrushchev on coming to power seemed an enigma to his comrades because of this paradoxical nature. His opinions were often irreconcilable, and he did not seem to see life or politics in terms of absolutes. Though a longtime member of the Central Committee of the Party, his career had never been pursued at that Olympian level. He dealt in particular collective farms, particular factories, individual military units. Unlike Stalin, he was often seen to speak to or notice a peasant or worker. He saw government as the management of some specific policy and took it from there. Like Nagy and Djilas he was not trapped in orthodoxies, or his own commitments and beliefs. Having only a personal share in the enforcement of Stalin's policies, not in their planning, he was able to see the strengths and weaknesses of the socialist state in something like their true proportions. From his new position of personal safety he was able to see the effects of the Leviathan state as a whole, in terms of its triumphs and its failures, and to realize that no mere tinkering with its structure would be sufficient if the USSR was to continue in the Cold War that was under way.

To build and maintain a modern economy, the USSR must have men willing to take risks, which could come about only by instilling in the populace the confidence that no honest decision could cost a man his life or his freedom. The professionally trained managers and technicians of Soviet industry and science he considered to be precious and indispensable as a nucleus for training the larger force of "model socialist producers" he had in mind. To throw their knowledge away because of a fear of imprisonment he regarded as criminal folly. Once they were cowed into silence and "coerced judgments" there would be no one to take their place. For Khrushchev, plans made with respect to some time in the future were not operative. It was not until the future came that realistic operative decisions could be made, and such decisions would not necessarily conform to what was projected by ideology. Without prematurely abandoning orthodoxy, Khrushchev reckoned that the Party could properly recognize change and explore its possibilities. This, in fact, was what he planned to do with the power now in his hands.[14]

But his comrades in the collective leadership had accepted Khrushchev's primacy not because of his opinions but because he was safe. They were more conscious of his strengths and faults of character than of his virtues of clairvoyance, and would have been glad to dismiss his ideas but for the fact that they could not do without him. Khrushchev led not because he was considered qualified by the holding of opinions which no one else held but because his presence in the Kremlin was indispensable to the pursuit of tranquil government.[15]

The Central Committee, however, put little credence in Khrushchev's hints for reform at a moment when everyone was thinking of the immediate problem of consolidating their rule in the wake of Stalin's still potent image and legacy. "It was never disclosed," said Andrei Gromyko long afterwards with perhaps needless bewilderment, "how or by what process of reasoning he made his forecasts and proposals."[16] Whether because Khrushchev was right when everybody else was wrong, or because his better-educated colleagues found it hard to credit Khrushchev with high mental processes, or because Khrushchev was never able or never deigned to explain his reasons, all his colleagues and contemporaries assumed that he reached his conclusions, as Gromyko said, "by some storm of instinct rather than by ordered thought."[17]

Whatever the process, Khrushchev accurately dissected the socialist state as it had evolved in the years from 1917. The speech he delivered in January 1956 was not merely an act of vengeance against a tyrant who could no longer bully or kill, or an expression of moral revulsion at the crimes Khrushchev, as one of Stalin's factotums, had helped carry out. The speech against Stalin was a deliberate political act which, in condemning the past, also laid down a course for the future. And it was to be an act of the Party and not of Khrushchev alone. Khrushchev denounced Stalin's despotism over the Party and promised a return to the practice of Lenin because the Party barons insisted that he should, as the price of their acceptance of his leadership.

Hesitant and cautious at first in his welcoming speech to the Twentieth Party Congress, Khrushchev spoke of Stalin in moderate, even respectful, terms. The issue came to a head soon afterwards. When Anastas Mikoyan, who had been defeated by Khrushchev in the struggle for the succession, rose to speak, he not only attacked Stalin's memory and legacy, but referred by name to two leading Party figures who had been put to death under Stalin, although innocent of the crimes they were alleged to have committed. These were Ovseyenko and Kossior, two relatively unimportant men except for the fact that Kossior had been purged by a commission which consisted of Yezhov, Molotov, and Khrushchev. Indeed, Kossior's successor as First Secretary of the Ukraine had been Khrushchev.

Like any politician confronted by the sins of his past, Khrushchev tried to cover up. Documents on the Kossior trial suddenly went missing. But Khrushchev could not ignore the warning: Mikoyan was hinting that Khrushchev would be denounced at the Congress if he refused to make an open break with Stalin. To Mikoyan and Khrushchev's other rivals, the issue was not one of reform but of insuring that Khrushchev could not evolve his own cult of personality to rival Stalin's. To Khrushchev, Mikoyan's speech was a challenge that he turned into opportunity. Throughout the evening of February 24, 1956, negotiations between Party factions ensued. The Congress was not summoned to order until after midnight. When at last it did begin its business, it heard from Khrushchev the speech which, although delivered in a secret session, was soon to become famous throughout the world.

To shield himself from responsibility for the death of Kossior and numerous other of Stalin's crimes, was Khrushchev's first objective. Stalin, he declared, had "decided everything." He continued:

> We have to consider seriously and analyze correctly this matter in order that we may preclude any possibility of a repetition in any form whatever of what took place during the life of Stalin, who absolutely did not tolerate collegiality in leadership and in work, and who practiced brutal violence, not only toward everything which opposed him, but also toward that which to his capricious and despotic character, [was] contrary to his concepts. . . . Whoever opposed . . . was doomed to removal . . . and physical annihilation. [18]

His own neck saved, Khrushchev moved ineluctably to limit the scope of personal power of the Communist party's General Secretary. "We must abolish," he told the delegates, "the cult of personality decisively, once and for all; we must draw the proper conclusions concerning both ideological-theoretical and practical work. It is necessary for this purpose . . . to fight the willfulness of individuals abusing their power. The evil caused by acts violating revolutionary legality . . . has to be completely corrected." [19]

Khrushchev's diagnosis of the criminal failures of Stalin was that the dictator had relied solely upon violence to construct socialism. It was a power now to be revoked. In denying the Party's power to punish and murder to achieve its ends, Khrushchev set forth a new vision of the socialist state. His audience was stunned and incredulous, but Khrushchev was relentless. In place of the Leviathan state, Khrushchev suggested a state and economy able to adjust its competing forces so as to rule out the return of any absolute dictatorship. In such a case, the use of coercion to build socialism was gone for good. And if socialism did not have to be imposed from above, from the state, then the Party might rule through a limited form of democracy which would ensure it the support of all classes, and not the proletariat alone. Carried away on a wave of optimism, Khrushchev declared that if violence and coercion were banished as tools of government, socialism would win the voluntary support of all members of society.

In passing, Khrushchev confirmed many things revealed by Gide, Koestler, Silone, Djilas, and Nagy. Yes, there are prison camps. Yes, torture is common. Yes, the innocent are beaten and killed. He acknowledged the helplessness of individuals before the brute power of a single monopoly party, particularly when that party owns the state and the state owns the presses, the courts, all the instruments of force, persuasion, and communication, all "criticism and self-criticism." To Koestler's revelation of brainwashing, Khrushchev gave an authoritative answer:

> And how is it possible that a person confesses to crimes he has not committed?
>
> Only in one way: because of the applying of physical pressure, torture, bringing him to a state of unconsciousness, deprivation of his judgement, taking away his human dignity.[20]

And among the other things he confirmed were genocide, the persecution of subject nationalities, the capricious and fantastic exploitation of the peasantry, the ubiquitous police, the universal terror reaching high and low in Party circles, even to the men nearest the Kremlin throne.

Khrushchev's speech burned with the heat of personal betrayal. How, he wonders, could the wisest, freest, most humane, most democratic, most advanced, most enlightened, most just system in the history of the world evolve into a monstrous tyranny? To Khrushchev, Stalin's crimes did not make socialism illegitimate. He would remain constant to his one abiding faith, even when that faith had been betrayed. Indeed, no matter how many times that faith had betrayed its ideals, socialism would still find Khrushchev loyal to the spirit of 1917: the man on the street with the red flag wrapped about his body.

For Khrushchev, revelation and truth would be socialism's salvation. Stalin's crimes could not be swept under a rug. Running through his speech is a series of near primal screams, a bonfire of Stalinism:

> Stalin's despotism . . . the criminal murder of S. M. Kirov . . . mass repressions and brutal acts of violation of socialist legality . . . shot in order to cover the traces of Kirov's killing . . . mass acts of abuse . . . prolonged tortures . . . kept Professor Vinogradov in chains . . . beat, beat, and beat again . . . men came to fear their own shadows . . . insecurity, fear, and despair . . . thousands executed without trial . . . everything has its limits, my torture has reached its extreme . . . let my cry of horrors reach your ears. . . .[21]

Here was moving testimony of Khrushchev's desire to break with the Stalinist past. If there was to be any hope of succeeding at this, however, it would come only through a bold, clean stroke of absolute repudiation—whatever the cost. And the cost was immense. It told Communists all over the world that for three decades Moscow had lied to them; the Kremlin was not infallible. It told them what sheep they had been. After this, how could anyone give unquestioning allegiance and obedience to Moscow's orders? How could anyone accept Moscow's leadership?[22]

The implication of Khrushchev's speech was clear. Checks on the exercise of personal power were to be developed and enforced. Like Martin Luther citing the Gospels to justify his break with a corrupt papacy, Khrushchev sought justification for his proposals in Lenin's writings. But the justification was only a fig leaf. Khrushchev meant, in effect, to abandon the Leviathan state. No society, he brazenly suggested some weeks after his speech, was a completely homogenous organism, conscious of itself as a proletariat or likely to become so. It was divided always between rural and urban, skilled and unskilled, factory and home, with different interests and different levels of earning power. The state, in treating all citizens identically, could only seem to them to be hostile or indifferent.

If the state and Party had to accept limits on their power, then it followed that the state was not the agent of socialism, but instead a tool to be used by men in socialism's construction. Here was the terrible horizon of reform. Every citizen, not only Party members, had political rights and responsibilities that had to be protected.

Khrushchev suspected that the socialist state contained fundamental contradictions that would lead to its eventual breakdown. It was based on a denial of the inherent competitiveness of man. The aim of the socialist state was always to suppress rivalries in the name of the all-important socialist vision, so that no individual obstacle would interfere with the construction of a communist society. But the more the state insisted on uniformity—the more ruthless it was in exacting its will—the more people would become sullen automatons and the more their individual gifts and resources would be reduced. That is, the more the state insisted on its vision of humanity, the less human its citizens would become. In order for the state to progress toward true socialism, it needed to be able to call upon the full talents of its citizens, but under the dictatorship of the proletariat in its present form, the talents of most comrades were squandered or allowed to atrophy. This situation was already producing economic stagnation in industries and sciences not favored with huge state subsidies; and the only way for the socialist state to revive its citizens' talents was to loosen their shackles—a reform which in the long run would supposedly assure socialism its success.

The more ruthlessly the state insisted on its rights and powers, the less resources would be generated among its people; and it would be far-thinking for the state to surrender its assumption that state control of society must always become greater and greater. For industries to keep growing, state control must shrink. The vision of one great, unified, social and industrial organization was just that—a vision, of no real value to the daily life of society. The bigger the state grew, the larger its area of managerial control, the smaller the chance for individual initiative. At last the contradictions involved in this process would jam the whole system so badly—there being no other source of creativity left to tap—that it would become an intolerable swamp of bureaucracy. All of the socialist idea would become bogged down in managerial inertia, the like of which had never before been seen in history. To remain unchanged, socialism could only hope for a future of alternations between lassitude and despotism.

Khrushchev's speech was as shocking as if one of the apostles had disputed Jesus. It began the break between Mao's Communist China and Moscow. Mao, indeed, objected strongly to the de-Stalinization campaign as a cowardly attempt to pin the blame for collective mistakes on a single man. He thought Khrushchev's secret speech a monstrous hypocrisy. Khrushchev and all the Soviet leaders had been up to their necks in Stalin's crimes. How did Khrushchev, he demanded, see his role "when he beats his breast, pounds the table and shouts abuse at the top of his voice?"[23] Was he a murderer and bandit himself? Or merely a fool and an idiot? Mao was clearly afraid that the Moscow campaign against the cult of personality might be used against himself. More fundamentally, he thought that Khrushchev's heresy strengthened his own claim to the pontifical supremacy of the communist world.

But Khrushchev's rhetoric, as always, was stronger than his purpose. He mortally wounded communism's moral claims, but failed in his efforts to alter its structure. All that the post-Stalin changes involved was the end of mass terrorism against Party members, that is to say those inside the ruling system. Leviathan's totalitarian structure, that absolute monopoly of power by the Party, remained in its entirety, sustained as before by the secret police and the army, each controlled by an internal structure of Party officers.

What moves were made in the direction of liberalization were tentative. Part of the gulag structure was dismantled, though its core remained. On December 25, 1958, new "Fundamental Principles of

Criminal Law and Procedure" were enacted, giving theoretical rights to the accused in criminal proceedings and provoking the first legal debate ever held in the Soviet press. But this reform from above was bound to produce instability, and so reversal, since Soviet Russia was not a society under the rule of law. Marxism, indeed, never produced a philosophy of law. The only true Soviet legal philosopher, Evgeny Pashukanis, argued that in a socialist society Law would be replaced by Plan. This was logical, since the notion of an independent legal process was incompatible with the notion of an inevitable historical process interpreted by a ruling Party elite. Pashukanis' own case proved it: Law had been replaced by a Plan—Stalin's plan—and he was murdered in the 1930s.[24] Khrushchev's 1958 reform was a nullity in practice because it would have given the courts the beginnings of an independent status and so allowed them to erode the monopoly of power enjoyed by the Party. No matter what Khrushchev envisioned, in reality no Soviet court ever returned a verdict of not guilty in a political case—thus preserving an unbroken record of subservience from 1917 onwards.[25]

So, as we have seen, the Leviathan state endured. Khrushchev, who in many ways behaved like an autocrat, had to be removed like one. His colleagues disliked his heresies and his foreign adventures. They came to see him as a disturber of their peace. He tried in the early 1960s to introduce more democracy to the Party. His idea of the "State of the whole people," implying the end of Party power-monopoly, was thoroughly heretical. While he was on vacation in the Crimea in October 1964, the Presidium voted him out of office and had their decision confirmed by the Central Committee the next day. Khrushchev was flown back to Moscow under police guard.[26] The object and manner of the coup confirmed the organic connection between Leninist norms and secret policemanship, something that would last until the Party's collapse with the failed coup against Gorbachev in August 1991.

One area of Khrushchev's reforms did have lasting effect. When the Presidium refused his request to change the system of censorship, he authorized some publications on his own responsibility. In 1962 the slim novel of an ex-gulag inmate was allowed to be published. Cleft by Khrushchev's schism, the Party appeared still to be in absolute control. But the current of protest, as persecution intensified under Brezhnev, ran on above and underground. *One Day in the Life of Ivan Denisovich* would become the most influential book to circulate in the USSR since 1917.

16

⇥⟫ ⟪⇤

Solzhenitsyn
The Young Prophet

Revolutionaries always seem to flourish through invective. Nikita Khrushchev was a socialist practiced in the movement's venomous accusatory style. Under Stalin he served on various purging committees; after his own secret speech, anti-Stalinism became (oh so briefly) the ruling political fetish. Everything from the impure Stalinist past was to be reviled, and Khrushchev intended to be the chief beneficiary of this relentless process of ideological reduction. But whispered reports of Khrushchev's revelations only bewildered and terrified when they reached the "masses." By personally authorizing the publication of the novel *One Day in the Life of Ivan Denisovich*, composed by a young writer only recently freed from a decade in the gulag, Khrushchev perhaps intended to dispel the confusion by taking to the public his program of political housecleaning through patriotic denunciation. Indeed, like Bukharin and Mayakovsky before him, Khrushchev mistakenly believed in the possibility of turning Party revulsion and rage on and off and in any direction he chose. To heap Alexander Solzhenitsyn's exposé of the gulag on top of his own discussion of Stalin's crimes seemed a safe risk. Coming on top of the doubts Khrushchev had incited, however, these new revelations only further discredited the socialist idea. Demoralization would become so strong that no mere sprucing up of socialism could save it. With Solzhenitsyn, the long process that was to bring Leviathan crashing down began to gather true momentum.

How can it be that the political creed chosen by history, the unseen inevitability of dialectical materialism, should have produced, in each succeeding generation, a system which makes life hell for its followers and which threw up a tyrant of truly monstrous stature? These are questions which have haunted every Soviet who has ever been in Boris Pasternak's fortunate position of being able to choose whether to stay in

Russia and fight the socialist state or to take the money and run. Alienated by the savage values of socialism as openly revealed by Khrushchev, humanists and intellectuals turned back, as did the historian Roy Medvedev in Moscow and the novelist Jorge Semprun in Spain, to Karl Marx's scriptures for meaning, or like Andrei Sakharov and Vladimir Bukovsky to an open dissent that, though it may have been motivated by genuine religious distress, helped to shiver respect for socialism everywhere in the world.

Similar tensions, we have seen, were embedded in the writings of Gide, Koestler, and Silone. Similar dissents were prefigured in the lives of Djilas and Nagy. In Alexander Solzhenitsyn, whose hatred of his country's government seems almost equally balanced by a fervent patriotism, a tragic knowledge that a Russian can only be himself when he is on his native soil, the shattering of ideological illusion is nearly complete. The pieces of the faith cannot be put back together.

Among the masked men of Russia's revolutionary century, Solzhenitsyn is perhaps the most heavily armored by a deep and almost innocent love of himself as a work of art. He seems to have adroitly decided to be an adult enigma from the cradle onwards and to be not merely an old man of the world as early as possible, but even to pass as ancient man, possibly on the principle that the last shall be first. One has the impression sometimes that he must have been laying down the law from his baby carriage. Now in his seventies, he looks—in color, precision, and dignity—like one of his own fictional characters. The marks of time on his face, together with his angular body and concentrated air of detachment, give him a refined, abstract quality. In Solzhenitsyn one sees the point of a question Oscar Wilde posed in regard to Max Beerbohm: he asked a lady whether Max ever took off his face and revealed his mask. Solzhenitsyn has no face; or if he does have one, it is *disponible,* as blank as an actor's is.

Osip Mandelstams's widow Nadezhda, a shrewd judge of character, has nicely hit at how Solzhenitsyn's role-playing inhibits his work: "When he thinks he is telling the truth," she confided in Bruce Chatwin, "he tells the most terrible falsehoods; when he thinks he is telling a story out of his imagination then, sometimes, he catches the truth."[1] Is there a biographical answer to this Solzhenitsyn paradox? Solzhenitsyn himself, like so many authors, dreads biographical attention but is wounded when he fails to get it: when he first emigrated to America he is reported to have paced the lanes around Cavendish, Vermont, to scare off the sightseers, returning to his farmhouse in a fury if there had been none to drive away. He is afraid of future biographers and in conversation he is cautious of intimacies.

This Garbo-like self-protectiveness is partly explained by examining the photographs of Solzhenitsyn. No writer has ever looked more like a prophet. It is as if he knows that he must match that Old Testament exterior.

If Solzhenitsyn's own character is provisional, like that of the most outstanding characters of his novels, we can see how important improvisation is to him—as important as his powers of minute scrutiny are to his work. As a man he is separated from observing his dreams and desires by an almost military concern for strategies and inventing obstacles. The obstacles provoke the psychologist. In life his stratagems have often misfired: in art they lead to the sort of reverie he caught from Tolstoy. They are also responsible for his euphoric excesses, his sometime celibacy, his gallows humor, and his obsession with death.

Solzhenitsyn was the son of a prosperous Stavropol farmer and ex-Tsarist officer who was killed by accident in June 1918, having survived the horrors of the Eastern front. While skinning a hare in a cart, Isaaki Solzhenitsyn "in a moment of carelessness leaned his cocked shotgun against the cart's side. The horse started. . . . The cart gave a jerk, and the shotgun fell and exploded."[2] Solzhenitsyn had not known him. He did know that his father had been obliged to surrender his lands to the Bolsheviks, and that stuck in the mind of his son. His mother was of a kulak family with some Cossack blood. Solzhenitsyn was proud of this connection, and as he grew up he cultivated the impassive Cossack pride and macho bearing. The mother brought up her son in Kislovodsk, a one-time resort that had declined. She was simple and known for her stunned silences. The household, Solzhenitsyn once said, was a speechless solitude. He saw her silence as an act of revolt against her life. Solzhenitsyn has said that there were few words of affection between mother and son; he simply worshipped her. She became mythical in his eyes. Their bond lay in their joint indifference, the badge of the suffering and the knowledge that they shared. Eventually, his mother's suffering assumed a religious form. Her stoicism was not merely a rebellion; it was an ascetic rejection of the things of the world, a characteristic she passed on to her son.

Solzhenitsyn was the complete wandering street kid, the tough and personable young prole, always ready to fend off a blow, fanatical about soccer and swimming and bodily fitness. The solid communal ethos of the Bolshevized working class was to remain with him all his life, even after his middle-class marriage and his final wealth. (He continues to adhere to that dandified, swagger style of dress that is sometimes seen on good-looking, natty European workmen.) By the age of eleven it was clear to his alarmed mother that he was a passionate reader and very intelligent. He was helped by a remarkable schoolmaster who was a dogged philosopher and a minor writer. The boy easily got through school; he read Pushkin and Dostoevsky, but the soccer and the swimming went on, the lonely wanderings in the countryside and the low communal quarters, and presently the easy sexual encounters with the girls from a steel-tubing factory. He saw himself as the impassive Cossack Don Juan to whom girls flocked. There is an old snapshot that shows Solzhenitsyn as a young man in blue bathing trunks on a rock by a river; the strong male grace of his posture, the proportion of his torso and limbs, sharp as if from marble, make a figure that looks somewhat Apollonian. He was the handsomest and strongest of his circle, and he perhaps unconsciously transferred his superior physical endowments into the plasticity that marks his art. One theory frequently circulated is that Solzhenitsyn's handsomeness early relieved him of useless doubts about himself—that, as in the case of Raphael, his masculine good looks afforded him assurance, accompanied as they were by the talent that gave him authority.

At university in Rostov his interests centered on literature and he was soon working with poor theatrical and literary groups; and, with his chosen friends, was for a time involved in Communist politics. For any boy with ambition it was natural to be a left-winger and to join the Komsomol, particularly as Party head-hunters were anxious to recruit the academically gifted. Solzhenitsyn would avenge his father's losses by joining his father's persecutors. Only through collaboration could his family's standing be restored. But, as Michael Scammell has written, membership in the Komsomol was "no empty formality" for Solzhenitsyn. He read and argued about Marxist doctrines, and felt that something, indeed, had to be done for the peasants and workers who were the victims of capitalism. He deplored the ruthless "Roman-style" of capitalism that exploited anything and everything, in favor of the Greek sense of limits and "nothing too much." Capitalism was mindless and barbarous, but the barbarity was of nature and could be "called primitive and innocent."[3] The deep sense of indifference in him responded to the indifference of the dialectic:

> You know, by the end of my school years a Soviet education had won me over, and so I joined the Komsomol. . . . I read an enormous amount . . . and got completely carried away. I was absolutely sincerely enthralled by it over a period of several years.[4]

Solzhenitsyn's statements always tend to be extravagant, as if too full of imagination or of truth. What he learned and felt as a student, living among peasants and poor workers, was the totality of poverty, and ugly, barren poverty was his first picture of some men's helpless fate. His recollection of it, added to the misery he knew in his early adult years (when he sometimes burned his old notebooks to keep warm) produced his pathetic and brief fellow-travelling period.

His senses were not stirred by communism alone. Solzhenitsyn responded to the harsh mountain landscape of Rostov, the stony plateau, and the steppe that was "another sea"; to the clear sunlight, the brassy summer heat, and the seductive silence of the evenings. There was nothing Wordsworthian in this. Each stone or tree was an object: his visual sense of landscape is intense in all his writings. Mortality was a presence as unanswerable as rock. His writing would sometimes lead him to lapse into rhetoric and sentimentality, but his best manner is plain, detached, lonely, and laconic: abruptly lyrical and briefly tormented. What are those torments? Not of conscience or poverty alone. His mother died while he was a student. Loneliness never left him; it is at the heart of the almost too vivid sense he conveys of the instants of hope.

Just before the outbreak of Hitler's war, Solzhenitsyn at twenty-one met the girl he was to marry. She was Natalia Reshetovskaya, the well-to-do daughter from that "educated stratum that formed the backbone of the bureaucratic and service class of Cossackdom before the Revolution."[5] An obsessed student, Solzhenitsyn set the time for their meetings at 10 P.M.—the hour the library closed. Still Natalia fell in love with him. They married on April 27, 1940.[6]

She saw at once that he had to have peace of mind for his thoughts and work and that she must behave with total self-abnegation, even at the cost of her own feelings; yet if she might appear to him as one of his future "meek" characters, she was far from that. It was soon evident to her that the immediate enemies of her husband were the leech-like Komsomol members and especially their arrogant leader. They saw Natalia as a frivolous intruder who would take Solzhenitsyn from their debates, which at this time were centered around the person of Peter the Great. (One thinks of the particular delight with which Stalin read the biographies of Peter, his favorite historical hero.)

Solzhenitsyn, in good Pushkinian tradition, had a feeling of love-hate for Peter the Great, and his feelings prompted him to plan a historical novel based on the tyrant. His notions about Peter were much the same as Tolstoy's feelings about Napoleon.[7] The idea of his novel would be to cut the superman down to size, to reveal him as cruel, vindictive, petty and, as far as his country's subsequent history was concerned, morally disastrous. The Slavophil, "Muscovite" side of Solzhenitsyn's character could happily slay Peter for wishing to make Russia a European nation while, at the same time—lofty intellectual manqué as Solzhenitsyn was at twenty-one—attacking Peter for his fundamentally Slavic barbarism, his unshakable tyranny, his having established a form of autocratic government that inflicted centuries' worth of suffering.

Solzhenitsyn's capacity to give himself to an intellectual enthusiasm, to master a subject, was in evidence throughout 1939–1940 as he accumulated vast notes on the subject of Peter. All secrets of Russian life he saw in Peter. Pushkin the poet had glanced at them, the seemingly terrible mystery that the Russian people almost want to be governed by brutes. But Solzhenitsyn, the young writer of prose, could not yet get into it. It may be paradoxical to say so, but Solzhenitsyn had too much common sense to be able to understand it. The essence of Pushkin's "The Bronze Horseman" is that the Russians are a slave race. Those without privilege had no choice but to submit. The secret of Russian life was therefore in a strange way quite alien to Solzhenitsyn, who could submit to little; and since he was only ever capable of writing about issues which directly affected himself, it is not surprising that the Peter the Great novel obstinately refused to come. It was a desperate position, which yielded only a slight, youthful poem:

> It's obvious—PROGRESS! But I'm a heretic:
> By what right was our country spurred into line?
> Let's make a note, I'll call it the Swedish thesis:
> "Was the cost of Poltava truly justified?"
> Two hundred years of conquest, conquest, conquest,
> Destruction and strife, wars with their endless ruin—
> Yet the Swedes we crushed on the Vorskla
> Have grown as fat as capons.[8]

When war broke out with Nazi Germany Solzhenitsyn was a fervent patriot, and fully on the side of his country against the threat of the invading Nazi armies. So long as it was possible for him to regard Mother Russia as threatened, it was easy for him to forget the plight of kulaks, dissidents, Jews, and other such blots on the Russian landscape. Like many other young men before and since, who went off to war expecting to see quick action, Solzhenitsyn did little in the line for the first months of the war. He wrote poetry. He toyed with a novel. He read voraciously: Sholokov, Melville, Gogol. He lolled about. He observed. In his lassitude, he alternated between thinking he was coming down with consumption and making religious and political resolutions. Solzhenitsyn, like all true writers, carried his life about with him, created the very cocoon of observant detachment, indolence, and sensuality in which a creative mind flourishes.

After a day of silent scribbling, the young Solzhenitsyn would emerge from his hut to eat with the Cossacks of his regiment, the 74th Horse-drawn Transport Battalion of the Stalingrad Army Command, based on the river Buzuluk 150 miles northwest of Stalingrad. Some of the group were fascinated by the subtle manner in which Solzhenitsyn could exercise power over his companions. It was Solzhenitsyn who got veteran Cossacks to play silly games and teach him to ride. It was Solzhenitsyn who, amid general merriment and drunkenness, got his sergeant to balance on one leg on a tent peg. Moreover it was Solzhenitsyn who was in charge of giving prizes for these japes, and his comrades were always surprised that the educated lad noticed, precisely, the little tastes and predilections of his companions.[9]

The power of this young groom was not of the kind looked for in men to promote. It was in the areas of observation and subversion that it was apparent. At mess there was sometimes criticism of the war. It felt good humored. There were a lot of laughs. Solzhenitsyn was usually at the bottom of them. Yet he was not a leader. He seemed to be something of a joke. The Cossacks were as amused by their young companion's incompetence with horses, as by his manners; his surly silences were broken by passages of fluent and well-spoken dinner conversation of a kind which would have been more appropriate at a university dining hall than in a hut on the steppes. They were half amused and half troubled by his moral vulnerability. Sometimes he would disappear and they did not know where he was. They would find him sitting with local peasants, or chasing girls, or playing cards.

The progress of the war became uglier. After months of retreat, the siege of Stalingrad began in earnest. The new political commissar of his unit, a former classmate at Rostov, became sympathetic to Solzhenitsyn's pleas to see action, and allowed him to attend an artillery school. Solzhenitsyn did not impress his teachers but managed to cadge his way to lieutenant's stars, though he was still not to be a fighting soldier. He saw refugees from Stalingrad, managed to survive the appalling retreat, and lost for good the illusion of military glory. How much fighting he saw can only be conjectured, but whatever its extent, the war conveyed to him an abysmal vision of human nature for which the polished precision and cool confidence of verse (he continued to yearn to be a poet) were somehow beside the point.[10]

After the battle of Orel—where the Wehrmacht's defeat at Stalingrad was confirmed—Solzhenitsyn went on leave. His mother was dead. On return he was promoted to captain, and took part in pushing the Germans out of Russia and across Poland. But NKVD tribunals were at work "on the heels of the advancing Soviet army."[11]

On February 9, 1945, Solzhenitsyn himself was arrested. His letters home had been opened by the NKVD and read. Solzhenitsyn later described his experiences in the Lubyanka in *The First Circle*. He is dryly dismissive:

> When he had thought beforehand about being arrested he had had a mental picture of a pitiless duel of wits. He had been inwardly tensed up, prepared for some sort of lofty struggle to defend his ideas and his future. But he had never expected that it would all be so simple, so banal, and so inexorable. These people who dealt with him . . . men of lowly rank and intelligence, were indifferent to his individuality and to the reasons for his being there. On the other hand they were minutely attentive to details that he had never thought of before and in which he was unable to offer any resistance. But what possible meaning could resistance have and what would be the use? At every step, for a different reason, they demanded of him things that were the merest trifles in comparison with the great battle that lay ahead of him, and there was no point at all in kicking up a fuss about such matters. But taken all together, the methodical indifference of the procedure was such as utterly to break the prisoner's will.[12]

This was his welcome to the gulag. For making derogatory remarks about Stalin he was sentenced to eight years. He was freed in 1952.

Solzhenitsyn the writer emerged from the camps. Like the Pasternak of *Dr. Zhivago*, Solzhenitsyn now envisioned himself as acting in the powerful tradition of the nineteenth-century Russian novel as it appeared in the prophet-preacher writings of Tolstoy and Dostoevsky—now one, now the other. As a writer of polemic, he wanted to mimic the tradition of Belinsky and Herzen. Unlike his literacy heroes, he was removed from the influences Western geniuses—Shakespeare, Cervantes, Sterne, Dickens, and Zola—had upon his predecessors. Solzhenitsyn's indoctrination as a young Komsomol, with that group's reliance on politics and science, remained his key influence. It is true that he had once wanted to be a poet and had read the poets of the revolutionary period, but the tendencies of his youth continued to draw him to the documentary and his unrest with Soviet society to a documentary which would defy the Stalinist political monopoly of that mainly "useful" form of writing. Because Solzhenitsyn was and is a passionate man, equipped with searing powers of irony, he was certain to find that man does not live by the record alone, but by the myths he creates, myths which contain his private thoughts and that sense of being elsewhere when dogma becomes despotic. From Tolstoy and Dostoevsky, and as a man of imagination, he learned to hate contemporary materialism. There is a passage in the last of the Gulag volumes which makes the point:

> We don't mind having a fellow countryman called Lev Tolstoy. It's a good trade-mark. (Even makes a good postage stamp.) Foreigners can be taken on trips to Yasnaya Polyana. . . . But my dear countrymen, if someone takes Tolstoy seriously, if a real-life Tolstoyan springs up among us—hey, look out there! Mind you don't fall under our caterpillar tracks.[13]

Not exactly the style of Tolstoy; it is closer to the crowd style of Dostoevsky.

With *Cancer Ward,* he became a novelist. Here documentary and the novel merge. The autobiographical element is strong but the symbols grow larger than the personal report of the author's own story. *Cancer Ward* is close to his own history. A twenty-six-year-old Captain of Artillery in East Prussia, with a university degree in mathematics and physics, is sentenced to eight years of forced labor. In exile in Kazakhstan where, in his time, Dostoevsky had also been seen—the Captain (like Solzhenitsyn before him) is treated for a tumor and recovers. In this picaresque novel—the sick are the picaros of contemporary life—we get a day-by-day account of the life of an overcrowded cancer hospital, an exhaustive analysis of how cancer distorts the life stories of the patients and the doctors, and this is a way of describing what Russian life is really like to the outside world. The hospital is like a prison; it isolates. Every man and woman has his tale on his tongue; having cancer is a way of life. The people are all far from home, owing to the war or exile, and one sees the part played by distance, anarchy, and chance.

The hospital is really an obscene collective. Illness and overwork destroy private relationships; the irony is that the unanswerable punishments of Nature free one from the malice of the secret police and one has a brief liberty before one dies. Comedy is black: a devoted philologist, for example, is stricken with cancer of the larynx! No more languages for him. If you are a Party man, like the careerist Rusanov, you are astonished that your power has gone. At night, Rusanov's bed lies between the beds of two men condemned to exile:

If Paval Nikolayevich were the same man he had been before he entered hospital, he would have gone and raised the question as a matter of principle—how could they put executive officials among dubious, socially harmful elements? But in the five weeks that the tumour had pulled him about as if he were a fish on a hook, Pavel Nikolayevich had either mellowed or become a simpler man.[14]

Rusanov is quietly drawn as a *Iudushka* or hypocrite; a tedious, self-complacent, and exacting apparatchik: he thinks he has the right to be the first to read the Party newspaper when it is brought into the ward; he is a glutton for the droning dullness in all the articles about economics and politics. Time spent pondering his disease is time stolen from the affairs of ideology. At first illness terrifies him, but as he recovers, his arrogance returns. Still, he has been a little mellowed until a fresh fear arises from reports that a new Presidium has been formed and that an investigation of Stalinism's "delinquencies" will take place. Fear invests Rusanov, for he knows that all Party rewards are obtained by servility and climbing: seeing rivals done in, pushed away, jailed—the sly waiting game of arranged demotions and promotions. His terror is soothed by his awful, go-getting daughter—a sort of Soviet yuppie—who has written a few poems and has recently intrigued her way into the Union of Soviet Writers. She tells her father not to fret; safety is only a question of knowing what strings to pull and she has learned all the necessary tricks. Rusanov need not worry about that shameful plot by which he arranged to have someone sent to the gulag in order to confiscate the man's apartment.

The cancer ward is, of course, a symbol of Russia diseased by Stalinism. The patients talk of their lives and beliefs, and above all of the conflict between those who believe in power and those who mutinously think of private happiness. Most accept the Communist society; it is daily life. Experience, however, has shown what has been lost: the moral ideal of socialism. Its loss is like the loss in modern fiction of the American dream.

The ward is a sort of confessional. The old care for nothing but their treatments; the young care only for their animal lusts. A young man who has lost his leg and who has been "thinking pleasant thoughts—how he'd learn, briskly and smartly, to walk on crutches"[15]—has a fleeting, clumsy erotic encounter with a girl waiting to lose her breast.

Such bleakness is broken—ever so briefly—by two incipient love affairs, with a nurse and a woman doctor, both of whom have practically invited the recovering captain to live with them. But although the emergence from the hospital, the renewal of the movements of life—he is fascinated as he watches the action in a zoo and comes to feel the pulsing life of the animals—intoxicates the ex-patient, he fails to visit either woman. Senses and ambitions dulled, he writes to one of them a bland, friendly note. At the last, stretching out on a luggage rack, a dufflebag for a pillow, he takes a train to the little Siberian village to which he has been exiled "in perpetuity" and in which he will make for himself a quiet, fairly comfortable life.

So far the limits of the novel are quite familiar; but at the mid-point Solzhenitsyn breaks new ground. He gives a portrait of a happy family, the simple, ingenuous Kadims who, expecting nothing from the harsh life of exile, had found an absurd happiness with their dogs and cats: it recalls the idyllic pages of Ivan Goncharov's classic novel *Oblomov*. Solzhenitsyn is opening a window on a subject that has hitherto been obsessive and claustrophic.

As *Cancer Ward* is more or less Solzhenitsyn's earliest polished fiction, it is interesting to find from the beginning an instance of the apparent separation of what has been called Solzhenitsyn's right and left hands. At first sight, it is easy to think that the Solzhenitsyn who simply loves life in all its manifestations and details is at war with Solzhenitsyn the "moralist." We often think of Solzhenitsyn as someone who spoiled his art by trying to develop as a prophet or thinker. But in *Cancer Ward* there is no such division. It is because he can so cram his short novel with detail of every human and natural kind which leads almost naturally to his moralizing. Cancer, death, is no abstract thing. In *Cancer Ward* we see a group of actual people with lives and personalities who are completely real to us. To know, to know deeply and closely, is to sympathize. And at the same time there is a callous Homeric eye in Solzhenitsyn which can see the behavior of the doctors and patients and recognize their terrors as an emanation of nature, of life. The conclusion of the novel depends for its beautiful effect on such a suspension of moral feeling so that, while sympathizing, we do not judge. Thus *Cancer Ward* reflects a strong dawning in Solzhenitsyn, which confinement of any sort was always to effect in him, of the need for common humanity. In *Cancer Ward* Solzhenitsyn has projected a frightening and sterile universe, and the line-by-line events of the story are powerful and blasting. The truth is that in place of the community of equal comrades that was the original socialist dream of the nineteenth century, the socialist state has yielded for any thinking citizen a nightmare of absolute solitude.

17

→≫ ≪←

Solzhenitsyn
Poet of the Gulag

A second story of building socialism through imprisonment brings to a close this "clinical" period of Solzhenitsyn's writing, and it is even more terrifying.

In the novel *The First Circle* the idea is taken from Dante. The first circle of hell in Dante's *Divine Comedy* is the fate reserved for the pre-Christian philosophers, who are doomed to remain there for eternity. For Solzhenitsyn, this circle is represented by the Mavrino Institute for scientific research on the outskirts of Moscow. The year is 1949, when Stalin is becoming feeble but ever more ruthless. Action in the novel is confined to three days; it seems an eternity. The Institute is staffed by scientists, engineers, and academicians who have been taken out of the forced labor camps to do technical work under conditions only slightly less hideous than the brutal conditions of the gulag, for though they eat better, they are still cut off almost completely from their families.

The novel opens with a sample of the old human values of trust and concern that linger on in Russia. Volodin, a scientist, incurs official wrath for warning a colleague that he is in danger for having promised to give some medicine to a fellow professor in Paris. For this act of professional courtesy the man is condemned to the Lubyanka. The scientist's realization that he is doomed, his confinement in a cell, where he is watched day and night through a peephole, his being stripped, searched, and otherwise humiliated, provides one of the most hideous scenes in all literature.

It is a shared degradation. Like Volodin, most of the prisoners of the Mavrino have been there for a decade or more; at the end of their sentence, their terms will almost certainly be extended. They know they are condemned for eternity. With them, under the efficient police system, are a number of workers from outside who go home at night and who act, together with some of the prisoners themselves, as informers. Eternal damnation could not be more certain. If their usefulness comes to an end, the prisoners will be returned to the savage camps and die at last in the prison hospital. It is like the system applied by the Nazis to foreign workers during the war: feed them little, exhaust their muscles and brains, then let them die.

Damnation, however, is a perverse kind of freedom, just as having cancer is. The prisoners of Mavrino have adapted themselves to their fate. Among them is the brilliantly drawn Rubin, a Jew and Party member, a philologist who was an organizer of sabotage in Germany during the war: then there are Nerzhin, a mathematician who has been a soldier; Pryanchikov, an engineer; Spiridon, a peasant and glass blower who has been taken on by mistake; Doronin, a young double agent; and Sologdin, a designer, a recalcitrant in for a twenty-five-year stretch. Their task is sinister: to design a device for codifying speech patterns and tracing telephone calls—a machine that Stalin has specially asked for. It will lead to a huge increase in arrests and the novel indeed opens with that scene in which Innokenty Volodin foolishly uses the telephone to warn a friend not to give certain medicine to a foreign professor. By the end of the novel the completed apparatus traps him. It is typical of Solzhenitsyn that women play only a small part in the book. They are lost, touching, lonely figures and in only two or three chapters do they play any part. Indeed, one characteristically Victorian aspect of the book is its scant interest in the perverting of sexual life in prison. Love is sorrow and sex is "outside" and regarded as rather disgraceful. The idea owes something to Russian puritanism.

Within Solzhenitsyn's scheme, we see the curious nervous eagerness of life in prison, listen to the life stories, watch the effect of prison on character—on the guards and officials in charge, too. The prisoners are known as *zeks*:

> One of those age old prison arguments was in progress. When is it best to be imprisoned? The way the question was put presupposed that no one was ever destined to avoid prison. Prisoners were inclined to exaggerate the number of other prisoners. When, in fact, there were only 12 to 15 million human beings in captivity, the zeks believed there were 20 or even 30 million. They believed that hardly any males were still free. "When is it best to be imprisoned?" simply meant was it better in one's youth or in one's declining years. Some zeks, usually the young ones, cheerfully insisted that it was better to be imprisoned in one's youth. Then one had a chance to learn what it meant to live, what really mattered and what was crap; then at the age of 35, having knocked off a ten

year term, a man could build his life on intelligent foundations. A man who'd been imprisoned in old age could only suffer because he hadn't "lived right", because his life had been a chain of mistakes, and because those mistakes could no longer be corrected. Others—usually these older men—would maintain no less optimistically that being imprisoned in old age is, on the contrary, like going on a modest pension into a monastery; one had already drawn everything from life in one's best years. . . . (In a prisoner's vocabulary "Everything" narrowed down to the possession of a female body, good clothes, good food and alcohol.) They went on to prove that in camp you couldn't take much hide off an old man, whereas you could wear down and cripple a young man, so that afterwards he "wouldn't even want to get a woman".[1]

Rubin, the logical Jewish communist, accepts prison, because "the ways of Socialist truth are sometimes tortuous." He has a violent row with Sologdin, the unrepentant designer, that goes to the heart of the novel. The row is about ends and means. An excellent distinction is made: Rubin's situation "seemed to him tragic in the Aristotelian sense." He had been

> dealt a blow by the hands of those he loved the most [the Party]. He had been imprisoned by unfeeling bureaucrats because he loved the common cause to an improper degree. As a result of that tragic contradiction, in order to defend his dignity and that of his comrades, Rubin found himself compelled to stand up daily against the prison officers and guards whose actions, according to his view of the world, were determined by a totally true, correct and progressive law.[2]

Other zeks persecute him. Quarrels wreck the health of this clever, emotional man. Sologdin is the worst persecutor:

> Sologdin knew very well that Rubin was not an informer and would never be one. But at the moment the temptation was great to lump him with the security officers. . . .[3]

Sologdin says:

> Since all of us have been imprisoned justly and you're the only exception, that means our jailers are in the right. Every year you write a petition asking for a pardon . . .
> "You lie! Not asking for a pardon, but for a review of my case."
> "What's the difference?"
> "A very big difference indeed."[4]

As a Party member, though in disgrace, Rubin makes his Jesuitical point.

"They turn you down and you keep on begging,"[5] Sologdin retorts. And, Sologdin says, *he* would never demean himself by begging. (And in fact, he doesn't: Sologdin is a student of human weakness. He shrewdly waits till he has a brilliant idea about the encoding device and boldly plays one prison official off against another in a feat of blackmail which is the only thing officials are frightened of.)

Now Solzhenitsyn's mastery as a novelist appears: he sees the consoling contradictions of human nature and how they fertilize character. Rubin is not only the subtle and passionate Jewish Marxist and "sea-lawyer": he is also the born Jewish comedian: he entertains the prisoners with a farcical historical parody of their own trials, filled with faked evidence from poetry, prison slang, and innuendos. And there is even more to this richly sympathetic man. His successes make him miserable and he becomes the practical Jewish mystic who is working on a plan for ritualizing communist life by introducing Civic Temples!

The novel is not a sprawling, flat panorama, in spite of its range of scenes inside and outside prison. It has a serene command of space and time. Close to the vernacular, spiced with slang and proverbs, Solzhenitsyn's style in two respects resembles the plain style of Swift and Orwell: it sways between savage, educated irony and the speech of the people. A passionate and agonized book such as Dostoevsky's *The House of the Dead* owes much to the Romantic belief in the supreme value of suffering which is often said to be fundamental among Slavs. Prison has the monastic lure. Many of Solzhenitsyn's characters are haunted by the acceptance of suffering, but there is nothing mystical or romantic in him. He is quite clear that the Mavrino is not the Château d'If or Gorky's Siberia, that something has gone morally wrong and that courage in a changed attitude to the self is the important thing.

He also delights in exposing official prose and its deceits. There are two passages in *First Circle* which comment on the "popular" or newspaper style used by the poets when they addressed "the People."

> Mayakovsky, for instance, considered it an honour to use a newspaper clipping as an epigraph for a poem. In other words he considered it an honour not to rise above the newspapers. But then why have literature at all?

For a good reason

> a great writer—forgive me, perhaps I shouldn't say this, I'll lower my voice—a great writer is so to speak a second government, that's why no regime anywhere has ever loved its great writers only its minor ones.[6]

The strength of *First Circle* lies in the ingenuity of its play-like architecture, in which the major characters make speeches and the minor characters act as a chorus. They are not a passive or moralizing chorus—they incite action. The Mavrino onlookers watch almost in silence. To them the imbroglio of the scientists is alien. If, as many critics have noticed, Tolstoy's influence on Solzhenitsyn is still marked, Solzhenitsyn has become more forgiving of his characters' indiscretions than, say, Tolstoy is of the wife in *The Kreutzer Sonata*. Pity, rather than condemnation, has become characteristic of the recently freed Solzhenitsyn. And these first two novels, written in the first blush of freedom in the 1950s, have a form his later work would come to lack; their economy drives their point home. By economy Solzhenitsyn enhances our understanding. He became the first Soviet writer to convey the feel and detail of the Stalinist system of terror, revealing especially that something is going on at the times even when nothing is going on: the distinctive ennui, which is the basic nutriment of social life in his works.

Solzhenitsyn's narrative slips back and forth in time and character, circulating like Sterne, like Proust even. Proust did this because he was enthralled by human inertia: Solzhenitsyn is out for every tremor of the ego: he is expert in making characters disappear and then reappear, swollen and with palms itching for more life. And the stories of each man build up the central idea. Our eye is on the most tragic character, Nerzhin, and his concern with what a man must do with his life. It is through his sorrow that we see that, bad as the lot of the prisoners is, the lot of their wives whom they can scarcely ever see or write to is a worse imprisonment—in the open. They dare not admit that their husbands are political prisoners; they will be shunned. Guilt by association is a disease: one is a carrier. Nerzhin is a genuine stoic—in contrast to the endangered diplomat Volodin who is a genuine epicurean. Both men know they are doomed. In his early days as a communist Nerzhin had noticed that educated or liberal prisoners always let him down in a crisis; he turned idealistically to the "people" in the labor camps and found they were worse:

> It turned out that the People had no homespun superiority. . . . They were no more firm of spirit as they faced the stone walls of a ten-year term. They were no more far-sighted than he during the difficult moments of transport and body searches. They were blinder and more trusting about informers. They were more prone to believe the crude deception of the bosses.[7]

With great tact Nerzhin nevertheless cultivates the simple peasant Spiridon who feels tragically the forced separation from his family, because in the family he saw the only meaning to life. He can never argue or think much but hits the nail on the head, peasant-fashion, with a proverb. His reply to the question, "How can anyone on earth really tell who is right and who is wrong? Who can be sure?" is devastating: "The wolfhound is right and the cannibal is wrong."[8] (Solzhenitsyn has read Hemingway and this scene reminds one of the only good thing in *For Whom the Bell Tolls*—the long talk with the Spanish peasant at the bridge in the Guadarrama.) Spiridon's view of life (Nerzhin sees) has an important and rare characteristic: it is his own. Nerzhin reflects:

> What was lacking in most of them [the People] was that personal point of view which becomes more precious than life itself.
> There was only one thing left for Nerzhin to do—to be himself . . . the People is not everyone who speaks our language, nor yet the elect marked by the fiery stamp of genius. Not by birth, not by the work of one's hands, not by the wings of education, is one elected into the people.
> But by one's inner self.
> Everyone forgets his inner self year after year. One must try to temper, to cut, to polish one's soul so as to become a human being.
> And thereby become a tiny particle of one's people.[9]

Nerzhin's integrity detaches him from the others; on matters of regulation and principle he risks everything with the officials and guards and insists on straight or cold ironic confrontations. They fear his irony. Naturally—and he knows it—he will be sent back to the labor camp. He has understood the awful words "for ever" as few of the others have; the words mean "You have exhausted your power to hurt me."

The secret of the early Solzhenitsyn's success is that he talks people into life and never stops pouring them in and out of his scenes. The beginning to the novel, however, does contain one great weakness in his method: the novelist has, with a journalistic daring, introduced a live portrait of the aging Stalin. I simply do not believe in the following words:

> But reviewing in his mind the not-so-complex history of the world, Stalin knew that with time people would forgive everything bad, even forget it, even remember it as something good. Entire peoples were like Lady Anne, the widow in Shakespeare's *Richard III*. Their wrath was short-lived, their will not steadfast, their memory weak—they would always be glad to surrender themselves to the victor.[10]

Freedom—of a sort—came in 1952. Solzhenitsyn was released from labor camp and allowed to settle as an internal exile in Kazakhstan. His first night of liberty was unforgettable:

> A night under the open sky! We had forgotten what it was like. There had always been locks and bars, always walls and ceilings. I had no thought of sleep. I walked and walked and walked. . . . I felt that if only I had a voice . . . I . . . would start baying at the moon: I shall be able to breathe here! I shall be able to move around.[11]

As Solzhenitsyn wrote in *Cancer Ward* of the patient Oleg Kostoglotov, "On that night he believed and hoped again, no matter how many times he had vowed never to do either."[12] Stalin's death in March seemed an omen of confirmation.

Solzhenitsyn's life, however, was only marginally less harsh. All he knows about agriculture, Solzhenitsyn says, is that the earth is black. Poverty depresses him, but he forgets it as he puzzles over the way to sow wheat and clover. The snow gives way to the mud of the thaw, the starlings return, the nightingales sing, the frogs are croaking. Soon family and a predatory crowd of visitors arrive, and just as he had in the camps, he is eventually obliged to leave his house and write in a one-room hut he has rigged up.

Solzhenitsyn complains that work in this period sometimes stopped him from writing. What he meant was that he was not finding it easy to finish what he wrote. Poetry is abandoned. He turns to autobiography, one in which the labor camp in his past becomes Russia itself. He was only seven months writing it.

Solzhenitsyn's reputation was made by his stark reporting of the horror and degradation of the labor camps in *One Day in the Life of Ivan Denisovich*. The title phrase "one day" is not only a clue to its immediacy, but far more to the tradition that the Russian novelists do not move by plot-time—which is an artifice—but by the felt hours of the day that run into each other. In its simplicity this story is the finest and most apprehensive thing he has written, for the prophet-preacher does not obtrude upon the simple character whose humble tale is being told.

Structurally and in content, the story is simple. But what Shukhov sees, the accidental detail of his experience, is impressive. Here he grows. He really has got a mind and it is hurt. It is a tribute to Solzhenitsyn's reserves of talent that the novel survives and over-grows its own weaknesses. Shukhov's sense of victimization is valuable. His despair is put to excellent use. If the theme is sometimes lost, we have his unforgettable scenes of the labor camp. Solzhenitsyn has something like genius for place. There is not a descriptive insinuator of what prison camp is like from minute to minute who comes anywhere near him— and that includes Pasternak and Dostoevsky. Some novelists stage it, others document it; he is breathing in it. He knows how to show us not only Ivan husbanding his mortar on the building site, but other people, too, moving from hut to hut, from bunk to bunk in their own circle of uncomprehending solitude. Grasping this essential of life in the isolated camp, he sees the place not as a confronted whole, but askance. His senses are alive to things and he catches the sensation that the things have created the people or permeated them. This was the achievement of *Cancer Ward* and it is repeated in *One Day in the Life of Ivan Denisovich*. A wanderer, he succeeds with minor characters, the many small figures in the crowded camp who suggest millions more of the imprisoned. The dialogue of a communist apparatchik, a camp guard, a low lawyer, a Jewish scholar, people brash, shady, or saddened by the need of survival and whose ripeness comes out of the dirty brick that has trapped them, is revealing and wonderful. Solzhenitsyn's talk carries the speaker's life along with it. Their talk makes them move. They involve Shukhov with themselves and show him living, as all human beings do, in a web spun by others as well as by himself.

That habit of seeing things askance or out of the corner of his eye gave Solzhenitsyn (in the early novels) an even more important quality: it kept alive a personal sense of comedy and thus fed his originality. It has all the fatality of Jewish comedy, that special comedy of human undress and nakedness of which the Jewish writers are the world's masters. Solzhenitsyn follows in this tradition by his ability to convey anguish. How to deal with his paranoia—if that is what it is—how to make it contribute not only to the character of Ivan but also to the purpose of the book? He seems to speak to both the living and the dead. It is the habit of the mad but Shukhov is not mad; he is at once comically and seriously disturbed by every kind of question. And since he is a man of some intellect these questions are often interesting in themselves; but chiefly they convey the dejected larking of a mind that is being tried by two contradictory forces: the breakdown of the public world in which he lives and the mess of private life. In which world does he live? He is absurd in some ways yet he is fine; he is somewhat vain yet he is raw. He is a great man yet he is torpedoed by minor mistakes. As a character Ivan is physically exact—we know his domestic habits—but mentally and emotionally amorphous. Any objection to this is overridden by his range as an observer-victim. It is a triumph that he is not a bore and does not ask our sympathy.

The guards are the necessary enemies. They are a loud, smart, nasty smell; each understands the first lesson of gangsterdom: to humiliate your victim. By their presence we are prepared for squalor, rancor, drunken fighting, the rabid greed of poverty. Yet there is nothing Zola-like in Solzhenitsyn's descriptions of the vile: they are not rhetorically vile, for Solzhenitsyn absents himself and becomes them and lets them speak in their own voices as they live out their passions. We expect a story such as *One Day in the Life of Ivan Denisovich* to be a study done in stark black and white; in fact it subtly evokes the inconsequent yet decisive and sudden passions of its people. The guards could afford to eat and simply glutted themselves. The prisoners took their chances, stole or crowded round the camp tables and begged. And powerful as such scenes are, they are all the more powerful for being part of a drama which is heard in the day-to-day voices of the prisoners as they work in their camp and yet also talk out of their inherited imaginations. How exactly Solzhenitsyn has caught the brigade leader's nature when he quotes the naiveté of the face of this snake-like and ruthless man: the naivieté of uncontrollable appetite incited by the pursuit of money.

In this, his most fully realized novel, Solzhenitsyn goes to the inborn nature of his people, not to their merely observable idiosyncrasies. Who would have suspected that poverty would have given Shukhov, the simple peasant, an inborn will? What Solzhenitsyn saw in the prisoner's isolation was something positive and precious: the private silence in which we live, and which enables us to endure our solitude. We live, as his characters do, beyond any tale we happen to enact. So in the saddest of Solzhenitsyn's stories, we are conscious of the simple persistence of a person's power to live out his life.

One Day in the Life of Ivan Denisovich was a sensation when it was first published in the USSR in 1962. Solzhenitsyn's mastery was recognized by all. The censor cut out only a page at the end. A clever preface by Alexander Tvardovsky linked the novel to Khrushchev's de-Stalinization campaign:

> The subject matter of Alexander Solzhenitsyn's tale is unusual in Soviet literature. It echoes the unhealthy phenomena in our life associated with the period of the personality cult, now exposed and rejected by the Party . . . whatever the past was like, we in the present must not be indifferent to it. Only by going into its consequences fully, courageously, and truthfully can we guarantee a complete and irrevocable break with all those things that cast a shadow over the past.[13]

And Khrushchev agreed, seeing in the book a means to attack his opponents in the Presidium. (So "chummy" did Khrushchev seek to be with Solzhenitsyn that "as late as 1966 he sent me New Year's greet-ings—which astonished me because I was on the brink of arrest. Per-haps [in his disgrace] he didn't know?"[14]

With the overthrow of Khrushchev in 1964, Leonid Brezhnev lost no time in pushing through a program of orthodoxy, a purge of books that might threaten the "reputation of the Party." Solzhenitsyn's works, naturally, fell foul of the censor. For example, on September 12, 1965, the police burst in upon the offices of *Novy Mir* (Solzhenitsyn's first publishers) and tried to seize all the copies of *One Day in the Life of Ivan Denisovich*. But the book was already in wide circulation, and copies soon found their way into secret hideouts and small printing presses.

By driving Solzhenitsyn underground, the Soviet authorities lent weight to his political reflections. As yet, though his name was famous at home, *Cancer Ward, The First Circle,* and *One Day in the Life of Ivan Denisovich* were barely known in the West. Because of his banning Solzhenitsyn burst upon the world. What struck Solzhenitsyn's thou-sands of new foreign readers were first the lucid urgency and sincerity of his prose, and secondly the indictment which they constituted of his barbarous country. (The pattern was one that has continued in Russia since the nineteenth century, but the authorities never seem to learn anything, as a roll call of dissident names from Herzen to Scharanski would testify.)

Solzhenitsyn openly encouraged discussion and publication of abuses in the system. But a group of people who did not share Solzhenitsyn's sense of gratitude was the Committee on State Security, the KGB. Solzhenitsyn was by 1967 not merely taking risks. He was going much further than that. He was using his position as a famous and interna-tionally regarded writer to challenge the Communist party; to challenge its claim to a "leading role" in Soviet life. "In my opinion," he later wrote in *The Oak and the Calf,*

> it's the most Russian thing imaginable to take a swing and—wham! For one brief moment you feel yourself worthy to be a son of your country. Brave? I'm not brave. There's no one more timid. . . . I know something about the camps as they now are, but I don't say anything. What Lydia Chukovskaya once said about political protests was right: "If I don't do it, I can't write about the things that matter. Until I pull this arrow out of my breast, I can think of nothing else."[15]

Solzhenitsyn was preparing himself to be a Christ-like figure. And a small group of like-minded writers and dissidents who now identified with the simple and incontrovertible logic of his position emerged.

Solzhenitsyn's immediate supporters became convinced in the course of 1968 that the scene of "Christ before Pilate" could not be far from re-enactment. Friends went to England and Italy, carrying with them the bulk of Solzhenitsyn's private papers and manuscripts, to keep them from the hands of the KGB. But what could they do to Solzhenitsyn? They could send him into exile, where they could be certain that he would be tireless in his attacks upon the wrongdoings suffered by the Russian people. They could lock him up, as they were beginning to lock up his friends. But locking up political dissidents can so often rebound upon the powers that do it . . .

The cunning and haunting truth of the scene of Christ before Pilate is that power, in the end, shifts to the side of the silent, dispossessed figure of Christ, rather than remaining with Pilate. And this was the problem which Solzhenitsyn calculatedly and brilliantly arranged for the Kremlin. Certainly the story went the rounds in Moscow that Solzhenitsyn should be banished to Siberia, and Solzhenitsyn's friends in the writers' colony at Peredelkino (where he was squatting) believed the rumor when it reached their ears. Wiser counsels prevailed in Moscow, evidently. It was said that Brezhnev himself squashed the proposal on the ground that imprisonment would make a global martyr out of Solzhenitsyn.[16] This was partly because Brezhnev's autocracy never came close to Stalin's thoroughgoing murderous brutality—or, same thing—political efficiency; partly because Solzhenitsyn had out-maneuvered the Party. By the time his next controversial book had reached the censors, it was already circulating in *samizdat* copies and was being published in translation in Italy, England, and the United States. The book was called *August 1914.*

Solzhenitsyn was now obsessed by the Soviet claims that the October Revolution had been inevitable, and looked to dispute that case by returning to the outbreak of war in 1914. The subject of *August 1914* is the invasion of East Prussia and the military disaster of Tannenberg. It is a perfect Tolstoyan subject. It contains all the ironies: a general staff corrupted by court favoritism and more concerned with seniority than battle; a muddled and ill-prepared campaign; yet a defeat which nevertheless did draw off so many German troops from the West that it enabled the French to save Paris at the Marne. There were two rival and out-of-date plans of campaign; drive into East Prussia with overwhelming manpower, cut off the East Prussian salient at the shoulder and encircle it: or force the way through to Berlin. If we check Solzhenitsyn's account with those of military historians, we find that he is completely accurate. The actions of General Samsonov, the commander of the second Russian army that was destroyed, are set out correctly; the fact that the sad general was the victim of rival generals and criminally ill-equipped and cut off from information, is set out in the history books, down to such details as the lack of wire for his field telephones and the neglect of signal codes, so that he had to send out all messages *en clair*.

The other figures in the high command—Danilov, the master strategist, the Grand Duke Nicolas, Zhilinsky who cheated, the obsequious Yanushekevich who buried his incompetence in paperwork—are drawn to the life and, at the end of the book, there is a searching account of their behavior at the conference table when the white-washing of their responsibilities is completed. Solzhenitsyn has examined the records, but his account of the confusion of the campaign is garbled: Tolstoy was a master of confusion in the field. He made the disposition of forces clear: one follows him without a map. To follow Solzhenitsyn without a map is difficult. Still, in Vorotyntsev, the staff officer and fictional character who carries the moral burden of the narrative, we have the well-drawn portrait of both a feeling man and an intelligent professional soldier who can not only guide his remnant out of the mess, but who can guide us too.

There are two exceptional moments in the narrative. We see General Samsonov in all his moods but when the debacle comes, he splits: half of him thinks he has an army still, the other wanders about with an innocent, mad smile on his face, raising his cap politely to his soldiers who themselves don't know whether they are soldiers anymore. The other is a long episode describing the escape of Vorotyntsev and his remnant, through the encircling German advance. They will succeed. But we are to see this as ironic, for we know from history what their fate is to be. Here Solzhenitsyn reveals his purpose, for underlying the book is the criticism of the dogma that history can be rationally predicted or governed. History, says a teasing old professor to one of the ingenuous young students in the story, grows like a living tree.

18

→≫ ⟨⟨←

Solzhenitsyn Decides to
Change the World

The great task that Solzhenitsyn took upon himself during his last period in the USSR was to act as a catalyst for opponents of the socialist state to emerge from their passivity.

The dissident movement of which Solzhenitsyn became a leader dated from 1965, the year after Nikita Khrushchev's fall, and there was something approaching mass protest by 1966–1967, when the *samizdat* type of underground publication was at its peak. The repression began almost immediately, with the show trial of two leading dissenters, Andrei Sinyavski and Yuli Daniel, in February 1966. This ended any pretense of a continuation of Khrushchev's judicial reforms and general liberalization. The trials evoked sinister echoes of Stalin's rule, with fabricated charges of spying for Western intelligence agencies, and suggestions of torture and forced confessions.[1]

In this respect Soviet policy toward opponents of the socialist state was utterly consistent. From the outset of Lenin's rule dissent was treated as a mental disease, and dissenters liable to suffer "treatment" in special Soviet psychiatric hospitals. The first known case was in 1919, when Lenin had Maria Spiridonova, a leader of the Socialist–Revolutionary Tribunal, interned in a sanatorium. The large-scale, systematic use of psychiatric punishment began in the late 1930s, when the NKVD built a special four hundred-bed penal establishment in the grounds of the regular mental hospital in Kazan. By the late 1940s, the Serbsky Institute, the main Soviet center for teaching and research in criminal psychiatry, had a special department for political work. By the early 1950s, at least three establishments "treated" cases of political prisoners, since we know of one man, Ilya Yarkov, who suffered in all of them. Psychiatric punishment was given primarily to offenders under the catch-all Article 58 of the Soviet penal code, which dealt with anti-Soviet acts. Yarkov's fellow inmates included Christians, surviving

Trotskyists, opponents of the quack genetics of Lysenko, heterodox writers, painters, and musicians, Latvians, Poles, and other nationalities. The system, far from being abandoned, greatly expanded under Khrushchev, who was anxious to persuade the world that Soviet Russia no longer imprisoned political offenders, merely the mentally unbalanced, and was quoted by *Pravda* in 1959 as saying: "A crime is a deviation from the generally recognised standards of behaviour, frequently caused by mental disorder. . . . To those who might start calling for opposition to Communism . . . clearly the mental state of such people is not normal."[2] Subordination of the individual mind to the state was now absolute. Bukharin's Leviathan had reached his zenith.

Solzhenitsyn first became aware of the spread of psychiatric forms of punishment in the USSR with the publication of Valery Tarsis' *Ward* 7 in 1965, and thereafter made strenuous efforts to obtain documentation of specific cases and to raise the issue among Soviet intellectuals. But psychiatric punishment was used primarily against humble worker-protesters unlikely to attract wide attention. The very use of such practices inspired Solzhenitsyn to become opposed to any form of protest or activity against the regime that might incite violence. That sort of action could only lead to the replacement of one system of violence with another, one lot of violent tyrants with another lot.

Here Solzhenitsyn raises the very heart of the difficulty of opposing the Communist regime, and he was (and is) unable to answer it. He was unable, even, to face it sensibly, and began to revert more and more to an Orthodox conception of Russia, that Third Rome ordained by God. As Solzhenitsyn saw things, the Soviet Union presented him with two alternatives. The first was to become a sort of revolutionary, to break violence with violence. The alternative was to work with the government; to attempt, by means of compromise, to reach a reform program. Both courses were equally abhorrent to Solzhenitsyn.

So he forged the position of the refusenik. His confidence that in doing so he was recapturing the original intentions of Christ won many hearts. And a reaction from the Kremlin, which expelled him from the Writers' Union. The only precedents for such action in the postwar years had been the expulsions of Anna Akhmatova and Mikhail Zoschenko, in 1946, and of Pasternak in 1958, after the Italian publication of *Doctor Zhivago*. But Zoschenko and Akhmatova were well established, and Pasternak owned his dacha in Peredelkino: each could absorb the blow. Solzhenitsyn, however, would be stripped of legitimacy. Without his union card he would have no official place in society: like the poet Joseph Brodsky, he would be technically unemployed and thus a "parasite."

All benefits (a housing allowance, the "right" to live in Moscow or Leningrad) would be taken away. In acting against Solzhenitsyn, Brezhnev, egged on by his ideologist Mikhail Suslov, was sending out the word that "Solzhenitsynism" was an indictable offense.

As Brezhnev so well knew, the majority of the Russian people would never opt for a violent confrontation with the Communist party. But equally, there was a growing sense that something must be done, that things could not go on as they had under Stalin, that the Party bureaucracy was unfit to govern. Solzhenitsyn became the focus for all this discontent precisely because he was not of any party, precisely because his howl of rage against the authorities was so personal, and because he produced no serious program of alternative action. He was no good at saying what should be done, but very good at saying what was wrong. Everyone with eyes in their head could see it. Andropov, the KGB chief, could see it. The fact that the only action that the Party could take against him was to excommunicate him from the pet Writers' Union was, in the eyes of Solzhenitsyn, evidence of the system's decay.[3]

The edict of excommunication caused a sensation. On the day it was announced, the Kremlin forbade mention of Solzhenitsyn in the press. Solzhenitsyn was himself in Moscow that day. As he turned into Lubyanskaya Square, he saw a crowd of several hundred. Cheers broke out. Friends managed to hustle Solzhenitsyn into a taxi, but this demonstration of solidarity must have been pleasing to the newly denounced heretic. So, too, were the flood of letters, flowers, telegrams, and expressions of support which poured in as a result of the excommunication.

Observers of the Soviet literary scene could not fail to be struck by the contrast between the Party's treatment of Solzhenitsyn and that of dissidents in the reign of Stalin. There were, to be sure, plenty of figures in the bureaucracy who would have liked Solzhenitsyn muzzled and locked up. Perhaps an element of subtlety contributed to the fact that, unlike his supporters and disciples, he was never himself imprisoned or sent to a psychiatric hospital for his repeated lambasting of the socialist social order, his urging upon the populace of a "literature of doubt." And Solzhenitsyn was aware of the Kremlin's inhibitions and took advantage of them as best he could. He wrote. Indeed, he now struck at the heart of the communist canon—Vladimir I. Lenin.

Lenin in Zurich consists of a number of chapters which Solzhenitsyn cut out of his novel *August 1914* because they ran too far ahead of the time scale of the chronicle he had in mind. These chapters have a natural intensity and unity, and something of the scenario for a film. Without preparation, we are plunged into Lenin's mind as he stands with his wife and mother-in-law on an Austrian station platform, staring at the engine of the train—frightening image of impersonal power—which will carry them to Cracow on a journey back to St. Petersburg and the Finland Station. The 1914 war has taken the methodical logician by surprise. So deep in the mechanics of conspiracy is Lenin that he has not anticipated in anyway the onset of a stupendous act of history and is unprepared for its accidental element. Once more—as in the brief rebellion of 1905—the conspirator finds real life has outpaced the tactician. When the train gets to Cracow his situation has changed; he will have to make for neutral Switzerland. But at Cracow, where the first Polish wounded are arriving and the crowds of women are weeping over the stretchers, he has been revived by an exultation that will keep him going:

> Piss-poor, slobbering pseudo-socialists with the petit-bourgeois worm in them would try to capture the masses by jabbering away "for peace". They must be hit first and fast. Which of them has the vision to see and the strength of mind to embrace the great decision ahead: not to try and stop the war, but to step it up? To transfer it—*to your own country*.
> "Peace" is a slogan for fatheads and traitors! What is the point of a hollow peace that nobody needs, unless you can convert it immediately into civil war with no quarter given?[4]

In the next three years Solzhenitsyn puts us inside Lenin's mind, crushes us against it, entangles us with it, takes us into the pit of his rancors, the frustrations and the hatreds that sustain him, as he keeps the political machine in his mind oiled and free of rust, while he is forced to live in limbo.

The thing was to be ever immediate on shifting ground. The war was a gift in itself to the revolutionaries, but now—where would the revolution start? Russia was inaccessible. The one idea the war made plausible was the idea of permanent revolution, i.e., permanent civil war. Why could it not begin in neutral Switzerland? The idea came to nothing: the "swinish" Swiss socialists were pusillanimous. They were in love with one hundred years of petit-bourgeois neutrality; and were more interested—how could you believe it!—in defending their country? This failure made Lenin furious with himself; why hadn't he seen that Stockholm was the place to set the world revolution going? But failure rarely broadens perspective; Lenin went on with his café politicking, chess playing, and Marx reading. In the end, the Germans were plotting to use him to perform a fifth-column job against the Tsarists and he had the humiliation of hearing news of Russia from others not condemned to inactivity (writing pamphlets in the Zurich library), and—in 1917—he was once more taken by surprise and did not for a long time believe that the Revolution had begun in Russia.

Solzhenitsyn's chronicle depends on his plausible if hostile estimate of Lenin's introspections, as they torment his mind and become minutely argued decisions. Certainly the dialogue is close to the dreary language of the dialectic in which Lenin and his conspirators habitually babbled. It is a relief to come upon two scenes in which Lenin is brought to life by two rogues, the fantastic Parvus, the millionaire conspirator, and the brilliantly cynical Radek. This journalist is at his merriest when it comes to writing articles or letters of eager duplicity. The sight of such happy and inspired shamelessness is almost cheering. As for the fat Parvus who has made millions in the Ottoman Empire and delights in getting funds for revolutionaries out of capitalist financiers—he is a sort of stage magician. Parvus knows that money is power and simply loves playing with it in order to buy women, châteaux and, in a most disinterested way, leaders. Thus he has been invaluable to the Bolshevik conspirators. The Red millionaire had no faith, we are told, in the organizational talents of the Bolsheviks. He attacked Lenin's concessions to the peasants. Parvus ended by building himself an opulent house on the island of Schwanenberger in Germany and lived there to enjoy his orgies for the rest of his life.

Parvus' fate reads almost like a subconscious prophecy of Solzhenitsyn's coming exile in the decadent West. With *Lenin in Zurich* he exiled himself. The slights to Lenin meant that the book could in no way get by the censors. *Samizdat* copies were seen by thousands of readers. The Soviet Union in 1971 was not a nice place to live, but there have been worse places, such as the USSR in the 1930s. It is worth noting that the assault on Lenin was seen by a large portion of the literate populace. Compare this with the extreme fate of Osip Manelstam, a little more than thirty years before, who committed the capital crime of reading aloud to a disloyal friend his sixteen-line poem "The Kremlin Mountaineer" which denounced Stalin. By Stalin's standards, Brezhnev was a softy.

But he recognized that in his emerging portrait of Lenin Solzhenitsyn was composing an unforgettable assault on the Communist regime. Both abroad and in the Soviet Union the book (on its publication in the West) was as widely discussed as anything Solzhenitsyn had previously written. For every person who had read *The First Circle*, there were five who had read *Lenin in Zurich*; and the book makes it abundantly clear that the myth of the inevitability of the Bolsheviks' rise to power was a big lie. The medicine prescribed by Solzhenitsyn to counteract the lie may be foolish; the diagnosis of the illness was accurate.

Brezhnev could not stop intelligent foreigners from reading Solzhenitsyn's works and concluding that the country Brezhnev led was in a terrible muddle. But, as the Party's General Secretary and thus de facto head of the Kremlin's own "Holy Office of the Inquisition," he could not ignore Solzhenitsyn's claim that Lenin's legacy was a pack of lies. It was in this area that the propaganda war between Solzhenitsyn and the government was to be waged, for, short of locking Solzhenitsyn up and making him into a political martyr, there was little the Kremlin could do, save take the most extreme possible measures to brand Solzhenitsyn as a counterrevolutionary.

The trouble with the propaganda war was that both parties played into the other's hands. To be anathematized by the Party was just what Solzhenitsyn wanted. Part of the demon, the impulse, which kept him writing was the liberating knowledge that he was striking out on his own and annoying, not just the Communist party, but all the other apologists for socialism as well. In *Lenin in Zurich* he depicted Lenin in as offensive a manner as he possibly could. He said nothing good about Lenin's philosophy, which he had spent many years studying. By devoting himself to such crude attacks, Solzhenitsyn enabled the Kremlin, in the person of Suslov, to sidetrack the terrible political assault which all his books represented. The Party could respond in a manner which was calculated to make Solzhenitsyn suspect in the eyes of ordinary Russians. His patriotism was called into question. An itemization of Solzhenitsyn's heresies was published in all the Party newspapers. His base in Russia was becoming dangerously narrow.[5]

Solzhenitsyn, however, could not be silent. When he was informed by the young Vladimir Bukovsky and others of the terrifying conditions in Soviet psychiatric hospitals, he received copious encouragement for his campaigns of publicity and passive resistance. This was the sort of abuse Solzhenitsyn had been attacking for two decades, and continued to cry out against, day after day, in letters and notes. The more he did, the more his disciples in both the USSR and the West wanted to hear, and the more his condemnations spread.

Solzhenitsyn would not and could not give in. "We must be loyal to the essential truth," he declared, "and nothing must debase that loyalty."[6] Essential truth, *istina*, is one of the few words in the Russian language that cannot be rhymed. It has no verbal mate, no verbal associations, it stands alone and aloof, with only a vague suggestion of the

root "to stand." Most Russian writers have been tremendously interested in Truth's exact whereabouts and properties. To Pushkin it was
of marble under a noble sun; Dostoevsky saw it as a thing of blood and
tears and hysterical politics; and Chekhov kept a quizzical eye on it,
seemingly engrossed in the hazy scenery all about. Solzhenitsyn, however, marched straight at it, head bent and fists clenched, and found a
place where the cross had once stood, found—indeed—an image of
himself.

Solzhenitsyn now took to his work like a prophet who knows time is
running out. Throughout the 1960s he had been working, off and on, on
a history of Stalin's labor camps. His despair as he wrote was the
knowledge that, as George Orwell had foreseen, he was living in a land
of enforced forgetting, a country in which the state lied about its past
and its present all in the name of Utopia.

19

➤➤➤ ⫷⫷⫷

Enemies of the People
Alexander Dubcek and the Prague Heresy

Illusion of permanence, of the inviolability of communism's power and status, was the great lie confronted by Solzhenitsyn. In Brezhnev's empire, incumbent Party leaders assumed that communism was forever; that challenges could always be suppressed by inquisition, imprisonment, and execution; that the only real domestic danger to the Party's rule was the threat of internal rupture in the shape of a reform-minded Communist regime coming to power within the Soviet bloc, which needed only to be fended off or controlled to leave the Party secure. No understanding of the protest, no recognition of their own unpopularity or vulnerability, disturbed the minds of Brezhnev and his cronies. Their views were so fixed and shortsighted as to amount almost to perversity. They possessed no sense of mission save the continuance of Communist power, performed no beneficial service for the proletariat they were supposedly destined to serve. Their outstanding attitudes—obliviousness to the growing disaffection of their subjects, primacy of self-aggrandizement, illusion of invulnerable status—were persistent aspects of Communist rule.

"What we have, we hold!"[1] This declaration by Brezhnev may stand as the excuse for communism's inertia. After Khrushchev, few in the Party's leadership had the wit, and none the courage, to see that the socialist state has a greater task than to enlarge and maintain what it holds. When Party interest is placed before national interests, and private ambition, greed, and the bewitchment of exercising absolute power determine policy at all times, flexibility in the national interest necessarily loses, never more conspicuously than under the ideological inertia that followed Khrushchev's fall. The succession from Khrushchev to Brezhnev multiplied the harm.[2] Brezhnev's conception of socialism was unchanged from that model first designed by Nicolai Bukharin in the fires of the civil war. To Brezhnev, the socialist state was the supreme pork barrel.[3] For twenty years, this vision would suffer no penetration by doubt, no enlightenment. Pursuing the spoils of office like a hound on a scent, Brezhnev's rigid rule was characterized by bribes and conspiracies as a substitute for thought or a realistic economic program. He shrank from the obvious task of political and economic reform because he feared for the Party's authority and its opportunities for private gain. Within Russia, he made his office a mockery and the cradle of communism's Luther.

Was there a feasible alternative? Brezhnev's excess of venality, amorality, avarice, and a spectacularly costly arms race with the United States did indeed dismay some among the Party faithful. Their warning voices were loud if inconstant, and complaints by Party figures such as the historian Roy Medvedev and physicist Andrei Sakharov about Brezhnev's derelictions were explicit. Indeed, such complaints made both men pariahs. But inept or corrupt regimes like those of the terminal Romanovs or the Kuomintang or of Brezhnev cannot generally be reformed short of total upheaval or dissolution. In the case of Brezhnev, reform initiated at the top by the head of the Communist party with concern for his office, and pursued with vigor and tenacity by like-minded Party members, could, perhaps, have cleansed the most detestable practices, answered the cry for worthiness in the Party and its cadres, and attempted to fill the craving for moral and spiritual purpose, possibly postponing the ultimate decay of the socialist state.

Disaffection was felt with the indifference of the Party and its widening separation from the general populace, with the commissars' lives given over to luxury and privilege, little different from the average capitalist's. This was a source of deep resentment because in the common mind, if not in Leninist doctrine, Party cadres were supposed to be ascetic intermediaries between men and history. Where could a good comrade find inspiration if this vanguard failed in its office? People throughout Russia and the Soviet empire in Eastern and Central Europe felt a sense of betrayal in the daily evidence of the gulf between what history's agents were supposed to be and what they had become. A famous joke current in 1960s Moscow had Leonid Brezhnev proudly displaying his collection of Jaguars, Cadillacs, Bentleys, and Range Rovers to his aged mother, a jittery peasant woman dressed all in black. The old woman rambled among the cars cautiously, then came back to tug at her son's shirt-sleeve: "But Leonid, Leonid," she would whisper, "what if the Reds come back?"

In Milovan Djilas, Imre Nagy, and Nikita Khrushchev protest had taken form and found a voice. In such heresies there was already being expressed many of the doubts that were to become prevalent under Brezhnev. But their dissents only found limited resonance within the Party at large. Politburo members and most apparatchiks were solidly indifferent to talk of reform. Their personal fortunes, privileges, and positions were embedded in the existing system and they equated any call for reform with dissolution of the socialist state and devolution of their power. Throughout the Communist world in the Brezhnev era, a revolution in people's understanding of communism was in the making but the Party's rulers failed to take notice. Off to jail or psychiatric hospitals went brave dissidents like Vladimir Bukovsky and Anatoly Scharansky. They regarded protest merely as dissent to be suppressed, not as a serious challenge to their validity.

Prison and exile and execution, however, cannot silence ideas whose time has come, a fact that generally escapes despots, who by nature are rulers of little foresight. The dissents of Djilas, Nagy, and Khrushchev lingered. Meanwhile, a new understanding of socialism and a new challenge in the rise of national Communist parties completely independent of the Kremlin was rising. Partners in revolution were antagonists in victory. Tito and Chairman Mao began the process by declaring their absolute separation from Moscow. Their systems might mimic the socialist state as decreed by Lenin and designed by Bukharin, but the very fact of their shunning Moscow lowered the USSR's status. Encroachment on the Soviet Union's prerogatives in its satellite states followed and increased, with the parties of Poland, Hungary, East Germany, and Czechoslovakia often filling senior posts with their own appointees, withholding (in the case of Romania) troops from the Warsaw Pact's unified command, and disputing obedience to Kremlin decrees. In Czechoslovakia, this independence was to be of grave consequence, for within its Communist party leadership the voice of dissent and reform fused with a new assertion of Czechoslovak national independence.

When Alexander Dubcek was forty-seven, after twenty-four years as a Party cadre, his character, habits, principles or lack of them, and ideas about power were well enough known to his colleagues in the Czech Central Committee to warn them of sudden storms ahead. To the wider circle of the Czech Party, and by repute abroad, the fact that, though soft-spoken and sometimes meek, he was thoroughly dubious of many Marxist-Leninist doctrines was no secret and no surprise, although his reputation for heresy was not yet what it would become. His frame of mind was heartily reformist: to celebrate his election, he gave a speech untroubled by socialist cant, and filled with promises of changes to come.[4]

Dubcek was said never to have missed a Party meeting during his twenty-four years of membership. There was nothing about the workings and opportunities of the Communist bureaucracy that he did not grasp. Intelligent and energetic, a student of Marx and Lenin, Dubcek did not, like so many of Lenin's successors, believe that a foolproof blueprint for building socialism could be worked out in advance. Rather he believed in the necessity for perpetual adaptability and improvisation to fit circumstances. To think meant to to give room for freedom of initiative, for the imponderable to win over the material, for individual will to demonstrate its power over circumstance.

The idea that history could be pre-planned was infantile, Dubcek warned even before his elevation to the leadership. From flights of Marxist metaphysics he would, in his speeches, descend at once to the earth of tactics, the necessity for realism, the elements of compromise. Preconceived notions based on dogmatic judgments of what history is bound to do were for him premature. "All decisions in politics must be inspired by the will to seize and retain the initiative." Marxist predestination is forgotten, abandoned, discarded; its only possible justification is an occasional "appeal to sentiment with a view to strengthening resolve."[5]

Personal characteristics, as much as his notions of socialism, were both an aid and a drawback in Dubcek's rise to power. Tall and elegant in figure, he was a handsome Slav with a strong sensual mouth, a broad brow, and impressively penetrating eyes. The face was youthful and seductive, which promoted his popularity among younger members of the Party. Quick and impatient, Dubcek was a constant boil of ideas, humor, passion, imagination and, above all, energy. As a young Minister he used to trot around Wençeslas Square in Prague, carrying with him the morning paper to read whenever he slowed down to a walk. His passions led him into excesses. Dubcek was loquacious and often made himself the theme of his own discourses. Dubcek's ability to antagonize assured that all the time that he was trying to graft democracy onto the trunk of the socialist state, his longtime enemies were priming their guns, crouched for a counterattack.[6]

Credit for Dubcek's youthful decision to become a communist must be given to Neville Chamberlain not Marx. Few Slovaks imagined that a betrayal as grand as that of England's appeasement of Hitler at Munich was conceivable; when the inconceivable happened, they were horrified and disillusioned. And Dubcek had been weaned on class hatred. As an emigré to America, his father had toiled in Chicago for a decade, only to return home in defeat, poverty, and bitterness. When an opportunity came to go to the Soviet Union, Dubcek *père* had embarked with his entire family to Khirgizia when Alexander was only four, there to raise his children as true communists. Later, the boy was educated in a Party school in Gorki. Thus Munich came as no surprise: his Soviet schooling taught him that betrayal was behavior typical of bourgeois-imperialists. Only Comrade Stalin promised help for Czechoslovakia in its hour of need. Any doubts that Dubcek may have had about the great leader's integrity were dispelled. The Communist party of Czechoslovakia was the only local political party to condemn unreservedly the treachery of Munich, and for this action it gained a respect and following it had hitherto been denied.

Dubcek, though some twenty years younger than Milovan Djilas and Imre Nagy, was a similar figure following a parallel career, a tendency which was specially characteristic of the first third of the twentieth century. All three had, early on in life, lost faith in the traditional politics of their countries and stood outside their nation's conventional cultures. Dubcek, indeed, was a prototype of that tiny band of young idealists who scorned his country's majority of silent collaborators with the triumphant Germans in order to join the Communist party because of its underground war against the Nazis. While employed in a yeast factory in Trečin he was made "organizing secretary of the local Party's district committee."[7]

Collaboration was virulent in the rump state of Slovakia spawned by Hitler after the occupation. Under the clerico-fascist leadership of Monsignor Josef Tiso, two Slovak divisions were sent to fight alongside the Germans on the Russian front. Slovak soldiers reacted to this wildly unpopular order by deserting in mass to the Red Army they were supposed to attack; at the battle of Melitopol alone some three thousand fled across the lines and joined the Czech Brigade fighting in Russia under the command of Colonel Ludvik Svoboda. When word of this disaffection reached home, the Slovakian communists knew that, if they called for a revolt, large sections of their nation's troops would rise up against the government and its German allies. And they would gain the credit for the revolt because they had, between 1939 and 1941, "methodically betrayed democratic partisans to the Gestapo."[8]

When the rising came in September 1944, Dubcek became a partisan. His war was not particularly glorious, as William Shawcross has written, but it was the making of his revolutionary temperament. The Slovak partisans corresponded precisely to his ideal vision of a true communist society. In mountain redoubts, Dubcek saw an unspoiled fraternity. And added to this in Dubcek's eyes were the virtues of the heroes of the French and Russian Revolutions: stoicism, fortitude in adversity, personal bravery, and self-sacrifice; incorruptibility; lack of personal ambition; contempt for faction and intrigue; loftiness of soul; even the taciturn reserve that rebuked the insincere loquacity of the local Communist officials he recalled from his Soviet boyhood. A great part of Dubcek's loyalty to the Party, even when he came to doubt his faith in Marxism-Leninism, stemmed from his burning determination to revive the honest communism of the partisans. The mountain fighters of Uhrovec became paragons of all the virtues: martial, personal, and political.[9]

Resistance was a boon to the Communists, for it left them as the strongest party in the country at the end of the war. In the genuinely free elections, with secret ballots, of May 26, 1946, the Communists polled more than twice as many votes as the next strongest party (that of prewar President Edvard Beneš), and obtained more than 35 percent of the total vote cast. Even had he wanted to, Beneš could not have kept the Communists out of his government. But Beneš had no intention of doing so. Appeasement had taught him not to depend on the West.[10]

Czechoslovakia's postwar prospects were dependent on Soviet good-will. In the case of a Russian victory over Hitler, Stalin would be free to impose his will on the country. Beneš, from his wartime London exile, understood all this. As the uprising in Slovakia raged, he and his exiled government determined to make the best possible terms with Moscow. Unlike the unhappy Poles, he managed to avoid any open defiance or provocation of Stalin during the war. He did not overestimate the possibilities that were open to him. From London he took the initiative to negotiate with Moscow a treaty that should govern postwar relations between the two countries. When Beneš approached Stalin for this purpose he found him friendly, well disposed, rather generous in his attitude.

Early in 1943 Moscow had assured Beneš that it was prepared to see Czechoslovakia restored as an independent country with all its prewar territories intact. Moscow would not interfere in the nation's domestic affairs, or so the Kremlin promised. These assurances were repeated on more than one occasion. In 1945, at a dinner that he gave for Beneš, Stalin offered a toast in which he said that Beneš had once been right to suspect the Soviet Union of wishing to Bolshevize Europe, but that Soviet policy had changed. After the war, he said, the various Communist parties would become nationalist parties, giving the national interests of their respective countries priority.[11]

Honesty and deception mingled within Stalin's motives for issuing this pledge. One can imagine that he was genuinely averse to undertaking the forced Bolshevization of a Czechoslovakia that, in addition to being oriented toward the Western conception of democracy, was the strongest, richest, and most advanced of the countries liberated from the Nazis by the Red Army. He may have felt that he could maintain, with a non-Communist government under Beneš' leadership, the kind of relations that he was later to maintain with the Finns; and this would be preferable to the burden of holding the country in sullen subjection. At the same time, he might also have been moved by a desire to allay Beneš' suspicions of the Moscow-trained Czech and Slovak communists who were to assume key places in the postwar government, men whom he denigrated in talking to Beneš.

Whatever the measure of Stalin's honesty, even if he was being wholly dishonest, Beneš had no choice but to accept such terms as he could draw from him. Czech communists were genuinely popular. In this one instance, then, elections did bring about a government "friendly" to Moscow. In March 1945, Beneš met in Moscow with the Czech Communist leaders to organize a provisional government. Out of twenty-five cabinet posts, seven went to Communists. These seven included the posts of Prime Minister and Interior Minister, with jurisdiction over the police.

In the spring of 1945, the provisional government, following on the heels of the Red Army, set up its administration at Kosice, in eastern Slovakia. There it issued the Kosice program, setting forth the policies of the new regime. It accepted Soviet annexation of Ruthenia, which had constituted the eastern tip of the country. After the 1946 elections, the government was re-established in Prague. It appeared for a brief moment that, as in Finland, a *via media* had been found between the demands of Moscow for "friendship" and the appeal of freedom on the Western model.

This hope was soon crushed. In June 1947 the offer of assistance in the rehabilitation of Europe made by U.S. Secretary of State George Marshall, later to be known as the Marshall Plan, exerted on the Czech government a strong pull, a tug which aroused Moscow's anxiety if not its alarm. In the winter of 1947–1948 there were signs that the strong communist position in Czechoslovakia was weakening. Throughout Europe as a whole, a reaction was brewing in response to the evidence of Stalin's ruthless suppression of Eastern Germany and Poland. The Cold War was then beginning.

In February 1948 the Communist Minister of the Interior, supported by the Communist Premier, defied the Czech cabinet, which was attempting to exercise over him the discipline that the Finnish cabinet, that same spring, was to exercise (successfully) over its own Communist Minister of the Interior. Six days later, a Deputy Foreign Minister of the Soviet Union arrived in Prague. The police, obeying the orders of the Communist Minister of the Interior, went into action. Bloodshed ensued. Beneš and his supporters were suppressed—some by arrest and imprisonment, some by exile, and some were killed. Jan Masaryk, the closest aide to Beneš and son of the country's founder, was pushed or fell from a window in the Foreign Ministry. Parliamentary democracy was abolished. Czechoslovakia was forcibly transformed into a police state under a puppet government subservient to Moscow.[12]

In these confusing circumstances, all Dubcek's efforts were channelled toward one goal only: continuance of support by the peasants of Slovakia for the Party. Without the peasants, it would have been impossible for the Communist coup to claim any legitimacy. His roots, his candor, his easy adaptability, the sweet reasonableness of his promises, the hint of deference in his tone so different from the usual communist bluster, opened all avenues to him and made Dubcek a perfect foil for keeping the peasants passive. In villages and on farms he reassured the rural population that their properties would not be nationalized, and promised that there would be no collectivization of land. He won farmers over with his invented tales of the hardy, prosperous peasants he had seen in Russia. He spoke in the gruff local dialects almost flawlessly, and could sit for hours in fields and farmhouses, letting others do the talking while he listened with an understanding smile kept in constant play over what was otherwise an oddly baffling countenance. The secret of his success was a willingness to be bored.

As a ranking Party official in Skoda, Dubcek was responsible for mollifying farmers and shopkeepers alike in the region; all instructions to and reports from local party cadres went through him, and on Dubcek would lodge the blame if the peasants balked. The bellows and blunders emanating from Prague did not help his efforts to keep the peasantry quiet. He was, it is said, in the position of a cultivated young man whose wooing of a farmer's daughter of the most sensitive morals is hampered by the social solecisms of his coarser relatives.

His Bratislavan Communist chief did not ease Dubcek's task. Gustav

Husak, a strong, silent Slav with the eyes of a fanatic, resented Dubcek's moderation. But the instructions from Prague were explicit and Dubcek was given leeway. Undoubtedly this forbearance helped many farmers believe that there was nothing to fear from supporting the Communists—they were going to build merely a more efficient form of social democracy. In February 1948, the Prague Congress of Peasant Commissions (a front organization composed of card-carrying communist peasants) enthusiastically endorsed the Party's takeover of power. Dubcek later said of this vote of confidence:

> the confidence which the working farmer demonstrated in the Communist Party at that time can without hesitation be described as one of the most positive factors in constructing socialism not only in the villages but throughout the country. Without this confidence, without a firm union between small and medium farmers and the working class it would not have been possible to carry out the revolutionary changes in our agriculture.[13]

More succinctly, without the peasants the Party's coup might have failed.

Dubcek and the peasants now waited in equal ignorance to see what the aftermath was going to be. The wait was not long. In March 1948, the Party considered that the Peasant Commissions had outlived their usefulness. Collectivization was ordered. An eruption of popular anger was quickly directed at the local Communist agents of collectivization. The brutality of this rising and its bloody suppression was a product of the Manichean language of socialism that went back to Bukharin and Mayakovsky. Communists had become so accustomed to damning stereotypes of independent peasants as monsters and incarnations of evil that reason collapsed back fatally to a sort of demonology. From a place of hiding Dubcek watched in silence, ostensibly armed with some degree of authority to stop the murders but disinclined and ultimately impotent to do so.

Stunned with grief at—or perhaps frightened by—the massacre of recalcitrant peasants, Dubcek was afflicted with remorse and a sudden rare introspection, for in this moral crisis, Dubcek had his first doubts. His confusion between the cause of communism and the cause of his country began here. Throughout the resistance to Hitler he had managed to identify the cause of his nation exclusively with that of the revolutionary tradition. In the name of socialism Czechoslovakia would be reborn. But the systematic murder of unwilling peasants brought an explicit realization. Socialism was turning into something that had nothing to do with the principles of Marx and Lenin; it was a new dictatorship that had no intention of withering away, ever. It maintained itself by threats and murder, a mockery of the socialist ideal.

No rupture of his faith in communism followed these insights. A critical moment in the life of any idealist comes when he realizes that his principles and career are doomed to conflict. One or the other must give way. To choose Party loyalty, you must work to soothe your conscience and to rationalize the need for your decision. To choose conscience is to find yourself an outcast from all you once held dear. Hesitating but little, Dubcek's ambition triumphed. Though superficially an orthodox Communist, Dubcek was a much more ambivalent character than he appeared. For a brief moment in the summer of 1948 he stood with a brave little minority in opposition to forced collectivization. As far as is noted, Dubcek did not open his mouth against the measure, but the remarks of the men he stood with were unequivocal in their denunciation of the betrayal of the peasants. They were damning words presumably approved by Dubcek, since he supported the speaker. Yet he did not resign from the Party when the denunciation gathered no support. On the contrary, Dubcek sought and received a full-time position within the Party apparat. Governed by an exacting sense of duty akin to that of Bukharin or of Koestler's communist martyrs in *Darkness at Noon*, Dubcek felt that as a disciplined comrade it was his duty to accept any and all Party decisions as necessarily right, once the decision was made irrevocable. Yet either duty worked slowly or else ambivalence was already operating, for it was six months before he decided to take up his new Party post. The lag was due in part to his newly acquired wife, to whom he was deeply attached—so much so that he bowed to her wish to be married in the Catholic church, a strange act for a committed atheist.[14]

Dubcek's initial ambivalence, however, merely had the effect, once the decision to choose Party loyalty was made, of making him more communist than his comrades. Because he wanted to be "one of them" he was the more anxious to be orthodox, the more easily taken into camp by the Party's ruling ideologues. They needed Dubcek because they felt that local Slovaks were a necessity for a Party dominated by Czechs, and also because they knew that he would carry out orders faithfully, unquestioningly. In his home region, it was hoped that Dubcek's appointment to the state apparat charged with the takeover of shops and small industrial enterprises would mean a softening of policy; actually it meant the reverse. Though humane, Dubcek was uncompromising. Private property was evil, pure and simple.

Listening to the drumbeat of orthodoxy, Dubcek fell in step. It was the making of him as a communist. He rose in power by sheer consistency in a world that admired rigidity of mind and heart. The absolute conviction that he brought to his speeches, that only communists of unimpeachable integrity and orthodoxy could be made responsible for the public good, provoked mirth among those Party officials busily confiscating once aristocratic estates and hunting lodges for their own private use, but as time went on the laughter became progressively more uncomfortable.

A kind of righteous indignation became Dubcek's natural form of utterance. Dubcek made communism a form of Manichean struggle between virtue and vice, freedom from want and the tyranny of private property. His vision found a responsive audience among those Slovak Party members with a chip on their shoulders because of the age-old discrimination against them by the Czechs. By 1951, at the age of thirty, he was already at work in the Slovak Central Committee in Bratislava. Like Stalin, his hero of the time, Dubcek prospered in the humorless, drone-like world of the Party bureaucrat. It can hardly be said that he had a private life, since it was an article of faith with him that private and public were, for the true communist, dissolved in a single existence of unselfish activism and moral regularity. He was, in fact, exactly the kind of punctilious worker bee glorified in communist posters and socialist realist novels. Settled in a small office with writing desk and chair, Alexander Dubcek spent a decade at Party paperwork, with which not even his election as a Parliamentary Deputy could interfere.

Insulated utterly, Dubcek's work within the Slovak apparat gained him little experience of the real mechanisms of an economy, and he learned to detest anything of the old system that lingered. He spent his life, like the old Bolsheviks of the pre-1917 insurrectionary diaspora, devising that imaginary communist world which would be as antithetical to the old one of privilege and profits as possible. Dubcek simply assumed that public support for this utopian vision would be contagious. The sincerity and purity of the socialist dream guaranteed its value and ultimate global victory; but the vision must be primarily constructive. He wanted, in the name of socialism, to see the whole of humanity redeemed, and he was able by the sheer force of his peculiar exhilaration to incite in his comrades a brotherly feeling.

Carried along by the current, and by the depth of his own ambition to climb the Party ladder, Dubcek was selected to take one of the places reserved for Czechoslovak communists at the Higher Party School in

Moscow.[15] Dubcek was now a certified highflier. With his genius for popular oratory, Dubcek now figured in the Party's plans as a future leader, and thus in need of formal ideological training. This was a deficiency of which Dubcek was quite conscious, and he was delighted at the chance to set it aright.

By a bolt of luck which he could not have foreseen, instead of hardening his faith this mission to Moscow restored the doubts that Dubcek had mentally buried in 1948. Within three months of his arrival in the Soviet Union, Nikita Khrushchev denounced Stalin at the secret session of the twentieth Soviet Party Congress. Rumors of the speech abounded; confusion among the students spread. The ghastly losses of Stalin's forced collectivizations and the war against Hitler—twenty million, thirty million, fifty million, no one could be sure—had been for nothing. Urgently, Dubcek and the other students questioned their teachers and each other, their questions dying away into concentrated silence as their anxiety mounted. Dubcek knew almost instantly that Khrushchev's speech was at once a deadly peril and a possible miracle. Only the miracle of cleansing communism of terror could outweigh the peril of doubt which, once let loose, might well accomplish what the capitalists hoped—discredit socialism in the eyes of socialists. That was the stake Khrushchev was playing at.[16]

These were the thoughts Dubcek dejectedly carried back home with him when he returned to Bratislava. Overnight, the fixed values of communism were called into question. A way of thinking had been dented, but for Dubcek nothing new had risen to take its place. When Khrushchev sent Soviet tanks into Budapest to crush the Hungarian Revolution and execute Imre Nagy, Dubcek felt doubly betrayed. He thought the decision to maintain Hungary as a communist country was a correct one, but hated that communism had to be imposed by force. As one of Dubcek's relatives told William Shawcross:

> Of course he didn't immediately think "We must do something about this." You must understand that propaganda in Moscow was hardly conducive to sympathy for the Hungarians. It was only much later that he began to see how things might be made better, and how it should be possible to do something with the ideas that Khrushchev had expressed.[17]

To do anything, however, Dubcek needed power. So he swallowed his doubts. After Moscow, he was conscious of belonging to the elite of the Party. At the age of thirty-two he was the youngest member of the Party's hierarchy and it was generally understood that he would join the Politburo in Prague at the earliest opportunity.

Czechoslovakia's failure to follow Khrushchev's program of de-Stalinization was Dubcek's opportunity to advance himself and his ideas. In May 1962, an angry Khrushchev dispatched his close Kremlin ally Leonid Ilyichev to Prague to push for de-Stalinization. Antonin Novotny and the conservative Czech Communist leadership could no longer resist. Orthodox though he seemed, Dubcek possessed a hard core of ambition and a keen scent for the main chance that pushed him to exploit Khrushchev's displeasure for his own gain. He supported the Kremlin's call for revision of the verdicts of purge trials undertaken at Stalin's behest. That he had failed earlier to speak his mind was a token of his impotence; that he demanded rehabilitation of those condemned now was a reflection of his ambition, not of a concern for justice.

Until 1962, Dubcek's principle was to avoid trouble so far as he could and to accept the inevitable when he had to. His method followed communist careerism, which allowed, not to say prescribed, arrangements with all factions. Evasive and smiling, he had eluded all absolute commitments to any faction and never explained what his own policy for government would be, if indeed he had one.

Dubcek's opportunistic support of Khrushchev's push for de-Stalinization excited tumults from reform-minded members of the Party, who saw him as their leader. When the commission charged with investigating the purge trials of the 1950s reported that miscarriages of justice had, indeed, taken place, Dubcek made certain that credit for the report went to him. Rewards soon followed. A chastened and desperate Novotny chose Dubcek to head the Slovak Central Committee. It may be that Novotny intended to tolerate Dubcek only briefly, in the mistaken belief that he could be removed once Khrushchev had been placated. But he was wrong.

High office, like sudden disaster, often reveals the measure of a man. An open dissent by Slovak intellectuals was Dubcek's summons to action; instead of suppressing debate, he sided with the dissenters. Their attacks on the slow pace of rehabilitating men purged during the 1950s brought Dubcek the reformer out into the open. For it gave an opportunity for Dubcek to attack, with impugnity, the sitting Prime Minister, Viliam Siroky. Complicity in mass murder was the charge levelled at Siroky:

> Comrade Siroky's report . . . uncovering bourgeois nationalists in the Party was not the result of an objective analysis of the facts. . . . On the contrary it was based on a prior thesis. . . . To this thesis all facts had to be subordinated. . . . Any disagreement with even one word of the report [was] accepted as an expression of open hostility. . . . Only two ways

were open to the comrades charged with bourgeois nationalism. They could either "agree" with the "criticism" or accept the charge that they were wilful enemies of the party. It would, therefore, be an expression of gross cynicism, if not of something much worse, if their "self-critical" statements . . . were to be considered as a confirmation of the correctness of their indictment for bourgeois-nationalism.[18]

Here was a fine obfuscation. Behind the lame rhythms of Party rhetoric was an undeniable challenge to the ruling clique in Prague. Dubcek looked terribly pale and exhausted as the denunciation proceeded, but his nervous energy never deserted him. And as his Slovak colleagues warmed to the damning remarks, Dubcek responded to the speech as if suddenly swept by some inner emotional storm which he was quite unable to control.

Dubcek's tacit support of such denunciations was not an act of political conviction. He calculated that a majority of the Party was ready for change along the lines advocated by Khrushchev. This was especially clear once it became obvious that Novotny and his cronies were not going to enact the necessary reforms, and thus forfeit support in the Kremlin. Younger members of the Party, such as Dubcek, were political animals who saw opportunities for advancement in supporting liberalization. Traditionally, even in extreme situations, younger Party cadres defined their interests not in automatic solidarity with their elders but in service to the Party. From that service they could expect regular preferment and the perquisites and status of Party office. What happened through Novotny's reign was that the rationale for continued loyalty was seriously strained by a logjam at the top. Novotny's attempt to maintain Party support by retaining his own followers in the Prague Central Committee finally served to isolate him, for it meant that his chance of rallying the lower echelons of the Party was nil.[19]

Knowledgeable and effective as a subordinate, Dubcek fell victim when taking a position of isolated leadership to timidity, perplexity, and habitual irresolution. When Novotny retaliated, Dubcek trimmed. Incapacitating ambivalence was even stronger than ambition, and for the moment it delivered Dubcek into Novotny's hands. Instead of launching a counterattack on Novotny within the Slovak Central Committee, Dubcek sat wanly as accusations mounted. In 1964 the moment of his collapse occurred when one committeeman held up the standard devices of Dubcek's rhetoric to ridicule. Seeing his position falling apart, Dubcek rose to speak. Nervously, he cleared his throat and gulped some water. In a monotonous mumble, he conceded almost every point to Novotny: "I want to underline that attempts to provoke discussion on grave questions of Party history call for collective assessment by the Party organs."[20] Everyone knew that the Party organs were under Novotny's control.

Dubcek's craven collapse should have been a warning to reformers that he was not the man to lead them out of bondage. But his ability to charm remained a subject of envy. Dubcek had a peculiar combination of child-like candor and surface honesty, which, together with his enthusiasm and his physical presence, enabled him to proffer an image of leadership. All his life Dubcek sought to recreate the fraternal socialism he had known as a guerrilla against the Nazis. He was able to inspire young socialists by the spell of his personality, part of whose power resided in the fact that it had the ingenuousness of a child's, and could lay out before them a luminous socialist utopia. His notion of Party politics was, in this sense, always imaginary, and he never himself seems to have known the difference between what was real and what was a dream. Dubcek's lack of a sense of reality was proved in his failure to unseat Siroky. Of his supporters, some were rightly shocked at his submission. But the tug of his personality assured that Dubcek's hesitations and surrenders were not fatal to his leadership of the reformers. For the time being, Dubcek's total surrender in 1965 brought to a stop all questions of political change in Czechoslovakia, and for the next few years onward Dubcek operated in an atmosphere of extreme political reaction, of Party dictatorship pure and simple. So far as the Party was concerned, time was standing still.[21]

In reality, however, a great deal was happening. The Party might have been marking time but the economy of the country was not. Vast changes were overtaking Czechoslovakia. The country had become an industrial focal point for the entire communist world. Peasants were migrating to the industrial centers in the thousands in search of better conditions than they could ever get on the land. An industrial power before World War II, Stalin's insistence on increased industrialization pushed Czechoslovakia firmly, in all its regions including backward Slovakia, into new ranges of industry.

Everywhere a new class of industrial managers was coming into being, and although they were underpaid, lacking in education, and overworked (mothers sometimes brought their children to factories with them), it was the start of the transformation of the Czech proletariat into an industrial bourgeoisie like that which existed in Western Europe. Modernization did not yet challenge the Communist party, but was functioning in essential contradiction. Ideological restraints on initiative remained in force. Nothing so vexed the Party's thinking, nothing so baffled and eluded settlement among reformers, nothing was so great a tangle of irreconcilables. Society needed individual initiative while Communist doctrine practically forbade it. Czech factories in the 1960s became a hothouse of the tensions and antagonisms brewed in communist societies by economic restrictions.[22]

The spirit of Djilas and Nagy, who had dared to deny the communist monopoly, was abroad. A weakened acceptance of the system, an awakening sense that authority could be challenged—that change was in fact possible—began to take hold. The struggle for "Socialism with a Human Face" began in February 1963, when Professor Eduard Goldstuecker of Charles University in Prague denounced the assumption that "a new higher social order can be achieved without humanity and legality and that great human accomplishments can be championed in theory but trampled upon in practice."[23] Elsewhere in Czechoslovak society there was a craving for change. Milan Kundera, Vaclav Havel, Alexander Kliment, and other artists complained bitterly about the lack of democracy. In Alexander Dubcek the political and spiritual strains of protest were to fuse into a philosophy—and a program.

Yet Dubcek, in the years 1966–1968, appeared to accept as a matter of course all the paranoid paraphernalia of the socialist state; the censorship of the press, the suppression of non-Marxist teaching in the universities, the anti-Semitic rantings, the rule of the secret police. In these years the Party continued on its inflexible course, and nothing it seemed could shake it. No reform of any consequence was contemplated or carried out, and no adjustment other than increased repression was allowed to meet the new conditions of the country's economy or the unrest gathering from below.

It was ethnic and not doctrinal abuse, however, that catapulted Dubcek into power in 1968. Novotny's crass favoritism of Czechs at the expense of Slovaks seemed to Slovak Party members the ultimate expression of a Party mired in sloth and corruption. Slovak hostility to Czech hegemony in the country was various and long standing. It was a summons for Dubcek. He stood openly as the champion of Slovak nationalism, tying the Slovak revolt of 1944 with the liberation of all Czechoslovakia. In speech after speech he sought to placate the Russians, assuring them of his undying loyalty. Yet he warned the Czech Party that, in order to maintain its leading role, it had to win constantly its leading position by the solution of problems, not by revolutionary rhetoric and slogans, by developing socialist society, not constricting it, ethnically or politically.[24]

Enclosed in rigid ideology, Novotny was unaware of the issues of Slovak dissent and incapable of understanding the protests that had been developing in the country since Dubcek's climbdown. Novotny hardly noticed the fracas in Slovakia except as a heresy to be suppressed like any other. His response was to use the Czech army to arrest all who failed to support his position.[25] It proved as effective as King Canute's admonition to the waves. General Vaclav Prchlik warned Dubcek of the scheme, and Dubcek was able to rally the Party by claiming that Novotny was planning to launch a coup against it. Novotny was finished. On January 5, 1968, Prague Radio announced to a stunned nation that Alexander Dubcek had been elected First Secretary of the Communist party. But there was nothing mysterious in Dubcek's triumph. He was the one-eyed man in the party of the blind.

In the nervous tension of his sudden accession, Dubcek felt that he had to show himself in command, especially to overcome the long shadow of Novotny. He did not at first feel a comparable impulse to be daring; to examine a wide variety of actions before he spoke. He lacked Novotny's blundering certitude. His ideological ambivalence was born of a certain historical and common sense and some capacity for reflective thinking. A man infatuated with himself, Dubcek was affected in his conduct of office by three elements in his character: an ego that was insatiable and never secure; a bottomless capacity to use the powers of office without inhibition; and a profound aversion, once fixed upon a course of action, to any contraindications.

Although a reformer by instinct, Dubcek acquired his ideas and policies for reform by transfusion from younger members of the Communist leadership. He was persuaded that the country was on the verge of the same emotional breakdown that had incited the Hungarian Revolution. The record of the Communist party in power, it was argued, could hardly be called enlightened; it could only be accorded a kind of brutal success. If the majority of citizens were materially better off than before, the cost in cruelty and tyranny had been enormous, and no less and probably greater than under the Hapsburgs.

Dubcek met past rigidity with improvisation. He proclaimed the freedom of the press, and eliminated the position of censor as an official Party post. He allowed the formation of free and independent trade unions, and began the process of redistributing land confiscated from the peasants. He spun off from direct Party control all sorts of industrial and managerial functions that had come under the aegis of the state. Within two months of taking office, 35 percent of Czech industry had been given independent cooperative status. People came to Prague from all over the country for redress of grievances that ranged from unwarranted imprisonment for ideological deviations to the complaints of old resistance comrades of Dubcek's who had nothing to live on in their old age. "A return to the old methods of administrative guidance," Dubcek declared, methods "which not only fail to produce . . . but . . . damage the unity of individuals," was "doomed to failure."[26]

Dubcek's political program—acclaimed everywhere as "Socialism with a human face"—was a direct rebuke to the gap between the communist ideal and communism in practice. For Dubcek, the ideal of communism was a vision of a just social order maintained by the proletariat, history's chosen people. So their political agents, the Communist party, were supposed to serve as defenders of this just order, as upholders of the socialist vision and champions of the oppressed.

His conception of the state was not that of a Leviathan but of a facilitator; the deepest socialist delusion. He wanted the state to assist, not own, the means of production. Investment would come not from the state's coffers but from having workers themselves loan money to their enterprises from the pension funds which they—through their own elected representatives—controlled. Dubcek's vision of the socialist state differed most from Bukharin's initial design in conceiving of the state not merely as the agent to make possible the way to communism, but as a "moral good" in and of itself. Bukharin had committed a fundamental error: in assuming that the state was endowed with complete freedom of will to reshape both man and society, he cut man off from his very nature. For there were laws of human character as well as history; there was an organic process of human development which was distinct from the process of production. and only through a fusion of this organic process with that of a benevolent state would socialism, real socialism, come into being.[27]

What Dubcek concluded as he watched his country rally to his liberal reforms was that society could not be organized scientifically; this was obviously a psychological and metaphysical problem as well as a mechanical one, as Lenin and the old Bolsheviks had seemed to believe. The absolutist demands of the socialist state had no relation to human social realities; and the Party's unchecked dictatorship had as little relation to fundamental human needs. Lenin and Bukharin assumed that the objects of society were production and consumption, whereas its actual objects were spiritual as well as material happiness. The solution to social problems was not the elimination of conflicting interests in favor of one all-embracing vision as dictated by the state, but the adjustment and amelioration of rivalries and cross-purposes. The concept of the socialist state was altogether wrong in its insistence on subordination to the whole; in a good society, individual liberty was necessary for social progress.

When the gap between the ideal and the real becomes too wide, political systems, like men, begin to break down. Dubcek's reforms were a damning indictment of the socialist state's tardiness in the building of Jerusalem. More clearly than most, he sensed the beginnings of a transfer of power, not from one party faction to another, but one more profound, a transfer outside the Party itself.

Where an orthodox socialist would have fled from this prospect, Dubcek embraced it. In the abstract, Dubcek believed in the Party and the socialist state but not at the cost of annihilating every opponent who stood in socialism's path. He might renounce private property and the need for individual opinion, but he saw no need for everyone else in society to do likewise. Here was the fundamental dichotomy of Dubcek's socialism. He thought it possible to meet the demands of workers and managers and thinkers for individual liberty while at the same time preserving the citadel of a collective socialist vision of a better world to be achieved through shared resources and struggle. Yet somewhere deep within himself Dubcek must have suspected the bitter truth of history: that progress and gain by one of his alternatives would only be accomplished by the loss of something of permanent value to the other.

Dubcek as First Secretary seemed an enigma to his comrades because his nature was paradoxical, his opinions sometimes irreconcilable, and because he did not see life or politics in terms of absolutes. As a result, he was often charged with being both naive and cynical, and communists who looked at the world from a fixed ideological point of view thought him perverse. Dubcek, did, as we have seen, hold certain basic convictions, but he could see arguments on both sides of a matter, which is the penalty of a thoughtful man. Between bouts of nerves and sudden bolts like a horse that hears the rustle of a snake, Dubcek set about the business of dismantling much of the infrastructure of the socialist state, and all in the name of socialism.[28]

A heavy sense of all that depended on the issue hung over him. Throughout the spring of 1968, Dubcek was warned of Kremlin anxiety. Not so much as a protest from the Kremlin was received. Nothing stirred. Soviet inactivity heightened the tension. Red Army troops cancelled their spring maneuvers. Lurking motionless in their Czech bases, they seemed to presage something more sinister.

Dubcek's intelligence advisor warned him in mid-June 1968. He suggested that approaches be made to fellow members of the Warsaw Pact to determine if they would support Czechoslovakia in the event of a showdown. Dubcek, however, continued his solitary policy of reform, straining to swerve communism from a path he believed certain to lead

to defeat. He was convinced that the only way to prevent Soviet interference was to show the efficacy of his policies themselves. The practical effect of his passivity was to make everything dependent on the
Soviets.

The immense train of results, the massive difficulties of implement-
ing his reforms, the dislocations and disloyalties of Communist apparatchiks who saw their positions threatened, the Kremlin's deep-seated
worries were not thought of by the author of the Prague Spring. When
he decided to divorce Catherine of Aragon, Henry VIII did not have in
mind the Reformation. When Dubcek presented his program to the
Czechoslovak Central Committee he was concerned with the political
necessity of reinvigorating the Party and restoring its prestige in the
nation at large. The order to end press censorship and to allow for
privately owned newspapers was submitted to the Committee on the
advice of Dubcek himself and authorized after only limited discussion.

The Interior Minister was not the only person unconcerned with
odds and ends of this kind. With each day in office, Dubcek became
more and more convinced that he must unseat the bureaucrats entrenched under the protective shadow of the Party, and achieve a new
democratic and voluntary socialism. Knowing that foreign tensions stifle
reform, he was bent on keeping the country out of any disputes that
would frustrate his program. If sucked into a dispute with Russia, all
plans for reform would be thwarted. And beyond that, he had a grander
and ulterior motive. He saw in his call for socialism with a human face
an opportunity for greatness on the world stage. Dubcek was lured by a
vision of Czechoslovakia, through himself, bringing to the motherland
of socialism the gift of a new model Marxism. If he could avoid Soviet
interference he could save his own program and save socialism from
itself. Ever since assuming power he had been trying by exhortation and
hints of reasonableness to persuade the Kremlin that his regime was a
laboratory of reforms that the Soviets might want to study and consider,
without a sign of success. As the summer of 1968 began, two under-
tows sucking Czechoslovakia toward confrontation with the USSR—
economic privatization of industry and agriculture, and criticism of
Brezhnev and the Kremlin in the liberated Czech press—were exerting
such a pull as to be almost impossible to resist. Dubcek was bent on
resisting; few communists have ever been less willing to be the victim of
events. But the more he resisted, the more he ordained his own coming
martyrdom. Dubcek made up his mind that if his Party continued to
support him in office he would focus all his influence upon his efforts to
substitute social dialogue for dictatorship, and that the fruits of this

policy must bring the Kremlin round to his way of thinking. Not Dubcek, but only his young aides knew that there was little time, little room to maneuver, left. This was a role Dubcek clung to with increasing desperation as the hammer of events weakened his grip, a role that he never, even after the final betrayal, abandoned in his heart.

To Dubcek, his reforms were the opposite of Nagy's counterrevolution. He wanted to remake Czech socialism in order to play a larger, not a lesser, part in the world socialist revolution. He wanted glory for himself as well as for his country, and he realized that he could have it only if his reforms were accepted by the Soviets. However prolonged and bitter, the debate with the Soviets remained for Dubcek only a shadow duel. He had no wish to push home the quarrel to some ultimate conclusion. So long as his program did not threaten the Soviets, he assumed that Brezhnev and his colleagues would acquiesce in the process. Holding these views, Dubcek hoped for Soviet understanding of his purpose until the very last, a Casabianca on the burning deck of socialist solidarity. But it was on the planks of a personal, not national, sense of fraternity. Where he could never regard the Russians as a threat, his people hated and despised them. The sentiments let loose by a free press trumpeted this hatred.

But at a meeting on July 29, 1968 in the Czech village of Ciernanad-Tisou with the Soviets, Dubcek found himself a target. Before his departure for the summit, Dubcek went on national television to declare: "Nothing will make us abandon the road we started in January this year. . . . I am convinced that our friends will understand the rightness of our way. We will not budge an inch."[29] But the Soviets had sent almost the entire Politburo to voice their displeasure with this uncompromising position. Amidst the tinted mirrors and scarlet curtains of the town's old railwayman's club, Brezhnev himself declared that he expected an attempt on his life and insisted on being seated facing the windows outside, so that the Soviets could watch the joint patrols of Soviet soldiers with Czech militiamen armed with submachine guns.

Within moments of opening the talks, Dubcek was stunned by an explicit demand that he renounce his program. Without allowing for any diplomatic niceties, Brezhnev bitterly attacked Dubcek and his government; for four hours he recounted their counterrevolutionary crimes, cited offensive articles in the Czechoslovak press, and abused "bourgeois-revisionists" such as Dubcek's colleagues Goldstuecker, Sik, and Cisar. At the end of this diatribe, the delegations broke for lunch.

They did not dine together. When the talks resumed, Dubcek attempted to defend his policies. Soothing words had no effect upon the suspicious Soviets. Another day of futile talks followed. "You are not going to treat us as your underlings," Dubcek brazenly declared at one point. "You'll get used to it, Alexander," old Ludvik Svoboda, now the Czechoslovak President, said. "Marshall Konev treated me as an underling throughout the war."[30] That night, the Russians withdrew across the border.

Dubcek knew that the real reason for Brezhnev's antagonism was annoyance at being goaded to undertake reform within the USSR. In one of his summaries of frustration he wrote, "I have told him the truth. I have brought all deficiencies to his notice. I have warned him about the conditions of socialist decay. I have demonstrated how these things can be corrected. All this he ignores and shuts his eyes to the deplorable condition of his country which is a terrible indictment of him."[31] This was exactly Dubcek's crime. His program was a constant reminder of socialism's deficiencies and it caused Brezhnev to lose face. Dubcek's presence in power had become a daily indictment.

Naive to the last, Dubcek refused to put his army on alert. The prospect of armed opposition to a Soviet incursion might have been the only thing that could have deterred the Russians. It was not to be. Having refused to take military precautions or to break relations, Dubcek shut himself up in Prague Castle, where, as one aide fumed in his diary, "He engaged in what he called thought and the air currents of the world never ventilated his mind."[32] The comment was that of a hurt and frustrated man but not without justice. Dubcek still would not heed the fact that his program threatened the very core of socialism as it had been practiced since 1917, and that the Soviets would fight him to the end rather than settle for less power by right. He was still determined to keep Czechoslovakia free of an overt struggle with Russia, in a position to re-create the socialist vision, withstanding all provocations short of an overt act. He did not expect one from Brezhnev. Dubcek's illusions delivered him into the Kremlin's hands.

It is the element of irresponsibility that is most striking in following the events that preceded the Soviet invasion of August 20, 1968. Presumably, Dubcek should have known that he was in some danger. But he could think of nothing but the internal problems of reform, which constituted a crisis of the most elusive kind. Both the Soviets and Dubcek were dealing in delusions. Dubcek behaved as if he were at the head of some sort of crusade, with a large and loyal army at his back, which was very far from being the case. He had his own handpicked Central Committee at his side, and the bulk of younger Party members, but the

Party apparatus was not nearly as loyal as he imagined. Even if his orders for reform reached their intended destination—and often they were deliberately mislaid—it was impossible for his loyal subordinates to always carry them out because of the hopeless inertia and inefficiency of the whole state machine. Some of his reforms did quickly break down or fail to materialize. The Prague Spring was the most disorderly governmental operation imaginable.

Brezhnev, on his side, was also living in a world of fantasy. He brushed aside eleventh-hour pleas from Tito and the Spanish communists to bring about a reconciliation with Dubcek and his program, and began to send out orders to Warsaw Pact members to be prepared to do his bidding. It was a blow to him to learn that Romania would not oblige.

Neither man, in short, had the power to control the situation they had so recklessly created. New talks between the two men were held in Bratislava on August 3, 1968. No common ground could be found. "There were times," one of Dubcek's colleagues told William Shawcross, when the Soviets "dragged him in the mud and trampled upon him. It made us sick; this is the end, we said to ourselves; let's give up. But after the initial shock, Dubcek always took hold of himself and ignoring the insults, weighed in."[33] Dubcek himself once described his behavior during such encounters: "I just try to smile at Brezhnev as he shouts at me. I say, yes, yes, I agree, and then I come home to do nothing."[34] A little deference, a little lie, a gracious personality—this was Dubcek's idea of socialist harmony.

For a while the harmony seemed real. Brezhnev became astonishingly amiable. This should have been a clue to watch for treachery, but to Dubcek it was merely another factor to feed his wishful thinking.

The invasion came and succeeded with a fabulous ease. On August 20, armies of five nations of the Warsaw Pact crossed into Czechoslovakia. No preparations for resistance having been made, Dubcek knew that an order to resist would have been suicide. But it is doubtful if he could ever have given such an order. Dubcek never fully grasped the gravity of the situation. There is no reason to doubt that he was telling the truth when he said, weeping: "That they should have done this to me, after I have dedicated my whole life to cooperation with the Soviet Union, is the great tragedy of my life."[35] He still had no idea that the Soviets intended to abduct and depose him. A heretic's fate akin to that of Djilas and Khrushchev, and perhaps the murdered Imre Nagy, awaited him.

Only when he was brought to the Kremlin in manacles did Dubcek understand. This was an indignity not even Nagy had suffered. To avoid execution, with rage in his heart Dubcek swallowed the necessity to act as the Kremlin's puppet. He was sent back to Prague to destroy himself, to destroy his reforms and his followers. Dubcek was to be the executioner of his own ideals.

As Dubcek was later to say from his place of exile in a Slovak forest, "No disillusionment was ever greater or more sudden."[36] It struck him with such violence that he thought himself no longer the same man. And yet it seemed to him that in the resulting state of hatred his conscience had become diminished. He would dedicate the rest of his life to the man he used to be.

Of all the profiles of disillusion we have studied, Dubcek's is perhaps the most poignant testimony of what communist intoxication did to the mind of his time. The Prague Spring and its suppression created passions, attitudes, ideas, and rivalries that determined communism's future decline and fall. The communist utopia that used to rule as an ideal, and the ideas that shaped it, disappeared as a popular notion, like the wraith of Dubcek's former self, in the bitter months that followed. Those illusions—the brotherhood of socialists, the dream of a new world—failed to function when put to the test. Power, like a brutal gust of wind, arose and swept them aside.

20

❧❧❧ ❦❦❦

Solzhenitsyn
Out of the Archipelago

Uproar at the invasion of Czechoslovakia was vociferous. Communists throughout the world were content to let the Kremlin bear sole responsibility for the act, to cover their own failure to object. Leonid Brezhnev, a stranger to the quality of mercy, granted no pardon. Milovan Djilas, always independent-minded, who could tell absurdity from utility when it stood in front of him, was the sole voice to campaign for Alexander Dubcek's pardon, but as he was himself recently released from prison, his effort was in vain. Dubcek's internal exile in Bratislava, however, kept discussion of his program alive, one more bitterness to divide and cause doubt. Dubcek was disgraced, publicly paraded before fellow Party members in his manacles, for no discernible purpose except to degrade. Such punishments could accomplish little, for without the threat of death it was doubtful that men could be made orthodox by fiat or deterred from experimentation by fear or punishment.[1]

If to no sure purpose, why was the degradation of Dubcek imposed? Because it was, seemingly, the only option other than death for the particular failing for which Dubcek was judged and held guilty. Exercising choice, however, is one of the burdens of being human and having a mind. Not to exercise it may be easier, but if unused it is likely to become sluggish, which may be one of the results of decades of enforced conformity, even upon those who think of themselves as determining the rules by which men are to conform.

Dubcek suffered for his doubts. The late 1960s was a period when Communist rulers went in fear of the young (who knew through Soviet propaganda about the May 1968 revolt in Paris, or the riots at the Democratic party's convention in Chicago that summer) and feared anarchy rising from their own working class. To suppress it, Brezhnev and his acolytes throughout Eastern and Central Europe enacted laws with ferocious penalties, and no matter what suggestion of reason or

276

compassion or common sense might be advanced against re-stocking the gulags, it would not be heard by the Party's leaders; the Party must not deviate. In a sense, this unthinking severity was a development of the very extensive doubts now running silently through the Party's various echelons, which the words and examples of Djilas, Nagy, Khrushchev, and now Dubcek, had fostered. But Brezhnev and those at the top of the USSR's acolyte parties consistently ignored these voices, pretending that each act of disenchantment and reform was some kind of misguided frenzy. No longer was Stalin in disgrace. His system was to be modernized—"Stalinism with computers."[2] They thereby lost any chance of winning back intellectual allegiance or inspiring a reconciliation.

Tolerance of socialism's failures, despite public airing of its crimes, bespoke a mental lethargy that underlay the Party's general unwillingness to change established habits and dogmas. Alternative theories were not beyond reach. To return even to the modest decentralizations of Khrushchev's regime might have been difficult but not impossible. Economic reforms could have been introduced by following a program adopted by Nagy's successors in Hungary, who dangled before the Hungarian people the chance to work in a limited free market in exchange for political passivity—goulash socialism. Means of checking administrative abuse might yet have been found if Party elders wanted, for at least in the USSR the conviction that the Party machine was essentially corrupt had not taken wholesale root among the people.

Criticisms of the Party and state occasionally broke through the serene Party facade under Brezhnev—not systemic ones, but complaints aimed at improving the functioning of particular ministries or industries. It was this combination of blindness and lethargy which formed the platform on which Alexander Solzhenitsyn was to preach his damning jeremiads.

Of all the critics of the Soviet system, Solzhenitsyn should have been perhaps the easiest for the system to seek to domesticate; for he himself suggested there were deep affinities between the revolutionary's character and that of his own. Whether he was remarking upon anything more than the character of the proletarian-born in each circumstance is impossible to say; there was certainly clenched class resentment in Solzhenitsyn, and he was nearer to the old Bolsheviks, if only because of his isolation and energy, than either Brezhnev or Khrushchev. Solzhenitsyn was a puritan and an anarchist; a sanguine creature, class-conscious and egocentric, and he had the peculiar revolutionary's madness: the madness of political morality gone rampant. Indeed,

Solzhenitsyn is a victim of that powerful cult of the will, duty, and conscience by which a religious temper turns life into an incessant war. The problem of evil is solved when we are drastically pure in private life. His genius for rendering the thinking surface of life recalls the gifts of Gide and Koestler and Silone on their very much smaller scale, though in Solzhenitsyn this genius sprang from the classical tradition of Pushkin and Tolstoy, from a primitive animality none of the other writers had, ever.

In his early novels, Solzhenitsyn's characters were left with their natures and their lives, and what they really were at heart was never spiritually or imaginatively grasped by the drastic old puritans of Stalin's prison camps, who believed in simplifying life by chopping off its limbs. Solzhenitsyn's imagination was not of the kind that adds to life in the sense of fusing something new and blinding with it; his imagination was a luminary which lit up and brought back the living detail of experience as the moon in midsummer will miraculously turn a dark landscape to the sparkle of its lost daytime life. What Solzhenitsyn recovered in his novels of the camps was the motion of time in men's lives themselves, the continuous approach, young-eyed and innocent, toward the moral corruption he feared so much. In that all-searching light of his, life was seen with clarity, understood with awe, and watched with compassion; for it moved upon a scene we have not been meant to witness and which was recreated with the desire of the animal to recall the terror of its moment.

And then, another point that is bound to strike us: what an advantage the prophet had over the preacher, the bad communist over the good communist, the Dostoevskian over the Tolstoyan when it comes to writing what are essentially religious novels. The preacher is forced to prove his point. Sinners are reformed, we all know; men and women do undergo conversions; they can be made better; and not, as in Dostoevsky, all the better for being worse. But the life of no man or woman can be mapped so neatly into black and white, as socialist theory demands: the value of a life, imaginatively, is in all of a life. What is most interesting about Solzhenitsyn's work is that it was written with that same socially messianic impulse that informed Lenin and Bukharin— and Gide and Koestler and Silone, too; he stood at the turning point of that impulse back toward individual and spiritual ends. *Cancer Ward,* *The First Circle,* and *One Day in the Life of Ivan Denisovich* may be said to continue the Soviet novelistic tradition of immediate propaganda for visible objectives. When he was young Solzhenitsyn dreamed as a good socialist of a religion that was not otherworldly, but which would create heaven on earth. No subtler master of the didactic has been produced since the revolution.

For Solzhenitsyn is one of those preachers, at least while he is preaching, who does really convert. Where others build up in the audience an obstinate resistance, Solzhenitsyn really does most cunningly persuade. We are glad that Sologdin's life changed when he saw his complicity and guilt; we recognize one by one all his feelings; we applaud his honesty, for we can see, in some corner of our souls, a facility for complicity and honesty, too. We are glad, too, that Spiridon is recalcitrant, angry, and bewildered at first by his imprisonment; that he can precisely estimate, in his detached and peasant way, what there is of opaque self-exultation left in him and what there is of transparent repentance. Rubin's sense that repentance is unnecessary makes him real as a character and when, at the crisis of his relations with the other prisoners, he resists what he regards as their attempt to imprison him mentally, just as the Party he loves has imprisoned him physically, our deepest sense of justice is aroused.

How did Solzhenitsyn manage to persuade as he wrote? He persuades, as all the great epic writers do, by his native possession of the sense of simple inevitability, and he had this sense of communism's inherent corruptions and brutalities from his profound affinity with its victims with whom, as a prisoner himself, he lived in communion. Yet, as a Russian, he believed in a lost golden age when all worked for the good. Solzhenitsyn's faith was like the primitive response to night and day: each man wakes up in the morning and sees the sky, sees what he takes to be the truth. But his simplicity was not all of a piece; it was not merely the eyes of a prophet scouting the wilderness. It was also cunning. Madame Mandelstam has recorded how the soon-to-be-exiled Solzhenitsyn conveyed an impression of knowing all there is to know and of having made up his mind about everything; how he could suddenly bark out harsh, bitter, and coarse sayings and chuckle with malice, grinning like some animal before the horrors of life. What Solzhenitsyn saw, in his egotism, his solitude, his strong animal passion, was the simple facts of life under socialism, and he put these down as if, in the naiveté of love and the satisfaction of ever-watching eyes, he were discovering them for the first time. So as he reveals the world of the gulag he sets down things so plain and so true that we are struck by their boldness—lives are wasted or destroyed as if carried by a brook rippling through the grave course of time itself. Solzhenitsyn persuades because he was always bringing his next words to our lips, precisely unveiling what we shall all recognize when we see them.

He persuades, but until the publication of the *Gulag Archipelago*, did not fully convince. The philosophy of Solzhenitsyn seemed too atavistic; he seemed to retreat into the collective common mind of the peasant. In this way, though hating communism and shunning its lies and its politics, he prescribed a similar ideal. Solzhenitsyn's puritanism was revolting; his egotism monstrous. There are moments when the supposed "criminal" histories of his inmates become as boring as a chaplain's memoirs, particularly when compared to the rich and intense portraits of Dostoevsky's *House of the Dead*. Compare them: which writer more fully expands our knowledge of the human spirit? Not the preacher. The good things in the early novels are the accounts of communist intoxication and its continuous debilitating delusions, also the brilliant, ironical, immensely wily descriptions of camp life and the back ways of socialist legality. We can smell the breath of those torpid judges and commandants; we catch the commissars in the very act of advancing their careers. And how revealing—for Solzhenitsyn was unable to resist the sense of delight in cowardice and confusion exposed—are those nighttime moments of conversation in the blockhouses which we are asked to regard as the hollow haunts of vanity and hypocrisy. It is this rounding against his own cause of doubt which is most unbearable in Solzhenitsyn, as all self-mutilation is, and which strikes as patently dishonest. Gluttonously he has swallowed his own deceits—such as hiding his own near recruitment to the NKVD—and now they exist no more. Yet, it is impossible to say that his puritanism with its self-display, has the aridity, the meanness, the smugness, the bent for the hypocrisies of moral certainty or the lapses into instant judgment, the cult of the pure, which communism itself commonly had. But Solzhenitsyn, too, preached the impossible.

Solzhenitsyn wrote the *Gulag Archipelago* to bring unimpeachable witness and global focus to his earlier themes. Here he acts as Gide did in *Retour de l'U.R.S.S.*, but without the velvet glove. The pride and cowardice and violence of life in the gulag is brought close upon us, whereas Gide reported on the pariahs of the socialist state at one remove. They were the exotic if telling anecdotes of a civilized connoisseur of communist ideology and passion. The wound in Gide's nature gave him the aesthete's curious admiration of socialist engineering and power and turned him outward to the primitive. Solzhenitsyn has the advantage of turning inward as he dissects, of going home, and he is filled with instinctive knowledge. In no way is he a mystic about the masses.

In the *Gulag Archipelago* Solzhenitsyn is no longer the teller of frightening dramatic episodes which isolate the passions of people as conditions of their shackled lives. The high passions, the murderous intrigues of survival, remain not only because of man's genetic inheritance, but because such traits are preserved the longest by the downtrodden and the wretched. In the gulag, the educated are more sensitive to change than the poor whose humane virtues appear to emerge only at those moments when civilizations crack. Solzhenitsyn finds himself inside the thoughts, words, and interests of the imprisoned proles as the socialist Saturn devours them. He does not stand with one foot safely beyond the barbed wire, but went into their lives, discerned their own moments of disillusion, and took them at their own valuation. From the moment we open the *Gulag Archipelago* we are pitched into the squabble and scrum of gulag life, straight among the talk of the misers, the spies, the honorable, the wasters, the modest, the hypocrites, the officials, the skirling camp shrews. Their voices deafen us, their quarrels and cries confuse our ears, their calamities catch us, and we are also subject to those strange truces in the rancor of a community when, for a day or moment, a disaster will quieten it with a common emotion. Collective suffering, Solzhenitsyn implies, is the only true and human moment of socialism.

Solzhenitsyn's aim was to write as closely as he could to the language of the Russian masses who were the supposed beneficiaries of the socialist state, for talk is the interminable litany of the poor. Especially he demolishes socialism's pretences by making wonderful use of common slang and the vivid proverbs of the masses. Solzhenitsyn has invented an epic style which carries these images and sayings naturally, and without Gide's didactic effect on the one hand, or Koestler's artificial coloring on the other.

Let us look back again at the literary heretics who have acted as a point of reference in discerning the decline of the socialist ideal. Gide, Koestler, and Silone were puzzled and stunned by the brutalities and grotesque lies which had taken place in the Soviet Union under socialism, and by the masks that true believers wear so as to shield their complicity in communism's crimes. Solzhenitsyn lifted the masks and charted the currents running below the surface of Soviet history—a chart which jettisons utopian predictions and deciphers the revolution's rhetoric as sinister slogans and abstract concepts that can be made to endorse any sort of crime. In Gide's and Koestler's work it was possible to see what guilt faith in revolution could yield, but they imagined that the abuses of socialism arose as much from the lusts of Stalin as from socialist theory. They failed to follow the clues as to the true origins of abuse.

But Solzhenitsyn, in the *Gulag Archipelago*, is able to pick up all the threads of socialist corruption, to follow them back to the revolution and the idea of socialism itself. Never, after we have read the *Gulag Archipelago*, can the promises, the scientific proofs, the pretensions, of socialist theory assume any transcendental or millenarial purpose. Woolly claims to social perfection, dogmatic assertions to have history on your side, look obsolete, crazed, and deceitful; after Solzhenitsyn it is possible, through all the shadow-play, to see that the socialist state's maniacal appetites were inherent in Marxist theory, that the only thing of historical inevitability about communism was murderous corruption.

The matter of the *Gulag Archipelago* is less a Koestlerian history-epic with its landscapes, its explanations, its expiations and its theories, than a stream of rabid camp talk. It is this series of confessional voices that makes the book whole, and fills that bleak, satiric side of Solzhenitsyn's mind, which so stunned in his early novels, with generosity, sorrow, and forgiveness. It is the power of Solzhenitsyn's argument fused with the poetry of remembered lives that makes the *Gulag Archipelago* incomparable and compelling. For in the *Gulag Archipelago* Solzhenitsyn's exposition of his argument—the *danse macabre* of dialectical inevitability, the cross-stitching of Marxist-Leninist quack logic —is always connected to a precise picture of socialism at work; and these testimonies, with their accumulation of interrogations, tortures, executions, and rapes, their remorseless revelation of the bloody conditions to which the men, women, and children of the working class have been forced to debase themselves, their chronicles of the sordid expedients by which the apparatchiks rule, and the hypocrisy in which they shroud their practices—these expand and become almost intolerable. We are made to feel that we are being taken, for the first time, through the *real* structure of socialist civilization, and that it is the most inhuman that has ever existed. The "amazing country of *Gulag*, which, though scattered in an archipelago geographically, was, in the psychological sense, fused into a continent—an almost invisible, almost imperceptible, country inhabited by the zek people"[3] is a nation of such savagery that there is little to choose between the physical degradation of the prisoners and the moral degeneration of the comrades.

But it was also Solzhenitsyn's intention to rally communists loyal to Nikita Khrushchev to his point of view. Khrushchev's secret speech to the twentieth Party Congress had only barely outlined the enormity of the terror. His thesis, as we have seen, was that the abuses under

Stalinism were the direct result of the dictator's personality. The massacres, the deportations, the tortures, the setting up of the penal camps—none of it sprang from authentic Marxist-Leninist precepts, or so Khrushchev said. They were, instead, the blood lust of Stalin, the megalomania and pathological suspicions of a tyrant who had savagely distorted the legitimate structures of the socialist state. With the close of Stalin's rule, this bloody chapter of Soviet history could be put to rest.

In the *Gulag Archipelago* Solzhenitsyn demolishes Khrushchev's version of history. Yet he wants to play on the doubts Khrushchev generated. The lawless, inhuman, tyrannical nature of communism did not originate with Stalin; it was not the product of a single personality, however monstrous in dimension and will. The great enslavement began with Lenin. It was Lenin who, in December 1917 and January 1918, demanded the merciless extermination of "anti-social elements," of "hooligans," "shirkers, parasites," and it is he who ordered the "cleansing" of Soviet society by execution "or punishment at forced labour of the hardest kind."[4] It was not Stalin's assumption of power that delivered his country to the gulag; it was the Bolshevik Revolution itself. Listen to Mayakovsky, says Solzhenitsyn, listen to the beloved songster of the Red Dawn:

> With cohesion, construction,
>   grit, and expression
> Wring the neck of this gang
>   run riot![5]

The gang, of course, being anyone not in agreement with bolshevism.

Terror, subjection of society to total surveillance, suppression of free thought, institutionalized torture and exile, are all intrinsic to communism and its view of man. Stalin merely fulfilled, with a crazed logical finality, the principles implicit in state socialism. Only a difference in degree, not kind, came with Stalin's death. This or that straw of truth may be allowed to blow in the wind momentarily. But the machinery of enslavement remains so long as socialism exists. It can gear up at any moment. Torturers go unpunished, and are ready to take up their posts at any time; the mines and the Arctic camps await the next wave. Socialism is in essence irreparably corrupt. It must stifle and mutilate the material and moral existence of its subjects because it has no legal foundation.

This is a primary thesis of Solzhenitsyn. The arrests of 1918–1919 are given the name "extrajudicial reprisals."[6] In fact, there was no need for such ornate cant. How could any behavior be termed "extrajudicial" when there was no law, when everything must bend to the revolutionary will? Citing one lynching after another, purges each more murderous than the last, choruses of confessions each more abject, more ludicrous than the one before, Solzhenitsyn hammers at his point: Soviet law is a mask for lawlessness, Soviet courts are nothing but instruments of naked power, Soviet judges are the sycophantic auxiliaries to the camp guard and the executioner.

And the consequence? A social fabric inherently illegal, a political structure without possibility of justice, for it has no idea what justice means, cannot look to gradual amelioration. It cannot redress itself piecemeal. Each thaw only heralds a new winter. Soviet socialism cannot be reformed by decree or pragmatic maneuver. Root and branch, it must be torn out. Already, it may be too late.

> We have to condemn publicly the idea that some people have the right to repress others. In keeping silent about evil, in burying it so deep within us that no sign of it appears on the surface, we are implanting it, and it will rise up a thousand fold in the future. . . . Young people are acquiring the conviction that foul deeds are never punished on earth, that they always bring prosperity.[7]

Here we get to the bottom of Solzhenitsyn's jeremiad—to the conclusion that socialism is wrong because it destroys the independent moral conscience of men and prevents the recognition of those rights which must be common to all human beings. If individual conscience does not matter, then what is wrong with its suppression in the name of the common good? Nothing, the communists would say. There is no way of proving that a conscience exists any more than there is a means to prove that all souls have equal value to God. Through the accumulation of his testamentary evidence, Solzhenitsyn seeks to prove that the progressive brutality of Stalinism arose from communism's denial of the worth of the individual mind and soul. He shows that the gulag gestated in socialism's womb. And if he exposes the dark depths of the socialist state, it is less to move us to fellow feeling with those the state has degraded than to destroy the pretenses of the state's masters. The dictatorship of the proletariat, in the *Gulag Archipelago*, is a caricature of governance; and the governed appear mainly as victims of its crimes. For Solzhenitsyn, there is in socialism an unbridgeable gulf between the good which it proposes for humanity and the ruthlessness and hatred which are its means to remain in power.

The *Gulag Archipelago* is the bitterest of all Solzhenitsyn's bitter books. It has hardly a trace of the moral confusion that gives his earlier books their humanity. Solzhenitsyn himself is not only the dehumanized prole, the state's victim; he is also entitled to use all the tricks employed by socialism in order to bring socialism down. This means he can lie, he can distort. For example, Solzhenitsyn cites the case of Yevgeny Ivanovich Divnich, "an emigré and preacher of Orthodox Christianity," who was tortured by both the Gestapo and the Ministry of State Security (the MGB). "The Gestapo was . . . trying to get at the truth, and when the accusation did not hold up, Divnich was released. The M.G.B. wasn't interested in the truth and had no intention of letting anyone out of its grip once he was arrested."[8] Here is a gross inference: the Gestapo used torture merely to seek "the truth." Only the MGB tortured for the sake of torturing. It is this sort of sibylline didacticism that leads the author of *The First Circle* and *Cancer Ward* to publish a paragraph of pure rage and muddle:

> We read in *Izvestya* for May 24, 1959, that Yuliya Rumyantseva was confined in the internal prison of a Nazi camp while they tried to find out from her the whereabouts of her husband, who had escaped from the same camp. She knew, but she refused to tell! For a reader who is not in the know, this is a model of heroism. For a reader with a bitter Gulag past it's a model of inefficient interrogation: Yuliya did not die under torture, and she was not driven insane. A month later she was simply released—still very much alive and kicking.[9]

This is truly ignoble—even if, or indeed precisely because, the register is that of sarcasm.

Moral genius cannot be separated from intelligence, from the power to inform judgment through a continuous life-giving sense of discrimination. At key moments in the *Gulag Archipelago* that intelligence shrivels. It is "they" who torture, who imprison, who blackmail; it is "they" who enact the apocalypse or the banality of evil. "They" number in the tens of thousands. "They" come forward whenever a Stalin or murderous technocrat calls. In the socialist state, there is always enough of "them" to do the job—to enslave, terrorize, or corrupt "us." But who are "they" and what finally are "their" motives? This is the central riddle in the tragedy and barbarism of state socialism, and Solzhenitsyn makes no effort to solve it. The men of the Cheka and KGB are simply addicts of status and acquisitiveness and power. With each exercise of abasement, their appetites grow. It is "they" who have the apartments, the cars, the women, the extra rations. "Their" bellies are warm and full while "we" cower in the Arctic cold, gnawing shoe leather. There is terrible truth in this diagnosis, but there is also over-simplification.

From a man of Solzhenitsyn's religious temperament one expects a subtler, less localized sense of the potential of disinterested evil, of sacrificial, abstract malignity in the human character. In the absence of such subtlety, a Stalin remains intangible, unintelligible. The lusts and obsessions of socialism are there, but only in their physical explicitness—suddenly, overpoweringly, the criminals of the socialist state appear dramatically out of a fog, with the rime upon them. Solzhenitsyn's voice of incantation disguises their pathologies, slurs and constructs a conventional nightmare. We are dealing with, in Joseph Brodsky's telling phrase, a system "that simply has put the production of tyrants on an industrial footing."[10]

With the *Gulag Archipelago* we are dropped into the stage after Gide, Koestler, and Silone, after the barely imaginable has been made real and distributed. So the early anti-communist heretics haunt, for the socialist world remained mired in that mess in which they found themselves in at the very beginning. But what a difference of tone lies between Gide, Koestler, Silone and that of Solzhenitsyn! The rage of frustration has succeeded their disappointed and stoical bitterness. There is all the distance that lies between the Calvinist's pulpit vision of disgust and doom, and the betrayal in the trench. What was literature to Gide, testament to Koestler, or vision to Silone, we are made by Solzhenitsyn to see with our own eyes. The search for faith which brought Gide, Koestler, and Silone to communism was something plausible in which to believe in the chaotic 1930s, when the USSR shone like a beacon for a new world. After Solzhenitsyn that same search appears merely as one of those question-begging frenzies which lead straight to the concentration camp. It is not surprising that even at his most irascible and sadistic, Solzhenitsyn became pre-eminent among the anti-communist prophets: he embodied the energy and pathos, the aggression and the guilt, of those who had exchanged belief in God for belief in history alone and, in many ways, Solzhenitsyn's attitude to religion is far more sympathetic than that of other apostates, for it was deeply tinctured by his sense of imagination and the sense of human pain. Solzhenitsyn at no time lost, as the more optimistic and accommodating Gide, Koestler, and Silone did, the powerful morbidity of the tradition into which, as a writer, he was born.

The Solzhenitsyn who went into exile after publication of the *Gulag Archipelago* is a very different character from the man Khrushchev set free to write. He is crabbed and complex, a neurotic made for the problem biography. Turning to his work we see that his pungency, urgency, his incomparable physical portraiture and power of image-making, might have made him a supreme satirist, a writer as great as Gogol or Swift, if he had maintained the humor of his youth. But that strain had dried up in him, and he could no longer be subtle with self-irony, untainted by the poisons of satire.

The main insight, on which Solzhenitsyn was to build both sane and—in his frustration—violent and sadistic conclusions, was into the power basis of socialist societies. In an age when many thinkers thought that socialism could be changed merely by an injection of goodwill, Solzhenitsyn understood the basis of force upon which all communist societies rest. In a time when economists thought that central planning must automatically eliminate the dysfunctions of the market, he realized that it aimed ultimately at the overthrow of private life. In a time of continual abstract arguments about the amount of liberty that might reasonably be allowed human beings, he saw that liberties are surrendered at the expense of all other freedoms and that they are not abstract ideas but concrete realities. Or they are nothing.

It was inevitable that Solzhenitsyn's cult of the individual sprang from his own pride, and his turn late in life to his Russian Orthodox faith was an alternative to the lost dialectical deity of his young adulthood. It is impossible not to be saddened at the sight of a man who has been released at great cost from socialism's chains to move, unchecked, toward megalomania. It is natural to smile when, free at last into the democracies of the West which he had imagined as repositories of all the stern social virtues, after years of grind, loneliness, and suffering which the image of freedom had made barely tolerable, Solzhenitsyn finds only sloth and corruption and decadence. He begins to believe in the wisdom of the ancient aristocracy, the ancient Orthodox rites, failing to recall that it was class blindness and spiritual inertia that had paved the way to socialism. But this was a result of the simplicity of Solzhenitsyn's character and of his social and moral frustration. Looking at the brutalities of the socialist state he longed for action against it; looking at Western chaos he called for decisive authority. Dangerous talk. At bottom, Solzhenitsyn's talk is clan talk. His mind was formed in a society akin to that which formed the young Stalin, and he lived in the mental climate of the Caucasus, with its vendettas and long memories. One more imaginative, fanatical, dogmatic Slav had failed to understand that democracy means compromise, an unprepossessing, semi-religious veneration of social stability. True democrats prefer worry to drama.

Solzhenitsyn succeeded, where Gide, Koestler, and Silone had failed, in destroying the legitimacy of the socialist state because he fully embodied the socialist and revolutionary ethic. Solzhenitsyn's unrelenting concentration and ascetism were akin to Lenin's own, for he, too, aimed at inciting a revolution. But a revolution of the mind was his goal. His mode of life during his last years in his homeland was that of the revolutionary emigré. His constant secret shifting of his research materials from place to place, the ceaseless fear of landing back in jail or in a psychiatric hospital; these constraints have their parallels in Lenin's and Bukharin's years of exile. Like them, he dispensed with ordinary comforts. While living in a gardener's shed at the home of Mstislav Rostropovich, he lived without heat and ate only scraps when he could not pay for his meals. He was indifferent to the clothes he wore, and friends had to outfit him with their own best cast-offs. Where Gide, Koestler, and Silone had been raised in worlds that were not remotely socialist, Solzhenitsyn was to the commune born. To oppose it, he was forced not only to pledge his conscience, but also his life. Compelled by his imprisonment and his solitude, he was forced to live like a revolutionary and therefore to understand the type. The portraits in his novels and histories are drawn with irony and hatred; Solzhenitsyn's bitterness was the anger of the insider, of the permanently damaged human being. Whether historical figures such as Stalin or invented characters such as Rubin, Solzhenitsyn's studies are meticulous artistic onions; peel off the top skin of ideological commitment, peel off the next skin of political caution, and the next layer to find the man who will accept a bribe or a promotion or a promise of safety—and underneath there appears, at last, the puzzled, rancorous, bewildered human being. Only in the conditions he must endure has Man been altered by socialism. All his portraits have something of this richness and are marked by Solzhenitsyn's minuteness—"a face already crinkled with envy."[11] His revolutionaries and agnostics are not all of a piece; Solzhenitsyn catches men isolated and drying up in futile obsessions with politics. Each and every character is boiling in his own political pot.

Solzhenitsyn was a great magician who sometimes rubbed the wrong lamps. Even in the days of *Cancer Ward* and *Ivan Denisovich*, when his voice rings most truly, Solzhenitsyn's voice was not fully political in the sense that he added to the practical or theoretical thought of politics. He added, rather, to that part of the inner life of people, to the imagination above all, which may take them to or away from religious or political action. His objection to socialism was fundamentally the poet's or the preacher's: socialism ignored the soul, socialism ignored the individual's need for a vision of his own private drama and significance. The most satisfying of Solzhenitsyn's counterrevolutionary acts was the creation of his enraging prose. He takes us back to another puritan in whom the violent pressure of socialism had created an intense extravagance of fantasy: to the writings of Mayakovsky. Solzhenitsyn was a socialist pagan with Mayakovsky's rhythms thumping in his head. Humility vanishes, acceptance goes, egoism expands. We are no longer to live in the prose in which it pleases the socialist state to call us, but suddenly to have the rights of our private poetic intuitions. We recognize our own distinct genius. Rather than subsume ourselves in the collective, we are to reclaim ourselves as singular human souls.

It is easy to see what Brezhnev and the Soviet authorities feared in Solzhenitsyn, but what about ourselves? Socialism is discredited; after the *Gulag Archipelago* it is impossible to see how the socialist state could ever have come to a good end. But is the book merely to become for us one of those classics whose vitality and vividness make them irresistible but of no lasting moment? Shall we regard Solzhenitsyn as part of the memory of modern Europe, stamping, yelling, biting till the blood comes, and uncontrollable? Will he merely suggest to us the natural bombast of dubious genius in a gangster state? Or shall we continue to find some lasting human substance in his refractory figure, to toughen and feed our need for faith? If the human spirit is to survive in a society grown hostile to its needs, Solzhenitsyn ought to be read, for the *Gulag Archipelago* is one of the elementary statements of one kind of artist's mind, above all of the power, range, and detail of sustained rage and hallucination. Solzhenitsyn was and is a pestilentially dedicated figure. Behind Solzhenitsyn rings the singular conviction of individual truth.

In the gulag, the individual man broke his bonds and his silence and in his own right came alive. If Gide gave birth within the socialist world to a reconquest of the self, that stoic and questioning invalid, with sad, luminous and broken eyes; if after him Koestler and Silone discharged upon us the chaotic imagination of the socialist penitent and the sensibilities that feed upon him, a figure like Solzhenitsyn is of the same exemplary kind. He parades within the belly of the socialist state a libido which has never surrendered to the censor unless it was there in the mask of that melancholy temperament to which he always laid claim. Solzhenitsyn had, no doubt, the melancholy of the serious artist and the image of him that emerges from his work suggests the naive and morbid sadness of some miracle-working friar. Despite the worm, or because of it, Solzhenitsyn jumped from homicide to art, from the complacencies of intrigue and the ironies of persecution mania to the animal transfigurations of pure undiluted rage. He can be held by no inner restraints, only by the unchecked libidos of the other animals, who gang up against him. His life becomes a vendetta. But even then, when his supreme knowledge of their crimes puts him equal to the power of his enemies, and he is left to waste his spirit in exile, his pride is unbroken, unconquered.

To this absolute pride which is carried away, so sympathetically, into condescending mania, there is only one response: his death or our deafness. Both commissars and capitalists can do nothing with an animal of such resources. It is either their vision or his. No surrender. The *Gulag Archipelago* might be said to commemorate the rediscovery of that part of the human self that declares there is no room for two.

Always the most honest man in any collection; always quarrelling, wounding, and occasionally damning; always persecuted by the jealous, always getting the better of his enemies and avenging himself of real or imagined wrongs, Solzhenitsyn is the individual at his most extreme. He alone can save Russia. We can laugh at his vision of a new Holy Russia arising from the communist trash heap, but it is not an empty vision. His prescription was painfully reasoned. It is, in the true sense of the word, creative, for it springs out of the interminable activity of Solzhenitsyn's extraordinary egotism. Whatever he does, his vision is at the bottom of his action. He is not merely a prophet; he is a witness of consuming ingenuity. And this ingenuity convinces us that we are dealing not with an extravagant but a total man. He portrays, without knowing it, a complete character, for the lie on one page is shamelessly given away a page or two later.

We see in Solzhenitsyn a many-sided man, released, fulfilled in all his powers to the utmost, despite socialism's pledge to remake man anew. He was continuously an artist, utterly wed to the point of pettifogging frenzy with his work, blind to the existence of anything else, humbled only by the monstrousness of the story he has to tell. Then the natural man, excited by the awakened sense of scientific curiosity—for what is the dream of remaking man and history but scientific experiment on the grandest scale—and finally the storyteller trained in all the fine points of the art. We, like the men and women to whom, on the brink of exile, he dictated what in time became the many *samizdat* copies of the *Gulag Archipelago* to circulate underground in the USSR, must be agog as we listen to that pouring, exterminating voice. The phenomenon of Solzhenitsyn—the voice as from God, the quality that dominated those who would normally have despised him—belongs to no category. Perhaps it can only be explained as the answer called forth by an exigent historic need. The moment required him and he rose. His strength came from the fact that in his voice were combined for the first time the modern cry of ideological disillusion and the old force of puritanical religious faith and patriotism, and what he commanded was both political action and a new life of the spirit to rescue his country and mankind from communist tyranny.

The flight of Solzhenitsyn's meteor continued in his exile. If his life did not instantly generate a national resistance, nevertheless communists thereafter were fighting a losing cause, whether they knew it or not. For the light shed by Solzhenitsyn is not the light shed by Gide, Koestler, and Silone, who hoped that their warnings would penetrate some universal goodness within mankind, and thus restore socialism to itself as a humane vision. To employ Milton's stunning phrase from 'Paradise Lost' about the illumination of Hell, Solzhenitsyn's is "no light, but rather darkness visible."

*Part
Four*

21

⇥⇥ ⇤⇤

Gorbachev

The Young Commissar from Privolnoye

The cracking of old and rigid structures is slow and internal, while the façade holds.

The last government in the Union of Soviet Socialist Republics to possess all the attributes of Lenin and Bukharin's socialist state in full and furious working order took office in the Kremlin in February 1984. The Soviet Union was at the zenith of its power when Konstantin Chernenko took over from the dead Yuri Andropov in that year, and the Politburo Chernenko formed was an image of contented, plump, and orthodox communism. Its members represented Part loyalists who had patiently toiled in the apparat for a generation. The General Secretary's post having eluded him once, on the death of his patron Leonid Brezhnev in 1982, Chernenko was determined to promote his cronies and himself to the full extent. As the nation and Party's superior citizens, his Politburo felt it owed a duty to the system that had promoted them to guard its interests and manage its affairs in the way things had always been managed. Chernenko's government ruled from duty, heritage, and habit—like any aristocracy—and, as they saw it, from right.

Might-have-beens haunted the succession. Age and ill-health had shortened the tenure of Andropov, who had hinted at reform. An austere man, a diplomat and secret policeman for thirty years, the stagnancy and corruption of Brezhnev's rule revolted Andropov. Announcement of his election excited reformists who were happy that the Kremlin had come into the hands of an ascetic whose monk-like and rigorous life promised a return to "Leninist" virtue.[1]

The new era was not to be. Andropov removed many low-level corrupt and inefficient officials, and promised workers greater control over factories and farms. But he was old and debilitated by kidney disease. Under the burden of Party congresses, Politburo meetings late at night, and long Red Square ceremonials watched from atop Lenin's tomb in bitter cold, he weakened daily and died after holding office for little more than a year.

The hope that welcomed Andropov's minimal pledges of change was a measure of a craving for reform within the Soviet population, and warning enough that a Communist party concentrating on its own sectarian aims was not serving the underlying interests of the people. If this was recognized by perhaps a third of the Soviet Central Committee, they were chaff in the wind of a single thwarted ambition. In the election to succeed Andropov, Konstantin Chernenko (to no little astonishment) swept all factions and erstwhile opponents into his camp, and thus secured the Kremlin leadership at last. He was chosen in a secret meeting lasting only a few hours, the shortest (it is said) ever recorded. The solid Party men who formed his government had learned the practices of Communist rule through long years in the state and Party machine, and they undertook to manage the USSR's affairs as inevitably and unquestioningly as beavers build a dam. It was their ordained role and natural task.

But it was threatened: by a rising rumble of protest from below, by the young Party men who had risen under Andropov who talked of radical retrenchment in the power of the socialist state, by independent-minded communists in the Soviet empire of Eastern Europe who recalled fondly the reform programs of Dubcek and Nagy, by trade unions in Poland and in Russia itself who demanded the legal right to strike and otherwise interfere with the state's control of economic forces, by upstart rulers in Romania and Cuba who flaunted Kremlin orders. The rumble was distant, but it spoke with one voice that said, "Change," and those whose business was government could not help but hear.

Planted firmly across the path of change, operating warily yet with hardened conviction, was Chernenko. His Soviet Union was a sated place, a fulfilled rather than a revolutionary society. He offered the Soviet people more of the same rather than reform. Like Brezhnev, he would make no specific goals for communism to attain. He gave Stalinist priority to armaments, which remained the most favored and by far the most flourishing sector of the economy. When staff economists brought him statistics showing that the economy was stagnant, Chernenko, it is said, ordered them to cook the books. It was a task they knew how to fulfill. As Khrushchev characteristically observed of the officials who run the Soviet Bureau of Statistics: "They're the sort who can melt shit into bullets."[2]

Chernenko was the epitome of the Communist ruling class. His devotion was to the Party above all things—including socialist ideology. He cared nothing for subjects beyond politics and little for people. His aloofness was enhanced by such extreme shortsightedness that he once failed to recognize a member of his own Central Committee, and once, his own driver. On one occasion he was rumored to have been seen in prolonged military conversation with a minor general under the impression that he was talking to Marshall Orgarkov. He reserved his limited energy for serious matters only, and the most serious to him was the maintenance of Party influence and power, both for its own sake, and because he believed it to be the only element capable of holding socialism in place against the rising forces of capitalism and bourgeois democracy which he saw splitting the USSR into a bundle of unfriendly and distrustful fragments.

Heresy against Marxist-Leninist dogma was the greatest evil and for this reason he detested any call for reform, less for its potential for uncertainty and menace than for its unstated message that the Party and state were not infallible, which meant to him a denial of the Party's absolute right to rule. He fought all proposals designed to decentralize the economy or political rule. As Brezhnev's aide in 1964, when he had little idea of succeeding to supreme power, he had formulated his political philosophy when he declared after Khrushchev's overthrow that the business of the state was to preserve the rights and priviliges of the Communist party as a bulwark against a return to the past. To allow trade unions the right to strike would be, as he saw it, to give workers not merely a voice in the economy but a preponderating one that would give to "mere numbers" a power the masses ought not to have. He believed the workings of democracy to be dangerous, indeed antithetical, to socialism. To give political voice to those outside the Party would end in a divorce of power from historical responsibility; workers would rule for today and forget about the future. He did not believe in equality in any form. There were the masses and there were history's chosen leaders. So sincere and certain was his conviction of the Party's superior fitness that he considered the minute reforms initiated by Andropov a betrayal and surrender of communist principles. He thought that any surrender of power might ultimately destroy the Communist party as a class. Issues would arise under reform in which the interests of workers against peasants would clash and could only be decided by political compromise, and history's mandate was absolute.[3]

The overriding consideration of Party membership was to prevent any exposure of privilege or misconduct to the nation at large. In this respect Party discipline was rigid. Within the closed confines of the ruling class the unforgivable sin was to give away any member of the group; there must be no publicity that would bring the Party into disrepute. In the party's lavish secret world, self-indulgence became the law. The vast wealth accumulated by Brezhnev and his children was merely representative of a class in whom the habit of having its own way had gone to extremes. Only now and then did the sound of that distant rumble in the atmosphere cause them vague apprehensions of changes coming to upset Party rule. Until Andropov, most Party members were aware of the nation's problems without seriously imagining any major change in the established order of things. But a few, like the worldly Andropov, were deeply disturbed.

Andropov, however, was a straw, not a trend. Chernenko's Politburo had an air of careless supremacy which galled and deeply disturbed the thrusting young Party men brought into the Kremlin by Andropov. The Party's haughty attitude was both a state of mind and a fact. Chernenko did not worry seriously about potential enemies, within or without the Party, felt little need for new allies and had no friends. So great was his illusion of permanence that Chernenko felt little need to rid himself of Andropov's youngish acolytes, and was disposed to give one, Mikhail Sergeievich Gorbachev, who briefly had challenged him for the succession, a post as Deputy Party Secretary. It was like letting a fox into the henhouse. Gorbachev had been Secretary to the Central Committee during Andropov's rule and had drawn up the lists from which his patron purged 20 percent of the Party's Regional Secretaries and nine of twenty-three Central Committee department heads. When Kremlin doctors told Andropov that he might have only five years left to live, he must have decided to vest Gorbachev with the legacy to finish the job. For only a year later when Andropov lay dying in hospital in Kuntsevo, he turned over administration of the nation's economic affairs to the man who had become something of his surrogate son, Gorbachev. On first examining the nation's books, Gorbachev's exclaimed, according to Nicolai Shislin, "I should go back to the provinces now."[4] But Gorbachev had the doomed Andropov's proxy to run the whole country. Fumbling, scrambling for remedies, the neophyte Central Committeeman was flabbergasted by the many failures he uncovered. Nothing in his education had prepared him for this. Nothing in his Party's ideology seemed to offer him a solution. Ideological intoxication, indeed, had robbed the Party of reason. "We must start modernising," he said despairingly to the then Prime Minister Nikolai Tikhanov. "We must change *something.*"[5]

Change, however, was not in the cards. Not yet, at least. When Andropov died. Brezhnev's old guard in the form of Chernenko reclaimed power. For the moment, Gorbachev had to hold his reformist zeal in check. Until Chernenko's death he would have to live in the shadow of unfinished business.

Having had no personal share in shaping the state or policies that had brought the USSR so near to ruin, Gorbachev was able to see socialism's failings in their true proportions and could not believe that a policy of "steady as you go" was likely to affect events for the better. Though a lifelong apparatchik, his career had been pursued at the provincial level. He dealt in the allotment of tractors to this or that collective farm; small matters only. Unlike most local Party bosses, he saw ideology as a servant of administration, not the other way around. Never had he been trapped in following a foolish course simply because it was the correct Marxist-Leninist thing to do—at least not when he had the authority to do otherwise. Standing for so long at such close range to communism in action he was able to see its practical consequences, and to realize the immense effort of national will—if not yet the policies—that would be required for the long contest to set things right.

Massive and paunchy in his baggy grey suits, with a fleshy face adorned by a large scarlet birthmark on his bald dome and strong eyebrows to match, with a clear youthful skin, calm blue eyes, and a candid, tranquil gaze, Gorbachev gave an impression of benevolence and naiveté—two qualities not noticeably part of his character. As a local Party official from Siberia, who dealt with such unromantic matters as railways and fertilizer, he belonged to a branch of the Party not usually drawn upon for the higher offices. His Party career had been marked by quiet accomplishment and efficiency in each post he filled. He had no known dissident or other disturbing connections; his reputation as a loyal Party man was as smooth as his well-manicured hands; he seemed solid and utterly phlegmatic. Throughout his rise his outstanding characteristic was a habitual silence that in other men would have seemed self-deprecatory but, worn like an aura over Gorbachev's calm bulk, inspired confidence.

When plucked from the provinces to go to Moscow Gorbachev was conscious of one lack: he had had scant training in the rarefied realms of the Kremlin and Central Committee,[6] at least in comparison to his rivals, the heirs of Chernenko and the status quo.

*   *   *

Mikhail Gorbachev was peculiarly the product of the socialist state which we have been describing. He could not have lived or ruled as he did had he not been born in a particular time and place and situation. When Gorbachev was born, in a hut situated on a narrow river on the Russian steppe, Stalin was supreme but the failings of communism were evident. Famine had come to the region, not as an act of God but as a deliberate act of state. Stalin wanted to break the stubborn wills of the peasants, and the famine was created to subdue them. All through the region, families who resisted collectivization were arrested and deported, or murdered. Streams and rivers ran with bloated bodies, and according to Zhores Medvedev, the emigré historian and scientist whose family lived there, terror and lawlessness racked the northern Caucasus throughout the 1930s.[7]

Gorbachev was born in March 1931 in the tiny Caucasian village of Privolnoye in a far corner of the state of Stavropol. His life, like Doctor Zhivago's, began in the midst of a funeral, then an everyday event in the village. For between the autumn of 1932 and the spring of 1933, for example, one-third of the population of his village died, when food vanished completely. In some nearby villages all of the children between the ages of one and two succumbed to starvation.[8] It is possible that Gorbachev himself may have lost some of his siblings, since peasant families were normally large and birth control non-existent.

The Gorbachevs were just the sort of stubborn, independent-minded kulaks that Stalin had ordered to be liquidated. The peasants of Privolnoye had never been serfs; instead, they belonged to a band of energetic people who had pushed down from the Ukraine and the Don valley in the late eighteenth century in search of richer soil and economic freedom in the wild lands of the Caucasus. As a crow would measure, the village was less than a few day's flight from Moscow, but the distance spiritually seems almost infinite. All around the tiny huts stretched the land which was to exercise so strong a hold on Gorbachev. Here are the abundant forests which bring something more than a sense of close proximity to nature. There is also a sense of displacement, of incompatibility between houses and land, as though the pretensions and claims of man would inevitably, in the face of nature, break down. Who could be said to own these trees, these pieces of ice, these fields? These were questions which were to haunt the young Gorbachev.

It was here, however, that Gorbachev's ancestors took root and prospered. Like so many others, they were to be punished for their prosperity and headstrong independence.

But Gorbachev's father was among the few in the village who welcomed the revolution and collectivization. His parents and grandparents stepped forward to be the first to surrender their own private lands and stock. They trusted the government and looked at the new Ford and Caterpillar tractors which the state supplied with awe. Tractors symbolized the advance of socialism, their common use became a sacred rite of the new religion of collectivized life.[9]

All the grain produced and harvested by the shiny new machines was later seized by the state, and the villagers left to starve. Young Mikhail grew up in a family atmosphere disturbed daily by the talk of famine and schemes to hide some of their crops for themselves. Probably he had little idea of what was going on, nor of the extent of the catastrophe. In the insular village world, few people did. Official statements were cautious in the extent to which they ever admitted the crisis, and used terms such as *neurozhai* (crop failure) and *bedstviye* (calamity, misfortune) rather than the emotive *golod* (famine). A conspiracy of silence was enforced by local informers. Any man might call his neighbor a kulak, and thus assure his destruction, simply because he had a pair of boots; evidence was irrelevant. What could a once prosperous farmer do in such a situation? Mask his past and turn his coat, of course. Early conversion to collectivization seemed to assure the Gorbachev family of its safety. On the new state farms young Misha, like some borstal boy Oliver, waited on line for watery millet soup to be ladled out from common pots. So it was that his family existed by compromise and collaboration. A gift for survival in turbulent times was the principal legacy passed from father to son.

His father's socialist conversion did not, however, extend to the religious life of his family. A gift for faith was his mother's bequest to young Misha. Within Gorbachev's maternal line was concentrated the blood of several priests. She found consolation for family hardship in the pious exercise of faith. Despite the risk, even in the harshest years of collectivization, she continued to practice the common peasant hobby or craft of painting ikons. She was never happier than when reading the lives of the saints or in entertaining the strange, half-crazed wandering pilgrims who continued to roam Stalin's Russia. When the time for baptism came, mother and grandmother made certain that the boy underwent the ancient religious ceremony. In later life, Gorbachev would recall with admiration her steadfast devotion in the face of grave risk. To her devout displays can be attributed the early and lasting signs of Mikhail Gorbachev's tenacity. The young boy might follow his father in breaking away from the closed system of religious culture, but the believer in Gorbachev retained for life some of his feelings for the spiritual reassurance of the Orthodox church and above all for its inculcation of personal responsibility. His later difficulty in breaking with his socialist faith reflects the profound influence of religious belief on his own thinking. If Gorbachev the man grew up to consider himself an atheist communist, he nevertheless remained curiously responsive to spiritual needs.[10]

As a self-converted socialist with an eye for self-preservation, Gorbachev's father saw the importance of a correct education for his children. Here his shrewdness served his son well. What was the use of the old church schools with their useless religious education? With an eye to getting his son into the Party later in life, Sergei Andreievich Gorbachev embraced the new state-controlled village school as the place for his son. His wife at first opposed him. She knew little about education, but she did know that, in the old days, boys who graduated from the church schools might, if they were clever enough, get a grant from the town council which would get them to university and thus free them from the nightmare of military service. Only when he was able to convince his wife that the new state schools controlled entry to the safety of the civil service or the professions did she agree. It must be said that for all his careful trimming, Gorbachev *père* understood the importance of education. Indeed, his sons were all very able and agreed later in life that they owed their talents to their tedious and mechanical father, who for almost half-a-century was content to work every day at a small tractor station, repairing and fueling the machines.

One of the natural results of Sergei's careful strictness with his wife and children was to unite them with one another and with their gentle mother. In many respects Mikhail took on her character. He might be silent at school, but he let himself go with his brother at home and led the way in making fun of the people of the village and communal farm, in the manner of his mother. It is commonly the role of the first child in a poor family to become his mother's confessor, and also the family humorist. Gorbachev followed both patterns. There is a story that he dressed up as a displaced beggar and got money out of his uncle; and another lark—which his mother would have forbidden if she had seen it—when the boy pretended to be a comic priest being examined by the local Commissar. From the interviews that he has given, it seems that Gorbachev's dark memories of his childhood are less concerned with himself than with the bad effects the severe conditions of his upbringing had on the remainder of his family. It was his younger brother who took the brunt of his father's nervous temper and was lastingly broken in will by it. Mikhail took pride in his ability to stare his father in the face when he was likely to be beaten. His will was never broken. The chin is raised in studied defiance when he stands in his school uniform in the family photographs.

Only the continuing ravages of Stalin rattled him. Even though he was only six in the year 1937, the boy Misha could not help but feel the crescendo of Stalin's Great Terror. People everywhere began to disappear. Uncles, cousins, the loose-tongued first. Then sometimes brothers and fathers. One night all the teachers in the school vanished. The children returned to class the next day to see an all new faculty to replace those who had been arrested. Some students, too, were expelled, condemned as enemies of the people. Fear pit brother against brother, parent against child. A schoolboy who turned in his parents was made a national hero. Denunciation of condemned relatives was the only way a student could stay in school.

No immunity was granted Gorbachev's family by their willing collaboration. His grandfather, a man who had quickly jumped to the socialist side during the collectivization drive, was arrested and deported to Siberia in 1937. Until his sudden return a year-and-a-half later, his family assumed that he had been executed. To be descended from a family of collaborators and victims must convey a bizarre unreality of status. Both frightened and ashamed, it would be years before Gorbachev would pluck up the courage to reveal his family's dark secret.[11]

If the perils of collectivization and famine were the great political specters of Gorbachev's boyhood, then Hitler's invasion in June 1941 was a great national event that most shaped him. It was an event exactly parallel in his imagination as Napoleon's invasion was to the imaginations of nineteenth-century Russians. In both cases, there are the same ingredients of shock, fury, awe, and ferocious national pride. To the outsider, looking at a map of Russia, the perennial Russian fear of invasion strikes a note which is difficult to comprehend. The country is so vast, the distances covered by any invader would have to be so enormous, that only a madman or a genius would contemplate a military operation of such audacity. Yet twice such madmen have arisen, bringing with them scenes of carnage paralleled only by the famines of the 1930s. The brutalities of the Nazi armies as they waged race war against the Slavs inaugurated new horrors in this history of invasion. In the Caucasus the casualties were as great, perhaps greater, then in any other battle on the Russian front save for the siege of Leningrad: tens of thousands died in a single day of battle. Tens of thousands more civilians were to die in the harsh winters and food shortages which followed, the whole campaign emphasizing with hideous and inescapable force the sheer futility of the pursuit of power, and the hollowness of military glory. There are few more vivid moments, in Gorbachev's life, of the emotional impact of Hitler's war.[12]

Fighting itself did not reach Privolnoye, but the Germans did come searching for food and in pursuit of Jews. On one farm outside the village, 370 Jewish families who had fled the fighting in the Ukraine were caught and slaughtered. Because Hitler's purpose in the region was to cut off the Soviet Union from its oil fields in the Transcaucasus, he sought the local people's aid through what was, for the Nazis, a relatively mild occupation. Young Gorbachev was able to continue his schooling. There was sufficient food. Collective farms were abolished.

With his father away in the Red Army, the lonely but self-reliant boy took responsibility for his family. He hated the separation from his father and uncles and feared for them: above all he felt responsibility for his isolated mother. This seems to have been the moment when he first felt he was the one with the duty and the wit to become the practical savior of those he loved. If his strict upbringing had broken the will of his younger brother, Mikhail had conserved his. In the fields he worked shoulder to shoulder with the village women, in place of the absent men.

The German occupation of Privolnoye, though only half-a-year in duration, was one of those events that became decisive in a young man's life. Self-reliance and self-confidence were its legacy to Gorbachev, and also another secret sin. The occupation left a pall of suspicion over the area that lasted for the remainder of Stalin's reign. Years later, when he was attempting to climb the Party ladder, Gorbachev had to rely on higher-ranking protectors to prevent the stain of implied collaboration from showing up on his record.[13] In this respect, Mikhail Gorbachev was truly a creation of the generation into which he was born, moving from triumph to suspicion and back; and, because he was cut off by upbringing and education from the usual source of Party cadres in Stalin's rule, his journey, which began alone, was to continue for much of his life as a solitary intellectual trek.

The defeat of Hitler's Reich was followed in the USSR by a reaction as savage as anything previously attempted by Stalin. State control of the economy and civil life, relaxed during the war, was stiffened anew. The resourceful peasants of the Caucasus fell back on their traditional taste for joking, lying, and the vulgar.

Meanwhile, through all the inconstancy which marked Soviet life during and after the war, Gorbachev's education was planned and organized. All memories of him at this date, his own and other people's, recall a young man of fairly insufferable severity who, for all his helpful posturings, devoted most of his waking hours to working and studying as a means to make his way out of the village.[14] Young Russian boys who wanted to make their way in the world were expected to "serve" the Party, just as nineteenth-century boys were expected to "serve" the aristocracy. This mindset was nicely caught by Pushkin in his famous poem "The Bronze Horseman." The poor anti-hero of the poem "serves" somewhere or other in an office in the gleaming metropolis erected by the great tyrant Peter, his determined attempts to run away from Peter's statue being suggestive, as all readers of the poem so terrifyingly feel, of the complete impotence of ordinary, private individuals in the presence of an overwhelmingly strong autocracy. The higher ranks of the aristocracy, no less than the dreary, nameless little Yevgenys of Pushkin's imagination, were expected to "serve," and even in Stalin's USSR it was with this in mind that Mikhail Gorbachev crammed and revised his studies.

He continued to work on the collective farm, sometimes driving a combine harvester with his father after Sergei Andreievich's return from the Red Army. Impatience got the better of Mikhail. To get on, he had to get out, and the Communist party was the one sure way of advancing. While still in his last year of grammar school young Misha volunteered for service in the regional Komsomol (the communist youth organization for ideological indoctrination)—which controlled the leadership tracks in secondary school and had reserved entrance spots at university, rather like the reserved place the boys of Eton and Winchester could once rely upon to get into Oxford and Cambridge. Komsomol membership was mandatory for anyone thinking about a career in politics. In the Komsomol, even more than in his secondary school in the little town of Krasnogvardeisk—a twelve-mile journey from his home village—would Gorbachev first become aware of the actual structure of life in the Soviet Union, life outside his own family and commune, life as directly affected by the policies and character of the socialist state.

The student group which he now entered represented something of that military caste which had been so prominent in imperial Russia. The Komsomol brought together a group of orthodox young communists of all backgrounds, though the predominant group at the time of Gorbachev's initiation was of the children of Party members. Komsomol indoctrination of Communist ideology did not, however, come near to brainwashing. Witness the fact that Alexander Solzhenitsyn had survived its regime with his wits intact. Indoctrination, though drummed in to the young men and women daily, was not wanton. The organization was in some ways merely a Stalinist version of the Hitler Youth. The rigid routines of its program were said to teach self-control, resistance to panic and, above all, acceptance of authority. The core of the Communist party is discipline and the essence of discipline is obedience. Since this does not come naturally to men of independent and rational mind, like the young Gorbachev, they must be trained in the habit of obedience. Reasonable orders are easy enough to obey; it is capricious, bureaucratic, or plain idiotic demands that form the habit of discipline. Of these, the long, silent military marches were the symbol and essence.

The first two years of Party initiation were the worst, but like someone coming into the sunlight from some dark tunnel, Gorbachev emerged eventually as a local Komsomol leader. The curriculum for Komsomol students at the Krasnogvardeisk secondary school at this time was designed to produce loyal Party cadres and thusly concentrated on Marxist-Leninist dogma.

Little heed to the possibly wider needs of a citizen was paid. A student such as Mikhail emerged marvelously proficient in quoting Lenin's aphorisms on any subject but less well versed in the history of man and his institutions. Technical subjects were confined to one course in the management of collective farms and another on the Party's control of Soviet industry. Otherwise, the apprentice communists took courses on Marx, courses on Lenin, courses on Stalin and his writings.[15] Every subject was ideologically correct.

Young Mikhail revealed a proficiency for dialectical discussions, was always the quickest in class to discern the ideological imperfections of an argument. This may have been the attribute of a budding fanatic, but it seems more likely to reveal the lawyer-like quality of Gorbachev's mind, which was always on the lookout for weaknesses that could be pounced upon. He stood first in his class in ideological subjects, but was rarely a participant in group activities. Sports and games were shunned. With what energy was left over from his subjects, he returned to work on the Privolnoye collective farm.

Here he brought himself to the regular Party's attention. In the summer of his eighteenth year Misha gained acclaim as a model *kolkhoznik*. Driving the combine harvester every day, sweating and coughing in the heat and dust, he helped the collective produce a banner harvest. Output supposedly exceeded that ordered by the plan. The

Gorbachevs, father and son, were nominated for state awards, including the prestigious Order of the Red Banner of Labor. The boy was given his first suit of clothes so as to be photographed to appear in the local Party paper. Only three other boys in the Stavropol region had ever received such a trophy. It brought him the privilege of applying for admission to Moscow State University, citadel of Soviet higher education reserved normally for the sons and daughters of the Party elite. Mikhail was now certain that his career would be made within the Party.[16]

Where the old Bolsheviks had read Marx and gone underground out of principle and revolutionary euphoria, young Gorbachev journeyed to Moscow, like one of Stendhal's ambitious rubes. This is something of which it is doubtful Mikhail perceived the full implications. While doctrinaire communists clung to original principles, careerists like Gorbachev were discovering that communism, like capitalism, was a form of self-interest. No illusions or millenarial dreams guided his decision to work the Party machine. Gorbachev was a living exponent of the view that life was only to be advanced within, not against, the socialist state.

A comparison with Lenin's beginnings as a communist is instructive. He, like young Gorbachev, was a severe and hard-working young boy, determined on a career in the law. In 1887 his revolutionary life was set in motion; that was the year when Lenin's elder brother Alexander, who had gone up to Petrograd to continue his studies, took part in the students' plot against Tsar Alexander III. It was a sad and terrible thing from every point of view. At the Petrograd University, Alexander Ulyanov became a blazing fanatic against Tsardom—he never recanted or pleaded for mercy at his trial—and he and six fellow conspirators were very young. They never threw their bomb (the police picked them up while some of them were carrying it down the Nevsky Prospekt), and it was perhaps an excess of severity that the Tsar should not have given him another chance. He signed the warrant condemning young Ulyanov and four of the others to death, and they were hanged on May 20, 1887.

The effect upon young Lenin, who had just turned seventeen, was considerable. From that moment he was a subversive. He struck out with absolute determination toward the underground Left and the revolution, and he never looked back.

Center stage, always, and for all his career as a communist, was Gorbachev himself. Far from being a passionate and committed communist in the manner of Lenin, Party membership was for Gorbachev a decision taken coldly and rationally. There was nothing romantic or emotional about it. The resolution of his youth, the ability to settle down and study for long hours, to go to Moscow was just one more step on his own road to advancement. In using the Party for his own advantage there are glints of the Gorbachev to come.

Higher education which, in the Soviet Union, as in the West, is an ideal held out to all who can attain it, was in reality in Russia something which affected only the tiniest portion of the population. Attendance at Moscow State University put Mikhail in an even more select group, a condition further narrowed by his becoming a candidate member of the Communist party at the tender age of nineteen.

Lecturers at the university were nearly all Party hacks. Professors who did display intellectual daring could be sure of vigorous persecution from the government. An outstanding mathematician, for example, acclaimed all over the world, had to devote much of his time to defending himself and his colleagues from the university curator, who kept up a series of attacks on all teachers who were not Party members. During his first year Gorbachev decided to specialize in law. But it was considered highly damaging if students read anything that exposed their minds to the fact that not everyone shared the Party's notion of socialist legality. Lecturers in the law faculty were forbidden to "enter into the details of the legal systems" of Western countries. The set texts were Party approved. In such an atmosphere philosophical speculation was bound to be seen as a declaration against the Party and the government.

If there was a puritan in Mikhail, he enjoyed his new freedom in the city. Gorbachev loved to make speeches—turgid, ideologically rigid, sloganeering speeches in his laughably rolling country accent. The boy from the boondocks demanded to be noticed. He aroused some considerable annoyance by habitually wearing his labor medal, no matter the occasion. War veterans giggled at his vanity, and pointedly told him of the battles at which they had *earned* their decorations. Other more worldly students snickered at him for wearing the same suit every day. By the end of his five years at university he had become so pudgy that he could no longer button the jacket.[17]

Nothing stung the young Gorbachev more than his sudden realization of his gauche appearance. The young man was painfully aware of the gaps in his experience, especially in his knowledge of culture. Gorbachev aspired to belong. Like Gatsby, he felt an instinct to perfect himself, to tidy up his flaws. The gulf between the peasant Gorbachev and his urbane classmates was enormous. Cunning young Misha drew up a program for self-improvement. He planned to visit museums, memorize poetry, learn to appreciate the French Impressionists and other paintings. Benjamin Franklin could not have invented a better regimen.[18]

He made himself into a list of acquired virtues, which he trotted inside like some gray nag in a paddock. He was a little model of self-made socialist engineering. He would list, it is said, his virtues in columns and give himself good or bad marks. There is about the student Mikhail a certain earnest naiveté. Like a child. And like a little old man.

He had to break in the human being completely, so that much more could be broken—in the long run.

22

⇥⇥ ⇤⇤

Gorbachev
Ideologue and Opportunist

Fear as well as faith impelled Gorbachev's rise. For it was not merely a reputation as a serious and gifted student that accompanied him as he advanced at Moscow State University; the other side of him as a devious and nimble Party operative was also evident quite early on. In brief, he was following that drone-like course pioneered by Stalin, of ingratiating himself with every faction, of being everywhere and reporting everything. By the end of his freshman year he had been elevated to the position of Komsomol organizer for his class. According to the account of Gorbachev's classmate Fridrikh Neznansky, which appeared in *Time*'s pathfinding biography (edited by Strobe Talbot), Gorbachev stole the job from the incumbent by taking the young man out for a night of fun, pouring vodka into him until he was publicly drunk, then denouncing the young man for gross and indecent behavior at the next day's Komsomol meeting.[1] Whether Gorbachev really aimed at his comrade's downfall, or at revenge for some past wrong, or at stirring trouble for its own sake like Iago, is a riddle concealed in one of the most complex characters spawned by communism. Seductive and eloquent, he could persuade his peers quietly or sway a student mob. And like the young Stalin he was a plotter, always ambitious, subtle, bold, absolutely without scruple, but never so swerving or unfixed of purpose as to undo his own plots.

That Gorbachev was constantly playing a double game cannot be a matter of doubt. According to *Time*, Lev Yudovich, a third-year student at Moscow State who knew Gorbachev only slightly, did know enough to regard him as two-faced: always buddying up to other students, but, or so they suspected, only to get information. It may only have been expedient for him to ruthlessly expel people from the Komsomol, but expel them he did.[2] Gorbachev was determined to advance within the Party by any means and at any cost. His attitude to his fellow students

310

was not unlike that of a Victorian missionary in darkest Africa; he had his Marxist-Leninist faith and that was sacrosanct. All others were ignorant, benighted children who had to be led toward the light. Anyone who opposed him was an agent of the devil, or if not the devil then whatever the equivalent is called in the communist anathema. And if he was obliged to be ruthless in this righteous course—if, for example he found it necessary to conspire against friends—then it was merely in order to advance the cause of communism and, of course, himself. It was the surgical approach, and it was not only applied to the practical matters of Party membership and Party hierarchy; it applied to the mind and spirit as well.

These ironclad attitudes of mind were, in any case, necessary for survival in the nightmare of Stalin's last years. A new round of purges, equal to those that devoured Bukharin during the 1930s, was under way, giving new meaning to the socialist state's unbridled and absolute power. Under the aged Stalin it did not make any difference why someone might disagree with Party policy. In the period of paranoid witchhunts unleashed by the decrepit Stalin, you conformed or were killed.

As one of the leading communists at university, Gorbachev was all too conscious of the danger of his position. Although many of his classmates responded with enthusiasm to the feeding frenzy of informing and denunciation that ensued, Gorbachev himself probably regarded Stalin's actions with suspicion, but refused publicly to say so. To divide the Party against itself was to invite attack by the capitalist enemies on some unknowingly exposed flank. Here was a litmus test of the young Gorbachev's basic character, and he was not found wanting. During the infamous doctor's plot, when a wave of anti-Semitism swept the university in the wake of the arrest of several Jewish doctors fraudulently charged with scheming to poison the Kremlin leadership, Gorbachev did not succumb to the fury. When classmates tried to implicate a Jewish student in the faked plot, Gorbachev was the lone voice to speak up in his defense. Eyes ablaze, he jumped to his feet and denounced the primary accuser as a "spineless animal."[3]

According to his classmates, Gorbachev's debut as a dissenter was a triumph. Even if his chosen manner was as hysterical as the charges leveled at his Jewish classmate, Gorbachev's theatrically calculated performance revealed him as a grave man of the law. When he finished, a smattering of applause broke out among the assembled students, to which he responded with self-deprecation, waving the acclaim on to the fundamental decency of the Party itself.[4] This was stagecraft of a very high order for which Gorbachev would become justly famous. In 1952 he seemed, even to hard-boiled Party operatives, to ooze sincerity and principle. Although he shrewdly affected the air of a novice in the art of political posturing, Gorbachev was already something of a master. Systematic exploitation of these skills was to be a permanent feature of his rise. Throughout his career he would use his oratorical gifts to climb the career ladder of the Party and yet ever pose as a public figure with a reputation for integrity and independence.

It was a brave gesture and it was noticed, for these were times of terror and suspicion, when a single denunciation was enough to have you not only expelled from the Party but also to earn exile for years in the gulag. When faced with his first case of life and death, Gorbachev neither cowered nor trimmed, and this is to his credit. The plight of the Jewish student Vladimir Lieberman may or may not have rankled Gorbachev's subconscious or caused any doubts in his communist faith at all; nevertheless, it was the first occasion on which Gorbachev spoke out in public against orthodoxy. Certainly it can fairly be assumed that he spent the next few nights lying awake worrying about a knock at his door.

Here was the beginning of Gorbachev's double life as ideologue and opportunist. In those days no one publicly doubted Stalin, and in the law faculty it was the dictator's words that were law, not the penal code or constitution. The dissents of Bukharin, Gide, Koestler, Silone, and Djilas were unknown. Doubts were kept behind closed doors, closed mouths. Gorbachev's head may have boiled at the injustice of the scapegoating and witch-hunting personified by the doctor's plot, but his head was cool enough to retain full self-possession. Like some young tortoise, he was determined to make the most of life by treating it with deliberateness and caution. This is why the brutalities of Stalin's declining years silently exasperated him.[5] For the USSR was again condemned to a period of anarchy akin to that which ravaged the Caucasus in Gorbachev's youth. If the purges came to some of his classmates as an onrush of feeling, a return of revolutionary euphoria, for Gorbachev the tocsin sounded an alarm in his intelligence. Personal damage control was his main interest.

So, for the most part, Gorbachev silently acquiesced in Stalin's last years of madness and sterility. The old dictator was a dangerous man to the end; and almost to the end, he remained unchallenged in his authority. The men around him served Stalin in a sullen, guarded silence, expecting nothing and waiting only for the hand of Time to take him. When Stalin did go, he had consumed—almost to the last crumb—those very prerequisites in Russian society on which his fearful, jealous, totalitarian power had maintained itself. He had created a situation in which, fortunately for the Russian people, it would have been very hard for a new Stalin to establish himself in his place.

It was near the time of Stalin's death that Gorbachev met the girl he was going to marry. She was Raisa Maximovna Titorenko, a prize student of the philosophy department who was rumored to be the niece of either Andrei Gromyko or Politburo member Maxim Saburov. So far, Gorbachev had had few serious romances. Here was a girl who could flatter his ego and advance his career. Gorbachev's campaign for her was as relentless as his political hustlings. He took up ballroom dancing to be near her. When she finally took notice of him, it was to assist in his own program of self-improvement. Bookstores, museums, galleries, the Bolshoi; the courtship was a mirror image of Gorbachev's wants. A sterile socialist formality, the signing of ledgers in a registrar's office, served as their wedding ceremony. No religious ceremony for him. Afterwards, their fellow students organized a large reception at the student residence hall, with dancing, and toasts, and more toasts. Then came the inevitable problem posed by Moscow's chronic housing shortage: where was the couple to spend the night? It took some maneuvering, and no doubt a bribe of the concierge, but that night Gorbachev commandeered one of the dormitory rooms. In the morning, however, they would both have to return to their own quarters, to live apart for almost a year.[6]

The announcement of Stalin's death brought to the students of Moscow State the sense of an era's end. Sirens blared and searchlights raked the sky. Two moments of silence followed, which Gorbachev observed at the window of his student digs. People trembled at the thought of going on without their omnipotent leader, but soon the victims of Stalin's crimes, like Marley's ghost, began to walk the city's streets. Men and women returned from hard years in the gulag camps. It must have been impossible for a bright and alert young man not to see that the law he had studied so diligently and for so long was nothing but a sham. Public prosecutors who had tried to be honest, and had been jailed for their courage, now returned from the camps to tell their tales. For the young Gorbachev, the choice was grim: either enforce the existing system and be corrupted by it, or change careers.

Once more, ambition won out. But it was ambition without purpose. Despite his cultivation of Moscow's elite and his seemingly glittering marriage, he remained a prisoner of his provincial background. In a runoff election for top leader of the Komsomol at Moscow State, a well-connected Muscovite defeated Gorbachev. Hopes for launching his political career in the capital vanished.[7]

Another rude awakening awaited. When he went to the Moscow Public Prosecutor's office to apply for a position, he was told that the office had no apartment to offer Gorbachev in Moscow. You should think about going back where you came from, he was advised. It was a form of banishment, of disgrace, to return home. But he had no choice.

Return home he did, to life in an apartment that was little more than a tiny, heatless room. Gorbachev became an investigator in the local Prosecutor's office. The full dimensions of Stalin's crimes now became clear. Hundreds of Stalin's wretched victims began straggling back to Stavropol from the gulag. He learned, for the first time, that at least 5 percent of the country's population at any time—even the present—was incarcerated in the camps. Appeals against false accusations flooded his desk. "Particularly for someone who wanted to be a lawyer," the historian Roy Medvedev has said of Gorbachev, the universality of abuse and injustice must have been "a shattering blow to previously held notions of justice."[8] He saw it all, the rigged evidence and tortured confessions, and locked them away in his memory as he picked his way through the Party's parasitic aristocracy. To his credit, however, he did leave the Prosecutor's office after only a few months. For to be a Prosecutor at this time was to be a participant in parodies of justice, and no doubt be a KGB informer, too. He decided to make his career solely within the Party itself. Like Pilate, he had washed his hands clean.

Gorbachev both did and did not belong to the societies he inhabited. Stavropol was a sleepy, rude, and dirty place of bureaucratic exile to which inferior members of the *nomenklatura* might be banished, but it provided for Gorbachev the security and strength and independence which familiarity can often bring. Yet his presence there was an emblem of his status as an outsider in Moscow-centric Russia. He both was and wasn't peasant-like; he both was and wasn't a Muscovite Party intellectual; he both was and wasn't an apparatchik, a devoted servant of the Communist party.

His ambivalence was apparent throughout his first years back home, and it produced conflicts, some comic, some touching, some prophetic. Gorbachev was not sure where he was, or who he was.[9]

There is a tendency to think of Gorbachev's desire to live and think independently as a feature of his years in power, a manifestation of his coming to grips with the failures of communism in the country he led, a sign of the safety and freedom supreme power had bestowed on him.

But, as his days in Stavropol demonstrate, the desire for independence was always there and very strong, even when self-protectively kept in check below the surface. It was an important symptom of the isolation which was so necessary to him, as a budding political leader. He could not function fully when forced to be rigidly committed. Part of him had to be an outsider. Whether or not he was fully conscious of the fact, part of the delight of taking an independent line was that it angered fixed Party members, like his wife. It placed him on a limb, *contra mundum,* but never beyond the pale. Always in Gorbachev's life there was this dual compulsion.

But it left him without a sponsor in the local Party machine, and he had to begin his career at the bottom. In the Soviet Union, particularly within the Communist party, however, protection from persecution and the whims of superiors is everything. To lack it in the "blood sport" of Communist politics is dangerous in the extreme. Legally, politically, physically, Gorbachev was vulnerable. So Gorbachev returned to the task he accomplished so well in Moscow, of cultivating and manipulating men with the power to protect them. The price he paid was to become their instrument, enforcing Party edicts and thus enduring a measure of popular hate. Throughout the 1950s and 1960s Gorbachev would live entirely dependent upon the protection of patronage, and was thus subject to the hazards of political favor. In the excitable period that marked Khrushchev's early rule, Gorbachev lived on the edge of political assault that was always just imminent. [10]

Yet rise he did. In 1956 the up-and-coming young man was chosen to represent the Stavropol *apparat* at the Twentieth Communist Party Congress in Moscow. There, at the back of the great hall of People's Deputies, among the delegates and observers from Africa and Asia, he listened in stunned silence to Khrushchev's bitter eulogy for Stalin and his cult. Fear, anger, suspicion—above all, astonishment—were, it can rightly be assumed, his reactions to Khrushchev's revelations of Stalin's innumerable crimes. That Stalin, the god of his country and his youth, should be portrayed as little more than a blood-soaked barbarian was cause, one suspects, for dazed wonderment liberally laced with distrust. But Khrushchev also, it seems, touched a chord in Gorbachev aching to respond. Purifying and purging the Party of Stalin's crimes would be a source of communist renewal. Instead of damaging the Party, Khrushchev's revelations soon became for Gorbachev a sign of its purity and strength. Stalin's socialist state was stagnant and diseased and the vision of perpetual dictatorship made reform a necessity. To other delegates at the conference, Khrushchev's secret speech was a threat to their positions and hidebound ideologies. For Gorbachev, the speech was a summons. Reform acquired a moral imperative.[11]

Its necessity was voiced by many spokesmen in many guises. Khrushchev's speech opened the floodgates for new books and magazines criticizing Stalin's criminal system, which at the same time suggested a new model for reform: truth in history. Gorbachev recognized the waning of ideological intoxication in people's lives, for the challenge posed by Khrushchev was like that posed in the nineteenth century by Nietzsche when he declared: God is dead! He would have substituted a reformed and re-invigorated communism, but ordinary people substituted self-interest. As faith in communism retreated before the advances of Khrushchev's and then Solzhenitsyn's revelations, there seemed to be nothing left to fill the empty spaces in the heart. There was something cathartic about this, even for Gorbachev: it is said that it was now possible, for the first time in his life, to begin to speak about the injustice done his grandfather in 1937. No longer was that imprisonment a source of secret shame; it became something of a badge of honor.[12]

Reform now absorbed the strength once belonging to orthodoxy and conformity. Throughout the Khrushchev era a sense of renewal filled the air. And that promise survived the coming of Brezhnev in 1964, and the banning and persecution of Solzhenitsyn. For prophets filled with the voice of God are not easily eliminated. The thunder of Khrushchev and Solzhenitsyn was silenced, but the hostility and discontent they had voiced remained.

Stripped of Khrushchev, Gorbachev was not long in finding a new and better (because he was more disciplined) hero—himself.

23

꘎≫≫ ≪≪꘎

Gorbachev Tries to Live
His History

At the age of twenty-nine, when Gorbachev became Komsomol leader for the entire Stavropol region, he found the person and formed the connection that was to be decisive to his future. Fyodor Kulakov, First Secretary of the Communist party in Stavropol, a hands-on manager who was determined to make *his* region an agricultural success story for the whole USSR, chose Gorbachev as his aide and protégé. Mere office acquaintance grew into a bond of mutual respect. Of any other two men the relation might have been called friendship, but these two closed personalities left few revealing references or asides to each other at this stage, and Gorbachev would never be a man easily claimed as a friend.

Doubts remained hidden, even to Kulakov. For Gorbachev was expert at knowing intuitively what his protector needed to hear, and was quick to adapt himself in every way—his tone of voice, his body language, his mode of dress, and even his facial expressions—to mimic the idiosyncrasies of his patron. Sober, judicious, reserved, Gorbachev had the perfect pitch of any successful private secretary—caution, subject to ambivalence for any subject other than his master. When it came to Kulakov he was utterly loyal. He became for Kulakov a professional son, and thus shrugged off his patron's authoritarian streak and the fact that, in private, Kulakov was a wild drinker.

Kulakov's patronage put Gorbachev on the Party's fast track. He became responsible for enrolling and supervising Party recruits, and thus acquired his own powers of patronage. It was plain for all to see that Gorbachev at thirty-one was a powerful member of Kulakov's regional "mafia," a man to be respected and feared. This is not to say that Gorbachev transformed himself into a mindless sycophant. Far from it, indeed. Precise and positive, Kulakov was a specialist in management through statistical control. Anything that could be quantified was his

317

realm. He had the ruthlessness of uninterrupted success, and his genius for numbers left him little respect for human variables and no room for unpredictables. He relied on Gorbachev, the product of a collective farm, to bring the gift of humanity to his policies. Gorbachev's provincialism was no longer a handicap; if anything, it was an asset to Kulakov, who wanted connections to the peasants. With his plans to reform the collectivized farms he felt impelled to make overtures to the peasants themselves.[1]

Evidence of the long-term failure of Soviet agricultural policies was mounting. Stalin's murderous collectivizations had created a sullen and sluggish peasant class. One of the world's great food exporters under the Tsars, Russia became a net importer of food in the early years under Lenin and the deficit widened with the decades. The harvest of 1963 was the first of the major postwar Soviet agricultural disasters. Khrushchev complained it would have been still worse but for his policy to spread collective farms to virgin lands.[2] But this policy, like Stalin's, was muddled and irrational—the coerced settlement of barren land. No Marxist ever seems to have held sensible views about farming, perhaps because neither Marx nor Lenin was interested in it. Socialism is an urban religion. Khrushchev oscillated between state farms and collectives, between decentralization and centralization, and Gorbachev duly followed his orders.[3] One moment Gorbachev would authorize the establishment of a new self-run collective, the next he would turn over its management to an established state farm. Never did he dare to suggest handing back the land to its original owners. In his retirement, Khrushchev complained bitterly of food shortages. Even in a Moscow hospital reserved for high Party officials, he whined, the food was disgusting. And Moscow, as always, was the food showplace of the nation. In places like Stavropol it was far worse. Khrushchev met people from traditional farming areas who "tell me loudly and bitterly how eggs and meat are simply unavailable, and how they had to take a couple of days and travel to Moscow by train" for the privilege of waiting on line for groceries. Why, he asked, should eggs and meat be unobtainable "after fifty years of Soviet power?" "I look forward to the day," Khrushchev wrote, "when a camel would be able to walk from Moscow to Vladivostok without being eaten by hungry peasants on the way."[4] Bad harvests became the norm in Russia, and Gorbachev was one of the regional administrators of this year in, year out disaster.

Gorbachev imposed himself as a regional Party leader with verve and energy, his competence, intelligence, and personality winning general respect. Only his plans were cold and sterile. He held himself above the factional conflicts inside the Party. His loyalty was to Kulakov and Kulakov's loyalty was to him. The association benefitted both. Gorbachev lent his powers of human analysis and pragmatic intelligence to Kulakov, and the Stavropol chieftain rewarded him with ever higher office. The invention of Gorbachev the Party leader was nearing completion. The elaboration of personality, the calculated conformity tempered by deliberate distancing from Party blunders, served the purpose of a serious political undertaking, a conscious service to the history of his party and his country and himself. Under Kulakov's tutoring Gorbachev became formidably his own man because his romanticism was governed by prudent political intelligence and by historical consciousness. Romanticism in political affairs, as we have seen in the case of Bukharin, most often becomes linked to immature or apocalyptic ideas— secular translations of the essentially religious impulse to bring history to a halt in general happiness, a political nirvana. The actual record of revolutionary intellectuals, as we have seen, is, however, awash in the blood of others. This is the existential aspect of the revolutionary's temper. It was Sartre who called the student upheavals of May, 1968 "the imagination in power" and a "call to murder."[5] But Sartre would not participate in the undergraduate antics. He sat out the riots as he had sat out the Nazi occupation—engaged only on paper. Words were his act of leadership. The striking thing about Gorbachev's rise to power as a committed communist was that his engagement was to the act of his own advancement—to ambition—and not to ideology. He supported Kulakov, he supported the Party, but used each in his own game. It is impossible to imagine him as a budding Marat or a Robespierre, or as Stalin, whom he had once admired. In the manner of Sartre he was a prolix Party loyalist but a slippery one; he played at being Kulakov's factotum, remaining his own man all the same. He was too intelligent to do otherwise. He was both conformist and rebel (and would instigate, single-handedly, a revolutionary repudiation of what his nation had stood for for seventy years). He remained private, his code internal, permitting no illusion that it would be accepted or applauded by others, or that it would ever succeed: he was ultimately indifferent to external judgment. Gorbachev had an exceedingly high view of what people, and his country, might become, but he was entirely without illusion that they would succeed in other than inspired moments.

A year before his fortieth birthday, Gorbachev arrived on the national scene. In 1970 Kulakov recommended to the Central Committee in Moscow that Gorbachev succeed him as First Secretary in Stavropol. The boy from Privolnoye became one of the hundred-odd territorial bosses who played so decisive a role in running the USSR.[6] His entire family travelled to the city for his investiture.

Outwardly, there were one or two obvious changes that came to Gorbachev after gaining power. He became ever chunkier. His face was warier, his voice more incisive. His very clear blue-grey eyes had always given the impression that they were constantly watching, constantly on the alert. Now they had added to them a certain hardness—the sharp and piercing glance of the martinet.

A black and whiteness to his character was for the first time coming out publicly. To his fundamentally sharp mind there were few half-tones. He hated strongly and unforgivingly. Equally he loved steadily and deeply. And both functions were performed without fuss or outward passion or sentimentality. For those he cared for he was capable of precise attentions, a wholehearted confidence. And with the same ego-centric concentration he pursued his chosen enemies.

This basic dichotomy in his nature, never permitted full expression before, begins from his coming to power in Stavropol to grow more and more marked. Even in the smallest things he went through a process of thought that passed for a kind of mysticism. Everything was to be reduced to its utter simplicity. Was it good or bad? Did it work or not? Was it right or wrong? Having taken a decision, he stuck to it blindly, persistently and, at times, bigotedly. And all his subsequent dealings with the same subject were on the same direct level. All the doubtings and misgivings and half-interests and desires which lie at the periphery of a normal bureaucrat's mind, did not exist here. To his colleagues, there seemed to be no outer periphery to Gorbachev's mind. His mental world, like the world of the geographer before Christopher Columbus, was flat. If you went past the edges, you fell off. Ruthlessly, calmly, and clearly he lopped away all the impedimenta that he judged were without importance to his life. Other things might exist, but he was not inter-ested. No point in investigating them. Stick to what you wanted. When it was necessary to advance into unexplored territory, plan a campaign in advance. Never get beyond the reach of your bases. Clear up the new country entirely before you set out again.

This incisive logic—a logic sometimes unsupported by evidence—was already giving him immense advantages over young Party rivals of his own age. He concentrated. He rarely squandered time in the pursuit of mere intrigue. Everything in Gorbachev's life was done with a purpose and persisted in to the bitter and sometimes barren end. He rarely made conscious emotional judgments. He shunned violence in any form; he never investigated why. His prejudices existed and that was that.[7]

At forty he was developing the fixity of mind and purpose of a man twenty years his senior and he was far beyond his age in everything but experience. It was this that gave him a bearing that lacked warmth and suppleness and patience—unless by chance you happened to be on the right side of his mental fence; and then he was capable of a precise consideration and indulgence.

In the Gorbachev that existed from 1970 onwards there is an irresistible comparison with Nikita Khrushchev in everything but one major particular. The same compact and stout frame, the same rigid and almost fanatical set of the head, the stark emotional fervor, the contempt for convention and authority, the self-assurance and the ruthless determination, the quick outbursts of charm and generosity, the restlessness and the misogyny, the impatience and quarrelsomeness, the indifference to comfort and the love of praise, the compelling instinct toward leadership, the painstaking study and the asceticism, and finally, subliminating all this, an inward glory in the risks and skill of Communist party leadership. It is a remarkable resemblance. It fails only in this: quite unlike Khrushchev, Gorbachev had complete control of himself. He had no need for vodka or any other kind of escape. It seems almost impossible that a man, without being a stupid bore, could be so impervious to weakness, so entirely without a chink in his armor. Yet there it was: he was self-sufficient. Save for Raisa, he had formed no deep attachments outside himself, nothing that he could not cut away and forget. He was perfectly content without close friendships. He shed his parents and siblings from Privolnoye. He was apparently inspired by a series of abstract loyalties—to his party, his country, and most importantly, to himself. Of the humble loneliness of other men he seemed outwardly to have no part.[8]

All these qualities had been obviously building up in him since his earliest days in Privolnoye, and the element of struggle had become part of his life. But now, unconsciously we can assume, the effect of his ambition was to gather the qualities tightly together and fix them into the permanent cast of his character. Up to now he had lived in dependence on others. Now by virtue of his post as First Secretary, he switches over to being the patron of others. The mimickry subsides. Others will doing the running about while he directs.

Yet Gorbachev remained suspended between Moscow and the men he commanded. To many in the Kremlin hierarchy his self-assurance appeared as nothing more than arrogance. There was fear that Party rivals would be unwilling to place themselves under his command. It was said that he made few attempts to understand their difficulties—or anyone else's difficulties. He would flatly contradict his equals in conferences and sneer at their opinions. Gorbachev had acquired Kulakov's reputation of high-handedly pushing people aside whenever it suited his purposes. All the men Kulakov had slighted became his enemies, and the same threatened to happen to Gorbachev. But Gorbachev's ability to acquire other patrons saved him from that fate.[9]

Gorbachev, on learning of these charges, was genuinely surprised. He felt he had made considerable concessions to allies and equals alike. Had he not been obliged to submit to much inept planning? Could they not see that he was fighting the battle to implement Kulakov's policies, Party policies, and could not afford time to negotiate or deviate. Results were everything. Providing you succeeded, what did these petty misunderstandings matter?

Although Gorbachev had no firm enemies in the Kremlin, there were scores of men who felt that this new and active man should be watched, and watched closely. But the distance between Moscow and one of Russia's provincial capitals is measured in more than kilometers; it is also measured in degrees of safety. Throughout Russian history the farther from the Tsar an administrator was, the more creative and innovative he could be. Gorbachev would use the blessings of distance well, improvising experiments that flew in the face of Marxist-Leninist orthodoxy, but never daring enough to succeed.[10]

This often brought him into open conflict with the bosses of Soviet agriculture back in Moscow, for to assure ample harvests was his primary responsibility. Gorbachev could never blindly accept the advice or dictates of those above him. Perhaps, as many said, his besetting sin was vanity; certainly he appeared at times to be intransigent and stubborn to the point of bigotry, to oppose others simply for the sake of opposing them. Such vices, if they existed in him, also distilled virtues which were noticeably absent among other middle-level Party apparatchiks: he was more than a sycophant, he could not obey commands by rote, and only when impressed by a show of force were his wits clouded. Nor was he unduly handicapped by the niceties of Party protocol. He was unbribable—even by the subtlest forms of bribery. And he still avoided intrigue. This was also a refreshing novelty. A very great part of Gorbachev's success with Kulakov came from his habit of "talking back" to his superior, of digging in his toes and demanding point-blank what he thought would work—otherwise get someone else to carry out orders. It was never easy to turn squarely against strong political pressure, to reject plans given to him from very high authority and to insist on the adoption of his own. This was the real basis of Gorbachev's rule in Stavropol and it became a dominant strain in his character.[11]

Senior aides would have the right of coming directly to Gorbachev and he would send for them from time to time. At these meetings they would have to be prepared to state their business inside ten minutes. He would listen to no details. All these would go to his private secretary. Memoranda and papers were out. They would have to get used to transmitting and receiving orders by word of mouth. Where papers were necessary they must go to his secretary.

Gorbachev himself would lay down policy if no direct order had been received from Moscow. His subordinates would be thoroughly briefed on it before putting it into action. But they themselves must handle the details. They would have great latitude inside the general framework laid down by Gorbachev. They would do things their own way, provided only this—that they succeeded. By distributing responsibility, by making his apparatchiks something more than automatons, Gorbachev created a new atmosphere for the toilers of the socialist state—a hope and an enthusiasm that many thought had died out of the USSR forever.[12]

Perversely, the long-term effect of this new regimen was a sense of anxiety. In Communist politics men probably fear the unknown more than anything else in life. Decades of dictatorship—a steady and implacable route, no matter how hard to take—brings with it a sense of passive contentment. At least it is something firm and unchangeable to cling to in a changing and chaotic world where everything is rudderless motion, where one's fate is determined seemingly by luck and ungovernable chance and personal whim. And so this sense of inertia confronted Gorbachev. Here at last after so many years of simply obeying orders was inescapable responsibility. Many, perhaps most, were afraid of it.

More subtly, Gorbachev's attempts at decentralization of authority revealed something else as well. The men of the apparat sent from Moscow to Stavropol seemed to feel a certain mass loneliness. They were isolated from their real homes. Some had been unable to return home on leave for years. Posting to Stavropol stretched interminably ahead and transfer or advancement was uncertain. Everyone sooner or later acquired the feeling that he was forgotten and neglected—that his family had forgotten him, that the Party's leaders in Moscow regarded their duties as dead and trivial, that Stavropol was a place where men could be left to rot. It was a kind of *cafard,* and now there was only the danger of personal responsibility as imposed by Gorbachev to distract the mind from fixation.

In a pattern to be followed when he came to power in the Kremlin, Gorbachev tried to shatter this ennui. He tried to convey the sense that what went on in Stavropol was very important indeed. His reforms were vital. In the eyes of the USSR the plans he had to transform agricultural production by granting new authority to the communes themselves were central to the struggle in which a man might live to some purpose. It was classic communist rhetoric, different from past polemics only in its sincerity. Young and idealistic communists—and there were some—were eager to see the new First Secretary behind the new order.[13] Gorbachev was very early on the move most mornings, meeting with local officials, and he did not look or act like Kulakov or any previous leader of Stavropol. There was none of the aloofness and condescension usually associated with high Party figures. He was constantly getting out of his office and talking in a casual way with anyone he happened to meet. If this was a pre-arranged act to gain popularity, it did not appear to be so to those watching at the time.[14]

The number of his friendships remained few and his social life, except on the occasion of his tours through the region, virtually non-existent. External expression of his personality was limited; Gorbachev's life was inner. He was like a steam kettle in which the boiling goes on within an enclosed space and the steam comes out through a single spout. The secret of his self-possession was that he always had his mind absolutely made up as to what he wanted to do, and what action he would take if his programs were not sustained. This fixity gave him an embedded strength which men who fear the worst, or always will yield principles to avoid the worst, can never possess. It endowed him with a sense of moral superiority over his comrades which Party members, without knowing why, could sense in the atmosphere.

Gorbachev's activism, however, was resented for its trident self-promotion and his rudeness and sarcasm had not made friends. Nor did his disgust for deals, his refusal to woo Moscow apparatchiks with smiles and handshakes, or Party leaders with promises, enlarge his circle of supporters. Such jaunty self-confidence eventually caught Brezhnev's eye. Gorbachev pushed and pushed for a meeting with the General Secretary in order to present a plan for sheep production in his region. An argument liberally laced with quotations from Brezhnev's past speeches both flattered and amused the Kremlin leader. If you're so smart, Brezhnev is alleged to have said, you should become a member of the Politburo.[15] Within a week, the suggestion was taken up. Gorbachev was duly named a candidate member. His Stavropol exile had, at last, paid off. Someday soon, he knew, he would be brought permanently to Moscow.

Gorbachev's style of management in Stavropol revealed, even then, that fundamental cleavage between *his* notion of the socialist state and how that state had evolved since the revolution. For Gorbachev, there could be no genuine stability or progress in a system based on the evil and weakness in man's nature—which ruled by man's degradation, feeding like a vulture on his anxieties, his capacity for suspicion and hate, his susceptibility to error, and his vulnerability to psychological manipulation. Such a system could represent no more than the particular frustrations and bitterness of the men who created it, and the cold terror of those weak or unwise enough to become its unthinking agents.

This is not to say that Gorbachev was, when in his forties, already persuaded of communism's gravest flaws. That understanding came as part of his complicated education as he climbed the Party ladder to supreme power. What Gorbachev as First Secretary of Stavropol seemed already to be disgusted about was how something which brashly claimed to be a hopeful turn in human events, something which could have led to a decrease rather than an increase in the sum total of human injustice and oppression, had mutated into the shabby purgatory of a police state. Only men with a profound sense of personal failure could find satisfaction in doing to others those things demanded by such a system. Whoever has had occasion to look deeply into the eyes of a KGB officer will have found there, in that dark well of disciplined hatred, suspicion, and paranoia, the tiny gleam of despairing fright which is the proof of this statement. Those who began by clothing a personal lust for power and revenge with the staggering deceits and oversimplifications of totalitarianism wound up fighting themselves—in a dreary, hopeless encounter which projected itself onto the people and made of their lives a perpetual battlefield.

Men of this sort bequeath something of the passion of their struggle to those who inherit their power. But the inheritance does diminish. People can move along, themselves, as by some force of habit, on the strength of an emotional drive acquired second hand; but it is not theirs to transmit to others. The impulses that push men of one generation into so despairing an attitude toward themselves and toward the masses they ruled and in whom they wanted to see themselves reflected, lose their power to incite succeeding generations. The cruelties, the untruths, the endless deriding of man's nature practiced in the concentration camps, indeed all the institutions of the socialist police state, though they may at first hold something of the lurid fascination that danger and anarchy always exert, sooner or later end up—like some stale and monotonous pornography—becoming boring, most of all to those chosen to practice them.

Many of the servants of totalitarian power, it is true, having debased themselves as well as their victims and knowing that they have damned themselves from the prospect of a better future, cling despairingly to their unhappy offices. But Gorbachev's career demonstrates that despotism can never live on just by the fears of jailers and hangmen alone; behind it there must be a driving political will. In the day when despotic power could be closely associated with a dynasty or an inherited oligarchy, such a political will could be enduring. But then, it had to take a more benevolent interest in people over whom it ruled and from whose labors it fed. It could not afford to live by their total intimidation and degradation. Dynastic continuity compelled it to recognize an obligation to the future, as well as to the present and to the past.

The socialist state, as Gorbachev appeared to begin to recognize, did not have these qualities. It represented only a fearful convulsion of society. Grievously, agonizingly ill from the effects of socialism, society, being organic and marked by change, renewal, and adjustment, can not remain comatose forever. The violent injustices which caused the convulsion must begin to lose their actuality, and the instinct for a healthier, less morbid, more interesting life assert itself. In Gorbachev's life and career are the embodiment of this tendency.

No great and enduring change in the spirit of the USSR was yet possible under Brezhnev, who carried with him all the hate of the past. Yet the revolutionary fires were already banked. Leonid Brezhnev ruled the Soviet socialist state for eighteen years—from 1964 to 1982—during which Gorbachev was making his climb to power. And Brezhnev was godfather to a mafia of colossally casual corruption. His coterie lived like Turkish pashas. At his Black Sea dacha, Brezhnev used to preen and impress visiting officials by touching a button that would roll back a wall to reveal an Olympic-size swimming pool. Outlawed musicians and poets were summoned to command performances for him. Brezhnev's motto to young apparatchiks was: "the less you know the better you sleep."[16]

The region over which Gorbachev presided may have been far from the center of power in Moscow, but it was popular with Kremlin leaders, who patronized the secret Party spas near the Caspian Sea. Hidden behind long, gated drives and *allées* of poplars, surrounded by banks of roses and the sweet smell of honeysuckle, the private health spas reeked of privilege. They were among the hidden perks of high office, and Gorbachev as regional leader helped supervise and maintain them.

Once more, he was in a position to curry favor with the great. Like some regional office manager anticipating the wants and whims of a visiting corporate bigwig, Gorbachev was good at making Kremlin leaders feel comfortable on their vacations, flattering them, being a fixer, sometimes a sort of pimp. The ruthless Mikhail Suslov, Brezhnev's Grand Inquisitor who had ruled in Stavropol when Gorbachev was a boy, indeed had supervised the imprisonment of the senior Gorbachev in the 1930s, was one frequent visitor assiduously courted by Gorbachev. And with success. The two men went for long walks and frequently played cards late into the night.

But it was another, more sinister figure, who most claimed Gorbachev's attentions. Yuri Andropov, long head of the KGB, found the mineral waters of the spa at Kislovodsk helpful for his kidney disease.[17] Andropov came to the spa at least four times a year, and Gorbachev made certain that he was at the train station to greet him on each visit, accompany him to his dacha, settle him in, then escort him to the spas for his baths. During these visits the alliance that would re-orient Gorbachev's life was formed.

In Andropov's ascetism and cultural interests Gorbachev found a model for his notion of the ideal socialist man. Where Brezhnev was bullying and openly corrupt, Andropov was known throughout the Party elite for his modest and clean living. For his part, Andropov preferred the company of the literate and restrained Gorbachev to that of Brezhnev's high-living flunkeys. Melancholy, intensely intellectual, subject to fits of depression which Gorbachev called "nerve storms," caustic, bored by routine and fond of solitude, with a penetrating, skeptical, questioning mind, Andropov was the Hamlet of communist politics, doubting Stalinist dogma even as he packed the gulags. He was above the conventions, and refused to succumb to Brezhnev's corruptions. When he listened to others he could become easily bored, revealed by a telltale wagging of his leg which seemed to one observer to be saying, "When will all this be over?" When he was seated and listening to some presentation, only Andropov's fingers would betray movement, incessantly twisting and turning a paper knife or beating a tattoo on his knee or on the arm of his chair. He worked from breakfast to one in the morning, returning to his desk after dinner as if he were beginning a new day.

Despite his sharp tongue and sarcasms, Andropov exerted a personal charm upon Gorbachev which was no small cause of the younger man's opting to align himself with the KGB chieftain, who was beginning to set himself up as a rival to and possible successor for Brezhnev. Andropov appeared to care deeply for Party affairs, not only because control of them implied real power, but because he seemed to want to make socialism work. He regarded himself not as responsible *to* the Party but as responsible *for* it. Fidelity to making socialism work was his care. Where in the Byzantine atmosphere of Brezhnev's court no one was anxious to inform his leader of deteriorating realities, indeed, the worse these became the less Brezhnev was told, Andropov was anxious to know the true state of things in Russia. As Gorbachev was not afraid to draw attention to the gap between the self-deluding fantasies of Soviet propaganda and statistics on the one hand and the actual miseries of Soviet life on the other, Andropov quickly took a shine to the young man, who seemed to remind him of himself.[18]

Andropov's sights were trained on the corrupt Brezhnev clan, and he yearned to bring them down. With his secret dossiers and KGB informers, Andropov knew everything. He knew about the family stains in Gorbachev's past, for example, and buried them. Once he picked Gorbachev as an ally he protected him from attack from Brezhnev's faction. But it was unnecessary. Gorbachev, ever cautious, did not neglect his relations with Suslov, who remained for Brezhnev the high priest of ideology.

For both Andropov and Gorbachev the old Spartan socialist virtues remained, and to practice them assured a correct life. Socialism remained an exactly prescribed world: on this side the practical issues which leaders must tackle with courage and common sense; on that side the socialist vision which was pre-determined by history. Like a good operational plan, every issue was covered by some department in the historically correct order of things. There were no mysteries; but simply human weaknesses and corruptions which, unless checked, led to a state of decay and failure.

Like most secret rebels, Andropov and Gorbachev were at war, constantly, against decadence; they aimed continually at the purity of orthodoxy, which would come about only in a composed and efficiently managed world. At heart, both men were revivalists. They accepted the world as it was and the communist faith as they found it. Their self-annointed task was to reorganize existing things on a more efficient path.

By September 1978, Andropov was ready to bring Gorbachev to Moscow, and he succeeded in having Suslov also act as patron. It took two months of efforts, but before the end of the year Gorbachev was chosen as Secretary of the Central Committee. His was the last name on the official list of promotions, but that did not matter. Real power had come to him at last. There was some debate among the Brezhnev clique about his appointment; it was impossible not to notice that he was not one of *them,* that he shunned their earthy and boisterous ways. But in becoming Andropov's trusted protégé, he was beyond reproach.

Soon afterwards, Andropov launched his corruption probe of Brezhnev's clan. Ill, enfeebled, the old General Secretary was powerless to stop it. When Suslov died, Brezhnev's power base was fatally compromised by Andropov's KGB investigations. It was just a matter of time. Not since the dreaded Beria had a KGB chief assumed such power. And after Brezhnev himself collapsed and died in November 1982, Andropov seized power—Gorbachev at his side.[19]

24

⇶ ⇷

Gorbachev
A Failure of the Will

Inertia in the scales of history often weighs more heavily than change.

The dream of revolution is a dream of power. Gorbachev understood, or so it appears, that talent and intellectual vigor rarely translate directly into political power in the USSR, even though a central element in the seductive role of the communist vanguard is that it promises to assure just that. Indeed, in theory it seems to demand it. Gorbachev appears always to have looked for or expected political power to come to him one day. Yet like Lenin and Bukharin, and Gide, Koestler, and Silone for that matter, the communist vision was never one of power for its own sake. His game was deeper.

The political personality of Gorbachev when he became Andropov's dauphin was a product of ideology and circumstance: ideology inherited from the revolution of 1917 itself, and circumstances of the power which he had exercised for nearly two decades in Stavropol. There can be few tasks of psychological analysis more difficult than to try and trace the interaction of these two forces within Gorbachev's character and the relative role of each in the determination of his conduct.

To summarize the set of ideological assumptions which Gorbachev took with him into power is difficult. His Marxism appears to have been in a state of subtle, continuing evolution. But the outstanding feature of his thought when he stood side by side with Andropov was clearly orthodox Leninism, and can be summarized as follows: (1) that the central fact in the life of man, the fact which determines the character of society, is the system by which material goods are produced and exchanged; (2) that the capitalist system of production was nefarious, leading to the exploitation of workers by capitalists, and ever incapable of developing the economic resources of society or of distributing fairly the material goods produced by human labor; and (3) that capitalism contains the seeds of its own destruction and must, in view of the inability of capitalists to adjust to economic change, result eventually and inescapably in a revolutionary transfer of power to the working class. Capitalism would perish only with proletarian revolution. That final push was needed in order to tip over the tottering structure. Sooner or later that push would be given.

In all the decades from the October Revolution this pattern of thought was fundamental communist dogma, and Gorbachev appears to have subscribed to it fully. Frustrated, discontented, hopeless of finding self-expression—or too impatient to seek it within the Tsarist system—the original Bolsheviks had chosen bloody revolution as a means of social betterment, and Gorbachev, too, found in Marxist theories a highly convenient rationale for his own ambitions and desires. It afforded pseudo-scientific justification for his impatience, just as it categorically denied for Bolsheviks like Lenin and Bukharin all the value in the Tsarist system. A yearning for power and willingness to cut corners in the pursuit of it were easily accommodated by faith in communism. It is therefore no wonder that he came to believe implicitly in the truth and soundness of Marxist-Leninist thinking, so convenient to his own impulses and emotions. Sincerity of his beliefs need not be impugned. Gorbachev is a phenomenon as old as human nature itself. It has never been more aptly described than by Edward Gibbon, who wrote in *The Decline and Fall of the Roman Empire:* "From enthusiasm to imposture the step is perilous and slippery; the demon of Socrates affords a memorable instance how a wise man may deceive himself; how a good man may deceive others, how the conscious may slumber in a mixed and middle state between self-illusion and voluntary fraud."[1] It was with such a set of illusions that Gorbachev entered power, and the story of his years of high office is the final and terrible realization of the impossibility of their enactment.

Brezhnev had warned the Communist party to be content with the state it had, but his successors were neither separately nor collectively Brezhnevs. He had pursued clearly seen goals unswervingly; they groped for larger horizons with no clear idea of what they wanted. Andropov was a Machiavelli without a policy who operated on only one principle: suspect everyone. Konstantin Chernenko, leader of the Brezhnev faction, had no principles; he was so slippery, it was said, that compared to him an eel was a leech. The flashing, inconstant, always freshly inspired Gorbachev had, it seemed, a different goal every hour, and conceived of policy as an exercise in perpetual motion.

Andropov took his position as head of the Party and nation as naturally as a father will assume responsibility for his family, and the idea of
the Communist party's divine right to rule was something more than a
survival from revolutionary times; it was a living faith that was passionately believed in and not only by the Party oligarchs themselves. To the
great mass of the Russian people it was just as much dogma—unalter-
able and absolute dogma—as the Gospel had been earlier on in Russia.
It might be said that this fidelity to Party dogma was forced on the
Russian people, that it was the tyranny of the socialist state which had
turned the majority of them into a race of nameless slaves, but the fact
remains that Andropov's state was a predatory one which he and the
small group of Party bureaucrats ruled for their own exclusive benefit.
The average comrade was nothing more than a serf who could not have
any ambition other than to die early and peacefully, or to survive with
a minimum of work, hunger, and beatings. Through the state the Party
owned all the wealth, enjoyed all the privileges, and monopolized all the
political power, and it did not intend to give up any of its prerogatives.
It considered the Soviet masses to be little better than dumb animals
who could not be trusted with the slightest responsibility.

All of Stalin's powers, at any rate in their broader aspects, had been
faithfully preserved down to the time of Andropov's ascension, together
with the inevitable accompaniment: the sullen discontent, the frustration, and finally the indignation of people who hated such a way of life.
Here again it is almost impossible for anyone brought up in a democracy
to understand completely the hunger that there was in Andropov's USSR
for liberty, for some power in framing and exercising the law. This is
the dream that in the end outlasted the socialist vision. Basically Gorbachev's career and the revolution he spawned is the story of the rising
from the dead of this belief.

The stand of the Party on this issue was very simple: socialism was in
the process of being constructed. If you slackened control one bit, the
past might rise up and overwhelm the future; then only chaos and
decadence would result.

Yuri Andropov was at least willing to go a certain distance in making
reforms, in fact rather further than any of his predecessors including
Nikita Khrushchev. As things turned out, however, his system of liberation was merely bondage of another kind, and Soviet workers found
themselves in some ways rather worse off than they had been before.[2]
As Minister in charge of agriculture, Gorbachev handed over more land
for the small private plots that peasants had been allowed to maintain
since Khrushchev. But they had to pay for it, and they were obliged to

sell their produce to the state and not at informal markets where demand would set the price. In practice this meant that farmers had to work twice as hard as before, because the managers of the collective farms began to cut back on rations and pay to those farmers working their own private plots. Thus there was very little inducement for peasants to effect improvements or increase production. Still, it was the principle of the thing which Gorbachev thought to be important, and it will be useful to remember that it was in the farming sector of the economy that Gorbachev first encountered massive bureaucratic resistance to his reforms.

Now it must be noted that through all the years of yearnings and preparations for power, the attention of Gorbachev, as indeed of Lenin and Bukharin themselves, had been centered less on the future form which socialism would take than on the necessary destruction of his rivals, and those of Andropov, which had to precede the introduction of reforms. Gorbachev's views, therefore, on the positive program to be put into effect, once personal power had been attained, were for the most part nebulous, visionary, and impractical. Beyond a dream of more efficient management and the elimination of corruption, there was no agreed program. The treatment of the peasantry, which according to formal Marxist dogma was not at all a part of the proletariat, had always been a vague spot in the pattern of Communist thought; and it remained an object of controversy and vacillation for Gorbachev during his years as Minister of Agriculture. He knew that the elimination of dictatorial power over farm production was a necessity, that the Party's attempts to eliminate private production and trade had debilitating economic consequences and caused bitterness among the rural community of which he was a part by birth. Yet every policy he pursued became merely an attempt to reconcile the conflicting forces of state control and individual initiative.[3] For in Gorbachev's mental world, as in the character of his ideology, no opposition to state power could be officially recognized as having any merit or justification whatsoever. Such opposition could flow only from the hostile and incorrigible forces of dying capitalism. Here was the dilemma of reform. Intuitively, Gorbachev appears to have understood that it was collectivism, regulation, and central management—the heavy hand of the state—that was stifling productivity and enterprise in Russia. To breathe the pure and heady air of market exchange, all had to go. But to sweep away the edifice of state control of agriculture was to dismantle the core of the socialist state itself. That was heresy, pure and simple, and Andropov and Gorbachev shrunk from it.

All of Andropov's and Gorbachev's actions, therefore, though some of them were eminently sensible (such as rooting out and punishing patently corrupt officials loyal to Brezhnev), were badly compromised by intellectual incoherence. A vacuum of understanding arose from their ideological ignorance. When both men came into power, it was not just as reformers but as seemingly incorruptible men. Only if they could depend on support from the apparat could they deliver policies that avoided the arbitrary excesses of the previous reign. So, with Andropov's warm endorsement, Gorbachev rescued local management of the collective farms from the limbo into which Stalinist centralization had sent them. His mistaken assumption was that they would back his reforms with increased production out of gratitude and rationality. But nothing was quite that simple in Soviet Russia.

It followed from Gorbachev's sympathy with Andropov's incorruptible ideal that the liberalization of central state control of the Soviet economy would, of itself, generate the kind of rural prosperity that would solve the government's chronic problem of food shortages. This would happen in two ways. Public confidence, that most alchemical of economic qualities, would revive as corrupt managers and officials were disposed of. Freed of corruption and oppressive rule, the collective farms would flourish to such an extent that they would yield a model of happy socialist production to be followed by the industrial sectors of society. All this was, of course, the direct descendant of Bukharin's vision of a benevolent Leviathan state, and had just about as much chance of successful implementation.

Lest this account sound too sardonic it should be said immediately that Mikhail Gorbachev was no ministerial Pangloss. A somber, self-questioning man whose principle recreation was his work, he had an excessively dim view of the nature of the average Soviet comrade but an excessively cheerful view of the possibilities of his improvement. Application of his ideas had been possible in the region of Stavropol because he was there, on the ground, monitoring their progress, seeing to it that his orders were followed through on. That was impossible in Moscow. To apply his ideas on a national scale, he needed to rely on the massive state apparat to carry out his wishes. But far from being pragmatic civil servants willing to do his bidding, most had nothing more on their minds than personal survival. Obstruction and a suspicious and sullen inertia were the result.

Strung by violent mutterings against his policies, Gorbachev believed that bureaucratic obstruction was all an elaborate conspiracy, and that local apparatchiks were pretending that his reforms were unworkable in

order to embarrass his ministry. His response to these impertinent impediments to his ministerial will was to root out and sack those of his
opponents that he could. His principal line of attack against them,
though, required a strengthening of central authority in his own person
that went some way to diminishing his goal of freeing the agricultural
economy. As always, Gorbachev was showing himself to be strong on
ends, but weak on means. For all his powerful intellectual exertions he
failed to see a contradiction in his commanding a decentralized farm
economy to come into being through the instrument of personal absolutism. Viewing himself as the most liberal member of the Central
Committee, Gorbachev was in fact the Minister who most freely used
arbitrary power to dismiss and arrest, and a number of his opponents
ended up smartly in the gulag.[4] He also made no allowance for the kind
of structural dislocations—such as the absence of the refrigerated trains
and trucks so necessary to the transport of fresh produce in a vast
country—that constituted economic reality in the planned socialist economy.

Yet he also chose the worst possible time for reform. The year 1983
saw the return of bad harvests, and with them the return of severe
shortages in city shops, and anger among the Party bureaucrats at peasants accused of hoarding to profit from price rises on the black market.
The natural political consequence of this was to discredit reform and
experimentation in any form. And when Yuri Andropov died, Chernenko grabbed power amid the usual Party hurrahs of wild eyed heretics laid low. With this went some of Gorbachev's men and many of his
measures. This put an end to the peaceful, stable reform Andropov had
hoped to accomplish.

Gorbachev's defeat by Chernenko in the succession struggle after
Andropov's death was, in part, the inevitable product of unrealistic
expectations that circulated about Gorbachev's abilities and purposes.
To Chernenko and his supporters Gorbachev was not a prudent and
determined reformer, rather he was seen as a fraudulent prestidigitator.
Although Chernenko, no less than Gorbachev, saw the fundamental
prosperity of the USSR as being contingent on economic revitalization,
he was not prepared to sacrifice Party privilege and power on the altar
of reform. What counted for Chernenko was the maximizing of state
power.

Knowing it was out of the question to abolish all venal offices whilst
Chernenko ruled, Gorbachev concentrated on those areas of agriculture
where waste was most conspicuous and where venal offices most obviously deprived the state of productivity. So he abolished the positions of

bureaucrats unwilling to bend to him, replacing them with men directly accountable to himself and his ministry. Collective farm managers who fought him were similarly dispatched. Thus was created the first phalanx of Gorbachev's powerful enemies.[5]

Gorbachev even considered taking on Chernenko himself, comparing the older man's court unflatteringly with a kind of weed that flourishes in a swamp. Chernenko's vision of socialism represented a return to strict governmental control of a huge bureaucratic empire of patronage that had simply become, in many places, the personal plaything of Party courtiers. The center of his accusation against Chernenko's regime was that the General Secretary and his cronies deliberately constructed a flimsy and false picture of the Soviet economy that bore no reality to the actual conditions of production in the country. To Gorbachev's hard and methodical mind, prosperity depended on public confidence in the policies of government. With that elusive quantity present, there was no reason for workers and peasants not to support socialism to the utmost. But when the government presented only a wall of lies—lies that were seen through by the public as fabrications—the climate of public opinion would only remain morose, and productivity lag.[6]

On the principle of infallibility the iron discipline of the socialist state had rested since the revolution. This was a direct offshoot of Bukharin's concept of Leviathan, for if truth was to be found outside the Party, there would be justification for its expression in organized opposition. But that was precisely what Bukharin could not or would not permit. Perfect discipline demanded recognition of the Party's authoritative dictates, and infallibility required the observance of absolute discipline. The two factors determined the behavior of the entire state apparatus. But the implementation had, until the time of Gorbachev, been determined by the fact that the Party hierarchy was free to put forward for tactical reasons any particular notion which it found useful at any moment, and to require unquestioning acceptance. This meant that truth was not a constant but an invented thing. It was not absolute or immutable, but a passing manifestation of the wisdom of those in whom ultimate authority reposed because they represented the logic of History. Once a Party line had been established, whether by Stalin, Khrushchev, Brezhnev or Chernenko, the whole socialist state would move inexorably along the prescribed path, like some toy truck wound up and headed in a given direction, stopping only when it met with some unmovable object. The individuals who were the components of this machine were to spout back the numbers demanded by the state, no matter their relation to reality. Like the white dog on the old RCA recording labels, they could hear only their master's voice. Thus the intrusion of such facts as declining industrial or agricultural production could make no impression at all. The most that could be hoped for was that the state's minions would transmit information to those at the top, who were capable of making adjustments to factual reality. But no fact, for them, was of unchallengeable validity. This last point was nicely summed up by Hannah Arendt when she said that the most significant quality of totalitarian thinkers was their "extreme contempt for facts as such, for in their opinion a fact depends entirely on the power of the man who can fabricate it."[7] Ordinary men lie about themselves. Ideologues lie about society—its past, its present, and its future.

Gorbachev's ideas for reform amounted to an exercise in public education. His conviction that the truth must be told to the common man testifies to his attempt to form an engaged citizenry.

So the issue between Chernenko and Gorbachev was more than a matter of economic management. It arose from a deep and passionate belief, one which perhaps flowed from Gorbachev's own secret history and was to make the two inseparable in the discourse and conduct of his coming *perestroika* revolution. That was the opposition of transparency and opacity, of candor against dissimulation, of public-spiritedness against Party self-interest, of directness against disguise. In the phrase of Vaclav Havel, Gorbachev wanted communism to "live inside the truth." His *glasnost* would make the deliberate deceits of the socialist state a form of treason. But already, in the shape of Kremlin intrigue, these ideas were enough to persuade Chernenko to oust his most determined rival. For to Chernenko and his clique the preservation of secrecy and the production of propaganda were *the* means to rescue the socialist state. This was not only immoral for Gorbachev, it was imprudent. To deny the need for a relationship of trust and consent between governors and governed was to abandon all hope of popular support.

Before he could oust Gorbachev from the Central Committee, Chernenko died in the spring of 1985, having served little more than a year. After losing the last conclave and election, Gorbachev was not this time going to let supreme power pass from him. He lined up behind him the two power bases in the socialist state—the Red Army and the KGB—most aware of the perilous state of the economy and the continuing decline of the USSR's economic power in comparison with that of the rival capitalists. Chernenko's stand-pat socialism had caused them only alarm and despair. In point of fact, both the KGB and Red Army were willing to stand behind any claimant who stood for a bold program of economic revitalization, and they fell in behind Gorbachev when only he took this route. Even old Andrei Gromyko fell in line, praising Gorbachev as a "man with iron teeth."[8]

Mikhail Gorbachev was fifty-four when he ascended to supreme power in the Kremlin. He was at the height of his energies, expansive, vain, gracious, willful, and no stranger to the worst in man. Having grown up with the vicious strife surrounding Stalin's forced collectivizations in the Russian countryside, the paranoia of the dictator's last years in the early 1950s, and the purges enacted by Brezhnev when he seized power, Gorbachev seemed, as far as the world at large could determine, unscarred by the experience. Certainly he understood the Byzantine intricacies of Communist party politics,[9] yet there were also hints at a knowledge of a larger sense of rulership. When, at the outset of his regime, Gorbachev launched his claim to remake communism in a more democratic form, it is uncertain how seriously he took it, but as a device it was of incomparable value in giving him the appearance of a righteous cause. Though he was impatient to see a socialism of science and enterprise brush aside the institutional impediments to their ascendancy, he believed there was no reason why this should not and could not happen in a reforming socialist state.

To prod the somnolent economy awake was his announced intention. True socialism would come about not by revolution or violence or even central dictatorship, but by the simple and gradual operation of collectivized groups acting on their own initiative for the general welfare. Gorbachev's fantasy on taking over in the Kremlin was of an almost painlessly modernized USSR transformed by collective wisdom and shared capital into the benefactor not only for itself, but of the entire world. His vision of the future embraced the decentralization of economic decision-making and the opening of political debate without much sense of apprehension. Indeed, his castle in the clouds was built on what he saw as the unfolding and potentially limitless achievements of enlightened socialist governance.[10]

In his book *Perestroika* (in part a compendium of Gorbachev's thought cobbled together by his staff), Gorbachev made his lone attempt to provide a systematic diagnosis of socialism's ills.[11] The almost complete absence from the book of explicit moral argument, let alone moral outrage and condemnation, of appeals to conscience or to principle, and the equally striking absence of detailed predictions of what will or should happen after the implementations of his reforms, follow from the concentration of Gorbachev's attention on the practical problems of action. The conceptions of natural rights, and of conscience, as belonging to every man irrespective of his position in the historic class struggle, are paid little more than lip service. Socialism does not appeal to such mushy doctrines; it demands. It speaks not of rights, but of a new form of life before whose inexorable approach the old social order had already given way. Moral, political, economic conceptions and ideals alter with the social conditions from which they spring: to regard any one of them as essential to the success of socialism is ideological delusion. If the historical determinism of Marx was real, and Gorbachev emphatically believed that it was, universal values cannot be accepted as part of a policy of action. A denial of this fact can be due only to a stupid or cynical disregard for historical truth, a peculiarly vicious form of hypocrisy and self-deception repeatedly exposed by history. This fundamental continuity of outlook between Gorbachev and his predecessors in the Kremlin was something disguised by Gorbachev's natural gifts and charm, and led to continuing misunderstanding, at home and abroad, of both Gorbachev and his mission.

Gorbachev, as *Perestroika* all too clearly shows, detested romanticism, emotionalism, and humanitarianism of almost every kind. In his anxiety to manage and appeal to such idealistic feelings, however, he systematically loaded his argument with all the old democratic code words. He neither offered nor invited concessions about the fundamental structure of the socialist state. The manifestoes, professions of faith and programs to which he appended his name contain numerous references to the ideas of moral progress, eternal justice, the rights of individuals or nations, the liberty of conscience, the fight for civilization, and other such notions that embody the democratic and free-market ideal. But the fact that his program offered little in the way of laws that would concretely guarantee the existence of such liberties demonstrates that, at least at the start of his regime, Gorbachev considered them little more than worthless cant.

And yet it required of Gorbachev no small degree of intellectual courage and acuteness of vision to penetrate the Party's smokescreen of rosy statistics and to perceive the real structure of events under socialism. The spectacle of looming chaos, the imminence of the crisis in which it was bound to end, are both presented penetratingly in *Perestroika*. Nevertheless, what history has proclaimed must be defended and not swept away: to say that something eternal should be discarded is to deny the immortal rational plan of the universe. To denounce the process of socialism—the painful conflicts through which mankind struggles to achieve the full realization of its powers—was for Gorbachev a form of self-indulgence, arising from a shallow view of life.

With the reality of socialism's triumph over history there could be no compromise: to go backwards and abandon the socialist choice of 1917 would be nothing more than an act of cowardice, due to a desire to avoid the perils and risks and responsibilities of victory. Nothing stirred Gorbachev's imagination so much as cowardice: hence the furious and often brutal tones with which he harangued the slackards he confronted in the socialist apparat.

To trace the direct source of Gorbachev's consuming desire to reform the decaying socialist system which he had inherited is a relatively simple task. The absolutist socialist state had promised heaven and delivered hell. It had created a new lord of the Party cadre and made subhumans of the proletariat. They were now doomed to live in inertia and suspicion.

In launching into his reform program Gorbachev's rhetoric was apocalyptic, his solutions (such as they were) peculiar but not without sense. He became something of a messianic schoolmaster, wielding a very big stick to inculcate virtue. If there was too much drunkenness at work and on the streets, then the supply of vodka and other spirits was to be restricted, on some days cut off completely. Habitual drunks were to be sent off to state psychiatric hospitals to take the cure. He came to conceive of the socialist state itself as a school, but one in which knowledge would always be augmented by morality. Both, moreover, depended on discipline. Productivity and virtue, he became fond of saying, were part of the same exercise in social self-improvement, "Virtue without which production can become harmful and decadent, production without virtue is historically impotent."[12] Once the criminal element, morally and politically speaking—the party libertines, the corrupt, the shirkers and malingerers—had been eliminated, it would be possible to begin his vast exercise of creating a virtuous socialist order.

Needless to say, nothing came of his morality schemes, not least because, by decimating the sale of spirits, he destroyed a reliable source of state revenue.[13] But the passion for moral improvement which fired Gorbachev in the first two years of his rule flowed into all his policies and speeches, until, in late 1986, politics itself seemed a rather squalid pastime compared with the transcendent calling of this missionary of socialist virtue.

For Gorbachev and those who shared his vision, there were two necessary stages to this enterprise of economic and moral regeneration. First, the economic paralysis caused by excessive centralization of the economy had to be stopped in its tracks; second, the political and intellectual conformity so long demanded by the socialist state had to give way to an inspiring yet orderly flowering of debate and discussion. Such intellectual investigation would leave no part of the socialist state untouched. It would probe and unveil all its inconsistencies and dysfunctions, both planned and unplanned, and thus stimulate the true socialist virtues: fraternity, honesty, and hard work. The exaltation of a virtuous and democratic collective life would be in the strongest possible contrast to the acts of indiscriminate corruption characteristic of the extreme phase of the Brezhnev era.

For Gorbachev, the socialist state as it existed was not a final settlement. True communism was still to come. Capitalism had not been crushed; it was actually expanding and prospering; the world of creativity and invention still worshipped at the capitalists' feet. Socialists were gnawed by envy of the system they were supposed to have doomed to history's trash heap. He considered the West decadent in culture and enfeebled by excess democracy, but in energy, industry, and wealth, it surpassed anything in the USSR. The mechanics of socialism must therefore adjust.

Living in the shadow of the unfinished socialist construction, the Soviet Union, Gorbachev understood, was weary of being eternally on guard, eternally exhorted by her leaders to defend socialism. As Gorbachev consolidated his power in the Kremlin, he knew that his nation's spirit was rebelling against six decades of being on the defensive with its implied avowal of inferiority. Gorbachev knew his country to be economically weaker than its rivals. It needed some weapon that socialism seemed to lack to give itself confidence in the future. His willingness to free the economy and the spirit from the shackles of central state control would be the equalizing factor. Gorbachev believed that the human spirit had not been, after all, crushed by the omnipotent socialist state with its demands for uniformity.* A voluntary revival of the true socialist will, a sort of Soviet *élan vital*, would enable socialism to work where dictatorship had failed. Russia's genius had always been her spirit, the spirit of 1812, of the incomparable defense of Sevastopol, the spirit of the Battleship *Potemkin*. Belief in the fervor of the Soviet people, in a revival of their faith in themselves, would stir and save the nation. It was to be a new revolutionary era, banners unfurled, bugles sounding, that would lead the USSR to prosperity and true socialism.[14]

And where did Gorbachev look for inspiration? To what thinker did he turn for a model of socialism remade?

In Lenin, the founder of the socialist state, Gorbachev saw not a

---

*A famous, cynical phrase of Gorbachev's era went: "They pretend to pay us and we pretend to work."

terrorist but "an inexhaustible source of dialectical creative thought, theoretical wealth and political sagacity. His very image is an undying example of lofty moral strength, all-round spiritual culture and selfless devotion to the cause of the people and to socialism."[15] Here is perestroika's false dawn. For Gorbachev, indeed, the idea of democracy is a Leninist one. Perhaps in his sagacity, Gorbachev knew that the breaking of the old way of doing things would be a long process and that, like Stalin, he could recast the socialist system only from the safety of seeming to conform to Lenin's doctrines. But something else is revealed in this summons to restore the primacy of Lenin. You can not change your nature and ways of thinking as you can change your shoes. It must be a gradual shedding. In a home with three generations, Gorbachev was like a son who turns to his grandparent as a means of escape. Gorbachev was setting out to destroy the socialist system as bequeathed by Stalin, not the original concept of Lenin. And he would do it by slow attrition, like a son who stays home and obeys the essential rules of his parents, all the while silently hating their authority, and silently, in his soul, destroying not only their authority but their way of existence. But the spiritual home of Gorbachev remained state socialism, for "perestroika means the elimination from society of the distortions of socialist ethics, the consistent implementation of the principles of social justice . . . the end result of perestroika . . . is a renewal of every aspect of Soviet life . . . the essence of perestroika . . . revives the Leninist concept of socialist construction both in theory and in practice."[16] That perestroika should be confirmed by Lenin is all the assurance Gorbachev needs.

The problem, as Gorbachev saw it, was that the moral aspects of Marxism-Leninism were in need of new clarification. The scientific authoritarianism it insisted upon provided no moral motivation for the average man. The truth was that the Stalinist façade that had been applied to socialism had disguised the doctrine of the natural rights of man, which Gorbachev saw as important to both revive and bring into the open. What was needed was a restored standard of socialist morality, but all that dictum really amounted to was that Party leaders become "modest, decent, honest, and intolerant of flattery and toadying."[17]

Now, for Gorbachev, with the capitalist world remaining as an antagonist, there could be no question whatever of a gradual evolution of socialist morals to that of the capitalist system; a moral code which should include both proletarians and profiteers was to him inconceivable. Disregarding his own diagnosis of socialism's ills, he reacted against calls to incorporate bourgeois values into the Soviet system with an aggressive, bullheaded fury. Such calls were calculated to demoralize the convictions of good socialists, and hence they threatened his entire rationale for reform; so he denounced the very things that he needed in order to make socialism succeed—private property, independent opposition political parties, separation of party and state—as the most damnable of heresies.

Gorbachev, for example, insisted on the progressive aspect of "democratic centralism," the theoretical cornerstone of the socialist state. "We do not want to weaken the role of the center," he declared, "because otherwise we would lose the advantages of the planned economy. . . . At the same time, one cannot fail to see that the central authorities are overburdened with minor work. We will relieve them of current duties, for, by dealing with them, they lose sight of strategic matters."[18] Free the Party elite of the burden of detail, Gorbachev argues, and they will find their eyes opened and thus make the best decisions to direct the future for all Soviet men.

Such is the muddle in which the genuine anguish and yearning of Gorbachev reverberates through *Perestroika*. To point out Gorbachev's confusions and inconsistencies, however, is not to gratuitously detract from the daring of his work. On the contrary, in political tracts as in other forms of writing, the importance of a book depends, not merely on the correctness of its prescriptions, but on the depth from which it has been drawn. Gorbachev is struggling with the fundamental discords of his society. His trauma about socialism's survival is the trauma of all those who have sought utopia in a vision of mankind made harmonious; and only so distraught a spirit, ill at ease with at least some aspects of the corrupt nature of the Soviet political world, could have recognized and publicly listed the causes of socialism's wholesale mutilation of humanity, the grim mass extortions, and the ceaseless convulsions to which unchecked state authority had doomed the very idea of socialism.

But while Gorbachev is realistic in his catalog of socialism's ills, in his contempt for its brutality and inertia, and in his demand that it emerge from the mere rote repetition of political slogans, he remained gulled by the illusion that the system could be made to succeed, that it must be rescued from itself, if necessary by coercion. Hacks and knaves, killers and fools had distorted the socialist dream. The system was redeemable, or so Gorbachev firmly believed. His faith in his own synoptic vision of a reinvigorated, disciplined, self-directing society, destined to arise out of the irrational and discredited socialist present, was of that boundless, absolute kind which puts an end to all questions and dissolves all difficulties in its own rigid solutions. Gorbachev may not have often pub-

licly betrayed any trace of the pathological fanaticism that motivated
Lenin and Stalin, but he was as utterly obsessed as both of his grim
predecessors, and as detached from reality. Like some prophet who must
act upon a task imposed by heaven, with an inner tranquillity based on
clear and certain faith in the rightness of his cause of restoration,
Gorbachev bore clear witness to the signs of decay and deceit that he
saw on every Soviet street corner. The old socialist order was, he realized, crumbling before his very eyes; it is the great irony of his life that
in his efforts to rescue it he would do more than any man to hasten the
process of disintegration, thankfully shortening the agony that preceded
socialism's end.

Translated into economic and political terms Gorbachev's socialist
re-awakening became a doctrine of decentralization. Much of this program, however, was little more than recycled Nagy, Khrushchev, and
Dubcek. Indeed, his proposal to detach public ownership from centralized management was derived from a scheme that had helped incite
Dubcek's overthrow two decades earlier. But earlier history did not
weaken the genuine radicalism of Gorbachev's reforms. And with the
precedents of Nagy, Khrushchev, and Dubcek before him, Gorbachev
must have expected grave resistance as a result of the breaches of
privilege contained in the limitations he proposed to make by the Party's
power to direct the economy. He may not have been altogether unhappy
with this, for murmurings against his program by the hated members of
the apparat would help to increase popular support for his regime—or so
he hoped.

Yet what was truly astonishing about Gorbachev's notions was that
they were marked by a conspicuous *acceptance* of aspects of such values
as markets and free prices and personal incentives that even a few years
before would have been unthinkable by a Soviet leader. His understanding of the failures of collectivized agriculture gave him a strong sense of
the impotency of socialist economics. In this sense, like so much else,
Gorbachev was already part of a post-socialist regime and seemed merely
to be waiting for the moment to institutionalize his characteristically
new concerns. And there arose next to Gorbachev men who thought
that the Party should be stripped of any kind of political privilege.

In other words, men were rising to match Gorbachev's radicalism,
step for step, in many cases even to advance beyond him. Gorbachev had
assumed that the socialist state, by initiating its own reform, would be
able to manage and contain the effort. But men such as Boris Yeltsin
insisted that economic regeneration be opened to all forces in society,

which included men outside the Party. Where disagreements occurred, it was not because Gorbachev had shocked these reformers with his radical overhaul of the Soviet political world; it was either because he had not gone far enough in their eyes or they disliked the operational methods built into his program. The debate, for example, between Boris Yeltsin and Gorbachev over the pace of the socialist state's retreat did not at all suggest that Gorbachev was digging in his heels at the threatened demise of absolute Party rule with all its privileges. It bore a much closer resemblance to the lengthy discussions of a national academy, convened to discuss the effects of alternative versions of the same general experiment. Personal antipathy, however, aggravated the schism.[19] When Gorbachev proposed to allow the leasing of land to individual farmers, Yeltsin and his supporters argued instead for the return of absolute private ownership of land. Moreover, while Gorbachev thought that the Party could be trusted to protect the tenure of leaseholders, Yeltsin believed that the past track record of Party interference dictated its removal from having anything to do with farm production.

Indeed, it was dissatisfaction with the limits of Gorbachev's program that Yeltsin most vocally expressed. He wanted to transfer, as quickly as possible, all the powers of government to freely elected authorities. Gorbachev and his supporters hewed to the line that the Communist party remained the only body with the force and authority to deliberate on any new form for the socialist state. And while Gorbachev tried to play safe by holding elections in 1988 limited to members of the Communist party, Yeltsin and his supporters made play of their desire to eliminate this restriction. What both men wanted was still a long way from democracy, but there was a real sense that elected bodies ought to contain a broad representation of all "interests" in the nation.

This scenario in which Party leaders competed with each other for prizes in democratic-spiritedness was clearly not what Gorbachev had anticipated. It was rather as if he had set out to drive an obstinate mule with a very heavy wagon, only to find that the mule was a racehorse willing to gallop off into the distance, leaving the rider in a ditch. While the desire for economic modernization undoubtedly played a part in the realism with which both men approached reform, it was also a shared sense of the historical moment that prompted their display of rivalry. Allotted the role of dumb chorus to Gorbachev's program, reform-minded communists, like Yeltsin, suddenly found that, individually and collectively, they had a powerful voice—and that the USSR was paying attention. This abrupt self-discovery of politics was intoxicating.

And so far from needing the Communist party to complete the process of reform, they very rapidly made it plain that its removal was the condition of the program's success. The Party's reputation was too thoroughly mired in scandal and suspicions of double-dealing to sustain any popular credibility. It was a measure of how the language of public debate had so significantly changed that, after Gorbachev removed Yeltsin from his post as Moscow Party chief, Yeltsin continued to publicly urge a speeding of the pace of reform. Sounding like a revolutionary orator of 1917, after resigning from the Communist party Yeltsin answered the question on everyone's mind: "The party itself must submit itself to the public will, the public judgment."[20]

Harassed on all sides, Gorbachev continued to hedge his bets. Gorbachev's mind, like a heart, contained two valves: one pumped spirit into policy; the other circulated pragmatism. On the one hand, he preached a mystique of renewal through an act of will. But the realistic half of his leadership was summed up in an aphorism made famous during his Kremlin meetings: "What is the essence of the problem?"

Incessant as he was on the need for increased productivity and the simple need for Soviets to work harder, it was Gorbachev's mystique of the spirit and power of debate that captured the minds of his followers. Gorbachev's principles, not because they were too abstruse but because they were too attractive, laid a trap for himself and for the USSR. His people grasped only the head and not the feet of Gorbachev's program. Debate and argument came willingly, but collective hard work was forgotten in the verbal scrum. At a stroke the politics of the socialist state had changed, but Soviet economics had not.

Here Gorbachev's program depended upon a proposal that was anathema to his Party rivals. To invigorate the economy he proposed that their day-to-day management of it be restricted to setting broad policy guidelines which independent factories and farms, though continuing to be state-owned, would attempt to enact. The Central Committee would become little more than a sort of corporate Board of Directors, without hands-on control.[21] Had Gorbachev proposed to inter a Rockefeller or Carnegie side by side with Lenin in the great Red Square mausoleum, he could hardly have raised more clamor and disgust.

Gorbachev's proposed reforms shattered the lassitude with which most of the Party apparatus regarded their position until that moment. Party members must have sat up and gasped, "He's blaming us!" for the perilous state of the economy. Nothing since the revolution had so openly conveyed a deliberately hostile intent toward absolute Party rule, and not even Khrushchev's denunciation of Stalin had so startled Party opinion across the country. That shock had been limited, and posed no threat to the Party itself, or so they had supposed. This was different. This was the General Secretary of the Communist Party of the Soviet Union proposing to hack away at the socialist state; worse, threatening to set uncontrolled rivals loose upon the socialist state's back. Here was a direct threat to the Party's legitimacy, which most Party members had never dreamed was Gorbachev's intention. It was all very confusing— and to the majority of Party cadres, high and low—as shocking as a knife in the back. The threat to their position was clear and absolute.

Paradoxically, this uncertainty was not inconsistent with Gorbachev's vision of a reborn Communist party. What he wanted to expel from the Party was the hauteur of unchallenged authority and replace it instead with a neo-Roman ideal of patriotic sacrifice and courage.[22] These values he associated with the original Bolsheviks: a party not defined by privilege and certainly not by comfort so much as by an unbending profession of devotion to the service of the state and the future.

Indeed, very little of Gorbachev's program was calculated to endear him to the Party, either in Moscow or the provinces. The former did not care for his abrupt juggling with their authority and even less for his puritanical attitude toward their perks. As for provincial leaders, the increase in authority was offset by the new risks they ran. The overall effects of his reforms were, thus, unsettling, perhaps even demoralizing to both the Party and public. The more visionary his reforms seemed, the less they were liked. Gorbachev's was a truly revolutionary temperament trapped in the body of absolute socialist government.

Contrary to his opponent's charge that he was planning to sacrifice socialism, Gorbachev at the beginning was motivated by the conviction that only through reform could socialism be defended and upheld. He viewed his program from the point of view of an accountant who has come across a set of fraudulent books. He was determined to seize immediately the opportunity power offered to him, believing that his own bugle call to socialist renewal must and would precipitate a general revival. His twin policies of *glasnost* (a freeing of public debate) and *perestroika* (the decentralization of the economy and the introduction of some market mechanisms) were bold, even rash, in design, for without fully understanding the forces he was unleashing he could not fully and fairly judge the chances of success. Gorbachev simply did not think there was a choice. It may be he had a great leader's instinctive feel for his moment; it is more likely he felt that the Soviet Union and socialism would not have another.

25

→≫ ≪←

Gorbachev

Ten Months That Shook the World

G orbachev's overt act against the socialist state, like an unthrown verbal hand grenade, lay quietly in the back of his mind. He was still clutching reform through the years 1987 and 1988 with his eyes squeezed shut against his own party's increasingly explicit hostility. It would take the growing chaos of the Soviet economy as it stumbled half-heartedly through his modest reforms to oblige him to believe that the Party itself was an obstacle. When these disruptions did become clear to him, in the summer of 1988 when Soviet economic figures reported for the first time a decline in the nation's gross national product, all Gorbachev had to do was pull the pin on his hand grenade and toss it into the lap of the socialist state—yet he did not. He could not move against the system that had raised and nurtured him.

Meanwhile the Soviet Union's economic situation was daily growing worse. Shortages were necessitating bread lines and rationing. The signs of the USSR's economic indigence forced him into vast disarmament negotiations with the United States.

National bankruptcies are a state of mind. The exact point at which a government decides that it has exhausted its resources and legitimacy so completely that it can no longer fulfill its most basic function, the preservation of its sovereignty, is quite arbitrary. For great powers never go into receivership. However dreadful an economic situation they may get themselves into, there generally will be moneymen lurking in the wings prepared to set them on their feet—at a price. Only to small powers has that price been some sort of partial abdication of sovereignty—to the decrees of the International Monetary Fund, for example, or in the age of Victorian imperialism, the international debt commissions that the British and their partners imposed over the fiscally prostrate corpses of the Egyptians and the Chinese. For Mikhail Gorbachev, the moment of truth came when he realized he would have to turn to the capitalist West for the funds to renew his economy. At this point the legitimacy of socialism as a political system was shattered forever. While there was no international financial agency waiting in the wings to shoulder the economic burdens and dictate the terms of reform, the need to convince the West of his determination to re-make Soviet society was the closest thing to such an agency. Only a demonstrable break with the past would gain the confidence necessary to secure foreign credits. Financial rescue, Gorbachev understood, was dependent on evidence of fundamental political change.

But so far the only result of reform in the country was a wholesale breakdown in the structure of command. Real outbreaks of disorder, once reported, fed an expectation of violent suppression. Party officials read reports of strikes and stoppages as evidence that counterrevolution was moving inexorably toward them. Country people heard accounts of food shortages in the cities and assumed that squadrons of displaced and hungry workers were fanning out from Moscow and the other great industrial centers toward their fields and cottages. Within the seriously crazy world of mutual misperceptions, individuals could appear in one guise in town and another in the country.

The real significance of the failure of Gorbachev's attempt to decentralize socialism was the vacuum of authority it exposed. Although he created, by default, a Soviet Union of quasi-independent regions and communes, this unstructured (and sometimes armed) decentralization was not at all what he imagined. Gorbachev's impotent invocations for the people to use their new freedoms responsibly suggest how deep was the emptiness opened up by the collapse of the socialist state's central power. The same people who gleefully pelted the automobiles of local Party leaders also yearned for the restoration of some great paternal authority that would feed them and shield them from the abuse of underlings. In this sense, the spreading chaos of 1988—at least outside Moscow—was in no way in the service of democratization, but of protection.

If the intention of the strikers and rioters was not revolutionary, its consequences increasingly were. Ordinary Soviets and Party members alike were vividly aware that some sort of boundary had been crossed when people felt free to vote out long-entrenched Party officials, such as the local Party leaders of Moscow, Leningrad, and Kiev. They reassured themselves that they were enacting a kind of primitive democracy authorized by Gorbachev which was undermining the socialist state that had for so long held them captive. But not far from the exhilaration of release was an apprehension of punishment. What if they were being deliberately led astray? Or what if the Party officials who were being stripped of their authority should somehow prevail again? In that case a terrible fate might yet befall them. It was in such suspicions that Gorbachev's policies of glasnost and perestroika foundered. For a fear-ridden inertia still ruled.

One response, indeed, to this kind of graphically imagined paranoia, is to externalize the terror and project it onto some third party on whom fear may be sacrificially concentrated. Put another way, individuals or groups held responsible for the danger in which communities find themselves are first separated from the host in which they are said to have grown powerful, and then attacked in acts that are simultaneously defiance and propitiation. The Soviet Union in the winter of 1988 supplied all kinds of scapegoats in this way—some real, some imaginary. For many in the countryside and in the cities, Gorbachev's reforms offered them a new opportunity against their eternal scapegoat, and they burst into a frenzy of anti-Jewish beatings and burnings and plunderings, in what can only be described as spontaneous pogroms. All the arguments which the Jew had inspired as the perennial stranger who persisted in retaining his own independent identity were revived. Jews were blamed for carrying the infection of communism to Russia; Jews were blamed for communism's abject failure. Jews were not Russians, or Georgians, or Ukrainians; they were aliens within the national body, always conspiring; they were the promoters of national failure.[1]

Neither the seriousness of the economic crisis in the early winter of 1988 nor the acknowledged resurrection of ancient hatreds was enough to disarm Gorbachev. The newly elected Congress of People's Deputies that had been designed by Gorbachev to obviate opposition had, by taking itself seriously, turned his priorities on their head. Obstruction became not a sometime thing of his government, but its working condition. Once Pandora's box had been opened in this way, it proved impossible to close the lid and Gorbachev's administration foundered on the sorts of contentions that Lenin had seemed to banish from Soviet politics. While the bulk of the Communist party members of the Congress were prepared to authorize limited reforms to rescue the socialist state from immediate decay, on the matter of absolute Party power they were adamant. Only the Party was to rule.

Gorbachev's alternatives now appeared starkly obvious. He could transform the socialist state into a truly representative regime by opening elections to all and assuming that this would generate public confidence—and hence the economic dynamism—needed to sustain his government. Or he could try to prevail over the anticipated opposition of the entrenched Communist bureaucracy to any contraction by a judicious mixture of subterfuge, incentives, and threats. The dangers of both policies were apparent, and it was unclear in the winter 1988–1989 by which course of action the vital matter of economic reform would be helped rather than hurt.

To change course, Gorbachev needed clear and undeniable evidence that his policies could work, and made the satellite states of Eastern Europe something of a laboratory for his experiments. At a time when it might have been expected that the governments of Eastern Europe would offer some help and leadership, they instead collapsed into the netherworld of compulsive alternation between threats and silence, jailings and exilings. On the occasion of his visit to East Germany Gorbachev was discovered weeping and bemoaning the sterility of the government's thinking. "History punishes those who come late,"[2] he flatly commented. But it was apparent to him that the implanted Communist regimes of East Germany, Czechoslovakia, Poland, Bulgaria, and Hungary were not ready to accept the kind of constitutional regime that could produce reform and regeneration through consent.

Only the path of confrontation remained.

As always, Poland was the site of the first eruption. To placate Gorbachev (and its own domestic opposition), the regime of General Jaruszelski had staged elections structured to maintain Communist party dominance. But the new Polish National Assembly was a remarkable instance of a group handpicked for compliance and docility discovering instead the excitement of opposition. The more vocal the complaints of Deputies opposed to continued Party rule, the more enthusiastically they were applauded by the public in pamphlets and broadsides. Parties, such as the Peasants party, which had long been lapdogs of the communists turned into terriers of the people. The leaders of the banned trade union movement Solidarity, who had been challenging Party rule for almost a decade, discovered that by sheer obstruction in the Assembly, where they held a good-size minority of the seats, they could exert more power than they had ever imagined. Their entry into political life was thus defined as opposition rather than the communists' planned co-optation. Throughout May and June of 1989 this approach of creative truculence persisted. The Communist party's attempt to form a nominally representative government with the support of parties of the National Assembly was defeated by Solidarity members who used sheer rhetorical force to seize the political initiative and to stigmatize collaboration with the communists as a betrayal of the Polish nation.

What made matters worse for the communists was that the most formidable opponent came from the ranks of the proletariat. Solidarity was led by a former electrician named Lech Walesa, a squat figure whose peppery eloquence more than compensated for his lack of inches. Walesa's position was cautious, not counterrevolutionary. But that did not compromise its popularity. On the contrary it probably strengthened it, since so much of what was anti-communist feeling drew its forces from wounded expectations rather than pure hatred of the socialist ideal. Walesa's rhetoric cleverly echoed that coming from Gorbachev in Moscow. He reiterated the Gorbachev view that public consent and consensus were needed in order to undertake fundamental economic reform. But he had more ambitious plans for political reconstruction; he meant to take the argument beyond resistance to Communist edicts and to pressure instead for a large positive share in the making of legislation: in effect, a reapportionment of state power. Even before the elections of the spring of 1989, he made it clear that it was no longer possible for the Communist party to dictate what must be. Rather the elections to the National Assembly and the creation, afterwards, of a large opposition, were to act as midwife to a new democratic government. This was his position after the vote. Walesa must have supposed that the gravity of the economic crisis facing his country would persuade the communists to call upon their rivals to share power until the crisis passed. But the lions of Solidarity were disciplined to political mercy. On the contrary, it was precisely the plight of the Jaruszelski government that they saw as offering a supreme opportunity to coerce the end of socialist absolutism. Walesa intended a counterrevolution but one not made in blood but law: a Polish variation of the transfer to democracy that followed General Francisco Franco's death in Spain in the 1970s.

The trouble with this prognosis was that belief in it was not shared by all those who, for the time being, rallied under the Solidarity banner. A younger and more aggressively radical group saw the election of a National Assembly not as an end but as the beginning of a new Poland. The talk was not of taking some power from the communists so much as rooting out communism from Poland.

As long as the Communist party itself remained the focus of resistance to democracy and reform, and thus the target of attack, the two groups would come together. Both had an interest in denying the communists any possibility of carrying out their programs without paying the price of constitutional change. But as soon as that price had been conceded, and the issue of giving the communists any say, no matter how small, came to the fore, the differences would emerge with sudden and brutal clarity. In the end it would shatter the cohesiveness of Solidarity. But for the moment, Walesa and his advisors agreed that any attempt to fully purge the communists from Poland's government and life would be self-defeating. Either the new parliament dominated by Solidarity would provoke the communists, and perhaps the Soviets, into drastic repression or the communists would yield gradually to representative institutions. The latter, clearly, was the preferable option. The break from socialism might be slower than Walesa desired, but it was inevitable. For the communists to accept a Solidarity-led government meant the eventual dismantling of communism.

The formation of the Solidarity government of Poland in June was one of those theatrical moments that, frozen in time and embellished, would be represented as the first counterrevolutionary act of 1989. The response of some Communist leaders unerringly struck the worst possible note—petulance followed by impotence. The effect of the Party's peculiar performance in sullenly knuckling under could not have been more damaging: despotism that failed to have the courage of its convictions.

There was a kind of surgical deliberateness on Walesa's part that uncannily anticipated the systematic counterrevolutions that soon followed throughout Eastern Europe.[3] In Czechoslovakia and East Germany and Bulgaria, hard-line regimes moved to prevent the disruption of their rule by strong campaigns to silence opposition. Printers were raided, journals closed down and, most strikingly, the speeches and appearances of Mikhail Gorbachev were severely edited. Any group that might be suspected of fomenting Gorbachev-like reforms were closed down. In Prague, it included those notorious nests of subversives, the jazz clubs. But even prison, as we have said, cannot stop an idea whose time has come.

Within weeks of the formation of Poland's Solidarity regime, politics in Eastern Europe exploded into a chaotic and impulsive mass activity. Efforts to muffle the outspokenness of the dissident press only resulted in the editors and writers becoming overnight popular heroes. Vaclav Havel, the Czech playwright, established his celebrity as a political prisoner. Invective flowed from the printed page to the world of images: caricatures pillorying communists circulated in coffeehouses and taverns. Daily life was saturated by political contention.

What was Gorbachev to do about the looming crisis in the Soviet empire? Gorbachev had made no secret of his distaste for the harsh conduct of the unregenerate Communist regimes of Eastern Europe and his passivity over Poland shows that he was disinclined to intervene on their behalf. But when Gorbachev met with Poland's new Solidarity Prime Minister he made it clear that the satisfaction to be derived from dislodging moribund Stalinist influence was not to be taken as a blanket endorsement of insurrection and counterrevolution. Despite these reservations, however, the impression had undoubtedly been given that Gorbachev would not use his military power to prop up the discredited regimes allied to him. And there were voices near to Gorbachev himself, that claimed the cause of socialist reform to be indivisible—as necessary in Berlin and Prague as in Moscow and Leningrad.

The dilemma for Gorbachev was acute. If nothing was done to forestall the collapse of communist power in Eastern Europe, the credibility of Soviet authority would suffer a humiliation on the Soviet Union's doorstep. Token signs of support for the old-line leaders of the region, together with rumors of mobilization, might be enough to have a deterrent effect and preserve communism even as it gradually reformed. But if the bluff was called the choice between invasion and capitulation would be even more galling, more dangerous. War in the cause of men implicitly repudiated by Gorbachev because of their refusal to budge seemed foolhardy. In the event, the deciding factor appears to have been money. Though the leaders of the Red Army and KGB perhaps thought it unseemly to put a price on the hegemony and security of the Soviet Union, Gorbachev must have overruled their objections. Reviving Nagy's prediction of the cost of maintaining Soviet suzerainty, and reinforced by the bleak lessons of hindsight, Gorbachev acted as if military action would immediately kill his reform program, and thus drive the socialist state into bankruptcy or back to Stalinist totalitarianism.

It did not take long for the people of Eastern and Central Europe to discover that the threat of the Red Army keeping them down had become a sham. For all the posturing of Communist leaders, armed resistance to demonstrations melted. Thousands of embittered Czechs and East Germans fled to Western embassies in the late summer of 1989, where they demanded asylum as political refugees. This unchecked flight of the best and brightest exposed the lost credibility of Soviet and communist power in the most brutally naked way. Things had come to such a pass, it seemed, that the Soviets were no longer able to afford an imperial policy that had been the bedrock of their system since the close of World War II. Gorbachev's exclusion of the military option to keep Eastern Europe in line was a somber recognition that socialism was a hostage to economic decline. It also meant that Russia's client regimes could not hope to maintain themselves through any kind of palliatives or the bogey of the Red Army. Pushing the argument a little further, it was apparent from the painful moment the Czechs and East Germans assented to the flight westward of thousands of their citizens, traditional socialist absolutism was dead in Eastern Europe. There were but two alternatives left, neither of which could possibly restore to the communists the plenitude of power enjoyed before the rise of Gorbachev. The first was reform from above, sufficiently dramatic to galvanize popular support and through which the Party might at least preserve the initiative in the reshaping of the socialist state. The second, more ominous option, was a kind of imposed abdication in which the authority of the socialist state would be transferred from the Party alone to some sort of quasi-socialist regime vested in a popularly elected legislature. In Poland, this had already happened. Once the Communist party opened up government (and its books) to Solidarity, the bleak situation advertised by the Party was no longer seen as merely a self-serving act of publicity. It was grim reality. The magnitude of the crisis gave the hybrid Solidarity-Communist government confidence that it could call on a kind of patriotic consensus to swallow stringent economic medicine.

Deterioration in the satellite states meant that the Polish option could not be repeated, though the Hungarian communists tried mightily to do so. Imre Nagy's memory was to be exhumed and honored, and thus co-opted. Not only was Nagy's secret burial site located and acknowledged, but the Party set about designing an elaborate funeral rite as a great demonstration of its newfound devotion to democracy and reform. In a reverse of the process accorded Stalin, Nagy's cadaver was to be dug up and exhibited to the public for two days, after which there would be a solemn and elaborate funeral procession, formal orations, and re-interment in the crypt of Hungary's national martyrs. On an early June morning, a long military procession, the infantry showing their rifles reversed and the drums muffled with black crepe, led the procession from Nagy's secret grave site. Behind the honorary pallbearers, composed of survivors of Nagy's cabinet, followed battalions of veterans of the Hungarian Revolution, such as General Béla Király, back from three decades of exile in the West; representatives of the old and outlawed political parties; and even more surprisingly, *en masse,* members of the usurping government that had ordered Nagy's execution. At the very end, the funeral procession simply dissolved into a gigantic crowd of Hungarians and those who had come to Budapest to be close to their dead hero, a crowd, it was estimated, of five hundred thousand, an enormous tide of humanity flowing through the streets bearing the flag of pre-communist Hungary, with the golden crown of St. Stephen. "It seemed," said Imre Nagy's daughter Erzbet, "that we were travelling out of the world of the dead."[4]

The funeral was orchestrated around the imperishability of the martyr. The immortality of Nagy's words and principles guaranteed that as long as Hungary lived, so would Nagy. Nagy's blood, one speaker claimed, had not simply drained away from the people of Hungary but had actually secretly nourished their vitality. This sacralizing of Nagy was a tool of communist propaganda. Indeed, Nagy dead was to be more useful to the Party than the heretical live politician. In his name, the Communist party could re-invent itself. To defend Budapest and Hungary against the "plots" that had destroyed Nagy, the democratic socialist system he once advocated had to be implemented in earnest. To identify with Nagy became for the communists a testimony to their democratic purity.

But it didn't wash. The rehabilitation of Nagy was seen and understood as a ploy for the sake of the communists' hold on office. Upon a rock of suspicion, the communist attempt to control reform in Hungary foundered. Elections to a new Constituent Assembly gave them only a minority of seats. The change in the Party's name from communist to democratic-socialist did not help matters. It was the classic case of the leopard being unable to change or hide its spots. The communists could not be trusted with the future, and even members of the Party would not publicly support their leaders even if they wanted. The elections brought old counterrevolutionaries like Király back to Budapest and into parliament.

To end a dictatorship and restore liberty in its place needs delicacy. The tactics of the Hungarian communists were so heavy-handed that they were doomed to fail. Hating and rejecting the notion of sharing power, the Party planned the rehabilitation of Nagy and the holding of elections as a gesture to quiet the cries for substantive reform, without delivering a positive result. Their record assured that they would not get one. And the appearance of the Party yielding power became a reality when ordinary Hungarians, sensing weakness, became ill-disposed to accept terms. For an offer of compromise will always give an impression of a weakening of purpose and will to triumph. This is one reason why reforming or ending a dictatorship is always more difficult than starting one. The change of the Party's name and the plan to hold internationally supervised elections unavoidably gave an impression that the Party's enthusiasm for solitary dictatorship was fading, which was indeed the case and which naturally gave Hungarians reason to reject compromise terms or even to discuss them.

Frustrated and affronted by the refusal of Hungarians to compromise with their ruling party, the regimes of Czechoslovakia and East Germany dug in their heels. Despite a visit by Mikhail Gorbachev to East Germany to urge a policy of reform, Erich Honecker and his long-entrenched regime remained deaf and blind to the alternative ideas to which Gorbachev had given rise. Blandly impervious to challenge, unconcerned by the dismay at their parties' misconduct and the rising wrath at its corruption, almost stupidly stubborn in maintaining the existing creaking system, both Honecker in East Berlin and Gustav Husak in Prague wanted time to stand still. They could not envision change by the system because they were so fully part of it, grew out of it, depended on it for their lives.

On the face of it, Prague was an unlikely place to become the "cradle of counterrevolution," as it subsequently liked to call itself after the collapse of communism in November 1989. It was no Warsaw or Budapest, with their ceaseless bubbling underground of popular dissent. Since the suppression of the Prague Spring it had become the stagnant pond of Kafka's memory, with dissent confined to a small literary class.

In many respects it was Prague's passivity that made it ripe for the great urban insurrection that was to topple the hard-line regimes of Eastern Europe. It had an unusual concentration of literate, poorly paid, and easily excitable journalists, pamphleteers, playwrights, and hack writers. While years of relative economic prosperity had increased employment opportunist, the sudden disruption of Communist rule in Poland and Hungary, combined with the sight of ordinary Czechs fleeing westward through grants of asylum facilitated by the new government in Hungary, made these men both angry and hungry for change. And in the person of Alexander Dubcek, who was still alive, the voices of dissent had a symbol around whom they could rally.

Since his forced resignation in 1969 Dubcek had been waiting in his hometown of Bratislava, like Lenin in Zurich, for the moment of his calling. It was the Kremlin that had forced him from office, and now it seemed that it was the Kremlin that was paving the way for him to come back. To Dubcek in late September 1989, came word that the KGB was preparing a scheme to undermine Husak and his clique, a move that might restore Dubcek to power and win him sweet revenge over Husak—and incidentally, it was hoped, preserve a government with some degree of allegiance and loyalty to Moscow.

The threat by Husak's government to shoot down demonstrators against his regime confronted Gorbachev with a foreign crisis and domestic hazards both of alarming potential. Gorbachev acted rapidly. He summoned Czech Communist leaders to the Kremlin to compel a truce and the establishment of a more liberal government. Gorbachev felt urgently the need to save the process of transformation on which he had staked his prestige from degenerating into bloodshed like that of Beijing's Tienanmen Square where China's government massacred peaceful demonstrators for democracy. As the principal architect of reform he felt an extra interest in protecting it.

To compel the Czechs to an agreement he used the movement of Soviet troops within the country as a lever. It was Gorbachev's understanding that if the Czech communists refused to make reasonable concessions, he would abandon them to their fate. This was essentially a decision for counterrevolution. In his public speeches and printed declarations, Gorbachev's aims appeared to support the continuance of Communist rule in Eastern Europe, but in practice his policies were leading inevitably to the breakdown of his client regimes. To support Husak would not merely be futile; it would ally Gorbachev in popular eyes with the oppressors and corrupt functionaries, thus disheartening liberal forces within his own country and violently antagonizing the Western leaders whose future assistance would be needed in the redevelopment of the Soviet economy. While many conservative members of the Soviet Communist party thought Gorbachev's effort to promote reform in Eastern Europe misguided, Gorbachev refused to trim. Conservative communists preferred the status quo even when the status quo was a sinking ship. Gorbachev desperately clung to what he saw as a feasible alternative. To sustain forever the corrupt and inefficient regimes of Husak and Honecker was no longer within the Soviet Union's capacity and would have meant suicide for his reforms at home. The only other possibility was to follow his own advice to Honecker, to remember that "History punishes those who come late."

In a further effort to compel compliance, Gorbachev shut off arms to the Czechs in mid-October 1989, without effect. Supported by a dominant group of Party "reactionaries" who frankly stated their belief that reform and democratization were inconceivable and that only force could settle the issue and secure socialism, Husak remained recalcitrant, counting on Soviet support to come around in the end whenever violence threatened Soviet security. The dominant group in the Czech Party was simply unwilling to countenance a compromise or settlement. They counted on the use of brute force to cow the populace. But the Czech

Party's army and security apparatus was already being undermined—by Mikhail Gorbachev's KGB.

Within a month, an aged and tired Alexander Dubcek stood side by side with the dissident playwright Vaclav Havel on a balcony above Wençeslas Square as a new and democratic Czechoslovakia was proclaimed. Upon this apparition, the vast crowd for a moment ceased its cheering. The silence that fell over Wençeslas Square was a more eloquent sound than any heard in the last forty-five years in the city. Its significance could hardly be believed. What were Dubcek's feelings? After years of privations, disgrace, and disappointments, to have helped bring communism to this consummation and to have his old enemies surrender could only have stirred profound emotions. Too deep for tears, or words, they were not confided to any person or page.

Gorbachev's feelings when Czechoslovakia's communists surrendered to men they had long persecuted and often jailed were equally unrecorded. As might be expected, Gorbachev's advisors laid the blame politely but unmistakably in the lap of the Czech Party. At the same time, he seemed conscious that his own passivity needed explanation, particularly to the Red Army which was seeing the demise of its continent-wide Maginot Line. The goal of a planned and orderly retreat of the socialist state which had animated Gorbachev's policy from the start of his rule had now receded beyond his reach, seemingly in mockery of his efforts.

No reform could now save communism in Eastern and Central Europe. In the tortured councils of the Central Committees in East Berlin and Sofia, November was the moment of decision. In a mood of nervous vacillation, East Germany's Erich Honecker successively threatened his increasingly unruly people, then backed off. In Dresden, despite mass demonstrations, and orders to suppress them from Honecker, local Party leaders announced that they would under no circumstances fire on the people. Not wanting to endorse complete defiance of authority, some Party leaders—including Markus Wolf, long the shadowy and infamous leader of the *Stasi,* East Germany's KGB clone—joined in the demonstrations and sought to concoct face-saving compromises by which the Party would yield power gradually. To no avail. The political swerve was irreversible. Throughout East Germany the Party's paralysis and evident lack of will was greeted with euphoria: more and more strikes and mass meetings and torchlight parades.

In the face of mounting evidence that his orders were not enforceable, Honecker nevertheless attempted to stay in power. But his position was untenable. Some of his closest aides began to separate themselves from his personal domination. Honecker could not be saved. Indeed, as it became apparent that authority in East Germany was disintegrating, the removal of Honecker's administration began to seem a pre-condition for any kind of effective government. There was a short-term crisis of order, with the dispersal of troops by Honecker to different provincial centers opening up a dangerous vacuum at the center. But what really finished Honecker off was not so much his inability to enforce his edicts as the sudden death of factory and agricultural production. Conditions throughout urban East Germany were rapidly approaching the level of a food war. It was a time of fear, unsettlement, and exodus.

News that Honecker had been summarily dismissed, instead of being greeted with cheers, produced an instantaneous wave of fury. Disaffection was by no means confined to the civil population but had seeped into the ranks of the army, both officers and foot soldiers. Whole regiments were deserting. There was nothing left of the Party but to surrender, with as good a grace as could be mustered.

Born of the Red Army's occupation of Germany in 1945, renegade in its origins, crippled by Stalin's brutalities before it was fully established, communism had spent its mandate in one generation. In the first week of November 1989, demonstrators in Dresden, Halle, Leipzig, and East Berlin faced down armed *Stasi* troops. On November 8, 1989, students and mutinous soldiers danced atop the Berlin Wall. In a climate of boozy, loquacious defiance, the Communist party was swept from political control. A new government and a new, reunified Germany followed swiftly on. The wall that had divided Europe for three decades was crumbling. Chunks of it were carted away as souvenirs.

Honecker's end was more private, if equally pathetic. Kept under house arrest in the home of a Lutheran pastor, he reportedly once found enough privacy to swallow a non-lethal dose of poison. Another failed gesture, but an appropriate one. After all, he had watched his own faith commit suicide.*

---

*When German prosecutors began to make noises about bringing Honecker to trial, he fled to Moscow where Gorbachev gave him sanctuary. His flight, and Gorbachev's peculiar loyalty in protecting the old dictator, became a continuing source of friction between united Germany and the USSR.

26

-》》 《《-

Gorbachev
Twilight of Leviathan

The collapse of the Berlin Wall was Mikhail Gorbachev's worst
moment—and his best. He seemed to look finality in the eye, lay
blame where it belonged, make no excuses. Gorbachev's words provoked
the risings, but he did not know how to take advantage of them. This
failure resulted not so much from a loss of nerve on Gorbachev's part,
as from a loss of faith.

As the wall's structure crumbled, great cavities were carved in it,
beckoning rodents, stray cats, peeping tourists, and overnight vagrants.
In March 1990, with Gorbachev's express approval, Soviet-made bull-
dozers manned by German workers began to put the disintegrating hulk
out of its misery. Somehow it seemed just that communism's dissolution
should be marked by the ruin of its most monumental symbol. After all,
the Russian Revolution had been a great demolition. In the wall's stead
there remained only a gaping space at the frontier between capitalism
and communism: a no-man's-land of ideology and memory.

There remained, however, one field in which Gorbachev could still
attempt to make good on his promise to reform socialism: he could make
the Soviet Union and its Communist party come to terms with economic
and political reality. And this in haste and even with desperation he now
proceeded to do; indeed, Gorbachev perhaps saw no hope of his own
survival unless he brought success to his policies of reform. In quick
succession, he rehabilitated Bukharin and Khrushchev, opened the
gulags for inspection, and renounced the Party's constitutional claim to
have the "leading role" in Soviet life.

With each reform, Gorbachev was playing for time. Quite simply, his
life and outlook had been too firmly shaped by socialist ideology to allow
the socialist motherland to progressively disintegrate and die. In the
West, Gorbachev was seen by the vast majority of the public as some

sort of political wizard: someone who could pull rabbits out of hats and conjure peaceful revolutions and free nations out of thin air. At home, however, his program seemed merely a ferment of impotent activity, little of it either clear or comprehensible. Only his opponents in the Party seemed to understand the ultimate objectives of Gorbachev's policy of perestroika. Among them there was a general feeling that, in some way or another, orthodox socialism had to be restored in order to save the situation. Beaten by circumstance, long since helpless and unwilling to accomplish socialism's original purpose, most members of the *apparat* settled for one thing—retention of power—without the strength or capacity to cope with multiplying troubles.

And multiply they did. Loss of the ability to command production through terror, without the corresponding ability to inspire production through personal incentives, ruined many industries and collective farms. As the Party's influence waned, that of nationalist and sectarian movements grew. The Union of Soviet Socialist Republics fell prey to rival ambitions and ancient antagonisms. In some of the movements for national independence, such as those of Lithuania, Estonia, and Latvia, able men and political predators combined; in others ignorant racial and religious hatreds tossed to the top of the general broil. Gorbachev could control nothing. A rout was beginning. Fragmentation proceeded.

Gorbachev's confidence and cheer began to wane. His position became more and more tenuous. He had invested all of his prestige in his program to save and reform socialism. Within and without the USSR people wondered if he would retain power long enough to see his reforms through. Collapse of the means of production produced inflation that ruined the working class and drew them angrily into a swelling contagion of black markets and graft in order to live. The long string of defeats left even the Red Army weakened in morale and leadership, and ate into the military's support for Gorbachev's regime. A breakdown in the transport of foodstuffs from farms to city pauperized the countryside. Armed outbreaks against local Party leaders increased. Violence proceeded in a haphazard, hit-and-run fashion, rather than by organized insurrection. Signs of famine appeared in Tashkent and Uzbekistan. Discontent provoked repression and repression more discontent, nourishing opposition and turning minds away from socialism. The Party was haunted by a sense of insecurity. Machine-gun emplacements on street corners in the cities of Georgia and Armenia in 1990 were not designed for use against a foreign enemy. The great surge that had greeted Gorbachev's assumption of power in 1985 petered out in fatigue, oppression, and profiteering. Held together by Gorbachev's aura and his political skill, the Communist party carried on by ignoring the spreading sores and sheltering in escapism.

Derelict among the evidence of economic decay lay the fragments of perestroika and glasnost. Standing amid the debacle of his plans and hopes, with responsibility for the catastrophe seeming to rest finally upon him, with the unity of the nation breached, with every industry in retreat or fighting sluggishly to hold on, Gorbachev remained magically defiant. By casting blame on the executors and absolving the planners of perestroika, he was able to retain a blemished confidence in himself— and in so doing, provide the essential and unique requirement in the calamitous days of 1990.

For the loss of confidence in the Party, the guarantors of order, opened the way to widespread demands for fundamental change, and increasing misery gave force to the impulse. The long-oppressed Soviet people were no longer enduring but rebelling, although, like Gorbachev, they were inadequate, unready for the consequences, and mentally un-equipped for the task. Gorbachev could not successfully impose reform upon a rigid and unyielding structure, and neither could the quasi-elected assembly of communists he summoned. Without a coherent philosophy with which to replace socialism, the socialist state could not yet be overthrown.

In the year after the fall of the Berlin Wall, the forces set in motion by Gorbachev played themselves out, some of them in exaggerated form, like human failings in old age. Administrative structures fell into dis-order, finance and justice were abused, offices abandoned and ignored, the Party became an open marketplace of corruption. In a famous letter to the editor published in the Leningrad newspaper *Sovyetskuyu Russiyu*, a hard line university lecturer declared that the USSR was sunk in crime and inertia, with Lenin blasphemed everywhere, "ideological con-fusion" rampant, and students who had lost their way because of a "loss of political bearings."[1]

Workers rose in the same effort to oust corrupt officials and establish measures of good government as Gorbachev had attempted—encoun-tered similar Stalinist rebukes. Impatient for immediate results, a tur-bulent collection of miners went on strike in the autumn of 1990. Gorbachev caved in to them, but inevitably the local Party leaders re-acted against the settlement, restored venal officials, cancelled reforms, and persecuted strike leaders.

Convinced that the Party itself was sabotaging his program, Gor-bachev berated his opponents without tact or dignity, his face sometimes growing purple and his voice hoarse with rage. In Party congresses he interrupted opponents with rude invectives and cries of "rubbish!" and "shut your mouth!" He called Yegor Ligachev a half-wit, and once seemed about to strike a critic, only to be pulled back in time. As chaos spread, Gorbachev moved less by ideological zeal than by simple hatred of obstruction. He publicly chastized Central Committee members for their blindness. Worse, he challenged them to come up with a working alternative to his policies.

There was nothing in his condemnations of the Party that was not justified; the fault lay in Gorbachev's failure to think through the implications. It made no sense to sound a message of implied unfitness to rule to the Party unless it was backed by readiness to cease investing support in the *apparat*. In the absence of such readiness, Gorbachev's message was a crippled ultimatum from which he did inevitably retreat.

Gorbachev was a man no less rigidly persistent than Lenin or Stalin in the pursuit of an objective. He had made up his mind to be rid of the Party's obstructionists—chief among them Yegor Ligachev—who were a continuing indictment of himself and his regime. If he was the orthodox communist's incubus, they were his goad. The Party's future control of the socialist state was in the scales. At bottom was the principle contained in the contending visions of Bukharin and Gorbachev: one offering total state management of life, the other proposing to allow men to make decisions for themselves. Had it been within the Party's vision to adopt Gorbachev's program years before, it might have been possible for it to resist the forces of decay that were to come, and quite possibly to survive them. But that opportunity had now gone by, nor is it likely that orthodox Party leaders either recognized or regretted it. Gorbachev, too, failed to see that the opportunity for reform had passed. His concern was to remove a source of pressure he could not tolerate.

The feelings of the men who had raised Gorbachev over their own heads probably cannot be adequately described. Rages and insults might have been borne sullenly, but not interference with privilege. When Gorbachev hemmed and hawed over Lithuania's declaration of independence from the USSR, refusing to use military power to crush the nationalist movement but instead relying on economic blackmail to keep the little republic in line, a cause for schism came. More than anything else, the Party saw itself as incarnating the unity of the Soviet empire. When the ritual five-year Party Congress convened in June 1990, the majority of Party members had reached such a point of exasperation and frustration with Gorbachev that the fatal course of removing him from power was openly discussed. Since there was yet no stomach for the bloody prospect of a coup, the conservatives' plan was to annul Gorbachev's program as invalid through the very mechanisms Gorbachev had created—they would vote down his policies in the assembly.[2]

The first hints of the Party invalidating his program brought Gorbachev to heel. He offered an olive branch to his conservative opponents by pledging that it was not his intention to end the one-party state, and that a return to private property was not being contemplated. With these retreats, lines were drawn. Under the pressure of extreme hardship, a minority of Communist party members such as Boris Yeltsin and Eduard Shevardnadze had been brought to the point where they would accept any new leadership provided it offered hope of taking the nation out of the hated socialist world they knew into at least the prospect of something different. This heretical undercurrent was not quite ready to break through to the surface and abandon Gorbachev. For the long-ingrained habit of looking up to the Kremlin leader, no matter who that was, as the main source of authority, either for good or evil, remained strong. Gorbachev was still the symbol that held the Party together, and it seemed to this heretical element that he could yet lead them out of the chaos in which they were wandering; and it is one of the aberrations of history that Gorbachev himself felt this too.

And yet, despite all this, it was difficult to see any alternative to Gorbachev's continued rule. A Kremlin revolution, a rising of Red Army marshalls or KGB generals, was feasible; but no single man either in the Kremlin or among the military and secret police looked liked being the leader of such a movement who could inspire some public legitimacy. Then too, there existed among both factions an instinctive fear of what might happen if they upset the Kremlin throne, if the surly masses of the Soviet people followed their lead and raised a rebellion in the streets. Let loose the mob and anything could happen; then all of them, conservative and liberal communists alike, might be swept away.

And so Gorbachev's attempts to mollify both factions of the Party only yielded a despairing stalemate. A few disgruntled liberals, such as Boris Yeltsin, tore up their Party cards in disgust. But for the most part a strange apathy settled over the Party Congress, leaving the socialist state to continue, but rudderless.

For Gorbachev was asking the impossible of the Party. In the communist *apparat* men and women were trained from initiation to believe in the established system and to obey orders; one did not argue, senior Party leaders knew best. Discipline and loyalty and subservience—these were the imperatives. Even Gorbachev's closest advisors found it difficult to express open disagreement with their boss in a cabinet or Central Committee meeting.[3] No matter whether they agreed with him or not they sat silent: and this silence was accepted as assent. To each other, Gorbachev's advisors were free of course to state their views, but it may not always have been easy to do this. Gorbachev made the pace of work hot and the very brilliance of his mind may not have encouraged his colleagues to express their half-formed ideas and fears, those vague inconsequential questionings which sometimes contain the beginnings of an understanding of the real truth, the truth that is not always revealed by logic.

This, at any rate, was at the core of the mistrust of Gorbachev—that he bamboozled—and no matter how often he called for discussion there was an instinctive feeling among some Party men that somehow or other he had upset the established practices. It is the old story of the conflict between the experimenter and the civil servant, the man of action and the administrator, the ancient dilemma of the crisis where, for the moment, the trained manager is dumbfounded and only the determined amateur seems to know the way ahead.

Government proceeded in concealed muddle and silent confusion. The truth was that the Party had something to fear which was even worse than Gorbachev's program. Placards had begun to appear in the streets denouncing Communist rule and demanding retribution. With every day that went by it became more evident that a great part of the population looked upon the failure of Gorbachev's reforms not as a defeat but as a liberation. Outwardly, Moscow might appear calm, inwardly it was possessed by a coma of suspense. The great mass of people who aspire to nothing but their own safety and who submerge their imaginations in the routine of their daily lives were eager for the latest Kremlin rumor, the least scrap of information on the political battle behind the citadel's walls.

Gorbachev's voice was trapped in this void, sometimes absurd and even a bit pathetic. What good were his decentralized industries if demand for the shoddy products they produced had collapsed? What good was the freedom granted to farmers and communes if the prices they received for produce had no relation to any fixed value? It was, he learned from Alexander Yakovlev, one of Gorbachev's chief advisors, far from certain that workers and peasants were universally thrilled with their new freedoms, since they also feared the loss of the security of socialism.[4] Seventy years of Communist rule had made most suspicious of running risks. Indeed, in the chaos of the winter of 1990, there was a marked tendency among some groups to fall back on the patterns of collective solidarity.

What had Gorbachev's revolution accomplished to balance its failures? His two great social alterations—the curtailment of the socialist state and the abolition of terror—both promised more than they delivered. Though many many workers were undoubtedly happy to be somewhat free of the hierarchy of the *apparat* that constrained their labor and reward, they were, if anything, even more nakedly exposed than before. Likewise, the abolition of terror as an instrument of state control was more in the way of a legal than a social change and merely completed the evolution that began with Khrushchev. There is no question that peasants were thankful for the slackening of central control. Equally certainly, they were determined at all costs to oppose the implementation of a scheme that would leave them without any protection from the state.

Had perestroika and glasnost, at least, created stable and democratic institutions to help resolve the problems hobbling socialism? Here it was easier to see debilitating continuities rather than decisive change. Creation of an opposition, indeed a myriad of oppositions, Gorbachev came to recognize as catastrophic, for the majority of antagonistic groups began to question the integrity of the USSR itself. What was killing the socialist state, he seemed to realize, was its inherent inability to adjust to limitations on its power. Throughout its history it regarded disagreements not as arguments made in good faith, but as a sort of fifth column bent on subverting socialist rule. With this doomed beginning, Gorbachev simply intensified the war between the *apparat* and society. Matters could not be reversed by goodwill and decentralization. The fundamental question of the relationship of the individual to the state had to be re-examined.

Obviously, Gorbachev learned from the unhappy experiences of his first five years of rule. But in practice, however, his reforming experiments remained darkened by the long shadow of the socialist state itself, so that factions inevitably crystallized, not around specific issues of reform, but on plans for the overthrow of socialism. With his program constantly in paralyzing conflict with the state he supposedly controlled, dictatorship continued to determine the political direction of the USSR far more than democratic decision-making.

What occurred in the Soviet Union between 1985 and 1990 was an unprecedented explosion of politics—in speech, print, and image—that broke all the barriers. Initially, this had been Gorbachev's own doing. For it was in the elections he sponsored that opponents to socialism found their voice. In so doing, they became part of a process that tied the satisfaction of their immediate wants into the process of destroying the socialist state.

That was both Gorbachev's opportunity and his problem. Suddenly, an aggregate of subjects held in place by injustice and intimidation had become a force in the nation. By this new force, justice, freedom, and plenty were not only expected, but demanded. By the same token, should these benefits not materialize, the state that had for seven decades withheld them would be held responsible for their long absence. Before the promises of socialism could be realized, then, it was necessary to root out the socialist state.

Gorbachev's courage had not gone—indeed, for many it was a tremendous thing to see him persevere in the face of unending disappointment—but among the Soviet people his political credibility had been exhausted, and there seemed little possibility of regaining it or getting more. Still he went out to factories and to farms proselytizing with a sort of religious fervor, a frenzy that belied his own dawning realization that his reforms were doomed. What went on behind Gorbachev's opaque exterior he never showed. If he owed his composure to a failure of imagination, that was fortunate for his country. Ordinary men, Clausewitz once wrote, become depressed by a sense of danger and responsibility; if these conditions are to "lend wings to strengthen judgment, there must be present unusual greatness of soul."[5] If danger did not strengthen Gorbachev's judgment and insight in any way, it did call forth a certain strength of soul or of character. When ruin was all around him, he maintained a stoical tenor.

Without Gorbachev Russia would surely have faced either a bloody coup or civil war. A more clear-sighted, more quick-thinking leader with economic ideas of his own might have avoided the basic error of believing that socialism could be reformed, but after the retreat of the socialist state began the one thing that the USSR needed Gorbachev had. It is difficult to imagine any other man who could have kept his country from toppling over into the abyss. Certainly he was insufficient to the task of re-orienting his nation's economy; the reforms he proposed always came too late. The broken figures of Dubcek and Nagy had seen more clearly the original folly of the socialist state's design and proposed ways to make recovery from its ills possible. But when circumstances turned against them, both men wilted. It was Gorbachev, whom nothing could panic, who fatally undermined the idea of socialism without unleashing a new terror or a new war. In Gorbachev's confusion and vagueness—a remarkable blending of precipitancy and hesitation—the death throes of totalitarianism were conducted with very few deaths. That sudden flash of inspiration that will on rare moments transport a national leader past all the accepted rules of his society into a field of such innovation and daring that his country is utterly transformed—one thinks of the Emperor Meiji and his transformation of nineteenth-century Japan from a backward agricultural society to an industrial power in less than a generation—was perhaps lacking in Gorbachev's character, but he can hardly be condemned for that. His understanding that the socialist state was doomed in its present form was a definite vote of no-confidence in the ideas that had ruled his country since 1917; it only remained for him to conceive of the system with which he would replace socialism.

Mental standstill or stagnation—the maintenance intact or in part of the ideas with which you start—was a fertile source of Gorbachev's failure. Leaders in government, on the authority of Henry Kissinger, do not learn beyond the convictions they bring with them into office; these are "the intellectual capital they will consume as long as they are in office."[6]

Instead of becoming more flexible in the face of failure, Gorbachev's mind became more rigid. And this rigidity led to an increase in his personal investment in the salvation of socialism instead of to a rethinking and change of course. Policy founded upon error multiples the error before it retreats. The greater Gorbachev's investment and the more involved in perestroika's success he became, the more unacceptable became the process of disengagement. This unconscious pursuit of failure enlarged the scope of his program's damage and brought him to the ultimate humiliation of seeking direct investment and aid from the Soviet Union's long rival, the United States.

An air of inspired desperation marked Gorbachev's rule after the Soviet empire in Eastern Europe foundered. He clung to the belief that if he could keep his program of reform socialism going, it was bound to show results at some point. His expectation of eventual success was all the more intense because it was so sorely needed. Changing course is always a difficult and delicate business. Even intelligent rulers in democratic societies, when they exist, often find themselves unable to terminate a failed program, should they want to. Gorbachev needed to be convinced that perestroika was either not achievable or not worth the damage to the state. To renounce his program might mean an end to his rule—or at least a diminishing of his power and place in the Kremlin hierarchy. For any ruler to stop short of a declared and costly aim, thus acknowledging his own as well as his party's incapacity, is as problematic as the camel's passage through the eye of a needle. And so Gorbachev persevered in his fixed pattern of failure: a reform announced to great fanfare, implementation flawed, stalemate ensues. Every proposal

Gorbachev made fell well short of success. By 1990, it hardly mattered what directives were issued or not, for the vast majority of the Soviet people were too exhausted or cynical to understand Gorbachev's rationale for them, too bewildered to do anything but continue dumbly as before. A wild unreality intervened between Gorbachev's wishes and the actual conditions of the economy and society at large. Both were making their own rules, and it was useless for Gorbachev to proclaim this or that objective. Every decision was a touch-and-go affair.

If Gorbachev appeared unimpressed by the urgent need to revamp his program it was, perhaps, because he was not bothered by doubts of his own staying power or fears of his own collapse. He thoroughly intended in his own mind to stay the course, no matter how much disruption his policies caused, no matter how much Soviet power was lost, until his revamped socialism bore fruit. Indeed his failure to be more frightened than he was gave rise to reports that he was relying on some arrangement with the army and KGB to impose a new dictatorship. Like any Communist ruler from Lenin onward, Gorbachev continued to equate success with firm leadership, ignoring motivation, and simply incentives. Believing that socialism could be saved by his form of revision, Gorbachev predicated his policy on survival in power.

Gorbachev's words and deeds negated everything that orthodox communism stood for, yet his regime had to adapt to the structure of the socialist state. Needless to say, the effect of these compromises on the public could only be deceptive. Gorbachev constantly told his people what sounded daring and virtuous, but continued to reserve ultimate power and ownership for the Party and the state. The very hopelessness of these reforms seemed to numb people's energies, for increasingly Gorbachev's program was seen as argument without action. The desire for food, warmth, and security dominated the mind of the ordinary man, and you had only to join a bread line to realize that the Soviet worker, with his docility, his famous capacity for enduring terrible hardships, was approaching one of his periodic outbursts of semi-madness, when he can think of nothing but to smash and burn and destroy. This—not the malcontents in his own party—was the danger Gorbachev most feared. And so Gorbachev pushed forward, with maximum vigor and diminished self-assurance, which he masked by adopting the tone of a headmaster speaking to sullen and incorrigible schoolboys. Communism without dictatorship had only doubt and despair to fall back upon.

Popular causes for disenchantment were real enough. After the great hope of relief brought on by Gorbachev's ascension to power, Russia was now worse off than before: the economy a shambles, the union shattered, racial hatreds rampaging. Cynicism about the prospect of reform and a lapse into increasing passivity was the result. An attitude of "Let the Party Clean up its own Mess" prevailed in factories and among groups that Gorbachev counted upon for support. To let Party bureaucrats stew in their own failures seemed not only advisable but justified. The exercise of this judgment became the general population's chief effort.

Passivity was the obstacle that now rose in Gorbachev's way. The people would work only insofar as failure to do so might cut off food or other basics. Unlike Stalin, or Brezhnev, he could not by negative threat alone obtain what he wanted; he had to promise more and more change in order to goad people to act. But Gorbachev was the opposite of a cynic—he was a believer and a doer. Promises once made acquired a reality of their own. By the summer of 1990, however, Gorbachev must have understood that the need for reform was so great that it was likely to be self-defeating.

The question arises, was there an alternative—or at the top of the Soviet government a search for an alternative—to Gorbachev's policy of reform and socialist regeneration? For so long the consensus of advice had been that only central planning and dictatorship could make socialism work, that policy-making was conditioned by it and by the persistent fear of the nation falling back into the turmoil and disunity of the pre-revolutionary years. A status quo regime, as the once-revolutionary state had become, tends however to stay with a tried and true system, no matter how bankrupt. Any other course is too risky and awkward, and in the case of the USSR would risk a capitalist restoration, the only alternative sufficiently dynamic and organized to represent a realistic challenge. It was not feasible for Gorbachev to openly transfer his support to the democratic free market system. The imaginary alternative was the endeavor, which his perestroika was already promoting, to bring the two systems together.

In a muddled attempt to fuse the capitalist system and pluralistic democracy with the the socialist state Gorbachev's revolution ended. Controversy over the amount of state control to be maintained was largely irrelevant; these were not causes of Gorbachev's failure but only mechanisms. Ruin of perestroika was the inevitable outcome of the assumption, growing out of ideological rigidity and popular passivity, that socialism was amenable to reform. Responsibility lay with Andropov for initiating the attempt, and with Gorbachev for agreeing to and promoting it. At a deeper level was the incompatibility, superficially of two systems, fundamentally of two purposes. What course the idea of socialism might have taken if its structure had not been umbilically tied with central planning and dictatorship is a question that lost opportunities have made forever unanswerable. The only certainty is that it could not have been worse.

So, under Gorbachev, reform came at last to the USSR, and the socialist state disintegrated. Perestroika and glasnost arrived as a kind of revolution; but they were uncontrollable notions because hidden within them were unsuspected, secondary revolutions. Wittingly or not, Gorbachev unlocked a myriad of antagonisms frozen by Communist rule. With shackles loosened, hatreds long interred in the gulag or the grave were abruptly released. Private loyalties—of conquered nation, abused race, banned religion, punished clan—clawed their way to the surface of Soviet life.

So reform led only to this: the Baltic and other republics itching to break away, the corruption of black markets, the criminalization and schisms of politics. No one in the USSR could be certain of anything anymore; all was fluid. Secret policeman, black marketeer, apparatchik, dissident: the roles appeared interchangeable or fused. Gorbachev could have tried to see these uncertainties as the by-products of renewed liberty. Instead, he saw such disruptive mutations as threats to the sort of stability true communists take for granted; and in a reflex of anxiety, he could only see his country descending from bad to worse.

Any outsider could make the right connections between cause and effect. Gorbachev, however, lingering in the Leninist faith, could juggle with these great events and confuse one with the other; and even as he undermined, quite fatally, socialism in practice, he could continue to proclaim and predict its ultimate victory as an idea. Gorbachev correctly understood that the straitjacket of socialism had left his country fragmented, economically stagnant, with its gifted peoples close to hysteria. Yet he romantically believed that the USSR was also the country that had been founded as the homeland of the promised communist future, and for that reason was to be preserved as *the* pioneer state of that new world. All the dislocations, all the crimes, the failures and pains, had to be (and were!) conjured away by the logic of faith—the final triumph of self-delusion.

And so the socialist state withered. But Gorbachev's faith did not. Mounting chaos only drew him back into the Leninist fold. If socialism failed, if perestroika and glasnost failed, it wasn't because the dream was totally defective, or the faith utterly flawed; it could only be because ordinary men and women had failed the faith. A purer and purer faith is what he called for. In that quest for a reborn, purified socialism, Gorbachev lost sight of the reasons he embarked upon his muddled process of reformation. And he returned almost full circle to dictatorship.

For Gorbachev's wish had been from the beginning to work his way back to the supposedly pure socialism bequeathed to Russia and the world by Lenin and Bukharin. As he stumbled, however, he proceeded with the tool of faith alone. Reform was like a child's wish—with intellect suppressed or limited, reason discarded, the historical sense falsified—to work from the imaginary to something concrete. By seeking to salvage socialism from its wreckage, Gorbachev's program became merely a pathetic attempt to re-create something that—except as an ideological fantasy—never existed at all.

The open societies and free markets of the West could not be fully mimicked because Gorbachev emotionally rejected them. They undermine the socialist vision of harmony; they arouse; they threaten. But at the same time, Gorbachev seemed to know, almost intuitively, that they were necessary for socialism's survival. For it is they who produce the new machines, the new goods, the new ideas, and also the food and capital that had to be imported for the USSR to remain fed and afloat. All his rejections of the social structures of the West were contained within the underlying and ever unstated (perhaps because it was only subconsciously recognized) assumption that that living, creative civilization, could always be tapped—if always from an anti-septic distance. Gorbachev's rejection, thus, was not absolute. It was a way of seeking to survive without ever having to make the revolutionary break with socialism that was necessary for his country to progress. To follow *perestroika* and *glasnost* was to be parasitic; parasitism being, from the earliest days of the socialist state forward, one of the unmentioned diseases of the revolution. It was a unique form of parasitism which Gorbachev imagined: he would open the USSR to investment and contact with the West, but it was to be the host that would feed off the outsider. For the Leninist fancy which Gorbachev continued was that simple one of a world that goes on, runs itself, has only to be inherited, has only to fall into your greedy, waiting arms.

The communism of Gorbachev—brushed with the borrowed ideas of Bukharin, Djilas, Nagy, and Dubcek—was a communism supposedly returning to its political roots. Lenin, he believed, had founded a new sort of state, given men the last word in community, equality, union. But the violent quarrels and purges that came early to the socialist state had entered its theology; so that socialism as religion, though it preached utopia, at the same time gave its acolytes the sharpest sense of worldly insecurity and made that fear, too, part of the religion. Gorbachev's program had the flaw of these origins—the flaw that runs right through socialist history: the dream it promised offered no practical path to fulfillment. It offered only faith. It offered only the socialist state, which would manage everything—but which had ceased to function effectively. Gorbachev's reform communism manifested itself only as rage, anarchy, and inertia.

Awaiting his execution fifty years before Gorbachev's rise, Nicolai Bukharin had his Damascene conversion and saw the socialist state as brutally sterile. The cult of the state, manifested as the cult of Stalin, had swamped the moral advance of a nation barely emerged into the modern world. The intellectual confusions of utopia that so attracted André Gide, Arthur Koestler, and Ignazio Silone, because they each craved an illusion of earthly harmony, were seen to bring the world to a point of future despair. Young men such as Djilas, Nagy, and Dubcek, awakened by socialism to ideas, history, a knowledge of injustice, and a sense of man's innate dignity, ultimately found themselves unsupported by their faith, and awakened finally only to betrayal and disillusion.

For communism simplified the world, the concept of responsibility, of society and the state, and simplified people. Its ultimate triumph had been made by Lenin and Bukharin to appear to be so easy; the plundering of the inherited civilization, the confiscations and nationalizations, the distribution of big shadowy jobs. Creativity itself appeared as something that might be looted, brought into being by decree. Individual responsibility—a source of despair in the abjectness of the socialist state—was lessened. All that was required was obedience, and obedience is easy. Thus throughout the years of Gorbachev's reforms he justified his actions by the call that socialism was dying, its intellectual resources near to bankruptcy, its antiquated industries in terminal decline. But socialism could linger on only through the brute assertion of police power.

So this is perhaps what happens when the ideas that animate a society atrophy: they do not go out with a bang; they do not die from being spurned and neglected. Perhaps they die like this: when everybody suffers their consequences mutely, when inertia becomes so general and comprehensive that working people forsake effort because they know the pain can never be adequately compensated; when no one believes in anything; and when no one can or will consider a realistic and workable alternative. Perhaps ideas die through mindless repetition, when they lose their ability to inspire mental excitement, a heightened sense of human possibility, and become simply phrases that mask the fact, just barely, that masses of people are suffering to no purpose.

Gorbachev's ultimate aim was to invoke a humane Marxist vision, one he imagined as part of the murky socialist past. And so, step by step, deliberate sometimes but more often chaotically improvised, out of a zeal to rescue socialism from itself, he fractured and dismembered the structure of the socialist state and replaced it with—absolutely nothing. It is possible that Gorbachev privately understood what really happens when a ruling idea, an idea translated into faith and dogma, declines and dies: when systems of government are dogmatic or foolish, killing when they cannot create, when rulers and ruled alike conspire to frighten away the money and the life that they need, when, in a further inversion, the poetry of revolution becomes its own permanent debilitating intoxication. At that moment of realization Gorbachev did not awaken like Imre Nagy and Milovan Djilas, or shun in revulsion like Koestler and Solzhenitsyn. Once more he retreated into the faith.

But a re-affirmation of his socialist beliefs would not allow Gorbachev to govern effectively while seeking help from both reformers and orthodox communists. Resenting the incoherence of Gorbachev's policies, both groups were withdrawing support. Reformers like Eduard Shevardnadze and Alexander Yakovlev abandoned Gorbachev's banner. The movement was in trouble. Unorthodoxy, as always, made disproportionate noise. Heresy and democracy, though increasingly significant, were not the norm within the Party. In the summer of 1991 the real danger to Gorbachev emerged from within.

27

⇥⇥⇥ ⇤⇤⇤

Yeltsin Dismantles the
Socialist Order

Communism in Europe sank to a close in keeping with its character. Born in conspiracy, it died in conspiracy—as if some Marxist god of history arranged a symmetrical retribution. Lenin and Stalin could not impose a workable utopia, and Gorbachev could not entice one from the ruins of their experiments. He continued to issue streams of orders, and while both supporters and rivals acknowledged the urgency for change, the Party's hierarchy was bound, in the nature of things, to grow in resistance to reform. Thus Gorbachev's originally worthy intentions precipitated the crisis that was to destroy the socialist state.

The coup d'état against Gorbachev of August 19–23, 1991, had as much to do with survival as with doctrine and politics. The issue was socialist unity arising from Gorbachev's intention to sign a new treaty of union between the Kremlin and nine of the USSR's constituent republics. Gorbachev's rages and insults might have been borne, but not interference with revenue and privilege. When Gorbachev flatly refused to amend the treaty to preserve centralized Party control, the crisis came. Rather than try, as once before with the obstreperous Nikita Khrushchev, any half-measure requiring Gorbachev to sign "capitulations" of his authority, eight members of Gorbachev's own cabinet, gathered as something of a Committee of Public Safety, decided on the fatal path of removal. Since the Party had never developed a procedure for ousting a General Secretary for unfitness, their plan, it seems, was to annul Gorbachev's program on grounds that it had been promulgated under the confusion of illness. Unquestionably they had been frightened of the economy's decay when they elected Gorbachev leader in 1985, but equally clearly they had never reconciled themselves to the course of action his investiture seemed to pre-ordain.

On August 19, 1991, agents of this "Committee of National Salvation," aided by members of Gorbachev's own household security staff, seized the president in his summer retreat in the Crimea with the intention of forestalling the ratification of the new union treaty and bringing Gorbachev's reform program to a halt, with his coerced acquiescence. They planned a kind of regency council while holding Gorbachev in custody. After three days' turmoil, Gorbachev was freed because of the resistance of ordinary Russians to the coup and the conspiratorial incompetence of the coup makers. The shock of the outrage was mortal. Moments before his arrest Boris Pugo, Minister of the Interior and one of the rebellion's ringleaders, put a bullet in his brain. Marshall Sergei Akhromeyhev hanged himself in his apartment. Within four days the Communist party of the Soviet Union, too, would be dead.

Repudiation of the Party leader was so fateful an act that it is impossible to suppose that the men who inspired the deed were unmindful of the probable consequences if they failed. Rather, they acted in the belief that they could not fail, that they could compel Gorbachev by threats and force of arms, and that the Russian people, as always in their history, would knuckle under to brute force. The ringleaders acted without securing the assent of the army, or at least its commitment to Gorbachev's overthrow. If the generals hedged, it was well-advised caution. For of all the strange events inspired by seventy-odd years of socialism, the effect of the coup on the public mind was among the most surprising. The Russian people did not buckle; thousands went to the barricades; and in Boris Yeltsin they found a voice to proclaim their defiance to the world. When the coup makers proved unwilling or unable to violently put down Yeltsin and his followers, the coup withered away.

The coup did not rally support for the victim. The tide had receded from the omnipotent Communist party that had been the Leninist dream. Claims by Gorbachev, on his haggard return to Moscow, that the coup's failure would allow him, at long last, to purge the Communist party so that it would become and remain a bastion of democracy and reform were obsolete before he made them. More than anyone else, Gorbachev himself was held responsible by the Russian people for creating the conditions that allowed the coup to take hold. The coup makers were his own placemen. Gorbachev's choice of advisors, as he appeased hard-line members of the Party, thus blighted all he had accomplished for the reconstruction of the USSR. For Gorbachev was not immune from that occupational disease of rulers: overestimation of his capacity to control events.

Overestimation of his powers affected Gorbachev even in the coup's aftermath; feasibility restrained him less and less. For while treating the freed Gorbachev with elaborate honor, Yeltsin was determined to squeeze from his victory over the coup makers every last inch of power that Gorbachev could be made to yield. The leader of the Communist party, snatched from imprisonment in the Crimea, was like a prize hostage. Gorbachev's entry into the Russian parliament, on the second day of his deliverance, was an occasion for further humiliation because Gorbachev was, once again, unready to seize the moment to jettison socialism.

Hostility to Gorbachev remained, or rather it was the hostility of indifference, and perhaps there was in the Russian parliament led by Yeltsin also an element of fear: the fear that somehow Gorbachev might emerge again and punish them by restoring the Party to absolute power. And so there was a determination to suppress him, and by that very act find some way to suppress socialism, too. Throughout the coup the Russian parliament had remained in session day and night, making decisions with the breakneck and imperious speed that seems to be peculiar to revolutions at their height. It was wildly exciting, every moment bringing fresh news, a fresh sensation. But the coup's failure, they all knew, was still a long way from meaning that socialism was ended. Somehow the occasion of Gorbachev's appearance before them had to be used to strike the final blow against the socialist state.

In resisting the coup, Yeltsin and his followers wanted a good deal more than to see Gorbachev restored. That prospect they could accept; it was the abolition of one-party rule that they demanded. The assembly wanted an entire reorganization of the USSR, and it wanted it now. The decrees that Yeltsin had issued during the coup—countermanding the orders of the Emergency Committee, taking upon himself the command of the army on Russian soil—were a foreshadowing of the shape of things to come, and it hardly meant less, in the long run, than the breakup of the socialist state. Yet Gorbachev, on his appearance, seemed to think that he had some choice in the matter, that he need not accept Yeltsin and the parliament's supremacy as a *fait accompli*.

Left to defend his crown amid the coup's wreckage, Gorbachev appeared before the Russian assembly intending to rule as if nothing had happened to diminish his power. When he vowed to "work for the renewal of the party,"[1] a roar of heckling surged toward the speaker's rostrum. The question-and-answer session that followed bordered on lunacy. Every attempt Gorbachev made to justify his caution in pursuing reform, or to explain his surrounding himself with men who had betrayed him in the coup, to say that socialism remained a viable and moral idea, was interrupted by howls, catcalls, and jeers. During most of Gorbachev's speech Yeltsin either smirked or looked bored. At one point he poked a chunky finger near Gorbachev's face and insisted that the President read a document that revealed the extent of treachery within Gorbachev's government—only one of his appointees had held out against the coup.

On a rising tide of cheers and hoots (at Gorbachev) Yeltsin rushed through one decree after another. Nothing like it had been seen in Russia since October 1917; it was a program that uprooted every institution in Soviet life. The closure of Communist newspapers was followed by the removal of Party bureaucrats from the army and KGB. All Communist party property—enormous holdings—was seized, and so were its claims to positions in government ministries ended. Decrees made by the Emergency Committee were annulled, trials were promised for those who collaborated in the coup. Gorbachev meekly protested this rush, but Yeltsin understood that haste, real haste, was needed in consolidating support behind the new regime inside Russia before any Communist counterattack could gather. Yeltsin's peculiar method of handling this situation was to act as if this possibility no longer existed. In a flourish made all the more dramatic because of its casualness, Yeltsin quieted his audience so that he could make a "light diversion."[2] He waved a solitary sheet of paper over his head. Two years before, despairing of reform from within the Party, Yeltsin had come to a radical conclusion: since communism was incapable of reforming itself, it must be laid low. He now saw Gorbachev as merely a pathetic remnant of the socialist state who could no longer compel obedience. Going beyond the abuses of the Party to attack socialist theory, Yeltsin was now prepared to sweep away the entire socialist superstructure Central Committee, soviets, KGB, factory cells. Having rejected the ideological authority of the Party, it was now that Yeltsin came to rejection of its very being. With a wave of his hand he brought the paper down and signed it with a flourish. In a culminating heresy, with one stroke of his pen, Yeltsin outlawed the Communist party in Russia and all the nations of the USSR.

A whole man in a fractured time, Gorbachev was compromised from the beginning of his rule by the delusions of his faith. His calls for renewal aroused only mute responses. Like an Isaiah, he grew tiresome, but his yearning for socialist renewal spoke for all the men and women— the Bukharins and Silones, the Nagys and Dubceks, the Koestlers and Gides—who had once yearned for it also, only to be brutally silenced or silenced by doubt. Each, at some point in his socialist dreaming, refused to compromise his personal integrity. Gorbachev, for all his revolutionary rhetoric, was led along a path on which he compromised and trimmed with every step he took. He was led to defend lying, the myth of historical miracles, tabooistic superstition, the suppression of truth, and ultimately, as in the case of the Red Army's attacks in Lithuania, to excuse brutal violence. No less an authority than his friend Eduard Shevardnadze tells us that he was led to distrust man and to fear argument.[3] In spite of his own hatred of tyranny, he was led piecemeal to look to miniature tyrants such as Pugo for help. By the internal logic of his continued support of the idea of socialism, the internal logic of power, he was led unawares to the same point to which Bukharin had been led in the winter of 1917. He did not succeed in arresting the socialist rot. Instead, he succeeded in blinding and binding himself, by his own spell, to powers which once he had hated.[4]

The lessons Gorbachev gave were thus the precise opposite of those he intended. Excellent as his diagnosis of socialism's failings was, his time in power proves that the therapy he recommended was insufficient to the disease. Reform was not the remedy. It was never possible to return to the imagined innocence and purity of Marx's socialist utopia. That dream of heaven was never possible of realization on earth. Once Gorbachev began to allow men to rely on their reason, to use their powers of criticism and initiative, once they felt the call of personal responsibility, there was no hope of returning to a state of implicit submission to the Communist party's tribal magic. For those who have eaten from the tree of liberty, communist utopia is lost.

Violent, destructive, greedy, fallible as we are, men demand a vision of harmony and order. It is a debased hope and a debased faith, born of our despair at the rationality and responsibility of our actions. To live, to act without such hopes of earthly perfection seems beyond our strength. But we do not need certainty. Politics should never be a substitute for faith and wishes. The millenarial element in socialism was a form of idolatry, of superstition. Socialism failed, but other dreamers of a perfect world will come along, posing as prophets; the search resumes.

Afterword

The failed coup against Gorbachev, as all the world knows, ended not only socialism in the USSR, but the union itself. When the communist experiment collapsed all the illusions and enthusiasms and coerced obligations of Soviet history sank beneath a sea of massive resentment. Between August and December 1991, the Kremlin forfeited control of vast lands conquered over many centuries. One by one, peoples and nations declared their independence from Moscow's sway. A new, loose commonwealth was cobbled together from the erstwhile nations of the USSR, but, like the Articles of Confederation that once united the newly liberated American colonies of 1783, the future of this minimal confederation, too, looked bleak. On Christmas Day 1991, the Red Flag was lowered from the Kremlin's battlements for the last time. The tricolor of Russia rose in its place. Overhead bells tolled, perhaps for the displaced Gorbachev who, deluded and dithering until the last, offered his resignation from the presidency of the USSR only after the office and the country had ceased to exist.

Notes

Preface

1. Anna Akhmatova, *Poems of Akhmatova*, trans., ed. Stanley Kunitz and Max Hayward (Boston, 1967), p. 99.
2. Edmund Wilson, *To the Finland Station* (New York, 1972), p. v.
3. Isaiah Berlin, *The Crooked Timber of Humanity* (New York, 1991), p. 1.
4. Wilson, *To the Finland Station*, p. 5.
5. Ibid., p. 3.
6. Ibid., p. 8.
7. Ibid., pp. 24–25.
8. Ibid., p.8.

Chapter 1
Lenin Decrees the Socialist Order

1. Richard Pipes, *The Russian Revolution.* (New York, 1990), passim.
2. Joseph Brodsky, *Less than One: Selected Essays* (New York, 1986), p. 88.
3. John Reed, *Ten Days That Shook the World* (New York, 1960), p. 172.

Chapter 2
Bukharin Sees Leviathan

1. Leon Trotsky, *Collected Writings* (London, 1967), vol. vi, p. 202.
2. Ibid., p. 207.
3. Stephen F. Cohen, *Bukharin and the Bolshevik Revolution: A Political Biography, 1888–1938* (New York, 1973), pp. 39–43.
4. V. I. Lenin, *The State and Revolution* (London, 1958), p. 74.
5. Karl Marx, *Capital*, vol. II, chap. XVI; see also *The Communist Manifesto; Critique of the Gotha Program.*

6. Cohen, *Bukharin and the Bolshevik Revolution*, p. 55.
7. Ibid.
8. Ibid., p. 26.
9. Ibid., p. 28.
10. Ibid.
11. Ibid.
12. Ibid., p. 29.
13. Ibid.
14. Ibid., pp. 29–30.
15. Ibid., p. 30.
16. Ibid.
17. Ibid., pp. 31–33.

Chapter 3
Bukharin Embraces Leviathan

1. Richard Pipes, *The Russian Revolution* (New York, 1990), pp. 359–360.
2. Simon Schama, *Citizens* (New York, 1898), p. 767.
3. E. H. Carr, *The Bolshevik Revolution, 1917–1923,* 2 vols. (London, 1952), vol. I, p. 141.
4. Ibid., p. 143.
5. V. I. Lenin, *Collected Works,* vol. XXVI, p. 208.
6. Carr, *The Bolshevik Revolution*, pp. 221–222.
7. Ibid., pp. 205–208.
8. Leonard Schapiro, *The Origins of the Communist Autocracy* (London, 1977), p. 343.
9. See Lenin's two wartime polemics, *Will the Bolshevists Retain State Power?* and *State and Revolution*.
10. Lenin, *Collected Works,* vol. XXII, p. 378.
11. Ibid., pp. 516–517.
12. Carr, *The Bolshevik Revolution,* vol. II, p. 68.
13. Lenin, *Collected Works,* vol. XXII, p. 493.
14. Carr, *The Bolshevik Revolution,* vol. II, pp. 102–108.
15. Lenin, *Collected Works,* vol. XX, p. 417.
16. Carr, *The Bolshevik Revolution,* vol. II, pp. 109–110.
17. Ibid., pp. 209–210.
18. Schama, *Citizens,* p. 766.
19. Stephen F. Cohen, *Bukharin and the Bolshevik Revolution: A Political Biography, 1888–1938* (New York, 1973), pp. 85, 110–115.

20. Ibid., pp. 85–86.
21. Ibid., p. 86.
22. Ibid.
23. Ibid., p. 87.
24. Ibid.
25. Ibid.
26. Ibid., p. 90.
27. Ibid.
28. Ibid., p. 91.
29. Ibid.
30. Ibid.
31. Ibid.
32. Ibid.
33. Ibid., p. 93.

Chapter 4
Visions of the Future: Vladimir Mayakovsky

1. Robert Hughes, *The Shock of the New* (New York, 1980), p. 85.
2. Ibid.
3. Ibid., p. 87.
4. Maurice Friedberg, *Russian Classics in Soviet Jackets* (New York, 1962), p. 12.
5. For the best profile of Mayakovsky, see Ronald Hingley, *Nightingale Fever: Russian Poets in Revolution* (New York, 1981).
6. Vladimir Mayakovsky, *The Bedbug and Selected Poetry*, trans. Max Hayward and George Reavey (Bloomington, Ind., 1975), pp. 187–189. Patricia Blake's preface to this volume provides a fine, brief portrait of Mayakovsky's life.
7. Edward J. Brown, *Russian Literature since the Revolution* (New York, 1963), p. 54.
8. Ibid., p. 55.
9. Ibid., p. 53.
10. Mayakovsky, *The Bedbug and Selected Poetry*, p. iv.
11. Brown, *Russian Literature since the Revolution*, pp. 53–60.
12. Ibid., p. 52.
13. Ibid.
14. Ibid., p. 56.
15. Ibid., p. 38.

16. Robert Tucker, *Stalin in Power: The Revolution from Above, 1928–1941* (New York, 1990), p. 553.

Chapter 5
Stalin Identifies Socialism with Violence

1. Winston S. Churchill, *The World Crisis* (London, 1956), p. 278.
2. Isaiah Berlin, *The Crooked Timber of Humanity* (New York, 1991), p. 16.
3. For the best biographies of the young Stalin, see Robert Tucker, *Stalin as Revolutionary: A Study in History and Personality* (New York, 1973); Adam B. Ulam, *Stalin: The Man and His Era* (New York, 1973).
4. Max Nomad, *Apostles of Revolution* (Boston, 1939), p. 205.
5. Alexander Kerensky, *The Cruxifixion of Liberty* (New York, 1934), pp. 44–45.
6. Henry W. Nevinson, *Change and Chances* (New York, 1923), p. 125.
7. Prince Peter Kropotkin, *Paroles d'un révolté* (Paris, 1985), pp. 275–276.
8. Ibid.
9. Ibid.
10. *Crapouillot, Numéro Spécial, l'Anarchie* (Paris, 1938), p. 15.
11. Kropotkin, *Paroles d'un révolté*, p. 285.
12. Ibid.
13. Max Nomad, *Rebels and Renegades* (New York, 1932), p. 13.
14. D. S. Mirsky, *Russia: A Social History* (London, 1938), p. 186.
15. Maxim Gorki, *The Lower Depths* (London, 1951), p. 181.
16. Paul Miliukov, *Histoire de Russie* (n.p., n.d.) p. 1056.

Chapter 6
Stalin Identifies Socialism with Himself

1. Edward Ellis Smith, *The Young Stalin* (New York, 1967), p. 4.
2. Raphael R. Abramovitch, *The Soviet Revolution* (London, 1962), p. 416.
3. Ibid.
4. Robert Tucker, *Stalin in Power: The Revolution from Above, 1928–1941* (New York, 1990), pp. 205–206.
5. Ibid., p. 582.

Chapter 7
Leviathan Devours Bukharin

1. E. H. Carr, *The Bolshevik Revolution, 1917–1923*, 2 vols. (London, 1952), vol. I, p. 213.
2. V. I. Lenin, *The State and Revolution* (1917). (London, 1958).
3. Joseph Conrad, *Under Western Eyes*
4. Stephen F. Cohen, *Bukharin and the Bolshevik Revolution: A Political Biography, 1888–1938* (New York, 1973), pp. 290–291.
5. Ibid., p. 205.
6. Ibid., p. 207.
7. Ian Grey, *Stalin: Man of History* (London, 1979), pp. 199–200.
8. Cohen, *Bukharin and the Bolshevik Revolution*, pp. 350–355.
9. Ibid., p. 362.
10. Ibid., p. 362.
11. Ibid., p. 364.
12. Ibid.
13. Ibid.
14. Ibid., p. 365.
15. Ibid.
16. Ibid.
17. Mme. Anna Bukharina, interview, Moscow Evening News, Feb. 4–5, 1990.
18. Cohen, *Bukharin and the Bolshevik Revolution*, p. 367.
19. Ibid.
20. Ibid.
21. Ibid.
22. Ibid.
23. Medvedev, *Nicolai Bukharin: The Last Years*; for additional information, see also Arkady Vaksberg, *Stalin's Prosecutor: The Life of André Vyshinksky* (New York, 1991).
24. Mme. Anna Bukharina, interview.
25. *Report of the Court Proceedings in the Case of the Anti-Soviet "Bloc of Rightists and Trotskyites"* (Moscow, 1938), (hereafter referred to as *Bukharin Purge Trial*), p. 370.
26. *Bukharin Purge Trial*, p. 372.
27. Ibid., p. 383.
28. Ibid., p. 424.
29. Ibid., p. 769.
30. Ibid., p. 778.

31. Ibid., p. 779.
32. Mme. Anna Bukharina, interview; see also: Medvedev, *Nicolai Bukharin: The Last Years,* Chapt. 12.

Chapter 8
The Decline of the Revolutionary Ideal

1. Robert Tucker, *Stalin in Power: The Revolution from Above, 1928–1941* (New York, 1990, passim, esp. Part Three.
2. Roy Medvedev, *Let History Judge: The Origins and Consequences of Stalinism* (New York, 1971), pp. 259–70, 286.
3. Lincoln Steffens, *The Letters of Lincoln Steffens,* ed. E. Winter and G. Hicks, 2 vols. (New York, 1938), vol. II, p. 1001.
4. George Bernard Shaw, *The Rationalization of Russia* (Bloomington, Ind., 1964), p. 112.
5. Jean Lacouture, *André Malraux* (New York, 1975), p. 230.
6. Quoted by Sidney Hook in *Encounter,* March 1978.
7. Sidney Hook, *Out of Step: An Unquiet Life in the 20th Century* (New York, 1987), p. 496.
8. Stephen F. Cohen, *Bukharin and the Bolshevik Revolution: A Political Biography, 1888–1938* (New York, 1973), p. 376.
9. Lionel Trilling, "Art, Will and Necessity," passim, *The Last Decade* (New York, 1979).
10. Quoted in Isaiah Berlin, *The Crooked Timber of Humanity,* p. 16.
11. Ivan Turgenev, *Smoke.*

Chapter 9
The Decline of the Revolutionary Ideal: André Gide

1. For a detailed look at Gide's life, see George Painter, *André Gide: A Critical Biography* (New York, 1968).
2. Maurice Paléologue, *An Intimate Journal of the Dreyfus Case* (New York, 1957), p. 241.
3. Painter, *André Gide: A Critical Biography,* p. 109.
4. Ibid., p. 113.
5. André Gide, *Les Caves du Vatican.*
6. Richard Crossman, ed., *The God That Failed* (London, 1950), p. 169.
7. Ibid.
8. Ibid.
9. André Gide, *Les Nourritures terrestres* (Geneva, 1943), p. 81.
10. André Gide, *Les Nouvelles Nourritures terrestres* (Geneva, 1943), p. 146.

11. Crossman, *The God That Failed,* p. 170.
12. Painter, *André Gide: A Critical Biography,* p. 114.
13. Ibid.
14. Crossman, *The God That Failed,* p. 171.
15. Ibid., pp. 171–1721.
16. Ibid., p. 172.
17. Ibid., p. 173.
18. Ibid.
19. *Pravda,* June 19, 1936.
20. Crossman, *The God That Failed,* p. 181.
21. André Gide, *Retour de l'U.R.S.S.* (Paris, 1937), p. 96.
22. Crossman, *The God That Failed,* pp. 190–191.
23. Gide, *Retour de l'U.R.S.S.,* p. 74.
24. Crossman, *The God That Failed,* p. 185.
25. Ibid., p. 184.
26. Ibid.
27. Ibid.
28. Ibid., p. 185.
29. Ibid.
30. Ibid., p. 187.
31. Ibid.
32. Ibid.
33. André Gide, *Return from the U.S.S.R.,* trans. Dorothy Bussy (New York, 1937), pp. 45–46.
34. Ibid. Preface, passim.
35. Crossman, *The God That Failed,* pp. 195–196.
36. Ibid., p. 196.
37. Ibid., pp. 197–198.
38. Painter, *André Gide: A Critical Biography,* p. 17.
39. André Gide, *Journals 1889–1939,* 3 vols. (Paris, 1963), vol. III, September 5, 1936.
40. Ibid.

Chapter 10
The Decline of the Revolutionary Ideal: Arthur Koestler

1. Sean Day-Lewis, *Cecil Day-Lewis: An English Literary Life* (London, 1980), p. 94. See also Paul Hollander, *Political Pilgrims* (New York, 1980).
2. Day-Lewis, *Cecil Day-Lewis,* p. 102.

3. Richard Crossman, *The God That Failed* (London, 1950), p. 25.

4. For a luminous examination of turn-of-the-century Hungary see John Kukacs, *Budapest 1900: A Historical Portrait of a City and Its Culture* (New York, 1988).

5. Arthur Koestler, *Arrow in the Blue* (New York, 1984), p. 90.

6. Crossman, *The God That Failed*, p. 28.

7. Ibid., p. 31.

8. Ibid., p. 32.

9. Ibid.

10. Ibid.

11. Ibid.

12. Ibid., p. 33.

13. Ibid., p. 36.

14. Ibid., pp. 38–39.

15. Ibid., p. 40.

16. Ibid., p. 41.

17. Ibid., p. 40.

18. Ibid., p. 41.

19. Ibid.

20. Ibid., p. 42.

21. Ibid.

22. Ibid., pp. 42–43.

23. Ibid., p. 43.

24. Ibid.

25. Ibid.

26. Ibid.

27. Ibid., p. 46.

28. Ibid., p. 49.

29. Ibid., p. 51.

30. Ibid., p. 52.

31. Ibid., p. 53.

32. Ibid., pp. 52–54.

33. Ibid., p. 55.

34. Ibid., pp. 55–56.

35. Ibid., p. 64.

36. Ibid., p. 68.

37. Arthur Koestler, *Spanish Testament*.

38. Ibid.

39. Arthur Koestler, *The Yogi and the Commissar.*

40. Arthur Koestler, *Darkness at Noon.*

41. Alexander Wat, "The Death of an Old Bolshevik," in *Kultura Essays,* ed. Leopold Tyrmand (New York, 1970), p. 72.

42. Anna Akhmatova, *Poems of Akhmatova,* trans., ed. Stanley Kunitz and Max Hayward (Boston, 1967).

Chapter 11
The Decline of the Revolutionary Ideal: Ignazio Silone

1. Arthur Koestler, *Arrow in the Blue* (New York, 1984), p. 317.

2. Richard Crossman, *The God That Failed* (London, 1950), p. 89.

3. Ibid., pp. 89–90.

4. Michael Walzer, *The Company of Critics* (New York, 1988), p. 105.

5. Ignazio Silone, *Emergency Exit* (London, 1965), p. 65.

6. Elio Guerriero, *Silone l'inquieto: l'avventura umana eletteraria di Ignazio Silone* (Turin, 1990), p. 171. [I owe this and the following reference to Professor Maurizio Viroli.]

7. Ibid., p. 186. See also: Sante Marelli, *Silone, intellettuale della libertà* (Rimini, 1989), passim.

8. Crossman, *The God That Failed,* p. 104.

9. Ibid.

10. Ibid.

11. For a detailed discussion of Gramsci's life, see: James Joll, *Antonio Gramsci* (London, 1978); John Cammett, *Antonio Gramsci and the Origins of Italian Communism* (Stanford, 1967).

12. See P. Spiano, *Gramsci in carcere e il partito* (Turin, 1988).

13. Nicola Chiaromonte, "Silone the Rustic," *Survey* 26, no. 2 (Spring 1982), p. 44.

14. Crossman, *The God That Failed,* p. 106.

15. Edmund Wilson, *To the Finland Station,* pp. x-xi.

16. Crossman, *The God That Failed,* p. 107.

17. Ibid.

18. Ibid., pp. 111–112.

19. Ibid., p. 112.

20. Ibid., p. 113.

21. Ibid.

22. Ibid.

23. Ibid., p. 114.

24. Ibid.

25. Ibid., pp. 114–115.
26. Ibid., p. 115.
27. Ibid.
28. Ibid.
29. Ibid.
30. Ibid.
31. Ibid., p. 116.
32. Ibid., pp. 116–117.
33. Ignazio Silone, *The Seed Beneath the Snow* (New York, 1937), p. 172.
34. Chiaromonte, "Silone the Rustic," passim.
35. Crossman, *The God That Failed*, p. 118.
36. Ibid., p. 119.
37. Ibid.
38. Ignazio Silone, *And He Did Hide Himself*.
39. Ibid.
40. Ibid.
41. Ibid.
42. Ibid.

Chapter 12
Enemies of the People

1. *La Critica*, August 17, 1946.
2. George Orwell, "Looking Back on the Spanish War," quoted in Raymond Williams, *George Orwell* (New York, 1971), p. 60.
3. George Orwell, *1984*, Appendix, "The Principles of Newspeak," (London, 1966), p. 139.
4. Isaiah Berlin, "Political Ideas in the Twentieth Century," in *Four Essays on Liberty* (London, 1969), p. 94.
5. Karl Popper, *The Philosophy of Karl Popper*, 2 vols., ed. P. A. Schilpp (La Salle, Ill., 1974), vol. I, p. 91.
6. Malcolm Muggeridge, *Chronicles of Wasted Time* (London, 1979), pp. 254–255.
7. Edmund Wilson, *The Shores of Light* (New York, 1952), pp. 518–533.
8. Leon Edel, ed. *Edmund Wilson: The Thirties* (New York, 1980), pp. 208–213.
9. Quoted in Zbigniew Brzezinski, *The Grand Failure: The Birth and Death of Communism in the Twentieth Century* (New York, 1989), p. 10.

Chapter 13
Enemies of the People: Milovan Djilas

1. Milovan Djilas, *Conversations with Stalin* (New York, 1962), p. 164.
2. Milovan Djilas, *Wartime* (New York, 1977), p. 8.
3. Nikita Khrushchev, *The Crimes of the Stalin Era* (New York, 1956), p. 48.
4. C. L. Sulzberger, *Paradise Regained: Memoir of a Rebel* (London, 1989).
5. Djilas, *Wartime*, p. 6.
6. Djilas, *Memoirs of a Revolutionary* (New York, 1973).
7. Djilas, *Of Prisons and Ideas* (New York, 1986), p. 18.
8. Ibid., p. 39.
9. Ibid., p. 40.
10. Ibid., p. 41.
11. Ibid., p. 66.
12. Djilas, *Wartime*, pp. 187–215.
13. Zbigniew Brzezinski, *The Grand Failure: The Birth and Death of Communism in the Twentieth Century* (New York, 1989), p. 195.
14. Winston S. Churchill, *The Second World War: Triumph and Tragedy* (New York, 1953), vol. VI., pp. 196–197.
15. Djilas, *Conversations with Stalin*, p. 164.
16. Nikita Khrushchev, *Khrushchev Remembers*, trans. and ed. Strobe Talbot (Boston, 1970), p. 205.
17. Djilas, *Conversations with Stalin*, pp. 170–173.
18. Vladimir Dedijer, *Tito Speaks* (London, 1953), preface, passim.
19. Duncan Wilson, *Tito's Yugoslavia* (Cambridge, 1979), p. 61.
20. Ibid.
21. Milovan Djilas, *The New Class* (New York, 1957), pp. 47, 124.
22. Ibid., pp. 70–71.
23. Djilas, *Wartime*, pp. 371–372.
24. Djilas, *The New Class*, p. 38.
25. Ibid., chapter 1, passim.
26. Quoted in Wolfgang Leonard, *Three Faces of Marxism: The Political Concepts of Soviet Ideology, Maoism, and Humanist Marxism*, p. 338.
27. Djilas, *The New Class*, pp. 212–213.
28. Djilas, *Of Prisons and Ideas*, p. 22.
29. Ibid., p. 42.

Chapter 14
Enemies of the People: Imre Nagy and the Hungarian Revolution

1. Tamás Aczel and Tibor Méray, *The Revolt of the Mind* (New York, 1959).

2. Miklós Molnár, *Budapest 1956: A History of the Hungarian Revolution* (London, 1971), pp. 17–19.

3. Ibid.

4. Ibid., p. 20.

5. Ibid.

6. Ibid., p. 25, p. 273.

7. *Reform,* June 20, 1989, pp. 3–4.

8. Molnár, *Budapest 1956: A History of the Hungarian Revolution,* p. 273.

9. Romsics Ignác, *Bethlen István: Politikai életrajz* (Budapest, 1991), p. 329. I am indebted to the Hon. Gen. Béla Király, MP (Hungary) for this citation.

10. Miklós Molnár, *A Short History of the Hungarian Communist Party* (Boulder, Colo., 1978), p. 39.

11. Mme. Béla Kun, *Béla Kun: Memoirs* (Budapest, 1966), pp. 416–418; see also: Arvo Tuominen, *The Bells of the Kremlin* (London, 1982); Zoltan Vas, *Szepirodalmi Konyokiado* (Budapest, 1970).

12. Erzbet Nagy, interview, *Antenne 2,* June 18, 1989.

13. Jean Romain, *Paris Fin de Siècle* (New York, 1960), p. 91.

14. Michael Charlton, *The Eagle and the Small Birds* (London, 1984), p. 67.

15. Ferenc Nagy, *The Struggle Behind the Iron Curtain* (New York, 1948), chaps. 37, 38; see also: Barton J. Bernstein, ed., *Politics and Policies of the Truman Administration* (Chicago, 1970), p. 38.

16. Hugh Thomas, *Armed Truce: The Beginnings of the Cold War* (New York, 1987), p. 274.

17. Ibid., pp. 272–276.

18. Müvelt Nép, *Literature and Responsibility* (Budapest, 1955), chap. 2.

19. Molnár, *Budapest 1956: A History of the Hungarian Revolution,* pp. 26–28.

20. Ibid., p. 256.

21. Imre Nagy, *On Communism: In Defense of the New Course* (New York, 1957), p. xxi.

22. Ibid.

23. Ibid., chaps. 10, 11.

24. Franklin L. Baumer, *Modern European Thought: Continuity and Change in Ideas, 1600–1950* (New York, 1977), p. 483.

25. Erzbet Nagy, interview. *Antenne 2,* June 18, 1989.

26. Molnár, *Budapest 1956: A History of the Hungarian Revolution,* pp. 47–40.

27. Erzbet Nagy, interview.

28. Molnár, *Budapest 1956: A History of the Hungarian Revolution,* pp. 41–45.

29. Ibid., pp. 47–48.

30. Quoted in Wolfgang Leonard, *Three Faces of Marxism: The Political Concepts of Soviet Ideology, Maoism, and Humanist Marxism* (New York, 1974), p. 282.

31. Ibid.

32. Ibid., p. 283.

33. Molnár, *Budapest 1956: A History of the Hungarian Revolution,* pp. 85–87.

34. Ibid., pp. 100–106.

35. Ibid., p. 106.

36. Béla Király, "Two Misconceptions about the Hungarian Revolution," *Scope,* Vol. III., Spring–Autumn 1957, p. 20.

37. Ibid.

38. *Reform,* June 20, 1989, p. 4.

39. Melvin J. Lasky, ed., *The Hungarian Revolution* (New York, 1957), p. 237.

40. Király, "Two Misconceptions about the Hungarian Revolution," pp. 22–25.

41. Ibid., p. 28.

42. Erzbet Nagy, interview.

43. Molnár, *Budapest 1956: A History of the Hungarian Revolution,* pp. 189–200.

44. Hannah Arendt, *The Origins of Totalitarianism* (London, 1958), p. xiv.

45. Béla Király, "How Russian Trickery Throttled Revolt." *Life,* February 18, 1957, pp. 119–129. See also Béla Király, "The First War Between Socialist States: Military Aspects of the Hungarian Revolution," in *The Hungarian Revolution Twenty Years After* (Canadian–American Review of American Studies, vol. III: 2 [Fall 1976]), pp. 115–123.

46. Béla Király and Paul Jónás, *The Hungarian Revolution of 1956 in Retrospect* (New York, 1978), pp. 73–82.

Chapter 15
Enemies of the People: Khrushchev's Secret Speech

1. Khrushchev's comments were made at a diplomatic reception in Moscow in 1957. *Encycopedia Americana,* vol. 16, p. 396.

2. Louis J. Halle, *The Cold War as History* (New York, 1967), p. 307.

3. Nikita Khrushchev, *Khrushchev Remembers,* trans. and ed. Strobe Talbot (Boston, 1970), pp. 322–324.

4. Ibid., pp. 332–341.

5. Halle, *The Cold War as History,* p. 311.

6. Ibid.

7. For the details of Khrushchev's life, I have relied upon Roy A. Medvedev, *Khrushchev: A Political Biography*. trans. Brian Pearce (New York, 1983); Edward Crankshaw, *Khrushchev: A Career* (London, 1966).

8. Khrushchev, *Khrushchev Remembers*, chapter 3, passim.

9. George F. Kennan, *Memoirs, 1925–1950* (Boston, 1967), p. 558.

10. Khrushchev, *Khrushchev Remembers*, pp. 342–343.

11. Walter LaFeber, *America, Russia, and the Cold War: 1945–1975* (New York, 1976), pp. 174–178.

12. *Pravda*, September 11, 1937.

13. Tucker, *Stalin in Power: The Revolution from Above, 1928–1941*, pp. 448–449.

14. Halle, *The Cold War as History*, pp. 322–323.

15. Adam B. Ulam, *Expansion and Coexistence: The History of Soviet Foreign Policy, 1917–1967* (New York, 1968), pp. 568–580.

16. BBC, Newsnight, December 4, 1988.

17. Ibid. For additional comments by Gromyko, see Andrei Gromyko, *Memoirs* (London, 1989).

18. Khrushchev, *Khrushchev Remembers*, p. 564.

19. Ibid., p. 617.

20. Ibid.

21. Ibid., pp. 574–587.

22. For the text of the speech when it first reached the West, see Russian Institute, Columbia University, ed. *The Anti-Stalin Campaign and International Communism* (New York, 1956).

23. *Peking Review*, Editorials, September 6, 13, 20, 1963.

24. See Evgeny Pashukanis, *Selected Writings on Marxism and Law* (London, 1980); Eugene Kamenka, "Demythologizing the Law," *The Times Literary Supplement*, May 1, 1981, pp. 475–476.

25. Tufton Beamish and Guy Handley, *The Kremlin Dilemma* (London, 1978), p. 24.

26. For details of the coup, see Michel Tatu, *Power in the Kremlin* (London, 1969).

Chapter 16
Solzhenitsyn: The Young Prophet

1. Bruce Chatwin, *What Am I Doing Here?* (New York, 1989), p. 84.

2. Michael Scammell, *Solzhenitsyn: a biography* (New York, 1984), pp. 32–33.

3. Ibid., p. 87.

4. Ibid.
5. Ibid., pp. 97–106.
6. Ibid., p. 102.
7. Ibid., pp. 25, 104, 894, 971.
8. Ibid., p. 104.
9. David Burg and George Feifer, *Solzhenitsyn: A Biography* (New York, 1972), chap. VI.
10. Ibid.
11. Scammell, *Solzhenitsyn: a biography,* p. 132.
12. Alexander Solzhenitsyn, *The First Circle.*
13. Alexander Solzhenitsyn, *The Gulag Archipelago.*
14. Alexander Solzhenitsyn, *Cancer Ward.*
15. Ibid.

Chapter 17
Solzhenitsyn: Poet of the Gulag

1. Alexander Solzhenitsyn, *The First Circle.*
2. Ibid.
3. Ibid.
4. Ibid.
5. Ibid.
6. Ibid.
7. Ibid.
8. Ibid.
9. Ibid.
10. Ibid.
11. Michael Scammell, *Solzhenitsyn: a biography* (New York, 1984), pp. 316–317.
12. Ibid., p. 317.
13. Ibid., p. 448.
14. Alexander Solzhenitsyn, *The Oak and the Calf* (New York, 1975), p. 87.
15. Ibid., p. 269.
16. Scammell, *Solzhenitsyn: a biography,* chap. 28.

Chapter 18
Solzhenitsyn Decides to Change the World

1. For complete details of the Daniel and Sinyavsky trials, see Max Hayward, ed. and trans., *On Trial* (London, 1967), passim.

2. *Pravda*, May 24, 1959.

3. Solzhenitsyn, *The Oak and the Calf*, pp. 257–272, 484–494.

4. Solzhenitsyn, *Lenin in Zurich*.

5. Michael Scammell, *Solzhenitsyn: a biography* (New York, 1984), p. 704–706.

6. *The Daily Mail (Paris)*, September 11, 1972.

Chapter 19
Enemies of the People: Alexander Dubcek and the Prague Heresy

1. Quoted in Robert C. Tucker, "Swollen State, Spent Society: Stalin's Legacy to Brezhnev's Russia," *Foreign Affairs*, 60 (Winter, 1981–1982), pp. 414–425.

2. Michael Tatu, *Power in the Kremlin*, passim. See also Ronald W. Hingley, *The Russian Secret Police* (London, 1970), pp. 43–45.

3. Hélène Carrère d'Encausse, *Le Pouvoir confisqué; Gouvernants et gouvernés en URSS* (Paris, 1981), passim.

4. V. Mencl and F. Ourednik, "What Happened in Prague," in Robin A. Remington, ed., *Winter in Prague* (Cambridge, Mass., 1969), pp. 18–39.

5. Radoslav Selucky, *Czechoslovakia: The Plan That Failed* (New York, 1970), p. 59.

6. Tad Szulc, *Czechoslovakia since World War II* (New York, 1971), chap. XII.

7. Ibid., p. 48.

8. Hugh Thomas, *Armed Truce: The Beginnings of the Cold War* (New York, 1987), p. 259.

9. William Shawcross, *Dubcek* (New York, 1970), pp. 18–35.

10. Thomas, *Armed Truce: The Beginnings of the Cold War*, pp. 257–270.

11. Herbert Feis, *Churchill, Roosevelt, and Stalin* (Princeton, 1957), pp. 198, 569.

12. Thomas, *Armed Truce: The Beginnings of the Cold War*, pp. 265–270.

13. Shawcross, *Dubcek*, p. 40.

14. Ibid., p. 37.

15. Szulc, *Czechoslovakia since World War II*, p. 118.

16. Shawcross, *Dubcek*, pp. 65–66.

17. Ibid., p. 67.

18. Ibid., p. 86.

19. Wolfgang Leonard, *Three Faces of Marxism* (New York, 1970), pp. 313–314.

20. Shawcross, *Dubcek*, pp. 89–90.

21. Szulc, *Czechoslovakia since World War II*, p. 194.

22. Ibid., pp. 204–212.

23. Wolfgang Leonard, *Eurocommunism: Challenge for East and West* (New York, 1978), p. 104.

24. Shawcross, *Dubcek*, pp. 114–120.

25. Leonard, *Three Faces of Marxism*, p. 318.

26. Shawcross, *Dubcek*, pp. 129–130.

27. Szulc, *Czechoslovakia since World War II*, pp. 278–279, 300–303.

28. Ibid., chaps. XVI, XVII.

29. Shawcross, *Dubcek*, p. 170.

30. Ibid., p. 171.

31. Ota Sik, *Winter in Spring* (Dublin, 1974), p. 304.

32. Ibid., p. 309.

33. Pavel Tigrid, *La chute irrésistible d'Alexandre Dubcek* (Paris, 1969), p. 18.

34. Shawcross, *Dubcek*, p. 175.

35. Ibid., p. v.

36. Dubcek interview, *L'Unita*, January 20, 1988, pp. 1, 4–5.

Chapter 20
Solzhenitsyn: Out of the Archipelago

1. Vladimir Bukovsky, *To Build a Castle*, (London, 1978), passim.

2. Lafeber, *America, Russia, and the old War: 1945–1975*, p. 273.

3. Alexander Solzhenitsyn, *The Gulag Archipelago*.

4. Ibid.

5. Ibid.

6. Ibid.

7. Ibid.

8. Ibid.

9. Ibid.

10. Joseph Brodsky, *Less than One: Selected Essays* (New York, 1986), p. 120.

11. Alexander Solzhenitsyn, *The Gulag Archipelago*.

Chapter 21
Gorbachev: The Young Commissar from Privolnoye

1. Zhores A. Medvedev, *Andropov* (New York, 1983), conclusion, passim.

2. Nikita Khrushchev, *Khrushchev Remembers* (Boston, 1970), p. 131.

3. Mark Frankland, *The Sixth Continent: Russia and the Making of Mikhail Gorbachev* (London, 1967), pp. 119–131.

4. *Vanity Fair*, February 1990, p. 188.

5. Ibid.

6. Zhores A. Medvedev, *Gorbachev* (New York, 1986), pp. 5–19, 165–183.

7. Ibid., p. 26.

8. Robert Conquest, *The Harvest of Sorrow: Soviet Collectivisation and the Terror-Famine* (New York, 1986), passim.

9. Gail Sheehy, *The Man Who Changed the World* (New York, 1990), p. 38.

10. Ibid., pp. 33–35.

11. Dusko Doder and Louise Branson, *Gorbachev: Heretic in the Kremlin* (New York, 1990), pp. 2–3.

12. Dev Muraka, *Gorbachev: The Limits of Power* (London, 1988), pp. 39–42; see also Medvedev, *Gorbachev*, pp. 30–32.

13. Sheehy, *The Man Who Changed the World*, p. 48.

14. Doder and Branson, *Gorbachev: Heretic in the Kremlin*, pp. 7–8; see also, Christian Schmidt-Häuer, *Gorbachev: The Path to Power* (London, 1986), pp. 46–47.

15. Sheehy, *The Man Who Changed the World*, pp. 50–51.

16. Hedrick Smith, *The New Russians* (New York, 1990), pp. 39–40.

17. Sheehy, *The Man Who Changed the World*, p. 59.

18. Ibid., pp. 55–89.

Chapter 22
Gorbachev: Ideologue and Opportunist

1. The Editors of *Time*, *Mikhail S. Gorbachev: An Intimate Biography* (New York, 1988), pp. 70–71; Doder and Branson, however, discount this story, see Dusko Doder and Louise Branson, *Gorbachev: Heretic in the Kremlin* (New York, 1990), p. 10.

2. Ibid.

3. Hedrick Smith, *The New Russians* (New York, 1990), p. 49.

4. Gail Sheehy, *The Man Who Changed the World* (New York, 1990), p. 75.

5. Schmidt-Häuer, *Gorbachev: The Path to Power* (London, 1986), pp. 51–52; Doder and Branson, *Gorbachev: Heretic in the Kremlin*, pp. 9–12.

6. Doder and Branson, *Gorbachev: Heretic in the Kremlin*, pp. 15–20; Sheehy, *The Man Who Changed the World*, pp. 78–83.

7. Ibid., p. 85.

8. BBC Monitoring Service, December 10, 1989.

9. Zhores A. Medvedev, *Gorbachev* (New York, 1986), pp. 47–49; Sheehy, *The Man Who Changed the World*, pp. 87–89.

10. Sheehy, *The Man Who Changed the World*, p. 90.
11. Smith, *The New Russians*, pp. 54–55.
12. Doder and Branson, *Gorbachev: Heretic in the Kremlin*, pp. 22–26.

Chapter 23
Gorbachev Tries to Live His History

1. Zhores A. Medvedev, *Gorbachev* (New York, 1986), pp. 50–53, 76–77; Dusko Doder and Louise Branson, *Gorbachev: Heretic in the Kremlin* (New York, 1990), pp. 29–32.
2. Zhores A. Medvedev, *Khrushchev* (London, 1982), pp. 165–173; Gail Sheehy, *The Man Who Changed the World* (New York, 1990), p. 94.
3. Sheehy, *The Man Who Changed the World*, p. 94.
4. Nikita Khrushchev, *Khrushchev Remembers* (Boston, 1970), pp. 120ff., 139–143.
5. Annie Cohen-Solal, *Sartre: a life* (London, 1987), pp. 459–460; see also *Le Nouvel Observateur*, June 19, June 26, 1968.
6. Hedrick Smith, *The New Russians* (New York, 1990), pp. 57–58.
7. Doder and Branson, *Gorbachev: Heretic in the Kremlin*, p. 31.
8. Sheehy, *The Man Who Changed the World*, pp. 95–102.
9. Mark Frankland, *The Sixth Continent: Russia and the Making of Mikhail Gorbachev* (London, 1967), pp. 158–159.
10. Thomas G. Butson, *Gorbachev: A Biography* (New York, 1985), pp. 37–38; Schmidt-Häuer, *Gorbachev: The Path to Power*, p. 53.
11. Christian Schmidt-Häuer, *Gorbachev: The Path to Power* (London, 1986), pp. 60–61.
12. Doder and Branson, *Gorbachev: Heretic in the Kremlin*, pp. 37–38.
13. The Editors of *Time*, *Mikhail S. Gorbachev: An Intimate Biography* (New York, 1988), passim.
14. Ibid.
15. *Vanity Fair*, February 1990, p. 186.
16. Sheehy, *The Man Who Changed the World*, p. 109.
17. Zhores A. Medvedev, *Andropov* (New York, 1983), p. 97.
18. Ibid., chap. 9.
19. Smith, *The New Russians*, pp. 72–75.

Chapter 24
Gorbachev: A Failure of the Will

1. Edward Gibbon, *The Decline and Fall of the Roman Empire* (London, 1931), p. 409.

2. Zhores A. Medvedev, *Andropov* (New York, 1983), chaps. 12–13.

3. Hedrick Smith, *The New Russians* (New York, 1990), pp. 67–69.

4. Zhores A. Medvedev, *Gorbachev* (New York, 1986), chap. 7.

5. Gail Sheehy, *The Man Who Changed the World* (New York, 1990), pp. 166–170.

6. Medvedev, *Gorbachev*, pp. 138–144; see also, Buston, *Gorbachev: A Biography*, pp. 105–122.

7. Hannah Arendt, *The Origins of Totalitarianism* (London, 1967), p. 351.

8. Dusko Doder, *Shadows and Whispers* (New York, 1986), p. 267.

9. Smith, *The New Russians*, pp. 66–67.

10. Mikhail Gorbachev, *Perestroika: New Thinking for Our Country and the World* (New York, 1988), passim.

11. Zbigniew Brzezinski, *The Grand Failure: The Birth and Death of Communism in the Twentieth Century* (New York, 1989), p. 62.

12. BBC Monitoring Service, February 18, 1986; See also Gorbachev, *Perestroika*, pp. 239–242.

13. Sheehy, *The Man Who Changed the World*, pp. 178–179, 235–236; see also Smith, *The New Russians*, p. 186.

14. Smith, *The New Russians*, pp. 447–448.

15. Gorbachev, *Perestroika*, p. 11.

16. Ibid., pp. 22–23.

17. Ibid., pp. 108–109.

18. Ibid., p. 75.

19. Smith, *The New Russians*, passim.

20. *Libération*, July 25, 1990; for details of Yeltsin's position, see: Boris Yeltsin, *Against the Grain* (New York, 1990), passim.

21. Doder and Branson, *Gorbachev: Heretic in the Kremlin*, chap. XIII.

22. Gorbachev, *Perestroika*, pp. 41–45.

Chapter 25
Gorbachev: Ten Months That Shook the World

1. Hedrick Smith, *The New Russians* (New York, 1990), pp. 404–408.

2. Sheehy, *The Man Who Changed the World* (New York, 1990), p. 218.

3. Brzezinski, *The Grand Failure: The Birth and Death of Communism in the Twentieth Century*, pp. 117–119.

4. Erzbet Nagy, Interview, *Antenne 2*, June 18, 1989.

Chapter 26
Gorbachev: Twilight of Leviathan

1. Quoted in, Dusko Doder and Louise Branson, *Gorbachev: Heretic in the Kremlin* (New York, 1990), p. 305.
2. Ibid., chap. 18.
3. Stephen F. Cohen and Katrina vanden Heuvel, *Voices of Glasnost* (New York, 1989) passim.
4. Alexander Yakovlev, Interview, BBC Radio 4, September 11, 1990.
5. Carl von Clausewitz, *On War,* trans. Col. J. J. Graham, 3 vols. (London, 1911), vol. III., p. 89.
6. Henry Kissinger, *White House Years* (Boston, 1979), p. 54.

Chapter 27
Yeltsin Dismantles the Socialist Order

1. *Le Monde,* August 24, 1991, pp. 1–3.
2. Ibid.
3. Eduard Shevardnadze, *The Future Belongs to Freedom* (New York, 1991), passim.
4. Indeed, even after the coup Gorbachev seemed unable to confront the consequences of his continuing faith in socialism. See Mikhail Gorbachev, *August Coup* (New York, 1991), passim.

Acknowledgments

The author is indebted to and thanks the following persons for criticism, corrections, information, or the loan of materials: Anna Bukharina, Vladimir Bukovsky, Miriam Chiaromonte, Stephen Cohen, my near neighbor in Sussex, General Béla Király, Michael Scammell, and Maurizio and Nadia Viroli. I have relied particularly heavily in certain chapters on Professor Cohen's biography of Nicolai Bukharin, Robert Painter's biography of André Gide, Richard Pipes' history of the Russian Revolution, William Shawcross' life of Alexander Dubcek, and Michael Scammell's biography of Alexander Solzhenitsyn. I owe a lasting debt to the late Richard Crossman's book, *The God That Failed,* and to the inspired writings of Milovan Djilas.

To Peter Dougherty of The Free Press I owe a writer's most important debt: for the steady companionship of an interested reader, for constructive criticism mixed with encouragement in times of need. As always, my agent Robert Ducas has been a princely sounding board for my usual anxieties.

Index